Incredible India

by

Diwan Bahadur Harbilas Sarda

Edited and Revised by

Dr. Ravi Prakash Arya

Amazon books, USA

In association with

Indian Foundation for Vedic Science

1051, Sector-1, Rohtak, Haryana, India, Pin-124001

Ph. No. 09313033917; 09650183260

Email : vedicscience@hotmail.com;

vedicscience@rediffmail.com

vedicscience@gmail.com

Web: www.vedicscience.net

Third Edition
Kali era : 5119 (c. 2017)
Kalpa era: 1,97,29,49,119
Brahma era: 15,55,21,97,29,49,119

ISBN 81- 87710-44-6

Editor's Note

Diwan Bahadur Harbilas Sarda was born in Ajmer on June 3, 1867. His father, Harnarayana was the librarian of Govt. College Ajmer. In his young age Harbilas used to attend the lectures of Swami Dayanand. He was also present in the Bhinaya Kothi at the time when Swami Dayananda breathed his last. He was an ardent follower of Swami Dayanand Saraswati, the forerunner of the Indian Renaissance and founder of Arya Samaj. It is said that no one has realised in life the teachings of Swami Dayanand more deeply than Harbilas Sarda.

In 1888, he passed his BA from Agra College Agra and went to Allahabad in the same year to attend the session of Indian National Congress. He had a chance to have a glance at the founder of congress, A.O. Hume and other leaders from the close quarters. He also attended the sessions of Rashtriya Mahasabha as an observer. He joined the Govt. College Ajmer as a Lecturer. Afterwards he joined the Judicial services of Ajmer State. In 1924, he was elected as the member of Central Assembly.

When he was a member of the Central Legislative Assembly (1924-34), he sponsored the Child Marriage Restraint Act, 1925, popularly known as Sarda Act and thus besides rendering imperishable service to his community, he immortalised his name when he succeeded in getting passed this most important piece of social legislation in India. For this monumental work alone, the name of Harbilas Sarda will never be forgotten by the future generations of India, particularly by the women folk and children.

Those were the days of trials and tribulations as India was striving for independence and giants like Lokmanya Bal Gangadhar Tilak, Lala Lajpat Rai, M.R. Jaykar. Tej Bahadur Sapru, Madan Mohan Malviya, Vithal Bhai Patel, and Bhai Parmanand and M.A. Jinnah were in the field, each trying to get rid of the British rule in his own way. At that time Pt. Motilal Nehru was the leader of Swaraj Party and Harbilas Sarda was the Deputy Leader of the Nationalist Party founded by Lala Lajpat Rai. He was the trusted man of Shyamji Krishna Verma in India. He was in close touch with Swami Vivekananda also.

Hindu Superiority was written by him in 1906. The book is colossal in content and classic in treatment. It refers to 550 authentic works in different languages besides inscriptions. This itself speaks volumes of the industry put in by the author in writing the book.

The book contains eight chapters subdivided into 52 subchapters on various aspects of Indian culture and civilisation. The first chapter deals with Indian Constitution, Antiquity of Indian civilization, Government, Indian Social system, Positions of women in Indian society, Foreign relations, cause of India's downfall. Second chapter deals with the questions of Indian colonization of ancient world. Third Chapter devoted to literature, Sanskrit language, Art of writing, Vedic literature, Poetry, Drama, *Purāṇas.* Chapter four discusses the six systems of Indian philosophy and *Bhagavad Gītā.* Chapter fifth takes into account ancient Indian sciences of Medicine, Mathematics, Arithmetic, Geometry, Algebra, Astronomy, Military Science, Music and other sciences. Sixth chapter covers various arts like architecture and sculpture, weaving, and other arts. Seventh chapter deals with commerce and wealth. Eighth chapter deals with religion and tells how the various religions and mythologies of the world were derived from India. The book is compendium of information on Incredible India.

It can be said of the author of Hindu superiority that he had a vast knowledge, burning patriotism at that time of trials and tribulations. One comes across in this book many strange name and many technical expressions of numerous branches of knowledge. This book makes every patriot Indian feel proud of himself and his country and fills one with hope and courage. This book presents the true picture of what Max Müller (p.8) had expressed in his famous book '*India: What can it teach us*?'

> "If I were to look over the whole world to find out the country most richly endowed with all the wealth, power, and beauty that nature can bestow, in some parts a very paradise on earth - I should point to India. If I were asked under what sky the human mind has most fully developed some of its choicest gifts, has most deeply pondered on the greatest problems of life, and has found solutions of some of them which well deserve the attention even of those who have studied Plato and Kant – I should point to India. And if I were to ask myself from what literature we here in Europe – we who have been nurtured almost exclusively on the thoughts of the Greeks and the Romans, and of one Semitic race, the Jewish – may draw that corrective which is most wanted in order to make our inner life more perfect, more comprehensive, more universal, in fact more truly human a life not for this life only, but a transfigured and eternal life, again I should point to India?''

This book provides the ample ground for the following path-breaking statement of Prof. Heeren (Vol. II, p. 45) given in his famous book '*Historical Researches.*'

> ''India is the source from which not only the rest of Asia but the whole Western World derived their knowledge and their religion."

In addition to *Hindu Superiority*, the author contributed some 121 articles (100 in English, 20 in Hindi, and 1 in Urdu) on different aspects of Indian Culture and civilisation. He also edited *Swami Dayanand Saraswati Commemoration Volume* (1925), wrote Swami Dayanand and *Satyārtha Prakāśa* (1944), '*Shankar and Dayanand*' and '*Life of Swami Dayanand Sarasvati: World Teacher*'(1946), *Life of Virjanand Sarasvati* and Shyamji Krishna Varma (this book was published in 1959 after his death).

The author passed away on 20th January, 1955 at the age of 78 years.

The present editor wants to share a historical movement with the readers that this book was written in Nov. 1906 and exactly after 100 years (Nov. 2006) its revised and updated edition was published by the present author for the first time. The book is the great compendium of Indian saga of progress and advancement. It is the real history of the origin and development of humans and extension of their knowledge over the globe. This book is an account of achievement of Indians in the past. This book will also help the readers understand the contribution of India in the development of modern science and technology. The subject book is no less significant than any of the sacred books of Indians. Here it may be clarified that the word Hindu has not been used here in the book or in the very title of the book to denote Hindu religion by the original author Har Bilas Sarda. The word 'Hindu' denoted nationality in the 19th and 20th century as India was known by that time as Hindustan. The people living in Hindustan were known as Hindus. Thus basically the word Hindu denotes nationality, just like the words Bharatiya or Indian. The glaring example of this fact is that till now the Muslims going for Haz in Arabia are registered there as Hindu Muslims. But the same word was used by foreign writers to denote religion professed by Indians. Slowly and steadily in the presence of Muslim and Christian religions in India, the word Hindu was taken to mean Sanatana or Vedic religion instead of national of Hindustan. As such the very title 'Hindu Superiority' means 'Indian Supremacy'. Keeping in view of this fact, the very title 'Hindu Superiority' has been changed into 'Incredible India', which undoubtedly includes every aspect of Indian life and thought.

The information given in this book has been revised and updated in view of the new research in the world of history. Each and every enlightened and awakened Indian must keep this book in his/her personal library if he/she wants to know about his roots.

Rohtak, May, 24, 2017 **Dr. Ravi Prakash Arya**

PREFACE BY ORIGINAL AUTHOR

This books has grown out of a pamphlet written years ago and put aside at the time. The object of the book is, by presenting bird's eye view of the achievements of the ancient Indians, to invite the attention of thoughtful people to the leading features of the civilization which enabled the inhabitants of this country to contribute so much the material and moral well-being of humankind. And if this attempt succeeds in any way in stimulating interest in the study of the leading Indian institutions and a proper appreciation of their merits I shall be amply repaid for my labour.

I must take this opportunity of expressing my gratitude towards Mr. J. Inglis, Superintendent Scottish Mission Industries, Ajmer for his valuable assistance in seeing the book through the Press.

Harbilas Sarda

Ajmer
November : 1906

CONTENTS

Introduction 1-7

Chapter I

1. CONSTITUTION

The leading principle of Indian Constitution. –Turning point of Indian history. India's fall beginning with the *Kaliyuga.* 8-9

1.1. ANTIQUITY

Wonderful antiquity of the Indian civilization –Opinions of historians. –The Indian King Dionysius reigned 7,000 B.C., or 1,000 years before the oldest king on Manetho's tables. —Dynasties, not individuals, as units of calculation. --Age of the earth according to the Indians. 10-18

1.2. GOVERNMENT

Tests of good government. –Populousness of ancient India. –No thieves in ancient India. –Form of government immaterial. –Spirit dependent on the ethical character of a people. –Over Government. —Republican institutions in ancient India.—Law, a test of good government. —Origin of the Greek, Roman and English laws. —Laws of Manu. — Indian code will bear comparison with the systems of jurisprudence in nations most highly civilized. —Fallacies in Mill's reasoning. —His prejudice, —His History of India most mischievous according to Max Müller... 19-30

1.3. SOCIAL SYSTEM

Indian social organization based on scientific principles. — *Varṇāśrama.* — Different forms the caste system. — Brāhmaṇas and Śūdras not by birth but by action and character. 31-36

1.4. CHARACTER

Love of truth — Absence of slavery — Indian valour — The most tolerant nation. — No race more to be trusted than the Indians. — If civilization to be an article of trade between England and India, England will gain by the import cargo — Commercial honour stands higher in India than in any other country. — Indian children more intelligent than European. — Indian cleanliness. —Diet of the Indians. — Physical agility. — India as the wisest of nations. —Indian origin of the game of chess. —Wisdom of Solomon inferior to that of the Indians. 37-54

1.5. CHIVALRY

Innate chivalry of Indian character. Ill-judged humanity of the Indians. —Its unfortunate political results. —Cases of Shahabuddin Ghori and Aurangzeb. 55-63

1.6. PATRIOTISM

Love of Country. —Rana Pratap and Thakur Durga Das. — Aurangzeb's dread of Durga Das. —Gar-ka-Bundi. —Col. Tod on Rajput chivalry and heroism. 64-75

1.7. VALOUR

The Indians were the bravest nation the Greeks ever came in contact with. —Their character shines brightest in adversity. —They know not what it is to flee from the battle-field. —Mukandas faces a tiger; the tiger retires. —Soningdeo breaks the iron bow at Delhi. — Homer's heroes compared to Kurus. —*Lakh Talvar Rahtoran.* —Recourse to poison by Mughal Kings. —The cause of Akbar's death. —Singularity of Rajput character. —Its tenacity and strength. —Hercules was an Indian. —Proofs of the identity of Balram and Hercules. 76-86

1.8. POSITION OF WOMEN

Position of women a test of civilization. —Chivalrous treatment of women by the Indians. —Status of wife.

—Her equal rights with her husband according to the *Śāstras.* —Woman, *ardhāṅginī,* or better half of man. —Comparison in this respect of the Indian and the European women. —Ideals of Indian women. —Purdah system unknown in ancient India. —The rights of women to property. —Peculiar position of Indian women. —Influence of Indian women and society. —Female loyalty. —Bernier's testimony to the courage of Rajput women. —Retreat of Jaswant Singh of Jodhpur after his defeat at Fatehabad. —The Rani refuses to see him and shuts the gate of the castle.

87-110

1.9. FOREIGN RELATIONS

The conquest of the world by the Indian emperor, Sudas. —The conquests of Pururavā and of King Sagara. —Persia, Afghanistan and Turkistan parts of the Indian Empire. —Greek embassies to India. — Antiochus becomes an ally of Sobhag Sen. —Seleucus gives his daughter in marriage to Chandragupta. —The Persian king, Nausherwan, gives his daughter to the Mahārāṇa of Chitor. —Indian Embassies to Greece. —The Assyrian Queen, Semiramis, invades India. —Her defeat. —Gaj Singh, the founder of Ghazni.

111-116

1.10. CAUSE OF INDIA'S FALL

Alexander's invasion of India. —Indian disunion, the causes of Alexander's victory. —The brilliancy of the court of Vikramaditya. —The treacherous conduct of Alexander. —Prithvi Raj of Ajmer. —His victories over Shahabuddin Ghori. —Disunion between Prithvi Raj and Jai Chand. —The kings of Kanauj and Annahilwara Patun and Hamir join the enemy. —Prithvi Raj kills Shahabud-din with the help of Chund. —Baber's invasion. —Indians under Rana Sanga. —Treachery in his camp. —India not conquered by a foreign invader but betrayed by her own sons. 117-121

2. INDIAN COLONIZATION

Destructions and emigration the chief features of the period when the *Mahābhārata* took place. —Whole races and tribes emigrated from India. —India's loss was the world's gain. —Emigration a necessary feature of a thickly-populated country. —Scarcity of historical records. —Destruction of Indian libraries. —Dr. Dow, Profs. Wilson, Heeren and Col. Tod on Indian works on history. — The date of the *Mahābhārata*. —Views of the Indian astronomers. —Traditions. —The Indian theory of emigration. —The Central Asian theory of emigration. —Indian civilization originated and developed in India. —It spread to Ethiopia, Egypt, Phoenicia, Persia, Greece, Rome, to the abode of the Hyperborean, to Siam, China and Japan. 122-134

2.1. EGYPT AND ETHIOPIA

Egypt colonized by Indians about 8,000 years ago. —The testimony to the Indian colonization of Ethiopia. 135-140

2.2. PERSIA

The ancient Persians were colonists from India. —Manu on the origin of the Persians. 141-144

2.3. ASIA MINOR

The Chaldeans and the Assyrians were originally Indians. 145

2.4. GREECE

The Indian origin of the ancient Greeks, Greek society essentially Indian. —Anchilles sprung from a Rajput stock. 146-149

2.5. ROME

The Romans were the descendants of colonists from India. —Rome derived from Rama. —The Etruscans were settlers from India. 150

2.6. TURKISTAN AND NORTHERN ASIA

Turkistan peopled by the Indians. —Turanians were Indians. —Ottorocurae (Uttara Kurus) of the Greek writers were Ootooru Cooru (Uttara Kurus), or Northern Coorus (Kurus), sons of Cooru (Kurus). —Khata inhabited by Indians. —Bajrapur in Siberia founded by Indians. —Succession of the sons of Sri Krishna to the throne. —Chaghtaes were Yadus. — Origin of the Afghans. —Seestan. —Origin of the name Asia. —Samoyedes and Tchoudes of Siberia and Finland were the Yadus of India. 151-152

2.7. GERMANY

German Mensch same as Sanskrit *Manuṣa.* —Morning ablutions. —Origin of the name Germans. —The Hungarians. —Sculpture of Saxon cathedrals. 154-155

2.8. SCANDINAVIA

Scandinavians descended from the warrior class of the Indians. —Colonized about 500 B.C. —The Scandinavian Edda derived from the Vedas. —Days of the week. —Origin of the Scandinavian myths. 156-157

2.9. HYPERBOREANS

Their Indian Origin. —Emigrants from Khyberpur. —Passaron. 158

2.10. GREAT BRITAIN

The Druids were Buddhistic Brāhmaṇas. —Alexander and Napier conquer the descendants of their forefathers. —Derivation of ''Hurrah''. —The Stonehenge. 159-161

2.11. EASTERN ASIA

Transgangetic Peninsula a part of India. —Influence of China over it. —The name Burma. —Camboja or Cambodia. —The Chinese assert their Indian origin— They were emigrants from northern and north-western

India. —Culture and religion of China. —Indian colonization of the isles of the Indian archipelago. —Java. —Java peopled entirely by the Indians. —Borneo, Celebes, Sumatra and Australia. 162-167

2.12. AMERICA

High civilisation of the ancient Americans. —Indian remains still found there. —Indian mythology the parent of the American mythology. —Proofs of the Indian colonization of America. —Worship of Ramachandra and Sita. —Arjuna's conquest of America and marriage with the daughter of the King. —Routes to America.

The question of Indian visiting foreign lands. — The Vedas enjoin it. —Testimony of *Śāstras*. —Manu and the *Mahābhārata*. —Travels of Vyāsji and Shukdevaji. The expeditions of the Pāṇḍavas. –Emperor Sagarji. –The God of the sea. —Marriages of Indian kings with foreign princesses. —Indian in Turkistan, Persia and Russia. —Origin of the different nations of Asia and Europe. —Testimony of the Puranas and the Mahābhārata. —The seven Dvipas. —The deluge. 168-180

CHAPTER III

3. LITERATURE

Literature a test of the greatness of a nation. —The Indian had the widest range of mind of which man is capable. 181-183

SANSKRIT LANGUAGE

Sanskrit language of wonderful structure. —Compared with Greek, Latin and Hebrew. —More perfect and refined than any. —Modern philology dates from the study of Sanskrit. —Alphabets of Western Asia derived from the *Devanāgarī*. —Sanskrit is the basis of all Indo-European languages. —Greek and Zend derived from the Sanskrit. —Connection of Sanskrit with the ancient languages of Europe. —High antiquity of the Sanskrit literature. 184-192

3.1. ART OF WRITING

Alphabetical writing known in India from the earliest times. —Its use extended to every purpose of common life. —Sanskrit was the spoken vernacular of the ancient Indians. 193-197

3.2. VEDIC LITERATURE

Max Müller on Vedic Literarure. —The Vedas the greatest work in all literature. —Vedas the most precious gift of which the West is indebted to the East. —The study of Vedic Literature indispensable to all. — The Vedas the oldest books in the world. —Vedas the fountain of knowledge. —*Brāhmaṇas* not a part of the Vedas. —*Sūtras.* —*Prātiśākhyas.* —"Study of Language" by the Greeks and the Indians. — Consonantal division of the Sanskrit language unique in the history of literature. —Inferiority of modern Europeans in this respect. —In philology the Indians excel the Ancients and the Moderns. —Grammatical science of the Indians. —Grammar of Pāṇini stands supreme amongst the grammars of the world. —"No other country can produce any grammatical system at all comparable to Pāṇini" 198-207

3.3. POETRY

Treasures of poetry in India are inexhaustible. —The Indians were a poetical people. 208-209

3.4. EPIC POETRY

Rāmāyaṇa and *Mahābhārata* compared to lliad and Odyssey. —*Rāmāyaṇa* the noblest of epics and far superior to the work of Nonnus. —One of the most beautiful compositions that have appeared at any period or in any country. —Rama and Sita perfect characters. —*Mahābhārata* is the grandest of the epics. —Indian epics compared with the Greek epics. —Indian and Greek mythologies compared. Iliad and Odyssey are founded on the *Rāmāyaṇa* and the *Mahābhārata.* 210-224

3.5. DRAMA

Causes of the excellence of Indian drama. —Superiority of Indian drama over the Greek explained and illustrated. —The higher purpose of the dramatic art never lost sight of in Indian dramatic literature. —"No-where is love expressed with greater force or pathos than in the poetry of India," —Kalidasa "one of the greatest dramatists the world ever produced." —"He has done honour to all civilized mankind." —*Śākuntala* an astonishing literary performance. —Language nowhere else so beautifully musical or so magnificently grand as that of the Indian drama. 225-234

3.6. LYRIC POETRY

Gīta Govinda. —Its luxuriant imagery and voluptuous softness. –*Ṛtu Saṁhāra.* —Impossible of translation. —*Meghadūta* "will bear advantageous comparison with best specimens of uniform verse in the poetry of any language, living or dead" 235-237

3.7. ETHICO-DIDACTIC POETRY

Indian achievements in this branch of literature establish their intellectual superiority. —Constitutes practical ethics. — Its use and cultivation peculiar to the Indians. —*Pañcatantra* is the source of the whole fabulous literature of the world. —Aesop's fables derived from India. —Translations by Barzoi under the orders of Nausherwan. —Arabian Nights Entertainment also of Indian origin. —Internal evidence to support the Indian origin of the fabulous literature of the world. —Causes of extraordinary development of this branch of literature in India. 238-244

3.8. *PURĀṆAS*

Purāṇas are semi-religious books. —They are the treasuries of universal information like the *Encyclopaedia Britannica.* —Their origin. —Causes which assigned them their present position —Three classes. —Their

number. —They contain 16,00,000 lines. —The *Up-Purāṇas.* —The character of the *Purāṇas.* 245-250

CHAPTER IV

4. PHILOSOPHY

Philosophers arise in highly-civilized countries, and they are even then few in number. —"The Indians were a nation of philosophers." —Indian philosophy exhausted the possible solutions of problems which have since perplexed the Greeks and Romans, Schoolmen and modern men of science. —Indian philosophy contains counterparts of all systems of European philosophy. —Greek philosophy derived from India. —Pythagoras, Pyrrho, Thales, Anaxarchus Damocritus, Empedocles and others went to India to learn philosophy and imported doctrines from there into Greece. —Origin of Philosophy. —The six schools of Indian philosophy. 251-258

4.1. *NYĀYA*

Classes of substances. —The soul and body affect each other through the mind. —Transmigration of souls. —Vedas are the Revelation. —Material cause of the universe. —Not a system of logic only. —European logic compared with that of *Nyāya* . —"The logical researches of the Indians are scarcely behind the similar works of modern times". 259-261

4.2. *VAIŚEṢIKA*

It is a fuller development of *Nyāya.* —Summary of its contents. —Difference between *Nyāya* and *Vaiśeṣika* —Kanāda's doctrine of atoms superior to that of Democritus. —Theory of sound. —Syllogism. —Difference between Greek and Indian syllogism. 262-265

4.3. *SĀṄKHYA*

The oldest system of philosophy. —Points of difference from *Nyāya.* —Opinion of Mrs. Manning and others. —Views of modern physiologists are a return to the evolution theory of Kapila. 266-267

4.4. *YOGA*

The importance of *Yoga* philosophy. —Its practical character. —Eight stages of *Yoga.* —Testimonies of Prof. Wilson, Dr. Mittra, Dr. Mcgregor and others to the powers of a Yogī. —The system is peculiar to the Indians. 268-271

4.5. *MĪMĀNSĀ*

Uttara and *Pūrva Mimānsas.* —*Vedānta* a grant system of philosophy. —"No one can read it without feeling a richer and a wiser man." —Difference of opinion regarding the *Vedānta.* —Views of Ramanuja, Shanker and Dayananda. —Sir W. Jones' explanation of the Vedanta. —The *Mimānsā* method. —The *Upaniṣads.* —The sublime character of their teachings. —Views of Prof. Deussen and of the philosopher Schopenhauer. —Greeks and Indians compared. 272-276

4.6. *BHAGAVAD GĪTĀ*

Views of Mrs. Manning, Prof. Heeren and Mr. Elphinstone. 277

CHAPTER V

5. SCIENCE

5.1. MEDICINE

Indian sanitary code. —Manu one of the greatest sanitary reformers of the world. Dhanvantari, Caraka and Susruta. —Indian surgery. —Surgical instruments of the Indians. —Veterinary science, Translation of Sanskrit works into Persian and Arabic. —Anatomy, —Origin of the science of medicine. —Arab medicine founded on Indian medicine. —Alberuni. —Indian physicians at the courts of the Khalifs. —Indian physicians in charge of hospitals in Baghdad. — Influene on Greek Medicine. —Cure of snakebite. —Indian chemistry. —Mercurial preparations first administered internally by the Indians. —Medicinal virtues of mercury unknown in Europe till after the time of Pliny. —Vaccination known to the ancient Indians. 278-293

5.2. MATHEMATICS

Indians invented decimal ciphers. —Views of Schlegel, Prof. Macdonell, Monier Williams, Mannings, Sir W. Hunter, Weber and Wilson on the invention of numerical symbols. 294-296

5.3. ARTHMETIC

High proficiency in arithmetic. —Professor Wallance on Indian arithmetic. 297-298

5.4. GEOMETRY

Sūrya Siddhānta contains an original system of trigonometry founded on a geometrical theorem not known to the geometrecians of Europe till about two hundred years ago.—Antiquity of Indian geometry. —The 47th Proposition of Book I known to the Indians two centuries before Pythagoras, who learnt it from the Indians. —Area of a triangle in the terms of its three sides. —Unknown even in Europe till modern times. 299-301

5.5. ALGEBRA

Professor Wallace on the high proficiency of the Indians in Algebra. —Arabs recipients not inventors. —Invention of algebra and geometry due to Indians. —History of two problems of Algebra. —The process Cattaca. —Problem solved by Buddha at his marriage is the basis of the Arenarius of Archimedes. —Differential calculus known to the Indians. 302-306

5.6. ASTRONOMY

Extraordinary proficiency of the Indians in astronomy. —Indian Astronomy disproves the chronology of the Hebrew Scriptures. —Indian observations made more than three thousand years before Christ evince a very high degree of Astronomical science. —Conjunction of the planets at the beginning of the *Kaliyuga.* — Tables of Solar eclipses sent to Europe by Laubere and Patouillet. —Brāhmaṇa calculations proved to be absolutely exact by the tables of Cassini and Meyer. —Proofs of the great antiquity of Indian astronomy. —Originality of the Indians. —*Nakṣatras* or moon stations and the Chinese Sieu. —The Arabs were the disciples of the Indians. —The nine Siddhāntas. —Roundness of the earth. —The annual and diurnal motions of the earth. -The stars are stationary. —The Polar days and nights. —Circumferences of the earth. —What keeps the earth in its place. —The moon is a dark body. —The atmosphere. —Eclipses. —Tides. —Jai Singh II. —Methods of the Indians. —A peculiar theory of planetary motions. —To find the longitude of place. 307-322

5.7. MILITARY SCIENCE

Indian traditions all warlike. —Naval power of the Indians. —Indian Science of war. —Use of elephants, —Archery of the Indians. —Indian swordmen. —Classification of weapons. —Indian weapons now extinct. —Firearms of the Indians and their extensive employment. —Guns and cannons in mediaeval India. *Vajra.* —Gunpowder. —The *Brahmāstra.* —*Rāmāyaṇa* mentions firearms. —The *Śataghni* and *Āgneyāstra.* —Rockets a Indian invention. —Other machines and contrivances to throw projectiles now extinct. —The *Astra Vidyā* of the Indians. 323-338

5.8. MUSIC

The Indians are a musical race. —Indian system of music the oldest in the world. —Sub-division of tones and number of sonal modifications too intricate to be appreciated by Europeans. Europeans cannot imitate Indian music. —Indian airs cannot be set to music. —Cultivated on scientific principles. —The *Rāgas* and *Rāgnis*. —Indian notation introduced into European music in the eleventh century. —Derivation of Greek music from India.339-347

5.9. OTHER SCIENCES

Engineering. — Mechanics. —Microscopes. —Telescopes. —Fire-engines. —Botany. —Magnets. —Doctrine of Vacuume in Nature. —*Vimāna Vidyā*. —*Sarpa Vidyā*. —Electricity and Magnetism. —Philosophy of sleep. Aureole round the heads of Indian gods. 348-359

CHAPTER VI

6. ARTS

6.1. ARCHITECTURE AND SCULPTURE

Indian architecture, wonderful and beautiful. —Views of Mahmud Ghaznavi. —Unequalled in elegance. — Cave temples. —Skill shown surpasses description. —Ornamenting grottoes. —The Saracen arch of Indian Origin. —English decorative art indebted to the Indians. —Resoration of taste in England due to Indians. —Art exhausted itself in India. 360-366

6.2. WEAVING

Unrivalled delicacy of sense of the Indians. —Indian cotton finest in the world. —Europeans must not attempt to teach art to India. 367-370

6.3. OTHER ARTS

Art of dyeing. —Indians discovered the art of extracting colours from plants. —Ivory works. —Casting iron. —Indian steel. —Danascus steel of Indian origin. —The wrought-iron pillar near Kutab at Delhi. —The gun at Nurwarand the girders at Puri prove the marvelous skills of the Indians. —Export of iron from India. —System of rotation of crops, derived from India. —Use of glass in windows in ancient India. —Perfection of art in India.

371-375

CHAPTER VII

7. COMMERCE & WEALTH

7.1. COMMERCE

Indians the masters of the sea-borne trade of the world. —India was "once the seat of commerce". — Indians were a commercial people. —Trade with Phoenicia, Syria, Egypt, Rome. —Pliny complains of the drain of gold from Rome to India. —Trade with Arabia and Africa. —Eastern Trade. 376-387

7.2. CEYLON

Ceylon. —Its commercial importance. —Emporium of trade.—Ceylon a part of India. —Commercial ports of India. 388-391

7.3. LAND TRADE

—Land trade with China. —Trade routes for the land trade with Europe. —Internal trade of India. —Milestones and inns for travellers. —Indian fairs at Hardwar, Allahabad and other places. 392-396

7.4. WEALTH

India was the richest country in the world. —Spoils of Somnath, Mathura and Kannauj. —Gold first found in India. —An Indian port the only pearl market in the world. —The most famous stones and pearls all of Indian origin. 397-399

CHAPTER VIII

8. RELIGION

Religion a test of civilization. —What is the Vedic religion? — knowledge of God. —The Śraddhā— Vedic religion the only scientific religion in the world. ''Christianity has nothing to offer to those who are dissatisfied with Vedic religion.'' —Buddhism is offshoot of Vedic religion. —Majority of mankind still follow religions that emanated from India. —Origin of the Greek Church. —Origin of Christianity. — Buddhism and Vedic religion. —Propagation of Buddhism. —Buddhism in Arabia and in Egypt. —The Hermes Scriptures. —Indian origin of the religion of the Chaldeans, the Babylonians and the inhabitants of Colchis. —The Samaritans were Buddhists. — Buddhism in Britain. —The religion of the Scandinavians. —Scandinavian Mythology. —Egyptian and Greek religions derived from India. —The Mosaic cosmogony. —Greek mythology derived from Indian mythology. —Christian mythology. —The Indians are the parents of the literature and theology of the world.

400-421

INTRODUCTION

In the history of the world India occupies the foremost place. From the dawn of history to the present day India has been connected in one way or another with almost every event of world importance. By endowing India with the best and the choicest of gifts it had in store, Nature herself ordained that this magnificent country, with a climate varied and salubrious, a soil the most fertile in the world, animal and plant life the most abundant, useful and diversified to be found anywhere on the face of the earth, should play the leading part in the history of mankind.

Mr. Murray says, ''It (India) has always appeared to the imagination of the Western World adorned with whatever is most splendid and gorgeous; glittering, as it were, with gold and gems, and redolent of fragrant and delicious odours. Though there be in these magnificent conceptions something romantic and illusory, still India forms unquestionably one of the most remarkable regions that exist on the surface of the globe. The varied grandeur of its scenery and the rich productions of its soil are scarcely equalled in any other country.''[1]

''India is an epitome of the whole world,''[2] and possesses all the leading features of other lands— the most bewitching scenery, the most fertile soil, the most dense forests, the highest mountains, some of the biggest rivers and intensely cold seasons, may be found along with arid, treeless deserts, sandy waterless plains, and the hottest days. To a student of humanity or of Nature, India even now is most picturesque and is the most interesting country in the world. Count Bjornstjerna says, ''But everything is peculiar, grand, and romantic in India— from the steel clad knight of

---

[1] Murray High (p.1): *History of British India*, T. Nelson and Sons, London, Edinburgh, 1854.

[2] Chamber's *Encyclopaedia*, London, 1880, p. 337.

Rajasthan to the devoted Brāhmaṇa in the temples of Benares; from the fierce Mahratta on his fleet and active steel to the Nabob moving gently on his elephant; from the Amazon who chases the tiger in the jungle to the Bayadere who offers in *volupte* to her gods. Nature, too, in this glorious country is chequered with variety and clad in glowing colours; see the luxuriance of her tropical vegetation and the hurricane of her monsoon; see the majesty of her snow-covered Himalayas and the dryness of her deserts; see the immense plains of Hindustan and the scenery of her lofty mountains; but, above all, see the immense age of her history and the poetry of her recollections.''[1]

Professor Max Müller says, 'If I were to look over the whole world to find out the country most richly endowed with all the wealth, power, and beauty that nature can bestow-in some parts *a very paradise on earth* - I should point to India. If I were asked under what sky the human mind has most fully developed some of its choicest gifts, has most deeply pondered on the greatest problems of life, and has found solutions of some of them which well deserve the attention even of those who have studied Plato and Kant, I should point to India. And if I were to ask myself from what literature we here in Europe-we who have been nurtured almost exclusively on the thoughts of the Greeks and the Romans, and of one Semitic race the Jewish-may draw that corrective which is most wanted in order to make our inner life more perfect, more comprehensive, more universal, in fact more truly human, a life, not for this life only, but a transfigured and eternal life, again I should point to India''. He adds, 'Whatever sphere of the human mind you may select for your special study, whether it be language, or

---

[1] *Theogony of the Hindus*, p.126, 'The scenery of the Himalayas,' says Mounstuart Elphinstone, 'is a sight which the soberest traveler has never described without kindling into enthusiasm, and which, if once seen, leaves an impression that can never be equalled or effaced.' *History of India*, London, p. 181

religion, or mythology, or philosophy, whether it be laws or customs, primitive art or primitive science, everywhere you have to go to India, whether you like it or not, because some of the most valuable and most instructive materials in the history of man are treasured up in India and in India only.''[1]

Professor Heeren says, ''India is the source from which not only the rest of Asia but the whole Western World derived their knowledge and their religion.''[2] A writer in the Calcutta Review for December 1861, said, ''Though now degraded and abased, yet we cannot doubt that there was a time when the Hindu race was splendid in arts and arms, happy in government, wise in legislation and eminent in knowledge.''[3]

''The ancient state of India,'' says Mr. Thornton, ''must have been one of extraordinary magnificence.''[4]

Colonel Tod asks, ''Where can we look for sages like those whose system of philosophy were the prototypes of those of Greece: to whose works plato, Thales, and

---

[1] Max Müller's *India : What can it teach us?* P. 15

[2] *Historical Researches*, vol. II, p.45

[3] The same Review says: ''That the Hindus were in former times a commercial people we have every reason to believe -the labours of the Indian loom have been universally celebrated, silk has been fabricated immemorially by the Hindus. We are also told by the Grecian writers that the Indians were the wisest of nations, and in metaphysical wisdom they were certainly eminent; in astronomy and mathematics they were equally well versed; this is the race who Dionysius records-

'First assayed the deep,
'And wafted merchandize to coasts unknown,
'Those who digested first the starry choir,
'There motions marked, and called them by their names.'

''Hindustan has from the earliest ages been celebrated as one of the most highly-favoured countries on the globe, and as abounding in the choicest productions both of Nature and Art.''

Encyclopaedia Britannica, p.446

[4] *Chapters of the British History of India.*

Pythagoras were disciples? Where shall we find astronomers whose knowledge of the planetary system yet excites wonder in Europe, as well as the architects and sculptors whose works claim our admiration, and the musicians 'who could make the mind oscillate from joy to sorrow, from tears to smiles, with the change of modes and varied intonation.''[1]

A writer in the *Edinburgh Review* for October 1872, says, "The Hindu is the most ancient nation of which we have valuable remains, and has been surpassed by none in refinement and civilization; though the utmost pitch of refinement to which it ever arrived preceded, in time, the dawn of civilization in any other nation of which we have even the name in history. The further our literary inquiries are extended here, the more vast and stupendous is the scene which opens to us."

An attempt has been made in the following pages, with the help of the laudable labours of philanthropists like Sir W. Jones, Prof. H.H. Wilson, Mr. Colebrooke, Colonel Tod, Mr. Pococke and other European scholars and officers to whom the country owes a great debt of gratitude, to get a glimpse of the civilization which, according to the writer quoted above, has not yet been surpassed. And what is the result? What do we learn about the ancient Indians? We learn that they were the greatest nation that has yet flourished on this earth.

"In the world there is nothing great but man,
In man there is nothing great but mind"

was the favourite aphorism of the philosopher, Sir William Hamilton.[2] And Mrs. Manning says, "the Hindus had the widest range of mind of which man is capable."[3]

We find that the ancient Indians, in every feature of national life, were in the first rank. Take whatever

---

[1] Tod's *Rajasthan*, pp.608, 609.

[2] See Jevon's *Logic*, p.9

[3] *Ancient and Mediaeval India*, Vol. II, p.148

department of human activity you like, you find the ancient Indians eminent in it, and as occupying a foremost place. This is more than what can be said of any other nation. You may find a nation great in arms or commerce; you may find a people eminent in philosophy, in poetry, in science or in arts; you may find a race great politically but not equally so morally and intellectually. But you do not find a race which was or is pre-eminent in so many departments of human activity as the ancient Hindus.

The ancient Hindus were "a poetical people," they were essentially "a musical race," and they were "a commercial people." They were "a nation of philosophers," "in science they were as acute and diligent as ever." "Art seems to have exhausted itself in India." "The Hindu is the parent of the literature and the theology of the world." His language is the best and the most beautiful in the world. The national character of the ancient Hindus as regards truthfulness, chivalry and honour was unrivalled; their colonies filled the world, their kings "are still worshipped as the gods of the sea," "their civilization still pervades in every corner of the civilized world and is around and about us every day of our lives".

It may be urged that in the picture of Hindu civilization painted in the book, only roseate hues have been used, that while lights are purposely made prominent the shadows are conspicuous by their absence, and that most has been made of the best points of Hinduism. Such critics will do well to remember that the mountains are measured by their highest peaks and not by the low heights to which they here and there sink; that the first rank among the mountains is assigned to the Himalayas by Mounts Everest, Dhavalgiri and Kanchanjanga, and not by the lower heights of Mussoorie and Darjeeling, and that the patches of level ground here and there found enclosed within this gigantic range are justly ignored.

It may also be remarked here that the object of this book being to enable men to appreciate the excellencies of Hindu civilization—by giving them an idea of the character and achievements of the ancient Hindus, who were the creatures of that civilization, which has admittedly seen its best days-any discussion of modern India for its own sake is without the scope of this book. Wherever, therefore, any fact relating to the society, religion, literature or character of the Hindus of the present day, or their capacities and capabilities is mentioned it has reference only to the elucidation of some feature of that civilization as illustrated in the life, work or character of the people of ancient India.[1]

It is the inherent truth of Hinduism, the vitality and greatness of the Hindu civilization that have enable the Hindus yet to preserve their existence as such, despite all the political cataclysms, social upheavals, and racial eruptions the world has seen since the Mahābhārata. These calamities overwhelmed the ancient Egyptians and the Phoenicians and destroyed the empires of ancient Greece, Persia and Rome.

---

[1] It is no part of the plan of this book to run down any creed or nationality. Consequently, whenever any other religion or race is mentioned, it is only for the elucidation of some point of Hinduism, or to show the comparative excellence of some feature of Hindu civilization. Thus, whenever the oppressive nature of the rule of some of the Mohamedan Emperors is mentioned, or the havoc caused by some of the invaders from the North-Western frontier of India is described, it is not to emphasize that fact itself, but to illustrate, explain, or educidate some feature of the character of the Hindus or their literature and society. It may also be remarked that the evils of the rules of the Afghans, Turks, and others were due not to the religion they professed but to their ignorance and backwardness in civilization. The Arabs, though professing the same religion as the Afghans and the Moghals, kept the lamp of knowledge and science lit in Europe and Western Asia during the middle ages. The work of Al-Beruni, Albdul Fazal, Faizi and others in India pulls to pieces the theory that whatever evils there were in Mohamedan rule were due to the religion of the rulers.

Compared to the sun of Hindu civilization giving a constant and steady stream of beneficent light, which penetrates the farthest nooks and corners of the world, carrying comfort and contentment to mankind, these civilizations were like brilliant meteors that appear in the skies lighting the while, with their short-lived lustre, the heavens above and the earth below.

Then-let me dive into the depths of time,
And bring from out the ages that have rolled,
A few small fragments of those wrecks sublime,
Which human eye may never more behold;
And let the guerdon of my labour be,
My b'loved country! One kind wish for thee.

I

CONSTITUTION

Clime of the unforgotten brave!
Where land from plain to mountain cave
Was freedom's home or glory's grave:
Shrine of the mighty! Can it be
That this is all remains of thee?

BYRON: *Giaour*

No one acquainted with the history of the ancient Indians can reasonable deny the great merits of their ancient Constitution, which combined happiness with activity, tranquility with progress —"one lesson which in every wind is blown"— and conservation with advancement. Their astonishing subjective capacities and their extraordinary powers of observation and generalization led them irresistibly to trace Nature in all her multifarious solemn workings. They followed her in every thing they did, and hence the halo of reality and conservation which surrounds their work. It is this reality and conservation, the happy results of following Nature—"which is a wisdom without reflection and above it" —that have imparted that polish to Hindu Laws and Institution, which makes them at once durable and brilliant.

There was, anciently, an adjustment of forces which enabled each institution to describe its peculiar orbit and work in its own sphere, without interfering with the others; but now, alas! Owing to the long-continued and unabated pressure of hostile circumstances, that adjustment is being broken, and the forces are being let loose so as to bring the different institutions together. Their foundations, however, are still intact, owing to their exceeding firmness.

The turning point in the history of Ancient India was the *Mahābhārata*, the Great War between the Pāṇḍavas and the Kauravas. This momentous event decides the future of

Ancient India, as it closed the long chapter of Indian growth and Indian greatness. The sun of India's glory was at its meridian about the end of *Dvāpara*, and, following the universal law of Nature, with the beginning of the *Kaliyuga*, it turned its course towards the horizon, where it set on the plains of Thaneshwar amidst the romantic splendour of Sanjugta's love and Prithviraj's chivalry. As the *Mahābhārata* marked the zenith of Indian greatness, Shahabud-din's victory at Thaneshwar marked the sinking of the great luminary below the horizon. The Nadir reached several centuries later, when the armies under Baji Rao were routed on the same sacred, fateful plains by the Durrani host. The great war which, as will be seen hereafter, influenced so powerfully the destiny of nations was, in reality, the beginning of the end of Indian greatness, and it was at this period that the political and social constitution of India began to yield to those innovations which, by their very contrast to the fundamental principles of the Constitution, are so prominent now.

1.1. ANTIQUITY

Time is the root of created beings,
And uncreated; of pleasure and of pain.
Time doth create existence. Time destroys,
Time shatters all, and all again renews.
Time watches while all sleep. Unvanquished Time!

—*MĀHĀBHĀRATA*: *Ādiparva*

The antiquity of the Indian civilization is wonderful, its vitality miraculous. The fabulous age of the Greeks, the time of Egyptian Soufi, and the "stone age" of the modern European thinkers are but as yesterday in the history of the Indian civilization. The age of this earth is not to be counted by a few thousand years, but by millions and trillions. And Indian civilization is the earliest civilization in this world. Nations have risen and fallen, empire founded and destroyed, race have appeared and disappeared, but the Indian civilization that saw their rise and fall, their foundation and destruction, their appearance and disappearance, still remains.

After fully discussing the claims of the ancient nations of the world to high antiquity, Count Bjornstjerna says, "No nation on earth can vie with the Hindus in respect of the antiquity of their civilization and the antiquity of their religion."[1]

Dr. Stiles, President of Yale College in America, formed such an enthusiastic expectation from the amazing antiquity of the Indian writings that he actually wrote to Sir W. Jones to request him to search among the Indians for the Admic books.[2]

Mr. Halhed exclaims with sacred reverence, after treating of the four *yugas* of the Indians, "To such antiquity

---

[1] *Theogony of the Hindus*, p.50.

[2] Ward's *Mythology*, Vol. I, p. 144

the Mosaic creation is but as yesterday; and to such ages the life of Methuselah is no more than a span."

In concluding his remarks on the antiquity of Indian astronomy, Count Bjornstjerna says, "But if it be true that the Hindus more than 3,000 years before Christ, according to Bailly's calculation, had attained so high a degree of astronomical and geometrical learning, how many centuries earlier must the commencement of their culture have been, since the human mind advances only step by step in the path of science![1] And yet, astronomy is not the science that is cultivated very early in the national literature of any country.

Pliny states that from the days of Bacchus to Alexander of Macedon, 154 kings reigned over India, whose reigns extended over 6,451 years. How many reigned before Bacchus history is silent.

Abul-Fazal, in his translation of the *Rājataraṅgiṇī*, quotes the names of the kings who appear in these annals, and whose successive reigns are said to have occupied 4,109 years 11 months and 9 days. Prof. Heeren says, "From Dionysius (an Indian king) to Sandracottus (Sikandergupta of Gupta dynasty) the space of 6,042 years is said to have elapsed. Megasthenes says, 6,042 years passed between Spatembas and Sandracottus.[2]

Professor Max Dunker[3] says, "that Spatembas," which is perhaps another name of Dionysius, "began his reign in 6,717 years BC." "The era of Yudhiṣṭhira indeed," he again asserts, "is said to have preceded that of Vikramāditya by the space of 3,044 years, and to have commenced about 3,100 years BC"[4]

---

[1] *Theogony of the Hindus*, p.37
[2] *Historical Researches*, Vol. II, p. 218
[3] *History of Antiquity*, vol. IV, p.74
[4] *History of Antiquity*, Vol. IV, p.219

Count Bjornstjerna says, "Megasthenes, the envoy of Alexander to Kandragupso (Sikandergupta of Gupta dynasty), king of the Gangarides, discovered chronological tables at Polybhottra, the residence of this king, which contain a series of no less than 153 kings, with all their names from Dionysius to Kandragupso, and specifying the duration of the reigns of every one of those kings, together amounting to 6,451 years, which would place the reign of Dionysius nearly 7,000 years BC, and consequently 1,000 years before the oldest king found on the Egyptian tables of Manetho (viz., the head of the Tinite Thebaine dynasty), who reigned 5,867 years BC, and 2,000 years before Soufi, the founder of the Gizeh Pyramid."[1]

According to Sir W. Jones[2], eighty-one kings reigned in Magadha. "The first 20 reigns are unaccompanied with any chronological determination, but the ensuing are divided by him into five separate dynasties, of which the first commenced with King Pradista about 2,100 BC and terminated with king Nanda, about 1500 BC, embracing a period of 16 reigns; the second only comprises 10, and ends with the year 1,365 BC; the third dynasty, that of Śuṅga, contains also the same number of kings, and terminates 1,253 BC; the fourth, that of Canna, only consisted of four kings, and lasted till the year 908 BC; the fifth, that of Andhra forms a series of 21 kings, and continued down to the year 456 before the Christian era and 400 before that of Vikrama."

Now, according to the Purāṇas, the race of the Bṛhadrathas had ruled over Magadha before Pradyotas, (who reigned 2,000 BC, according to Sir W. Jones), from Somapi to Ripunjaya[3] for a thousand years. And before the first

---

[1] *Theogony of the Hindus*, p. 45

[2] *Sir W. Jones' Works*, Vol. I, p. 304

[3] Max Dunker's *History of Antiquity*, Vol. IV, p. 76

Bṛhadrathas, Sahadeo, Jarasandh and Bṛhadratha are said to have reigned over Magadha.''[1]

The fact that dynasties and not individuals were units of calculation, is in itself a proof of the great antiquity of the ancient Indian empire.

Count Bjornstjerna, after discussing the antiquity of Indian astronomy says, ''Besides the proofs adduced of the great antiquity of the civilization of the Hindus, there are others perhaps still stronger, namely, their gigantic temples hewn out of lofty rocks, with the most incredible labour, at Elephanta, at Ellora and several other places which, with regard to the vastness of undertaking, may be compared with the pyramids, and in an architectural respect even surpass them''[2]

Professor Heeren says, '' We do not perhaps assume too much when we venture to place the origin of Ayodhyā from 1500 to 2000 BC.''

Professor Heeren[3] says, ''I cannot refuse credence to this fact, namely that great States, highly advanced in civilization, existed at least three thousand years before our era. It is beyond that limit that I look for Rama, the hero of the *Rāmāyaṇa.*''[4]

According to the *Mahābhārata*, Ayodhyā prospered for 1,500 years, after which one of its kings, of the dynasty of Surgas, founded Kanauj. The foundation of the city of Delhi (Indraprastha) is as old as the fabulous age (Pober, Vol. I, p. 263), at which time it was already celebrated for its splendour (Vol. I, p. 606).

Rennell[5] states that Kanauj was founded more than a thousand years before Christ. But apart from these

---

[1] Max Dunker's *History of Antiquity*, Vol. IV, p. 77.

[2] *Theogony of the Hindus*, p. 38

[3] *Historical Researches*, Vol, II, p 227

[4] *Asiatic Journal*, 1841.

[5] *Memoirs*, p. 54 (2nd edition)

haphazard shots of European writers-who, as Professor Wilson says, "in order to avoid being thought credulous run into the opposite vice of incredulity," and would never concede anything for which there is not a demonstrable proof, especially as the history of ancient India is a history of ages so remote as to hopelessly put out of joint their early-conceived and limited notions of chronology and antiquity— there is an important piece of evidence in favour of the great antiquity of Indian civilization. Says Count Bjornstjerna, "The Bactrian document, called Dabistan[1] (found in Kashmir and brought to Europe by Sir W. Jones), gives an entire register of kings, namely, of the Mahabadernes, whose first link reigned in Bactria, 5,600 years before Alexander's expedition to India, and consequently several hundred years before the time given by the Alexandrine text for the appearance of the first man upon the earth."

That these Bactrian kings were Indians is now universally admitted[2]. Dabistan thus proves that India enjoyed splendid civilization 6,000 BC, or nearly 8,000 years before the Victorian age.

This alone is sufficient to prove that the ancient Indians were incontestably the earliest civilized nation on earth. Another conclusive proof of their unrivalled antiquity will be found in the fact that all the great nations of the old world derived their civilization from India, that India planted colonies in all parts of the world, and that these colonies afterwards became known as Egypt, Greece, Persia, China, America, etc. and that Scandinavia, Germany, and ancient Britain derived their civilization and their religion from the Indians, In short, as will be seen hereafter, it was India which supplied the rest of the world with learning, civilization and religion.

---

[1] *Theogony of the Hindus*, p. 134

[2] See Mill's *History of India*, Vol.II., pp. 237-238

The most ancient coinage in the world is that of the Indians (Aryas), and the modern discoveries of the coins of ancient India are conclusive proofs of the vast antiquity of Indian civilization.[1]

But in India everything is astounding to the European. Notwithstanding the destructive ravages of barbarous fanaticism, enough material remains from which we can infer, upon scientific data, the age of the present earth.

Swami Dayanand Saraswati has treated the subject elaborately in his "*Introduction to the Vedas*", and also discussed it with the Reverend Mr. Scott of Bareilly at Chandapur (vide *Arya Darpan* for March 1880, p. 67-68).

The *Saṅkalpa*, which every educated Indian in India knows well, and which is recited at every ceremony, even at a dip in the sacred Ganges, is the key to unfold the whole mystery that enshrouds the view of the time at which the earth assumed its present form.

ओं तत्सत् श्री ब्रह्मणो द्वितीये प्रहरार्द्धे वैवस्वत मन्वन्तरे अष्टाविंशतितमे कलियुगे कलिप्रथमचरणे आर्य्यावर्त्तान्तरैकदेशे अमुकनगरे अमुकसंवत्सरायनर्त्तु–मासपक्षदिननक्षत्र मुहुर्तेऽत्रेदं कार्य्यं कृतं क्रियते वा।

To understand what follows, it must be remembered that this world is alternately created from and dissolved into its material cause (कारण) — *the Prakṛti* — after a fixed period. The world exists in one form for a fixed period, and then for that very period, it exists only in its material cause. The former is called "*Brāhma Dina,*" and the latter "*Brāhma Rātri.*".

As the *Atharvaveda* says, the *Brāhma Dina* is equal to 4,320,000,000 years.

---

[1] The coinage of the Hindus, whatever may be its value and character, is certainly of a very remote antiquity-Elphinstone's *India*, p. 176.

शतं तेऽयुतं हायनान्द्वेयुगे त्रीणि चत्वारिकृण्मः।

अथर्व. प्र. अनु. 1 मं 21

This *Brāhma Dina* is made up of 1,00 *Chaturyugis* (4 *yugas*) or *Divyayugas*, as they are also called, Manu (*Adhyāya* I), says :

देविकानां युगानन्तु सहस्रपरिसंख्यया। ब्राह्ममेकमहर्ज्ञेयं तावती रात्रिरेव च।। मनु. अ. 1, श्लोक 72

A *Caturyugī* or *Divyayuga* means a period of four *yugas*, *Satyuga*, *Tretā*, *Dvāpara* and *Kaliyuga*, and consists of 12,000 *Divya* years— *Satyayuga* consisting of 4,800, *Tretā* of 3,600, *Dvāpara* of 2,400 and *Kaliyuga* of 1,200 *Divya* years. Manu (Chapter 1, SI. 71) says :

यदेतत् परिसंख्यातमादावेव चतुर्युगम्। एतद् द्वादश साहस्रं देवानां युगमुच्यते।। 79 and again

चत्वार्याहुः सहस्राणि वर्षाणां तत् कृतं युगम्।
तस्य तावत्शती सन्ध्या सन्ध्यांशश्च तथाविधः ॥६६।।

इतरेषु ससन्ध्येषु ससन्ध्यांशेषु च त्रिषु।
एकापायेन वर्तन्ते सहस्राणि शतानि च ॥७० ॥

मनुस्मृति 1.69–70

Now, a *Divya* year is equal to 360 ordinary years. Thus

Satyuga = 4,800x360=1,728,000 years

Tretā = 3,600x360 = 1,296,000 years

Dvāpara = 2,400 x 360 = 864,000 years

Kaliyuga = 1,200 x 360= 432,000 years

A *Caturyugī* = 4,320,000 years

Thus, the *Brāhma Dina* = 4,320,000,000 years. This is the period for which the world will remain in its present form.

Again the *Brāhma Dina* is divided into 14 *Manvantaras* and a *Manvantara* into 71 *Caturyugis*. Manu says :

यत् प्रागद्वादशसहस्रमुदितं दैविकं युगम्।
तदेकसप्ततिगुणं मन्वन्तरमिहोच्यते।। मनुस्मृति, 5.79

the *Sūrya Siddhānta* also says :

युगानां सप्ततिः सैका मन्वन्तरमिहोच्यते।
कृताब्दसंख्या तस्यास्ते सन्धि प्रोक्तोजलप्लवः।।

ससन्धयस्ते मनवः कल्पे ज्ञेयाश्चतुर्दश।
कृतप्रमाणः कल्पादौ सन्धिः पंचदशः स्मृतः।।

इत्थं युगसहस्रेण भूतसंहारकारकः।
कल्पो ब्राह्ममहः प्रोक्ता शर्वरी तस्य तावती।।

सूर्यसिद्धान्त, 1.18–19

According to the *Saṅkalpa* quoted above, six *Manvantaras*[1] have passed, the seventh is passing, and the remaining seven have still to come. Each *Caturyugī* =4,320,000 as shown before, and 4,320,000x71= 306, 720,000=one *Manvantara*. Now, six *Manvantaras* = 1,840,320, 000 have passed, and this present *Kaliyuga* is the *Kaliyuga* of the 28th *Caturyugī*. Of this *Caturyugī*, 5,106 years of the *Kaliyuga* (the present *Saṁvat* being 2063 *Vikrama*) have passed, and 432,000—5,106=426,894 years of the *Kaliyuga* have yet to pass. Thus, of the seventh *Manvantara*, 116,640,000 (27 *Caturyuga* is 4,320,000x27) + 3,893,106 (the period of the 28th *Chaturyugī* already passed, 4,320,000—426,894) total 120,533,106 years have passed. The period yet to pass before the day of Final Dissolution comes is 214,704,000 (remaining 7 *Manvantaras*)+ 186,186,894 (of the present (sixth) *Manvantara*) = 2,333,226,894 years.

---

[1] The six Manvantras already passed are Svāyambhuva, Svārocis, Autamī, Taijas, Raivata, Cākṣus, Vaivasvat. The seven Manvantras to come are named Sāvarṇī, Dakṣa Sāvṛṇī, Brāhma Sāvarṇī, Dharma Sāvarṇī, Rudra Sāvarṇī, Deva Sāvarṇī and Indra Sāvarṇī (Bhautyaka).

The Europeans, "accustomed as they are," to use the words of Professor Sir M. Williams, "to a limited horizon", will find this vast antiquity bewildering. Billions surely are incredible, if not incomprehensible to pious ears accustomed to a scale, the highest not of which rises no higher than 6,000 years. But matters are improving, and even these pious souls will in time break the shell and come out into a world in which centuries will be replaced by millenniums.

Mr. Baldwin says, "Doubtless the antiquity of the human race is much greater than is usually assumed by those whose views of the past are still regulated by mediaeval systems of chronology. Archaeology and linguistic science, not to speak here of Geology, make it certain that the period between the beginning of the human race and the birth of Christ would be the more accurately stated if the centuries counted in the longest estimate of the rabbinical chronologies should be changed to millenniums. And they present also another fact, namely, that the antiquity of civilization is very great, and suggest that in remote ages it may have existed, with important developments, in regions of the earth now described as barbarous. The representation of some speculators that the condition of the human race since its first appearance on earth has been a condition of universal and hopeless savagery down to a comparatively modern date, is an assumption merely, an unwarranted assumption used in support of an unproved and unprovable theory of man's origin."[1]

---

[1] Baldwin's *Ancient America*, p. 181

1.2. Government

For forms of Government let fools contest;
Whate'er is best administer'd, is best

— Pope, E. M.

The saying of the greatest English exponent of Political Philosophy, Edmund Burke, that no country in which population flourishes can be under a bad Government, introduces us to the subject of the political constitution of Ancient India. Burke lays down two important standards to test the good or bad government of a nation : (I) Population, and (II) wealth.

All the Ancient Greek writers and travellers are agreed that the Ancient Aryas were the largest nation on the earth.

Appollodorus[1] states that "there were between the Hydaspes and Hypanis (Hypasis) 1,500 cities, none of which was less than Cos."

Megasthenes says that "there are 120 nations in India." Arrian admits that the Indians were the most numerous people[2] and that it was impossible to know and enumerate the cities in Āryāvartta. Strabo says that Eukratides was the master of 1,000 cities between Hydaspes and Hypasis. Professor Max Dunker[3] says "the Indians were the largest of the nations." Ctesias states that "they (Indians) were as numerous as all the other nations put together."[4]

---

[1] Elphinstone's *India*, p. 241, See. Strabo, Lib, XV.

[2] See his chapter on India, C. VII. See also his History of Nations, 6,22,23.

[3] *History of Antiquity*, Vol. V., p.18

[4] Strabo states that 'Polibhothra was eight miles long and had a rampart which had 570 towers and 64 gates.'As late even as the 16th century, Kanauj was reported to have contained no less than

But the most important proof of the over-abundant population of Ancient India is to be found in the successive waves of emigration from India to the different parts of the world, founding colonies and planting settlements in what are now called the Old and the New Worlds.

As regards wealth, India has always been famous for its immense riches. "Golden India" is a hackneyed phrase.[1] Both in population and in wealth, India, at one time was not only pre-eminent but was without a rival.

What higher authority, what more positive proof of the good government of Ancient India is required than the fact that "ancient India knew no thieves,"[2] nor knew why to shut the doors of its houses even at the time when, according to Dr. Johnson, "the capital of the most civilized nation of modern times is the true Satan-at-home."

'Prepare for death, if here at night you roam,
And sign your will before you sleep from home.'

The form of Government depends upon the character of a people, the conditions of life obtaining among them, and the principles of their social system. With changes in respect of these matters, the form of government also undergoes a change. Broadly speaking, the best form of Government is that which enables only men of high character, noble minds, wide sympathies, men of sterling qualities and talents to rise to the top, and prevents men of shallow minds, mean capacities, narrow sympathies, and unscrupulous characters from coming into power, it being always understood that the proper functions of Government are only (I) national defence, and (II) protection of one individual or of one class from another.

30,000 shops of betelsellers and 'sixty thousand sets of musicians.' See *Historical Researches*, Vol. II, p. 220

[1] For further information on this subject, see "Wealth."

[2] See Strabo, Lib, XV. P. 488 (1587 edition).

The form of Government may vary, but the spirit depends on the ethical side of a people's character. It is well said :

Political rights, however broadly framed,
Will not elevate a people individually depraved.

If high moral principles guide the people in their daily conduct as a nation, the government of that nation is free from those party strifes, that incessant warfare raged by one individual against another and by one class against another for power or for protection, which is a leading feature of all European and American Governments of the present day. It is this law that discovers to us the eternal principle, that spiritual elevation not only helps material prosperity but is essential to the happiness of a people, and that it is an index to the realization of the aim and object of all government.

Mr. Herbert Spencer says, "There has grown up quite naturally, and indeed almost inevitably among civilized peoples, an identification of freedom with the political appliances established to maintain freedom. The two are confused together in thought; or, to express the fact more correctly, they have not yet been separate in thought. In most countries during past times, and in many countries at the present time, experience has associated in men's minds the unchecked power of a ruler with extreme coercion of the ruled. Contrariwise, in countries where the people have acquired some power, the restraints on the liberties of individuals have been relaxed; and with advance towards government by the majority, there has, on the average, been a progressing abolition of laws and removal of burdens which unduly interfered with such liberties. Hence, by contrast popularly-governed nations have come to be regarded as free nations; and possession of political power by all is supposed to be the same thing as freedom. But the assumed identity of the two is a delusion—delusion, which, like many other delusions, results from confounding means with ends. Freedom in its absolute form is the absence of all external checks to whatever actions the will prompts; and freedom in its socially-restricted form is the absence of any other external checks than those arising from the presence of other men who have like claims to do what their wills prompt. The mutual checks hence resulting are the only checks which freedom, in the true sense of the word, permits. The sphere within which each may act without trespassing on the like spheres of others, cannot be intruded upon by any agency, private or public, without an equivalent loss of freedom; and it matters not whether the public agency is autocratic or democratic: the intrusion is essentially the same.''[1]

It is due to a through recognition of this truth that the Indian sages laid so much stress on the necessity of formation of national character on ethical and altruistic principles, to secure political as well as social prosperity. The higher the ethical development of character, the greater the freedom enjoyed by a people. It is in this sense true that the best-governed people is the least-governed people. Over-government is an evil, a positive evil, and a very frequent evil. Over-government defeats its own ends. The real object of government is frustrated: its proper functions are neglected.

Mr. Herbert Spencer says, ''Among mechanicians it is a recognized truth that the multiplication of levers, wheels, cranks & c., in an apparatus, involves loss of power, and increases the chances of going wrong. Is it not so with Government machinery, as compared with the simpler machinery men frame in its absence? Moreover, men's desires when left to achieve their own satisfaction, follow the order of decreasing intensity and importance: the essential ones being satisfied first. But when, instead of aggregates of desires spontaneously working for their ends we get the judgements of Governments, there is no guarantee that the order of relative importance will be followed, and there is abundant proof that it is not followed.

[1] Herbert Spencer's *Autobiography*, Vol. I, p.439

Adaptation to one function pre-supposes more or less unfitness for other function and pre-occupation with many functions is unfavourable to the complete discharge of anyone. Beyond the function of nation defence, the essential function to be discharged by a Government is that of seeing that the citizens in seeking satisfaction for their own desires, individually or in groups, shall not injure one another; and its failure to perform this function is great in proportion as its other functions are numerous. The daily scandals of our judicial system, which often brings ruin instead of restitution, and frightens away multitudes who need protection, result in large measure from the pre-occupation of statesmen and politicians with non-essential things, while the all-essential thing passes almost unheeded.''[1]

In ancient India, owing to the high ethical and spiritual development of the people, they were not over-governed. They enjoyed the greatest individual freedom compatible with national cohesion and national security. It is owing to this want of ethical and altruistic development of character of the Westerners that freedom, in its true sense, is not yet enjoyed in Europe and America.

Mr. Herbert Spencer says, ''Only along with the gradual moulding of men to the social state has it become possible, without social disruption for those ideas and feelings which cause resistance to unlimited authority, to assert themselves and to restrict the authority. At present the need for the authority, and for the sentiment which causes submission to it, continues to be great. While the most advanced nations vie with one another it is manifest that their members are far too aggressive to permit much weakening of restraining agencies by which order is maintained among them. The unlimited right of the majority to rule is probably as advanced a conception of freedom as can safely be

---

[1] *Autobiography*, Vol. I. p.422

entertained at present, if indeed, even that can safely be entertained[1].

After the *Mahābhārata*, the Indian statesmen tried to preserve as much of the old Constitution as they could, while providing for the assimilation of new elements consequent on the slightly-changed conditions of life. Burke truly says that the true statesman is he who preserves what is acquired and leaves room for future improvement. Thus, though the comparative neglect of the ethical and spiritual culture of the Indians after the beginning of the *Kaliyuga* affected their individual freedom, yet the groundwork of the Constitution being sound, it was able to adapt itself to changing circumstances, and, as the necessities of the situation plainly demanded, more heed was paid to the conservative principles than the progressive ones. But the spirit of the Constitution was never affected till its practical dissolution with the advent of the foreigners in India.

"Arrian[2] mentions with admiration that every Indian is free." Lieutenant-Colonel Mark Wilks,[3] while discussing the political system in its provincial working, says, "Each Hindu township is, and indeed always was, a particular community or petty republic by itself." "The whole of India," he says again, "is nothing more than one vast congeries of such republics."

These facts do not seem to support the theory that representative government does not suit the genius of the Indians. Even Mr. James Mill is forced to admit that "in examining the spirit of these ancient Constitutions and laws, we discover evident traces of a germ of republicanism."[4]

---

[1] *Autobiography*, Vol. I, p. 441

[2] See *Indica*, Ch. X See also Diodoras, lib, II. P.214 (edition 1604). See also Elphinstone's India, p. 239

[3] *Historical Sketches of the South of India*, Vol. I. p. 119

[4] That the people took active interest in politics is exhibited by their instigating *Saṅhas* to fly from Alexander and Musicanus to break the peace made with Alexander.

As regard the executive system, Professor Max Dunker says, "The king placed officers over every village (called *pati*), and again over ten or twenty villages (*grāmaṇī*), so that these places with their acreage formed together a district. Five or ten such districts formed a canton which contained a hundred communities, and over this, in turn, the king placed a higher magistrate; ten of these cantons form a region which thus comprised a thousand villages, and this was administered by a Governor. The overseers of districts were to have soldiers at their disposal to maintain order (Police). This is of itself evidence of an advanced stage of administration."[1]

The Police of India was excellent. Megasthenes says, that in the camp of Sandrocottus, which he estimates to have contained 400,000 men, the sums stolen daily did not amount to more than Rs. 30.[2]

As regards the strength of the representative institutions, Sir Charles Metcalfe[3] says, "The village communities are little republics having nearly everything they can want within themselves and almost independent of any foreign nation. They seem to last where nothing else lasts. Dynasty after dynasty tumbles down, revolution succeeds revolution, and Pathan, Moghul, Mahratta, Sikh, English are all masters in turn, but the village communities remain the same. This union of village communities, each one forming a separate little State in itself, is in a high degree conducive to their (Indian) happiness, and to the enjoyment of a great portion of freedom and independence."

The benevolent nature of the Indian civilization is proved by the fact that the Indian Colonies and dependencies enjoyed the same Constitution as the mother country. Sir

---

[1] *History of Antiquity*, Vol. IV, p. 215

[2] Elphinstone's *India*, p.241. There was no organized Police Service in England before the reign of Queen Victoria.

[3] Report of the Select Committee of the House of Commons, 1832, Vol. III, appendices, p. 33

Stanford Raffles[1] says about Bali, an island east of Java : "Here, together with the Brahminical religion is still preserved the ancient form of Hindu municipal polity."

Indian works on diplomacy, polity and government (though few are now extant) show the high development that political thought reached in those days. Some of them have been translated into Persian and thence into European languages. Abu Sabhhad had the *Rājanīti* translated into Persian in 1150 AD Buzarchameher, the renowned minister of Nausherwan the Just, received his political education and training in India.

Law is a test of good government. The great Indian work on law is a marvel of simplicity and wisdom. Without being complex, it satisfied all the diverse wants of the people. It provisions did not change every week, and yet they suited the varied circumstances of Indian society. Sir W. Jones[2] says, "the laws of Manu very probably were considerably older than those of Solon or even of Lycurgus, although the promulgation of them, before they were reduced to writing, might have been coeval with the first monarchies established in Egypt and India."

The English derived their laws from the Romans, who, in their turn, derived them from Greece. During the Decemvirate, Greece seems to have been indebted to India for its laws. Sir W. Jones[3] says, "Although perhaps Manu was never in Crete.[4] Yet, some of his institution well have been adopted in that island, whence Lycurgus a century or two after may have imported them into Sparta."

---

[1] *Description of Java*, Vol. II, Appendix, p.237.
After quoting some passages from Manu, Colonel Briggs says, 'These extracts afford us sufficient proof of a well-organised system of local superintendence and administration.' 'Brigg's *Land Tax of India*, p.24

[2] Houghton's *Institutes of Hindu Law*, Preface, p. x.

[3] Preface to Houghton's *Institutes of Hindu Law*, p. xii.

[4] The oneness of Minas and Manu is highly probable.

The Bible in India says that the *Manusmṛti* was the foundation upon which the Egyptian, the Persian, the Grecian and the Roman Codes of law were built, and that the influence of Manu was still every day felt in Europe.

Professor Wilson[1] says, the Indian had a "a code of Laws adapted to a great variety of relations which could not have existed except in an advanced condition of social organization."

Coleman[2] says, "The style of it (Manu) has a certain austere majesty that sounds like the language of legislation and extorts a respectful awe. The sentiments of independence on all beings but God, and the harsh administrations even to kings are truly noble, and the many panegyrics on the *Gāyatrī* prove the author to have adored that divine and incomparably-greater light which illumines all, delights all, from which all proceed, to which all must return, and which can alone irradiate our intellect."

Dr. Robertson says, "With respect to the number and variety of points the Hindu code considers it will bear a comparison with the celebrated Digest of Justinian, or with the systems of jurisprudence in nations most highly civilized. The articles of which the Indian code is composed are arranged in natural and luminous order. They are numerous and comprehensive, and investigated with that minute attention and discernment which are natural to a people distinguished for acuteness and subtlety of understanding, who have been long accustomed to the accuracy of judicial proceedings, and acquainted with all the refinements of legal practice. The decisions concerning every point are founded upon the great and immutable principles of justice which the human mind acknowledges and respects in every age and in all parts of the earth. Whoever examines the whole work cannot entertain a doubt of its containing the jurisprudence of an enlightened and

---

[1] Mill's *India*, Vol. II, p. 282

[2] Coleman's *Mythology of the Hindus*, p.8

commercial people. Whoever looks into any particular title will be surprised with minuteness of detail and nicety of distinction which, in many instances, seem to go beyond the attention of European legislation; and it is remarkable that some of the regulations which indicate the greatest degree of refinement were established in periods of the most remote antiquity.''[1]

Mr. Mill says that ''the division and arrangement of Hindu law is rude and shows the barbarism of the nation''; upon which Professor Wilson, with his usual candour, remarks, ''By this test, the attempt to classify would place the Hindus higher in civilization than the English''.[2]

Mr. Mill's review of Indian religion and laws is a piece of stupendous perversity, ignorance and stupidity. Professor Wilson speaks of it in the following terms, ''The whole of this review of the religion as well as of the laws of the Hindus is full of serious defects arising from inveterate prejudices and imperfect knowledge.''[3] Of Mill's *History of British India*, Prof. Max Müller says, ''The book which I consider most mischievous, nay, which I hold responsible for some of the greatest misfortunes that have happened in India, is Mill's *History of India*, even with the antidote against its poison which is supplied by Professor Wilson's notes.''[4] Professor Max Müller deplores that ''the candidates for the Civil Service of India are recommended to read it and are examined in it.''[5] What wonder, then, that there is often misunderstanding between the rulers and the ruled in India!

While discussing Mill's views, Professor Wilson again says, ''According to this theory Mill's theory contained in his explanation of the causes of complex procedure in the

---

[1] *Disquisition concerning India*, Appendix, p. 217

[2] Mill's *India*, Vol. II. Pp.224-25.

[3] Mill's *India*, Vol. II, p. 436 (Note.)

[4] *India: What can it teach us*? P. 42

[5] Max Müller's *India: What can it teach us*?. P.42

English courts of law) the corruption of the judge is the best security for justice. It would be dangerous to reduce this to practice.''[1]

An eminent authority, the late Chief Justice of Madras, Sir Thomas Strange, says of the Indian Law of Evidence, ''It will be read by every English lawyer with a mixture of admiration and delight, as it may be studied by him to advantage.''

---

[1] Mill's *India*, Vol. II, p. 512.- Mill says that because the Hindus lend money on pledges, therefore they are barbarous. On this, Professor Wilson says, 'Lending on pledges can scarcely be regarded as proof of a state of barbarism, or the multitude of pawn-brokers in London would witness our being very low in the scale of civilization.'' Mills declares that Mohammedan code to be superior to the Hindu Code. 'In civil branch,' replies Wilson 'the laws of Contract and Inheritance, it is not so exact or complete as the latter (Hindus). Its (Mohamedan) sprit of barbarous retaliation is unknown to the Hindu Code. But Wilson clearly proves that this is a creation of Mill's diseased imagination.

It is further objected that uncertainties of the Hindu law are very great. Prof. Wilson (Essays, Vol. III, page 5th) remarks, 'If the uncertainties of the English law are less perplexing than those of the Hindu law, we doubt if its delays are not something more interminable. A long time elapses before a cause comes for decision and abundant opportunity is therefore afforded for the traffic of underhand negotiations, intrigues and corruption. It is needless to cite instances to prove the consequence or to make any individual application: public events have rendered the fact notorious. It can scarcely be otherwise.' But he returns to the charge and says, 'They says that Pandits don't agree in the discharge of Hindu law. But see in the case of Virapermah Pillay versus Narain Pillay, the opinion of the two English judges, the Chief Justice of Bengal declares that a decision pronounced and argued with great pains by the chief Justice at Madras, will mislead those by whom it may be followed, and that the doctrine which it inculcates is contrary to law.' Professor Wilson again says, The Chief Justice of Bengal says that 'he would connive at immoral acts if he thought they led to useful results.'

A writer in the Asiatic Journal (p.14) says, "All the requisite shades of care and diligence, the corresponding shades of negligence and default are carefully observed in the Indian law of bailment, and neither in the jurisprudence nor in the legal treatises of the most civilized State of Europe are they to be found more logically expressed or more accurately defined. In the sprit of Pyrrhus observation on the Roman legions, one cannot refrain from exclaiming, "I see nothing barbarous in the jurisprudence of the Hindus."

Of the commentary of Kulluka on Manu, Sir W. Jones says, "It is the shortest yet the most luminous; the least ostentatious yet the most learned; the deepest yet the most agreeable commentary ever composed on any author ancient or modern, European or Asiatic."[1]

---

[1] Preface to Houghton's *Institutes of Hindu Law*, p.18

1.3. Social System

Hail, social life! Into they pleasing bounds
Again I come to pay the common stock
My share of service, and, in glad return
To taste they comforts, thy protected joys.

—THOMSON: *Agamemnon.*

The Indians perfected society. The social organization of the people was based on scientific principles and was well calculated to ensure progress without party strife. There was no accumulation of wealth in one portion of the community, leaving the other portion in destitute poverty; no social forces stimulating the increase of the wealth of the one and the poverty of the other, as is the tendency of the modern civilization. The keynote of the system, however, was national service. It afforded to every member of the social body, opportunities and means to develop fully his powers and capacities, and to use them for the advancement of the common weal. Everyone was to serve the nation in the sphere in which he was best fitted to act, which being congenial to his individual genius, was conducive to the highest development of his faculties and powers.

There was thus a wise and statesman like classification which procured a general distribution of wealth, expelled misery and want from the land, promoted mental and moral progress, ensured national efficiency, and, above all, made tranquility compatible with advancement; in one world, dropped *manna* all round said made life doubly sweet by securing external peace with national efficiency and social happiness — a condition of affairs nowhere else so fully realized.

This classification—this principle of social organization-was the *Varṇāśrama*. Humankind were divided into two classes, (1) the Aryas and (2) Dasyus, or the civilized and the savage. The Aryas were subdivided into :

1. *Brāhmaṇas*, who devoted themselves to learning and acquiring wisdom following the liberal arts and sciences.
2. *Kṣatriyas*, who devoted themselves to the theory and practice of war, and to whom the executive government of the people was entrusted
3. V*aiśyas*, who devoted themselves to trade and the marketting.
4. *Śūdras* (men of low capacities), who were producers and helped the other three classes in production.

This classification is a necessary one in all civilized countries in some form or other. It was the glory of ancient Āryāvrtta that classification existed there in its perfect form and was based on scientific principles—on the principle of heredity (which has not yet been fully appreciated by European thinkers), the conservation of energy, economy of labour, facility of development, and specialization of faculties. Literary men, soldiers, doctors, lawyers, clergymen, traders, and producers are to be found in England, France, America, and in every other civilized country of modern times, as they were in Ancient India. The only difference is that in one case the division was perfect and the working of its marvelous mechanism regular, while in the other the classification is imperfect and its working irregular and haphazard.

The *Varṇāśrama* was not the same as the caste system of the present day - a travesty of its ancient original. No one was a *Brāhmaṇa* by blood nor a *Śūdra* by birth, but everyone was such as his merits fitted him to be. "The people," says Col. Olcott, "were nor, as now, irrevocably walled in by castes, but they were free to rise to the highest social dignities or sink to the lowest positions, according to the inherent qualities they might possess."

The son of a *Brāhmaṇa* sometimes became a *Kṣatriya*, sometimes a *Vaiśya*, and sometimes a *Śūdra*. At the same time, a *Śūdra* as certainly became a *Brāhmaṇa* or a *Kṣatriya. Shankara Digvijaya* says:

जन्मना जायते शूद्रः संस्काराद् द्विज उच्यते।
वेदपाठी भवेद्विप्रः ब्रह्म जानाति ब्राह्मणः।।

"By birth all are *Śūdra*, *Sanskaras* (education etc.) makes him a *Dvija* (twice-born). By reading the Vedas one becomes *Vipra* and becomes *Brāhmaṇa* by gaining knowledge of God."

A passage in the *Vanparva* of the *Mahābhārata* runs thus: "He in whom the qualities of truth, munificence, forgiveness, gentleness, abstinence from cruel deeds, contemplation, benevolence are observed, is called a *Brāhmaṇa* in the *Smṛti.* A man is not a *Śūdra* by being a *Śūdra* nor a *Brāhmaṇa* by being a *Brāhmaṇa.*" The *Mahābhārata Śāntiparva* says :

न विशेषोऽस्ति वर्णानां सर्वं ब्राह्ममिदं जगत्।
ब्रह्मणा पूर्वसृष्टं हि कर्मभिर्वर्णतां गतम्।।

"There are no distinctions of caste. Thus, a world which, as created by Brahmā, was at first entirely Brahmanaic has become divided into classes, in consequence of men's actions."

In his paper on "*Sanskrit as a Living Language in India.*" Read before the International Congress of Orientalists at Berlin, on the 14th September 1881, Mr. Shyamji Krishna Varma said, "We read in the *Aitareya Brāhmaṇa* (ii. 3. 19), for example, that Kavaṣa Ailuṣa, who was a *Śūdra* and son of a low woman, was greatly respected for his literary attainments, and admitted into the class of Ṛṣ is. Perhaps the most remarkable feature of his life is that he, *Śūdra* as he was, distinguished himself as the Ṛṣi of some of the hymns of the *Ṛgveda* (*Ṛg.*, X. 30-34). It is distinctly stated in the *Chāndogyopaniṣad* that Jābāla, who is otherwise called *Satya-Kāma*, had no *gotra*, or family name whatever (*Chān. Up.*, IV. 4); all that we know about his parentage is that he was the son of a woman named Jabal, and that he is called after his mother. Though born of unknown parents, Jābāla is said to have been the founder of a school of the *Yajurveda*. Even in the *Āpastamba Sūtra* (ii. 5-10) and the *Manusmṛti* (x. 65), we find that a *Śūdra* can become a *Brāhmaṇa* and a *Brāhmaṇa* can become a *Śūdra*, according to their good or bad deeds. Pāṇini mentions the name of a celebrated grammarian called Cakravarman in the sixth chapter of his *Aṣṭādhyāyī* (p. vi. 1. 130); now Cakravarman was a *Kṣatriya* by birth, since he has the prescribed *Kṣatriya* termination at the end of his name, which is a patronymic of Cakravarman."

Who were Viśvāmitra and Vālmīki but *Śūdras*. Even so late as the time of the Greek invasion of India, the caste system had not become petrified into its present state. The Greeks describe four castes. Megasthenes says that a Indian of any caste may become a Sophist (*Brāhmaṇa*.) Arrian counts seven classes: Sophists, agriculturists, herdsmen, handicrafts and artizens, warriors, inspectors and councillors. (See *Strabo*, Lib XV.)

Colonel Tod says, "In the early ages of these Solar and Lunar dynasties, the priestly office was not hereditary in families; it was a profession, and the genealogies exhibit frequent instances of branches of these races terminating their marital career in the commencement of a religious sect or "*gotra*" and of their descendants reassuming their warlike occupations."[1]

There was no hereditary caste. The people enjoyed the advantages of hereditary genius without the serious drawbacks of a rigid system of caste based on birth.

"The one great object which the promoters of the hereditary system seem to have had in view was to secure to each class a high degree of efficiency in its own sphere."

---

[1] *Manusmṛti*, II, 158 says, 'As liberality to a fool is fruitless, so is a *Brāhmaṇa* useless if he read not the Holy Texts; or again he is no better than an elephant made of wood or an antelope made of leather.'

"Hereditary genius" is now (1906) a subject of serious enquiry amongst the enlightened men of Europe and America, and the evolution theory as a applied to sociology, when fully worked out, will fully show the merits of the system. In fact the India of the time of Manu will appear to have reached a stage of civilization of which the brilliant "modern European civilization" only gives us glimpses. Even the system in its present form has not been an unmitigated evil.

It has been the great conservation principle of the constitution of Indian society, though originally it was a conservative as well as a progressive one. It is this principle of the Indian social constitution which has enabled the nation to sustain, without being shattered to pieces, the tremendous shocks given by the numerous political convulsions and religious upheavals that have occurred during the last thousand years. "The system of caste," says Sir Henry Cotton, "far from being the source of all troubles which can be traced in Hindu society, has rendered most important service in the past, and still continues to sustain order and solidarity."

As regards its important from a European point of view, Mr. Sidney Low in his recent book, *A vision of India*, says, "There is no doubt that it is the main cause of the fundamental stability and contentment by which Indian society has been braced for centuries against the shocks of politics and the cataclysms of Nature. It provides every man with his place, his career, his occupation, his circle of friends. It makes him, at the outset, a member of a corporate body; it protects him through life from the canker of social jealously and unfulfilled aspirations; it ensures him companionship and a sense of community with others in like case with himself. The caste organisations to the Indian his club, his trade-union, his benefit society, his philanthropic society. There are no work-houses in India, and none are as yet needed. The obligation to provide for kinsfolk and friends in distress is universally acknowledged; nor can it be questioned that this is due to the recognition of the strength of family ties and of the bonds created by associations and common pursuits which is fostered by the caste principle. An India without caste, as things stand at present, it is not quite easy to imagine."

1.4. CHARACTER

To those who know thee not, no words can paint,
And those who know thee, know all words are faint.

—HAN, MOORE: *Sensibility*

The happy results of government depend chiefly upon the character of the people. And what nation, ancient or modern, can show such high character as that of the ancient Indians? Their generosity, simplicity, honesty, truthfulness, courage, refinement and gentleness are proverbial. In fact, the elements so mixed in them that nature might stand up and say to all the world, "these were men."

The first and highest virtue in man is truthfulness. As Chaucer says:

"Truth is the highest thing that man may keep."

From the earliest times, the Indians have always been praised by men of all countries and creeds for their truthfulness.

Strabo says, "They are so honest as neither to require locks to their doors nor writings to bind their agreements."[1]

Arrian (in the second century), the pupil of Epictetus, says that "no Indian was even known to tell an untruth."[2] This, making a due allowance for exaggeration, is no mean praise.

Huven-Tsang, the most famous of the Chinese travellers, says, "The Indians are distinguished by the straightforwardness and honesty of their character. With regard to riches, they never take anything unjustly; with regard to justice, they make even excessive concessions---

---

[1] *Strabo*, Lib, xv. P. 488 (ed. 1587)

[2] *Indica*, Cap. XII, 6. See also McCrindle in '*Indian Antiquary*', 1876, p. 92

straightforwardness is the leading feature of their administration."[1]

Khang-thai, the Chinese ambassador to Siam, says that Su-We, a relative of Fanchen, king of Siam, who came to India about 231 AD on his return reported to the king "the Indians are straightforward and honest."[2]

"In the fourth century, Friar Jordanus tells us that the people of India are true in speech and eminent in justice."[3]

Fei-tu, the ambassador of the Chinese Emperor Yangti toIndia in 605 AD, among other things points out as peculiar to the Indians that "they believe in solemn oaths."[4]

Idrisi, in his *Geography* (written in the 11th century), says "The Indians are naturally inclined to justice, and never depart from it in their actions. Their good faith, honesty and fidelity to their engagements are well known, and they are so famous for these qualities that people flock to their country from every side."[5]

In the thirteenth century, Shams-ud din Abu Abdullah quotes the following judgement of Bedi-ezr Zeman:

"the Indians are innumerable, like grains of sand, free from deceit and violence. They fear neither death nor life.[6]

Marco Polo (thirteenth century) says, "You must know that these Brahmins are the best merchants in the world and the most truthful, for they would not tell a lie for anything on earth."[7]

Kamal-ud-din Ibd-errazak Samarkandi (1413-1482), who went as an ambassador of the Khakan to the prince of

---

[1] Vol. II. P. 83

[2] Max Müller's *India: What can it teach us*? P. 55

[3] Macro Polo, ed. H. Yule, Vol. II. P. 354

[4] Max Müller's *India : What can it teach us*? P. 275

[5] Elliot's *History of India*, Vol. I, p. 88

[6] *India : what can it teach us*? P. 275

[7] Marco Polo, ed. H. Yule, Vol. II. P. 350

Calicut and to the king of Vijayanagar (1440-1445) bears testimony to "the perfect security which merchants enjoy in the country."[1]

Abul Fazal says, "The Hindus are admirers of truth and of unbounded fidelity in all their dealings."[2]

Sir John Malcolm says, "Their truth is as remarkable as their courage."[3]

Colonel Sleeman, who had better and more numerous opportunities of knowing the Indian character than most Europeans, assures us "that falsehood or lying between members of the same village is almost unknown." He adds, "I have had before me hundreds of cases in which a man's property, liberty and life has depended upon his telling a lie and he has refused to tell it." "Could many an English Judge," asks Professor Max Müller, "say the same?"[4]

What is the pivot on which the whole story of *Rāmāyaṇa*, the book which even now exercises the greatest influence in the formation of Indian character throughout India, turns? — To remain true, though life may depart, and all that is near and dear in this world may perish. What is the lesson taught by the life of the greatest character unfolded to view by the *Mahābhārata*, Bhīṣma Pitāmaha? — To remain true and steadfast, come what may.

Professor Max Müller says, "It was the love of truth that struck all the people who came in contact with India, as the prominent feature in the national character of its inhabitants. No one ever accused them of falsehood. There must surely be some ground for this, for it is not a remark that is frequently made by travellers in foreign countries, even in our time, that their inhabitants invariably speak the truth. Read the accounts of English travellers in France, and

---

[1] *Notices des Manuscrits tom.* xiv, p. 436.

[2] Tod's *Rajasthan*, Vol. I, p.643

[3] Mill's *History of India*, Vol. I, p. 523

[4] Max Müller's *India : What can it teach us*? P. 50

you will find very little said about French honesty and veracity, while French accounts of England are seldom without a fling at *Perfide Albion*!''[1]

But it is not for truthfulness alone that the Indians have been famous. Their generosity, tolerance, frankness, intelligence, courtesy, loyalty, gentleness, sobriety, love of knowledge, industry, valour and a strong feeling of honour are even now remarkable.

''Megasthenes[2] observed with admiration the absence of slavery[3] in India, the chastity of the women, and the courage of the men. In valour they excelled all other Asiatics, sober and industrious, good farmers and skilful artisans, they scarcely ever had recourse to a lawsuit, and lived peacefully under their native chiefs.''

That acute observer, the historian Abul Fazal, says, ''the Hindus are religious, affable, courteous to strangers, cheerful, enamoured of knowledge, lovers of justice, able in business, grateful, admirers of truth, and of unbounded fidelity in all their dealings.''[4] Colonel Dixon dilates upon ''their fidelity, truthfulness, honesty, their determined valour, their simple loyalty, and an extreme and almost touching devotion when put upon their honour.''[5]

''The Indians,'' says Niebuhr, ''are really the most tolerant nation in the world.'' he also says that ''they are gentle, virtuous, laborious, and that, perhaps of all men,

---

[1] Max Müller's *India : What can it teach us*? P. 57

[2] Hunter's *Gazetteer*, 'India', p.266

[3] Rev. F. D. Maurice says that 'the Sudras are not in any sense slaves, and never can have been such; the Greeks were surprised to find all classes in India free citizens.' *The Religions of the world*, p. 43. Mr. Elphinstone says, 'It is remarkable that in the Hindu dramas there is not a trace of servility in the behaviour of other characters to the king.' '*History of India*. P.243

[4] Tod's *Rajasthan*, Vol. I, p.643

[5] Colonel Dixon was Commissioner of Ajmer-Merwara about 1850 A.D.

they are the ones who seek to injure their fellow-beings the least."

The high character, the noble self-sacrifice, the unbounded love of an Indian for those who are near and dear to him are well illustrated by the refusal of Yudhiṣṭhira to accept salvation, while his wife and brothers were outside Heaven. The *Mahābhārata* says:

"Lo, suddenly, with a sound that ran through heaven and earth, Indra came riding on his chariot and cried to the king, 'Ascend'. Then indeed did Yudhiṣṭhira look back to his fallen brothers and spoke thus unto Indra with a sorrowful heart: 'Let my brothers, who yonder lie fallen, go with me. Not even into thy heaven, O Indra, would I enter, if they are not to be there; and you fair-faced daughter of a king, Draupadi, the all-deserving, let her too enter with us!"

Sir Monier Williams[1] says, "Natives never willingly destroy life. They cannot enter into an Englishman's desire for venting his high spirits on a fine day by killing the game of some king— 'live and let live' is their rule of conduct towards the inferior creation."

"The villagers," says Mr. Elphinstone,[2] "are inoffensive, amiable people, affectionate to their family, kind to their neighbours and towards all but Government, honest and sincere."

In 1813 AD, when evidence was given before the British Parliament[3], Mr. Mercer said, "They (Indians) are mild in their disposition, polished in their general manners; in their domestic relations, kind and affectionate."

Captain Sydenham said, "The general character of the Indians is submissive, docile, sober, inoffensive, capable of great attachment and loyalty, quick in apprehension,

---

[1] *Modern India and the Indians*, p. 33
[2] Elphistone's *History of India*, p. 199.
[3] Mill's *History of India*, Vol. I, p. 523

intelligent, active; generally honest and performing the duties of charity, benevolence and filial affection with as much sincerity and regularity as any nation with which I am acquainted.''

Abbe Dubois says, ''The Hindus are not in want to improvement in the discharge of social duties amongst themselves. They understand this point as well as and perhaps better than Europeans.''

Sir John Malcolm said, ''From the moment you enter Behar, the Hindu inhabitants are a race of men, generally speaking, not more distinguished by their lofty stature and robust frame, than they are for some of the finest qualities of the mind-they are brave, generous, humane, and their truth is as remarkable as their courage.'' At a subsequent examination, he said, with respect to the feeling of honour: ''I have known an innumerable instance of its being carried to a pitch that would be considered in England more fit for the page of a romance than a history. With regard to their fidelity, I think, as far as my knowledge extends, there is, generally speaking, no race of men more to be trusted.''

Sir Thomas Munro when asked if he thought the civilisation of the Indians would be promoted by trade with England being thrown open, replied, ''I do not exactly understand what is meant by the 'civilisation' of the Indians. In the knowledge of the theory and practice of good government, and in an education which, by banishing prejudice and superstition, opens the mind to receive the instruction of every kind, they are inferior to Europeans. But if a good system of agriculture, unrivalled manufacturing skill, a capacity to produce whatever can contribute to either luxury or convenience, schools[1]

---

[1] 'In Bengal there existed 80,000 native schools, though doubtless for the most part of a poor quality. According to a Government Report of 1835 there was a village school for every 400 persons.' '*Missionary Intelligencer*, IX, p. 183-193.

established in every village for teaching reading, writing and arithmetic, the general practice of hospitality and charity amongst each other and, above all, a treatment of the female sex, full of confidence, respect and delicacy, are among the signs which denote a civilized people, then the Indians are not inferior to the nations of Europe, and **if civilization is to become an article of trade between the two countries, I am convinced that this country (England) will gain by the import cargo.''**

Professor Max Müller[1] says, ''During the last twenty years, however, I have had some excellent opportunities of watching a number of native scholars under circumstances where it is not difficult to detect a man's true character, I mean in literary work, and, more particularly, in literary controversy. I have watched them carrying on such controversies both among themselves and with certain European scholars, and I feel bound to say that, **with hardly one exception they have displayed a far greater respect for truth, and a far more manly and generous spirit than we are accustomed to even in Europe and America.** They have shown strength, but no rudeness; nay, I know that nothing has surprised them as much as the coarse invective to which certain Sanskrit scholars have condescended, rudeness of speech being, according to their view of human nature, a safe sign not only of bad breeding but of want of knowledge. When they were wrong they have readily admitted their mistake; when they were right they have never sneered at their European adversaries. There has been, with few exceptions, no quibbling, no special pleading, no untruthfulness on their part, and certainly none of that low cunning of the scholar who writes down and publishes what he knows perfectly well to be false, and snaps his finger at those who still value truth and self-

---

Sir Thomas Munro estimated the children educated at public schools in the Madras Presidency as less than one in three'' 'Elphinstone's *History of India*', p.205

[1] *India : What can it teach us?* P. 63

respect more highly than victory or applause at any price. Here, too, we might possibly gain by the import cargo.

"Let me add that I have been repeatedly told by English merchants that commercial honour stands higher in India than in any other country, and that a dishonoured bill is hardly known there."

The first Governor-General of India, Warren Hastings, said, "The Hindus are gentle, benevolent, more susceptible of gratitude for kindness shown to them, then prompted to vengeance for wrongs inflicted, and as exempt from the worst propensities of human passion as any people upon the face of the earth. They are faithful, affectionate," etc. (Minutes of evidence before the Committee of both Houses of Parliament, March and April 1813).

Bishop Heber said, "The say that the Hindus are deficient in any essential feature of a civilised people is an assertion which I can scarcely suppose to be made by any who have lived with them."[1] Again, "they are decidedly by nature a mild, pleasing, intelligent race, sober and parsimonious, and, where an object is held out to them, most industrious and persevering[2]... They are men of high and gallant courage, courteous, intelligent, and most eager for knowledge and improvement, with a remarkable aptitude for the abstract sciences, geometry, astronomy, etc., and for imitative arts, painting and sculpture; dutiful towards their parents, affectionate to children, more easily affected by kindness and attention to their wants and feelings than almost any men I have met with"[3] Again, "I have found in India a race of gentle and temperate habits, with a natural talent and acuteness beyond the ordinary level of mankind."

Of the labourers and workmen in the Calcutta mint in India, Professor Wilson says, "There were considerable skill and ready docility. So far from there being any

---

[1] Journal, II, p. 382.
[2] *Ibid*, p. 329.
[3] *Ibid*, p. 369

servility, their was extreme frankness, and I should say that where there is confidence without fear, frankness is one of a universal features in the Indian character. In men of learning, I found similar merits of industry, intelligence, cheerfulness, frankness. A very common characteristic of Hindus especially was simplicity, truly childish, and a total unacquaintance with business and manners of life; where this feature was lost[1] it was chiefly by those who had been long familiar with Europeans---- there can be no doubt that the native mind outstrips in early years, the intellect of the Europeans and, generally speaking, boys are much quicker in apprehension and earnest in application than those of our own schools. Men of property and respectability afforded me many opportunities of witnessing polished manners, clearness and comprehensiveness of understanding, liberality of feeling, and independence of principle that would have stamped them gentlemen in any country in the world.''[2]

Indian children are more quick and intelligent than European. ''The capacity of lads of 12 and 13 are often surprising.''

Sir Thomas Munro, Mercer and others, quoted above, says Professor Wilson, were ''men, equally eminent in wisdom as in station, remarkable for the extent of their opportunities of observation and ability and diligence with which they used them, distinguished for possessing, by their knowledge of the language and the literature of the country, and by their habits of intimacy with the natives, the best, the only means of judging of the native character, and unequalled for the soundness of their judgement and comprehensiveness of their views.''[3]

---

[1] 'The longer we possess a province, the more common and grave does perjury become.' Sir G. Cambell, quoted by S. Johnson, Oriental Religions, India, p. 288.

[2] Mill's *History of India*, Vol. I, pp. 530-32

[3] Mill's *History of India*, Vol. I, p.523

Professor Monier Williams[1] says, " I have found no people in Europe more religious, none more patiently persevering in common duties."

Mr. Elphinstone says[2], "if we compare them (Indians) with our own (English people), the absence of drunkenness and of immodesty in their other vices will leave the superiority in the purity of manners on the side least flattering to our self-esteem." He adds, "No set of people among the Hindus are so depraved as the dregs of our own great towns."[3]

"The cleanliness of the Indians", he says again, "is proverbial.[4] They are a cleanly people and may be compared with decided advantage with the nations of the south of Europe, both as regards their habitations and their person. There are many of their practices which might be introduced even into the North with benefit."

---

[1] *Modern India and the Indians*, pp. 88 and 128

[2] *History of India*, p. 202

[3] Elphinstone's *Hisotry of India*, pp. 375-81. the percentage of criminals in India is lower than in England. 'By a series of reports laid before the House of Commons in 1832 (Minutes of Evidence No.4, page 103) it appears that in an average of four years the number of capital sentences carried into effect annually in England and Wales is as 1 for 203, 281 souls, and in the provinces under the Bengal Presidency 1 for 1,004,182: transportation for life, in England 1 for 67,173 and in Bengal, 1 for 402,010. the annual number of sentences to death in England was 1,232, in Bengal 59. the population of England is 13,000,000; the population of Bengal, 60,000,000.

The Hindu convict is a better man than the European. The great Darwin was struck with the Hindu convicts at Port Louis and he wondered that they were such noble-looking figures. He says, 'these men are generally quite and well-conducted from their outward conduct, their cleanliness, and faithful observance of their strange religious rites it is impossible to look at them with the same eyes as on our wretched convicts in New South Wales.' *A Naturalist's Voyage Round the World*, p. 484

[4] Elphinstone's *History of India*, p. 202

Mr. Elphinstone says, "the native are often accused of wanting in gratitude. But it does not appear that those who make the charge have done much to inspire such a sentiment when masters are really kind and considerate they find as warm a return from Indian servants as any in the world; and there are few who have tried them in sickness or in difficulties and dangers who do not bear witness to their sympathy and attachment. Their devotion to their own chief is proverbial and can arise from no other cause than gratitude, unless where caste supplies the place of clannish feelings. The fidelity of our sepoys to their foreign masters has been shown in instances which it would be difficult to match even among the national troops in any other country." He again says, "It is common to see persons who have been patronised by men in power not only continuing their attachment to them when in disgrace but even to their families when they have left them in a helpless condition."[1]

To the diet[2] and the sobriety of living is due to the greater healthiness of the Indians. There are 3 instances in every10,000 in England and Wales.[1]

---

[1] 'A perfectly authentic instance might be mentioned of an English gentleman in a high station in Bengal who was dismissed and a afterwards reduced to great temporary difficulties in his own country: a native of rank, to whom he had been kind, supplied him, when in those circumstances, with upwards of Rs. 100,000, of which he would not accept repayment and for which he could expect no possible return. This generous friend was a *Marāṭhā Brāhmaṇa*, a race of all others who have least sympathy with other castes, and who are most hardened and corrupted by power.' Elphinstone's *History of India*, p. 201.

[2] Mr. J.H. Bourdillon, in his report on the Census of 1881, observes that the superior healthiness of middle-age among the Hindus is more strikingly shown, for out of each 100 living persons the number of those aged 40 years and over is among the-

Hindus..............................	21.97
Christians	14.31
Muhammadans	19.81

Mr. Ward says:

"In their forms of address and behaviour in the company, the Indians must be ranked amongst the politest nations."

Speaking of the inhabitants of the Gangetic India, Mr. Elphinstone says, "It is there we are most likely to gain a clear conception of their high spirit and generous self-devotion so singularly combined with the gentleness of manners and softness of heart together with an almost infantine simplicity."

Aboriginals 15.86

As regards the diet of the Hindus, Mr. Buckle tells us, 'In India the great heat of the climate brings into play that law (of nature) already pointed out, by virtue of which the ordinary food is of an oxygenous rather than of a carbonaceous character. This, according to another law, obliges the people to derive their usual diet not from the animal but from the vegetable world of which starch is the most important constituent. At the same time, the high temperature incapacitating men for arduous labour, makes necessary a food of which the returns will be abundant, and which will contain much nutriment in a comparatively small space. Here, then, we have some characteristics which if the preceding views are correct, ought to be found in the ordinary food of the Indian nations. So they all are. From the earliest period the most general food in India has been rice, which is the most nutritive of all cerealia, which contains and enormous proportion of starch, and which yields to the labourer an average return of at least sixty fold.'- *History of Civilization in England*, Volume I, page 64.

Neibuhr says, 'Perhaps the Indian lawgivers thought it was for the sake of health absolutely necessary to prohibit the eating of meat, because the multitude follows more easily the prejudice of religion than the advice of a physician. It is also very likely that the law of the Oriental insists so strongly on the purification of the body for hygienic reasons.'

[1] See the comparative tabular statement on page 204 of the report on the Census of Bengal, Vol. I (1881)

Even honest writers, who have had no opportunity of studying the Indian character, sometimes hastily generalise from stray instances of untruthfulness and dishonesty they happen to come across in life. In respect of such, Professor Max Müller says, "We may, to follow an Indian proverb, judge of a whole field of rice by tasting one or two grains only, but if we apply this rule to human beings we are sure to fall into the same mistake as the English chaplain who had once on board an English vessel christened a French child, and who remained fully convinced for the rest of his life that all French babies had very long noses."

The physical structure of the Indian is still as admirable as that of any other people on the globe.

Mr. Orme says, "There is not a handsomer race in the universe than the Banians of Gujrat."[1] We read in Chambers Encyclopaedia that "the body of the Hindus is admirably proportioned."[2]

A strong opponent of the Indians admires their physical agility. Mr. Mills says, "The body of the Indian is agile to an extraordinary degree. Not only in those surprising contortions and feats which constitute the art of the tumbler do they excel almost all the nations in the world, but even in running and marching they equal, if not surpass, people of the most robust constitutions."[3]

The Indians were renowned for wisdom in ancient times.

"Wisdom, my father, is the noblest gift
The gods bestow on man, made better far
Than all his treasures."

SOPHOCLES: *Antigone*

---

[1] On the effeminacy of the Inhabitants of Hindustan, pp. 461-65

[2] Chamber's *Encyclopaedia*, p. 539

[3] Mill's *India*, Vol. I, p. 478

"We are told by Grecian writers that the Indians were the wisest of nations."[1]

Mr. Coleman[2] says, "The sages and poets of India have inculcated moral precepts and displayed poetic beauties which no country in the world of either ancient or modern date need be ashamed to acknowledge."

The didactic poetry of the Indians furnishes sufficient proof of their transcendent wisdom. Mr. Elphinstone[3] says that "the Greeks had a great impression of their (Indians) wisdom."

Mr. Burnouf says that the "Indians are a nation rich in spiritual gifts, and endowed with peculiar sagacity and penetration."

It is the wisdom of the Indians that invented the best and the greatest of indoor games, the game of Chess, which is now universally acknowledged to be of Indian origin, the Sanskrit *caturaṅga* becoming shaturanga in Persian.

Sir W. Jones says[4], "The Hindus are said to have boasted of their inventions, all of which indeed are admirable; the method of instructing by apologues; the decimal scale and the game of Chess, on which they have some curious treatises."

Professor Heeren[5] says, "Chess-board is mentioned in *Rāmāyaṇa*, where an account of Ayodhya is given."

Chess is thus proved to have been in use in India long before Moses and Hermes made their appearance in the world. Mr. J. Mill, however, with his characteristic prejudice against the Indians, observes that "there is no evidence that Indians invented the game, except their own

---

[1] See *Introduction.*

[2] *Mythology of the Hindus*, p. 7

[3] *History of India*, p.242

[4] As quoted by Mill in his *History of British India*, Vol. II, p.43

[5] *Historical Researches*, Vol. II, p.151

pretentions.'' On this, Professor Wilson says, ''this is not true; we have not the evidence of their pretentions. The evidence is that of Mohamedan writers; the king of India is said, by Firdausi in the Shahnama–and the story is therefore of the tenth century at least–to have sent a Chess-board and a teacher to Nausherawan. Sir W. Jones refers to Firdausi as his authority, and this reference might have shown by whom the story was told. Various Mohamedan writers are quoted by Hyde, in his Historia Shahiludii, who all concur in attributing invention the Indians[1].''

''The wisdom of Solomon'' is proverbial. But the story most frequently quoted to show his wisdom, itself stamps that wisdom as inferior to that of the Indians. Says Professor Max Müller, ''Now you remember the judgement of Solomon, which has always been admired as a proof of great legal wisdom among the Jews! I must confess that not having a legal mind, I never could suppress a certain shudder when reading the decision of Solomon: 'Divide the living child in two, and give half of the one, and half to the other.''[2]

''Let me now tell you the same story as it is told by the Buddhaists, whose scared Canon is full of such legends and parables. In the Kanjur, which is the Tibetan translation of the Buddhist. *Tripitaka*, we read of two women who claimed each to be the mother of the same child. The King, after listening to their quarrels for a long time, gave it up as hopeless to settle who was the real mother. Upon this, Visakha stepped forward and said, 'What is the use of examining and cross-examining these women. Let them take the boy and settle it among themselves'. Thereupon, both women fell on the child, and when the fight became violent, the child was hurt and began to cry. Then one of them let him go, because she could not bear to hear the child cry.

---

[1] Mill's *India*, Vol. II, p.44, footnote.

[2] Kings iii. 25.

That settled the question. The King gave the child to the true mother, and had the other beaten with a rod.

"This seems to me, if not the more primitive, yet the more natural form of the story, showing a deeper knowledge of human nature and more wisdom than even the wisdom of Solomon."[1]

Mr. Elphinstone speaks of the Indian character in Misfortune in glowing terms. "When fate," he says, "is inevitable, the lowest Indian encounters it with a coolness that would excite admiration in Europe."[2]

The national character of a people necessarily suffers from the unsympathetic domination of a less civilised people. Successful falsehood, says Bentham, is the best defence of a slave; and it is no wonder that the character of the Indians deteriorated under the Moslem rule. The wonder is their character is still so high. Professor Max Müller says, "I can only say that after reading the accounts of the terror and horrors of Mohamedan rule, my wonder is that so much of native virtue and truthfulness should have survived."[3] He also says:

"When you read of the atrocities committed by the Mohamedan conquerors of India after that time (1000 AD.) to the time when England stepped in and, whatever may be said by her envious critics, made, at all events, the broad principles of our common humanity respected once more in India, the wonder, to my mind, is how any nation could have survived such an Inferno, without being turned into devils themselves."[4]

---

[1] *India : What can it teach us*? P.11

[2] Elphinstone's *History of India*, pages 198-199. Of the great grandfather of the present Maharaja of Jodhpur, Colonel Tod says, 'The biography of Man Singh would afford a remarkable picture of human patience, fortitude and constancy never surpassed in any age of country." '*Rajasthan*, Vol. II, p. 711

[3] Max Müller's *India : What can it teach us*?, p.72

[4] Max Müller's *India : What can it teach us*?, p.54

It must not be supposed from the condemnatory language used in more than one place in this book with regard to the treatment of the Hindus and their literature by some of the Mussalman invaders and rulers of India, that the history of those reigns is one continuous record of cruelty and oppression, unredeemed by an humanitarian considerations or sympathetic treatment. As Sir Arther Helps observes, no dark cloud is without its silver lining. There are instances on record which show a chivalrous and generous regard displayed by some of the Mohamedan Kings for the Hindus. It is related that when, during the reign of Rana Bikramjit, son of Rana Sanga of Chitor, who was at the time in Haravati, Mewar was invaded by Bahadur King of Gujrat, and Chitor was invested by the combined armies of Gujrat and Malwa, Maharani Karnavati, the mother of the infant son of Rana Sanga, who was in the fortress, appealed for help to Humayun, whom she had adopted as her *Rakhiband bhai* (bracelet-bound brother). Humayun, like a true cavalier that he was, accepted the obligation laid on him by the laws of chivalry and honour, to come to her aid, and abandoning his conquests in Bengal, hastened to answer the call of her adoptive sister, the dowager Mahārāṇī of Chitor. 'He amply fulfilled the pledge, expelled the foe from Chitor, took Mandu by a assult and, as some revenge for her king's aiding the King of Gujarat, he sent for the Rana Bikramjit, whom, following their own notions of investirue, he girt with a sword in the captured citadel of his foe.''

Not should it be forgotten that it was a Mussalman who preserved the Kingdom of Marwar at the most critical period of its history. Not satisfied with the blood of Jaswant and of his eldest son, Pirthi Singh, the unrelenting tyrant (Aurangzeb) carrying his vengeance towards the Maharaja Mewa even beyond the grave, commanded that his infant son, Ajit, should be surrendered to custody. 'Aurang offered to divide Maroo (Marwar) amongst her nobles if they would surrender their prince, but they replied 'our country is with our sinews, and these can defend both it and our lord.' With eyes red with rage they left the *Am-e-Khas.* Their abode was surrounded by the host of the Shah.' A fearful battle ensued. The first care of the Rajputs was to save the infant prince, and to avoid suspicion, the heir of Marwar, concealed in a basket of sweet-meats, was

When, however, centuries of foreign (Moghul) domination have left the people as virtuous, truthful and refined as any free people to be found anywhere in the world, what further evidence is necessary to prove the high national character of the ancient Indians, whose lives were regulated by ethical principles of the highest order!

---

entrusted to a Moslem, who rigorously executed his trust and conveyed him to the appointed spot, where he was joined by the gallant Durga Das and his Rajputs, who had cut their way through all opposition.

1.5. Chivalry

Let laurels, drenched in pure Parnassian dews,
Reward the memory, dear to every muse,
Who with a courage of unshaken root,
In honour's field advancing his firm foot,
Plants it upon the line that justice draws,
And will prevail or perish in the cause.

-Cowper

The innate chivalry of Indian character is well known to those who have studied their history, or lived with them and studied their manners and customs. Their treatment of the female sex, their unwillingness to injure or take away life unnecessarily, their magnanimous treatment of their fallen foes, their unwillingness to take advantage of their own superiority to their adversaries, prove the chivalrous character of the Indian race. The undaunted heroism and the unequalled valour of the ancient Indians, their magnificent self-confidence, their righteousness of conduct, and, above all, the sublime teachings of their *Śāstras*, containing the loftiest spiritual ideals yet conceived by humanity, made them the most chivalrous and humane people on the face of the earth. So much is the warrior caste of the Indians even now identified with a chivalry that Rajputs and Chivalry have become convertible terms.[1] Rajputana is eminently the land of chivalry, and the Rajputs, the descendants of the ancient Kṣatriyas, have preserved some of the latter's virtues, prominent among which is chivalry. Rama, Arjuna, Karana, Krishna, Bhima, Bali, Baldeo (Hercules), Sagara, and others were ideal characters: but coming down to modern times we find that Rana Pratap of Mewar, Durga Das of Marwar and Prithvi Raj of Ajmer were characters for whose equals in chivalry and patriotism we may search in vain the annals of other nations, European or Asiatic.

---

[1] See Tod's *Rajasthan*, Vol. II, p.601

The annals of no nation record instances to outshine the romantic chivalry displayed by Sadoo, heir of the lord of Pugal, till lately a fief of Jaisalmer, or the chivalrous conduct of his bride, Kurram Devi, daughter of the Mohil chief Manik Rao, who "was at once a virgin, a wife and a widow."[1]

Colonel Tod says, "Nor is there anything finer in the annals of the chivalry of the West than the dignified and the heroic conduct of the Raja of Duttea," who met with a glorious death in defence of the laws of sanctuary and honour, when on the death of Madhaji Scindhia, the females of his (Scindhia's) family, in apprehension of his successor, Daulat Rao, sought refuge and protection with the Raja.[2]

The author of the Annals and Antiquities of Rajasthan pays the highest tribute to the valour and chivalry of the Rajputs when he says, "Coeur de lion (King of England) would not have remained so long in the dungeons of Austria had his subjects been Rajputs."[3]

Professor H.H. Wilson says, "The Hindu laws of war are very chivalrous and humane, and prohibit the slaying of the unarmed, or women, of the old and of the conquered."

The innate chivalry of the Indian character has given rise to a peculiar custom observed among all classes of people, irrespective of caste, nationality or age. It is the *Rakhi* (*Rakṣābandhan*), by which Indian ladies command loyal, disinterested, and whole sole service of men, whom they deign to adopt as their brothers, though in most instances they never behold them. "There is a delicacy in this custom," says Colonel Tod, "with which the bond uniting

---

[1] See Tod's *Rajasthan*, Vol. II, p.629
[2] Tod's *Rajasthan*, vol. I, p.117
[3] Tod's *Rajasthan*, Vol. I, p.161.

the cavaliers of Europe to the service of the fair in the day of chivalry will not compare.''[1]

The following incident will show the character of the Rajputs and the nature of their warfare. During the reign of Rana Rai Mal of Chitor, his younger brother, Suraj Mal, whom the prophetess of Charuni Devi at Nahra Mugra had promised a crown, made several attempts to gain one. With the help of Muzaffar, the Sultan of Malwa, he took Sadri and Baturo and attempted even Chitor. Rai Mal met the attack on the River Gumbeeree. The second son of the Rana, Pirthi Raj, ''the Rolando of his age,'' as Colonel Tod calls him, selected his uncle, Suraj Mal, whom he soon covered with wounds. Many had fallen on both sides but neither party would yield: when worn out they retired from the field, bivouacked in sight of each other. Colonel Tod continues, ''It will show the manners and feelings so peculiar to the Rajput, to describe the meeting between the rival uncle and nephew-unique in the details of strife perhaps since the origin of man.[2] It is taken from a manuscript of the Jhala Chief who succeeded Suraj Mal in Sadri. Pirthi Raj visited his uncle, whom he found in a small tent reclining on a pallet, having just had 'the barber' (nae) to sew up his wounds. He rose and met his nephew with the customary respect as if nothing unusual had occurred; but the exertion caused some of the wounds to open afresh, when the following dialogue ensued:

''Pirthi Raj — 'Well, uncle, how are your wounds?'

---

[1] Tod's *Rajasthan*, Vol. I., p. 581 'It is one of the few (customs) when an intercourse of gallantry of the most delicate nature is established between the fair sex and the cavaliers of *Rajasthan*-- The Rajput dame bestows with the Rakhi (bracelet) the title of adopted brother; and while its acceptance secures to her all the protection of a 'cavaliere survente', scandal itself never suggests any other tie to his devotion''.- p.312

[2] Tod's *Rajasthan*, Vol, I, p. 296-97

"'Suraj Mal— 'quite healed, my child, since I have the pleasure of seeing you.'

Pirthi Raj— 'But, uncle (kaka), I have not yet seen the Dewanji.[1]' I first ran to see you, and I am very hungry; have you anything to eat?'

Dinner was soon served, and the extraordinary pair sat down, and 'ate off the same platter;' nor did Pirthi Raj hesitate to eat the 'pan' presented on his taking leave.

"'Pirthi Raj —'You and I will end our battle in the morning, uncle.'

Suraj Mal — 'Very well, child; come early.!'

"They met, and the rebels were defeated and fled to Sadri. Pirthi Raj, however, gave them no rest, pursuing them from place to place. In the wilds of Baturro they formed a stockaded retreat of the 'dho' tree, which abounds in the forest; and Sujah and his companion, Sarangdeo, were communing on their desperate plight when their cogitations were checked by the rush and neigh of horses, Scarcely had the pretender exclaimed, 'this must be my nephew!' when Pirthi Raj dashed his steed through the barricade and, reaching his uncle, dealt him a blow which would have levelled him but for the support of Sarangdeo, who upbraided him, adding, 'a buffet now was more than a score of wounds in former days' to which Suraj Mal added, 'only when dealt by my nephew's hand.' Suraj Mal demanded a parley; and calling on the prince to stop the combat, he continued, 'If I am killed, it matters not–my children are Rajputs, they will run the country to find support; but if you are slain what will become of Chitor? My face will be blackened and my name everlastingly reprobated.'

"The sword was sheathed, and as the uncle and nephew embraced, the latter asked the former, 'what were you about an uncle, when I came?' 'Only talking nonsense, child, after dinner'. But with me over your head, uncle, as a foe, how

---

[1] The Rana is called Diwanji

could you be so negligent?' 'What could I do? You had left me no resource, and I must have some place to rest my head.''[1]

An episode from the annals of Jaisalmer will illustrate the chivalrous nature of the Rajput and his desire to die fighting, as becomes a Rajput.

After a long course of victorious warfare, in which he subdued various tracts of country, even to the heart of the Punjab, disease seized on Rawul Chachick. In this state he determined to die as he had lived, with arms in his hand; but having no foe near with whom to cope he sent an embassy to the Langa prince of Multan, to beg as a last favour the Jood-dan, or ''gift of battle,'' that his soul might escape by the steel of his foeman, and not fall a sacrifice to slow disease. The prince, suspecting treachery, hesitated; but the Bhatti messenger pledged his word that his master only wished an honourable death, and that he would be only five hundred mentos the combat. The challenge being accepted, the Rawal called his clansmen around him, and on recounting what he had done, seven hundred select Rajputs, who had shared in all his victories, volunteered to take the last field and make (*Saṅkalpa*) oblation of their lives with their leader.[2]

On reaching Dhooniapur, he heard that the prince of Multan was within two Koss (two miles). His soul rejoiced. He performed his ablutions, worshipped the gods, bestowed charity and withdrew his thoughts from the world.

The battle lasted two hours, and the Yadu prince fell with all his kith and kin, after performing prodigies of valour. Two thousand Khans[3] fell beneath their swords and the Bhatti gained the abode of Indra.

---

1 Tod's *Rajasthan*, Vol. I, p.298

2 Tod's *Rajasthan*, Vol. II, pp. 258-9.

3 These were Hindu (Solanki Rajputs) as was their prince. The Rawal Chachick had married Sonaldevi, the grand-daughter of

The chivalry of the chief of Nimaj (a fief of Marwar in Rajputana), in the reign of Raja Mann Singh, excites the admiration of Colonel Tod, to which he gives expression in the following memorable words, "The brave Chief of Nimaj has sold his life but dearly. In vain do we look in the annals of Europe for such devotion and generous despair as marked his end and that of his brave clan."[1]

Of Rana Raj Singh, the great opponent of Aurangzeb, Colonel Tod says, "As a skilful general and gallant soldier, in the defence of his country, he is above all praise. As a chivalrous Rajput, his braving all consequences when called upon to save the honour of a noble female of his race, he is without parallel."[2] "The son of Rana Pratap, Umra, the foe of Jehangir," says Colonel Tod, "was a character of whom the proudest nation might be vain."[3]

Even of the Indians of the present day, Mr. Elphinstone says,[4] "They often display bravery unsurpassed by the most warlike nations, and will always throw away their lives for any consideration of religion or honour."

The chivalrous character to the Indian has handicapped him in his fight against his unscrupulous foes. To the advantage derived by the opponents of the Indians from the latter's mutual jealousies and disunion was added also that of their (Indian) unwillingness to do anything against the dictates of humanity or the demands of chivalry. Unlike

---

Hybat Khan, the Chief of the Seta tribe, or the Swatees, See Tod's *Rajasthan*, Vol. II. P. 233.

[1] Tod's *Rajasthan*, Vol. I, p. 197. Mercenary bands, to the number of 8,000, with guns, attacked Surtan Sing in his haveli (dwelling) at Jodhpur, under the order of Raja Mann Singh. With 180 of his clan he defended himself against great guns and small arms as long as the house was tenable, and then sallied forth, sword in hand, and with his brother and 80 of his kin fell nobly in the midst of his foes.

[2] *Annals and Antiquities of Rajasthan*, Vol. I, p.389

[3] Tod's *Rajasthan*, Vol. I, p. 133

[4] Elphinstone's *History of India*, p. 199

other nations they do not believe in the maxim, "everything is fair in love and war." "To spare a prostrate foe," says Colonel Tod, "is the creed of the Hindu cavalier, and he carried all such maxims to excess"[1]

If the chivalrous nature of the latter-day Indian had only been tempered with political discretion, India would not have suffered the misrule that characterised some of the subsequent reigns. Sultan Shah-bud-din Ghori, when captured by Pirthi Raj on the field of Tilaori, was liberated and allowed to return to his country, only to come back with a fresh army, and with the assistance of the traitors of Kanauj and Patun and of the Haoli Rao Hamir, to overturn the Hindu throne of Delhi. Again, when Mahmud, the Khilzi King of Malwa, was defeated and taken prisoner by the Maharana of Chitor, not only was he set at liberty without ransom but was loaded with gifts and sent back to Malwa.

When during the invasion of Mewar by the Imperial forces of the Emperor Aurangzeb-when all the resources of the mighty Mughal Empire were placed at the disposal of the Mussalman generals, and the Emperor himself repaired to the scene of action to direct the operations in person- the heir-apparent of Delhi and his army, cut off from all assistance, were at the absolute mercy of the heir of Mewar, the magnanimous Rajputs, in pursuance of mistaken notions of chivalry and humanity not only spared the whole army, but gave them guides to conduct them by the defile of Dilwara, and escorted them to Chitor. Nay, we learn from the historian Orme, that Aurangzeb himself owed his life to the clemency of the Rajputs. He says, "The division which moved with Aurangzeb himself was unexpectedly stopped by insuperable defences and precipices in front; while the Rajputs in one night closed the streights in his rear, by felling the overhanging trees; and from their stations above prevented all endeavours of the troops, either within or without, from removing the obstacle. Udeperri, the favourite

---

[1] Tod's *Rajasthan*, vol. 1, p. 287

and Circassian wife of Aurangzeb, accompanied him in this arduous war, and with her retinue and escort was enclosed in another part of the mountains; her conductors, dreading to expose her person to danger or public view, surrendered. She was carried to the Rana, who received her with homage and every attention. Meanwhile, the Emperor himself might have perished by famine, of which the Rana let him see the risk, by a confinement of two days, when he ordered his Rajputs to withdraw from their stations, and suffer the way to be cleared. As soon as Aurangzeb was out of danger the Rana sent back his wife, accompanied by a chosen escort, who only requested in return that he would refrain from destroying the sacred animals of their religion which might still be left in the plains; but Aurangzeb, who believed in no virtue but self-interest, imputed the generosity and forbearance of the Rana to the fear of future vengeance, and continued the war. Soon after, he was again well-nigh enclosed in the mountains. This second experience of difficulties beyond his age and constitution, and the arrival of his sons, Azim and Akbar, determined him not to expose himself any longer in the field, but to leave its operations to their conduct, superintended by his own instructions from Ajmer, to which city he retired with the households of his family, the officers of his court, and his bodyguard of four thousand men, dividing the army between his two sons, who each had brought a considerable number of troops from their respective Government."[1]

Well may Colonel Tod exclaim, "But for repeated instances of an ill-judged humanity, the throne of the Mughals might have been completely overturned."[2]

Twice owing to a political indiscretion on the part of the Ranas of Mewar, in the reigns of Akbar and Jehangir, did the Hindus lose their chance of supremacy. Were it not for the ill-fated interview between Rana Pratap and Mann Singh

---

[1] Tod's *Rajasthan*, Vol. I, p. 383

[2] Tod's *Rajasthan*, Vol. I, p. 379

of Jaipur on the Udaisagar lake, on the latter's return home from the conquest of Sholapur, Akbar would never have succeeded in consolidating his power and founding the Mughal Empire[1] in India, which, after a brilliant career of two centuries, was finally shattered to pieces by the Marathas.

Again, when during Jehangir's reign, Mewar conceived the idea of putting up Prince Khurram against the Emperor Jehangir, and, in the civil War, to wrest the supremacy for the Hindus, Bheem's indiscreet taunt to Raja Gaj Singh of Marwar at the critical moment alienated the Rathores, and the design was frustrated.

---

[1] 'To him Akbar was in indebted for half his triumphs, from the snow clad Caucasus to the shores of the 'golden Chersonese.' Let the eye embrace those extremes of his conquests, Kabul and the Paromamisan of Alexander, and Arracan (now well-known) on the Indian Ocean; the former reunited, the latter subjugated, to the empire by a Rajput prince and a Rajput army,'' p. 336. 'Prince Salim (afterwards Jehangir) led the war against Rana Pratap guided by the councils of Raja Mann and the distinguished apostate son of Sagurji, Mohabat Khan.'' Vol. I. p. 337

1.6. PATRIOTISM

Breathes there the man, with soul so dear,
Who never to himself hath said,
This is my own, my native land!

SCOTT: *Lay of the Last Minstrel*

Love of one's own country is inborn in all civilised men. *Mātṛ Bhūmi* - Motherland - was the constant refrain of the Hindus' song. The intensity of the feeling may be gauged from the fact that when during his fall, political foresight became a waning substance in the mental horizon of the Hindu, he ruled that no one should go out of the sacred limits of this holy land, that life here and death here alone shall be the necessary conditions of gaining Heaven hereafter. It is of course universally known that the creed of the Rajput or the warrior caste of India even now is, that dying sword in hand in the cause of the country is the surest and the nearest way to India's abode. Colonel Tod says, "The name of 'country' carried with it a magical power in the mind of the Rajput. The name of his wife or his mistress must never be mentioned at all, nor that of his country but with respect, or his sword is instantly unsheathed."[1]

Patriotism! In vain you ransack the annals of Greece and Rome, of Modern or Mediaeval Europe to find such noble patriots as Rana Pratap and Thakur Durga Das. Patriotism, chivalry and honour found their ideal embodiment in these two heroes. Pratap fought single-handed, with a handful of his Rajputs, against the mighty hosts of Akbar, "the greatest monarch that ever sat on an Asiatic throne," aided by the arms and counsels of his own countrymen, the Kutchwahas, Rathores, Haras Deoras of Abu and others, whose kingdoms lay round Mewar. He fought for a quarter of a century and died, leaving a name, unrivalled in the history of patriotism and chivalry. Colonel Tod says, "Pratap succeeded to the title and renown of an ancient house, but without a capital,

---

[1] Tod's *Rajasthan*, Volume II, p. 429

without resources, his kindred and clans dispirited by reverses; yet possessed by the noble spirit of his race, he meditated the recovery of Chitor, the vindication of the honour of his house and the restoration of its power. The wily Moghal (Akbar) arrayed against Pratap, his kindred in faith as well as blood. The princes of Marwar, Amber, Bikaner and even Boondi, late his firm ally, took part with Akbar and upheld despotism. Nay, even his own brother, Sagarji, deserted him. But the magnitude of the peril confirmed the fortitude of Pratap, who vowed in the words of the bard, 'to make his mother's milk resplendent;' and he amply redeemed his pledge. Single-handed for a quarter of a century did he withstand the combined efforts of the empire, at one time carrying destruction into the plains, at another flying from rock to rock, feeding his family from the fruits of his native hills, and rearing the nursing hero, Amra, amidst savage beasts and scarce less savage men, a fit heir to his prowess and revenge. The bare idea that 'the son of Bappa Rawal should bow the head to mortal man 'was insupportable, and he spurned every overture, which had a submission for its basis, or the degradation of uniting his family by marriage with the Tartar, though lord of countless multitudes."

Colonel Tod adds[1], "it is worthy the attention of those who influence the destinies of States in more favoured climes to estimate the intensity of feeling which could arm the prince to oppose the resource of small principality against the then most powerful empire in the world, whose armies were more numerous, and far more efficient than any ever led by the Persians against the liberties of Greece. Had Mewar possessed her Thucydides or her Zenophon, neither the war of the Peleponesus, nor the Retreat of the Ten Thousand would have yielded more diversified incidents for the historic muse than the deeds of this brilliant reign amid the many vicissitudes of Mewar. Undaunted heroism, inflexible fortitude, that which 'keeps honour bright,'

[1] Tod's *Rajasthan*, Vol, I.P. 349.

perseverance with fidelity such as no nation can host were the material opposed to a soaring ambition, commanding talents, unlimited means and the fervour of religious zeal; all, however, insufficient to contend with one unconquerable mind. There is not a pass in the alpine Aravalli that is not sanctified by some deed of Pratap-some brilliant victory of often more glorious defeat. *Haldighat is the*[1] *Thermopylae of Mewar, the field of Deweir her Marathon.*

"The last moments of Pratap" says Colonel Tod, "were an appropriate commentary on his life, which he terminated, like the Carthaginian, swearing his successor to the eternal conflict against the foes of his country's independence. But the Rajput "prince had not the same joyful assurance that inspired the Numidian Hamilcar; for his end was clouded with the presentiment that his son, Amra, would abandon his fame for inglorious repose. A powerful sympathy is excited by the picture which is drawn from this final scene. The dying hero is represented in a lowly dwelling; his chiefs, the faithful companions of many a glorious day, awaiting round his pallet the dissolution of their prince, when a groan of mental anguish made Saloombra inquire 'what afflicted his soul that it would not depart in peace?' "He rallied, 'lingered,' he said, 'for some consolatory pledge that his country should not be abandoned to the Turks;' and with the death-pang upon him, he related an incident which had guided his estimate of his son's disposition, and now tortured him with the reflection, that for personal ease he would *forego the remembrance of his own and his country's wrongs.*

"On the banks of the Pesola, Pratap and his chiefs had constructed a few huts (the site of the future palace of Udaipur) to protect them during the inclemency of the rains in the day of their distress. Prince Amra, forgetting the lowliness of the dwelling, a projecting bamboo of the roof

---

[1] 'What says the Thermopylae of India Corygaum? Five hundred firelocks against 20 thousand men! Do the annals of Napoleon record a more brilliant exploit.' *Rajasthan*, Vol. I, p.80.

caught the folds of his turban and dragged it off as he retired. A hasty emotion which disclosed a varied feeling. was observed with pain by Pratap, who thence adopted the opinion that his son would never withstand the hardships necessary to be endured in such a cause: 'These sheds' said the dying prince, 'will give way to sumptuous dwellings, thus generating the love of ease, and luxury with its concomitants will ensue, to which independence of Mewar, which we have bled to maintain, will be sacrificed; and you, my chiefs, will follow the pernicious example. 'They pledged themselves, and became guarantees for the prince, 'by the throne of Bappa Rawal,' that they would not permit mansions to be raised till Mewar had recovered her independence. The soul of Pratap was satisfied, and with joy, he' expired"[1].

As regards Durga Das and the Rathores, the noble historian of Rajputana says, "Let us take a retrospective glance of the transactions of the Rathores from the year 1737, the period of' Raja Jaswant's death at Kabul, to the restoration of Ajit, presenting a continuous conflict of 30 years' duration. In vain might, we search the annals of any other nation for such inflexible devotion as marked the Rathore character through this period of strife, during which, to use their own phrase, 'hardly a Chieftain died on his pallet.' Let those who deem the Hindu warrior void of patriotism read the rude chronicle of this thirty years' war; let them compare it with that of any other country, and do Justice to the magnanimous Rajput. This narrative, the simplicity of which is the best voucher for its authenticity; presents an uninterrupted record of patriotism and disinterested loyalty. It was a period when the sacrifice of these principles was rewarded by the tyrant king with the highest honours of the. State; nor are we without instances of the temptation being too strong to be withstood: but they are rare, and serve only to exhibit in more pleasing colours the virtues of the tribe which spurned the attempts at

---

[1] Tod's *Rajasthan*, Vol. I, pp. 348, 49

seduction. What a splendid example is the heroic Durga Das of all that constitutes the glory of the Rajput! our, loyalty, integrity, combined with prudence in all the difficulties which surrounded him, are qualities which entitle him to the admiration which his memory continues to enjoy. The temptations held out to him were almost incompatible; not merely the gold, which he and thousands of my brethren would alike have spurned, but the splendid offer of power in the 'proffered 'munsub of five thousand,' which would at once have lifted him from his vassal condition to an equality with the princes and chief nobles of the land. Durga had, indeed, but to name his reward; but, as the bard justly says, he was '*Amolak*' beyond all price, '*Unoko*' unique. Not even revenge, so dear to the Rajput, turned him aside from the dictates of true honour. The foul assassination of his brother, the brave Soning, effected through his enemies, made no alteration in his humanity whenever the chance of war placed his foe in his power; and in this, his policy seconded his virtue. His chivalrous conduct in the extrication of prince Akbar from inevitable destruction had he fallen into his father's hands, was only surpassed by his generous and delicate behaviour towards the prince's family which was left in his care, forming a marked contrast to that of the enemies of his faith on similar occasions. The virtue of the grand-daughter of Aurangzeb, in the sanctuary of Droonara, was in far better keeping than in the trebly-walled harem of Agra. Of his energetic mind and the control, he exerted over those of his confiding brethren what a proof is given, in his preserving the secret of the abode of his prince throughout the first six years of his infancy! But, to conclude our eulogy in the words of their bard: he has reaped the immortality destined for good deeds; his memory is cherished, his actions are the theme of constant praise, and his picture on his white horse; old, yet in vigour,' is familiar amongst the collections of the portraits of Rajputana."[1]

---

[1] Tod's *Rajasthan*, Vol. II, p. 81, 82

"In the history of mankind,"adds Colonel Tod, "there is nothing to be found presenting a more brilliant picture of fidelity than that afforded by the Rathore clans in their devotion to their prince from his birth until he worked out his own and his country's deliverance."[1]

Colonel Tod says "Many anecdotes are extant recording the dread, Aurangzeb had of this leader of the Rathores, one of which is amusing; The tyrant had commanded pictures to be drawn of two of a mortal foes to his repose, Shivaji and Durga. Shivaji was drawn seated on a couch; Durga in his ordinary position, on horseback, toasting *bhawties* or barley-cakes with the point of his lance, on a fire of maize-stalks. Aurangzeb at the first glance, exclaimed, 'I may entrap that fellow (meaning Shivaji), but this dog is born to be my bane."[2]

Patriotism, the honour of his race, anxiety to maintain the good name of his country are inherent traits in the character of a true Hindu. A simple incident of no great political importance shows the living faith of the Rajput in his country and his race, for whose honour he is prepared at all times and in all circumstances to lay down his life unhesitatingly.

Humiliated by a night attack on his forces by a handful of men under Hamoo, the Chief of Bundi, when his army was put to flight. in the course of a campaign against Haraoti, the Maharana of Chitor reformed his troops under the walls of his celebrated fortress and swore that he would not eat until he was master of Bundi.

The rash vow went round, but Bundi was sixty miles distant, and defended by brave hearts. His chiefs expostulated with the Rana on the absolute impossibility of redeeming his vow, but the words of kings are sacred: Bundi must fall ere the King of the Gehlotes could dine. In this exigence, a childish expedient was proposed to release him

---

[1] Tod's *Rajasthan*, Vol. II, p. 94
[2] Tod's *Rajasthan*, Vol. II, p. 66

from hunger and his oath; 'to erect a mook Bundi. and take it by storm.' Instantly the mimic town arose under the walls of Chitor; and, that the deception might be complete, the local nomenclature was attended to, and each quarter had its appellation. A band of Haras of the Pathar were in the service of Chitor, whose leader, Koombo Bairsi, was returning with his kin from hunting the deer when their attention was attracted by this strange bustle. The story was soon told, that Bundi must fall ere the Rana could dine. Koombo assembled his brethren of the Pathar, declaring that even the mock Bundi must be defended. All felt the indignity to the clan, and each bosom burning with indignation, they prepared to protect the mud walls of the pseudo-Bundi from insult. It was reported to the Rana that Bundi was finished. He advanced to the storm; but what was his surprise when instead of the blank cartridge he heard a volley of balls whiz amongst them! A messenger was dispatched and was received by Bairsi at the gate, who explained the cause of the unexpected salutation, desiring him to tell the Rana that 'not even the mock capital of a Hara should be dishonoured.' Spreading a sheet at the little gateway, Bairsi and the Kaawunts invited the assault, and at the threshold of *Gārā-kā-Bundi* (the Bundi of clay) they gave up their lives for the honour of the race."[1]

Where can you find a more inspiring and ennobling example of a patriotic Hindu doing his duty than that of the eldest son of the Mehtri Chief during the Civil War between Bakht Singh and Ram Singh in Marwar? Colonel Tod says, "There is nothing more chivalrous in the days of Edward and Cressy than the death of the heir of Mehtri, who, with his father and brothers sealed his fealty with his blood on this fatal field. He had long engaged the hand of a daughter of a chief of the Nirookas, and was occupied with the marriage rites when tidings reached him of the approach of the rebels to Mairta. The knot had just been tied, their hands had been joined-but he was a Mairtea - he unlocked his hand

[1] Tod's *Rajasthan*, Vol. II, pp. 463, 64.

from that of the fair Nirooki, to court the Apsara in the field of battle. In the bridal vestments, with the nuptial coronet (Mor) encircling his forehead, he took his station with his clan in the second day's fight, and 'obtained a bride in Indra's abode.' The bards of Maroo dwell with delight on the romantic glory of the youthful heir of Mehtri, as they repeat in their Doric verse,

'Kan a mooti bulbulla
Gulla soni a mall a
Asi kos kurro ho aya
Kunwar Mehtri walla.'

The paraphernalia here enumerated are very foreign to the cavalier of the West: 'With pearls shining in his ears, and a golden chaplet round his neck, a space of eighty Koss (160 miles) came to the heir of Mehtri.'

''The virgin bride followed her lord from Jaipur, but instead of being met with the tabor and lute, and other signs 'of festivity wail and lamentation awaited her within the lands of Mehtri; where tidings came of the calamity which at once deprived this branch of the Mairteas of all its supporters. Her part was soon taken; she commanded the pyre to be erected;' and with the turban and toorah, which adorned her lord on this fatal day, she followed his shade to the mansions of the sun."[1]

Owing to certain reasons, Rai Singh, the heir-apparent of Jaisalmer, during the reign of Mul Raj (who became king in AD 1762), was persuaded to put the minister to death. This was effected by the prince's own hand, in his father's presence; and as the Mehta, in falling, clung to Mul Raj for protection, it was proposed to take off Mul Raj at the same time. The proposition, however, was rejected with horror by the prince, whose vengeance was satisfied. The Rawal was allowed to escape to the female apartments; but the chieftains, well knowing they could not expect pardon from

---

[1] Tod's *Rajasthan*, Vol. 1, pp. 749, 50

the Rawal, insisted of investing Rai Singh, and if he refused, on placing his brother on the gadi. The '*Āna*' of Rai Singh was proclaimed, but no entreaty or threat would induce him to listen to the proposal of occupyinging the throne; in lieu of which he used a pallet (khat). Three. months and five days had passed since the deposal and. bondage of Mul Raj, when a female resolved to emancipate him; this female was the wife of the chief conspirator and confidential adviser of the regent prince. This noble dame, a Rathore Rajputni, of the Mahecha clan, was the wife of Anoop Singh of Jinjiniali, the premier noble of Jaisalmer, and who, wearied with the tyranny of the minister and the weakness of his prince, had proposed the death of the one and the deposal of the other. We are not made acquainted with any reason, save that of *svadharma*, or 'fealty,' which prompted the Rathorni to rescue her prince even at the risk of her husband's life; but her appeal to her son, Zoorawar, to perform his duty, is preserved, and we give it verbatim': 'Should your father oppose 'you, sacrifice him to your duty, and I will mount the pyre with his corpse.' The son yielded obedience to the injunction of his-magnanimous parent, who had sufficient influence to gain over Arjun, the brother of her husband, as well as Megh Singh, Chief of Baroo. The three chieftains forced an entrance into the prison where their prince was confined, who refused to be released from his manacles until he was told that the Mahechi had promoted the plot for his liberty. The sound of the grand nakarra, proclaiming Mul Raj's re-possession of the *gadi*, awoke his son from sleep; and on the herald depositing at the side of his pallet the sable *siropava*, and all the insignia of exile-the black steed and black vestments–the prince, obeying the command of the emancipated Rawal, clad himself therein, and, accompanied by his party, bade adieu to Jaisalmer, and took the road to Kottoroh. When he arrived at this town, on the southern frontier of the State, the chiefs proposed to "run the country"; but he replied that the country was his mother and every Rajput his foe who injured it.[1]

"This Rajputani,"adds Colonel Tod, "with an elevation of mind equal to whatever is recorded of Greek and Roman heroines, devoted herself and a husband whom she loved, to the one predominant sentiment of the Rajput *swadharma* (duty).

The reply of the Deorah prince of Sirohi when instructed to perform that profound obeisance from which none were exempt at Delhi, where he had been carried by Mokundas, one of Jaswant Singh's generals after having been secretly captured whilst asleep in his palace, and his subsequent conduct, shows the high spirit and the independence of character of a true Rajput and his intense love for his country. He said that "his life was in the king's hands, his honour in his own; he had never bowed the head to mortal man, and never would."As Jaswant had pledged himself for his honourable treatment, the officers of the ceremonies endeavored by stratagem to obtain a constrained obeisance, and instead of introducing him as casual, they showed him a wicket, knee high, and very low overhead, by which to enter, but putting his feet foremost, his head was the last part to appear. This stubborn ingenuity, his noble bearing, and his long-protracted resistance, added to Jaswant's pledge, 'won the king's favour; and he not only proffered his pardon but whatever lands he might desire. "Though the king did not name the return, Soortan was well aware of the terms, but he boldly and quickly' replied, 'what can your Majesty bestow equal to Achalgarh? let me return to it is all I ask.' The king had the magnanimity to comply with his request; Soortan was allowed to retire to the castle of Abu, nor did he or any of the Deoras ever rank themselves amongst the vassals of the empire; but they have continued to the present hour a life of almost savage independence."[2]

---

[1] Tod's *Rajasthan*, Vol. II, pp. 264, 5

[2] Tod's *Rajasthan*, Vol. II, pp. 56, 57

Colonel Tod says, "These *men of the soil*, as they emphatically designate themselves, cling to it and their ancient and well-defined privileges, with an unconquerable pertinacity; in their endeavours to preserve them, whole generations have been swept away, yet has their strength increased in the very ratio of oppression. Where are now the oppressors? The dynasties of Ghazni, of Ghor, the Khiljis, the Lodis, the Pathans, the Timurs, and the demoralising Maratha? The native Rajput has flourished amidst these revolutions, and survived their fall; and but for the vices of their internal sway, chiefly contracted from such association, would have risen to power upon the ruin of their tyrants."[1]

How far will this high character of the Rajputs be influenced by the new condition of things remains to be seen? Colonel Tod says, "When so many nations are called upon, in a period of 'great calamity and danger, to make over to a foreigner, their opposite in everything, their superior in most, the control of their forces in time of war, the adjudication of their disputes in time of peace, and a share in the fruits of their renovating prosperity, what must be the result, when each Rajput may hang up his lance in the hall, convert his sword to a ploughshare, and make a basket of his buckler? What but the prostration of every virtue? To be great, to be independent, its martial spirit must be cherished; happy if within the bounds of moderation."[2] It is to be hoped that education, travel and contact with enlightened Europeans will succeed in counteracting the baneful influences dreaded by the gallant Colonel.

"The Rajput, with all his turbulence, possesses in an eminent degree both loyalty and patriotism."[3]

What can be a more eloquent testimony' to the patriotic fervour and the heroic valour of the Rajputs, than the

---

[1] Tod's *Rajasthan*, Vol, II, p. 160

[2] Tod's *Rajasthan*, Vol I, p. 127

[3] Tod's Rajastha, Vol, I, p.194

following extract from the Annals and Antiquities of Rajasthan, by Colonel Tod:

"There is not a petty State in Rajputana that has not had its own Thermopylae and scarcely a city that has not produced. it's Leonidas. But the mantle of ages has shrouded from view what the magic pen of the historian might have consecrated to endless admiration: Somanath might have rivalled Delphos; the spoils of Hind might have vied with the wealth of the Lybian King; and, compared with the army of the Pandavas, the 'army of Xerxes would have dwindled into insignificance."[1]

---

[1] Tod's *Rajasthan*, Introduction, p. 16

1.7. VALOUR

No thought of flight,
None of the retreat, no unbecoming deed
That argued fear; each on himself relied on,
As only in his arm the moment lay
Of victory.

MILTON: *Paradise Lost*

The Hindus were declared by the Greeks to be the bravest nation they ever came in contact with.[1] It was the Hindu king of Magadha that struck terror in the ever-victorious armies of Alexander the Great.

Abul Fazal, the minister of Akbar, after admiring their other noble virtues, speaks of the valour of the Hindus in these terms: '"Their character shines brightest in adversity. Their soldiers (Rajputs) know not what it is to flee from the field of battle but when the success of the combat becomes doubtful, they, dismount from their horses and throw away their lives in payment of the debt of valour."

"The traveller, Bernier, says that "the Rajputs embrace each other when on the battlefield as if resolved to die."The Spartans, as is well known, dressed their hair on such occasions. It is well known that when a Rajput becomes desperate, he puts on garments of saffron colour, which act, in technical language, is called *kesrian kasumal karna* (donning saffron robes).

After describing how, when Dara disappeared from the field of Dholpur where the Imperial forces had made a last stand against the combined armies of Aurangzeb and Murad in their advance to Agra, and the Imperial forces took to flight, the Bundi chief, like Porus of old, continued fighting heroically till he was killed, saying, ''accused be he who flies! Here, true' to my salt, my feet are rooted to this field, nor will I quit it alive, but with victory", and. how Bharat

---

[1] Elphinstone's *History of India*, p.197

Singh, his youngest son maintained the contest nobly, Colonel Tod says, "Thus in the two battles of Ujjain and Dholpur, no less than 12 princes of the blood, together with the heads of every Hara clan, maintained their fealty even to death. Where are we to look for such examples?"[1]

During a visit of the Bundi chief, Rao Sooju, to Chitor, Rana Ratna, at the instigation of an intriguing Poorbia, determined to slay the Rao in a hunt when the respective chiefs were attended only by a couple of servants. Finding a convenient opportunity, the Rana said to his companion "now is the moment to slay the boar", and instantly an arrow from the bow of the Poorbia was sped at the Rao. "With an eagle's eye he saw it coming and turned it off with his bow!' This might have been a chance, but another from the foster brother of the Rana convinced him there was treachery. Scarcely had he warded off the second, when the Rana darted at him on horseback, and cut him down with his *khāṇḍā*. The Rao fell, but recovering, took his shawl and lightly bound up the wound, and as his foe was making off, he called aloud, 'escape you may, but you have sunk Mewar." The Poorbia, who followed his prince, when he saw the Rao bind up his wound, said "the work is but half done; and like a coward, Rana once more charged the wounded Rao. As his arm was raised to finish the deed of shame, like a wounded tiger the Hara made a dying effort, caught the assassin by the robe, and dragged him from his steed. Together they came to the ground, the Rana underneath. The Rao knelt upon his breast, while, with preternatural strength, with one hand he grasped his victim by the throat, with the other he searched for his dagger. What a moment for revenge! He plunged the weapon into his assassin's heart and saw him expire at his feet. The Rao was satisfied; there was no more life left him than sufficed for

---

[1] Tod's *Rajasthan*, Vol. II, p. 481. 'The annals of no nation on earth can furnish such an example as an entire family, six royal brothers, stretched on the field and all but one in death.' Vol. II, p. 49

revenge, and he dropped a corpse upon the dead body of his foe-man.

The tidings flew to Bundi, to the mother of the Rao that her son was slain in the Aihara. "Slain!!"exclaimed this noble"dame, "but did he fall alone? Never could a son who has drunk at this breast depart unaccompanied;" and as she spoke, "maternal feeling caused the milk to issue from the fount with such force that it rent the slab on which it fell."[1]

Colonel Tod thus relates an incident he witnessed in Haravati, "There was one specimen of devotion (to the prince of Kotah) which we dare not pass over, comparable with whatever is recorded of the fabled traits of the heroism of Greece or Rome. The Regent's (Zalim Singh[2] of Kotah) battalions were advancing in columns along the precipitous bank of a rivulet when their attention was arrested by several shots fired from an isolated hillock rising out of the plain across the stream. Without any order, but as by a simultaneous impulse, the whole line halted to gaze at two audacious individuals, who appeared determined to make their mound a fortress. A minute or two passed in mute surprise, when the word was given to move on; but scarcely was it uttered ere several wounded from the head of the column were passing to the rear, and shots began to be exchanged very briskly, at least twenty in return for one. But the long match locks of the two heroes told every time in our lengthened line, while they seemed to have 'a charmed life,' and the shot fell like hail around them

---

[1] Tod's *Rajasthan*, Volo. II, pp. 468, 69

[2] Col Tod says, 'Zalim Singh was a consummate politician, who can scarcely find a parallel in the varied pages of history. He was the Primum mobile of the region he inhabited, a sphere far too confined for his genius, which required a wider field for its display, and might have controlled the destinies of nations.

'When an English division in 'their pursuit of the Pindari leader, Karim Khan, insulted his town of Baran, he burst forth: 'If twenty years could be taken from his life, Delhi and Deccan should be one.' Tod's *Rajasthan*, Vol. II, pp. 517, 18.

innocuous, one continuing to load behind the mound, while the other fired with deadly aim. At length two twelve-pounders were unlimbered; and as the shot whistled round their ears, both rose to the very pinnacle of the mound and made a profound salaam for this compliment to their valour; which done, they continued to load and fire, whilst entire platoons blazed upon them. Although more men had suffered, an irresistible impulse was felt to save these gallant men; orders were given to cease firing, and the force was directed to move on unless any two individuals chose to attack them manfully hand-to-hand. The words were scarcely uttered when two young Robillas drew their swords, sprung down the bank, and soon cleared the space between them and the foemen. All was deep anxiety as they mounted to the assault; but whether their physical frame was less vigorous, or their energies were exhausted by wounds or by their peculiar situation, these brave defenders fell on the mount whence they disputed the march of ten battalions of infantry and twenty pieces of cannon."[1]

Mukandas was the head of the Kunpanwat Rathores of Marwar. He incurred the displeasure of Emperor Aurangzeb, by a reply which was disrespectful. The tyrant condemned him to enter a tiger's den, and contend for his life unarmed. Without a sign of fear he entered the arena where the savage beast was pacing, and thus contemptuously accosted him "Oh tiger of the Mian, face the tiger of Jaswant;" exhibiting to the king of the forest a pair of eyes, which anger and opium had rendered little less inflamed than his own. The animal, startled by so unaccustomed a salutation, for a moment looked at his visitor, put down his head, turned around and stalked from him. "You see exclaimed the Rathore, "that he dare not face me, and it is contrary to the creed of a true Rajput to attack an enemy who dares not confront him." Even the tyrant, who beheld the scene was surprised into admiration, presented him with gifts and asked if he had any children to inherit his prowess.

---

[1] Tod's *Rajasthan*, Vol., II, pp. 579, 80

His reply, 'how can we get children when you keep us from our wives beyond the Attack?' fully shows that the Rathore and fear were strangers to each other. From this singular encounter, he bore the name of Naharkhan, "the tiger lord."[1]

"It was with the Sesodia Rajputs and the Shekhawats that Mohabat Khan performed the most daring exploit in Mughal history, making Jehangir prisoner in his own camp in the zenith of his power." This Mohabat Khan was an apostate son of Sagarji: half-brother of Rana Pratap. "He was beyond doubt", says Tod, "the most daring Chief in Jehangir's reign."[2]

"The celebrated heroic charges of the Rathore horse at the battles of Tonga and Patun in 1791 AD, against the disciplined armies of the French General De Boigne, carrying everything before them, show the unequalled dash and elan of the Rathore cavalry when inspired by patriotism.

There is no end to the recounting of the brave deeds performed by the Rajputs. Name a few heroes like Pratap, Durga Das, Jaswant, Hamir, Raj Singh, Mann, Prithi Raj, Shivaji, and a volume is said. The rest

'Were long to tell; how many battles fought,
How many kings destroyed and kingdoms won.'

But as the Rajputs were men of valour, so were they men of herculean build and strength. It was a Bhatti Rajput Soningdeo, a man of gigantic strength–who not only bent but broke the iron bow sent by the king of Khorasan to the Emperor of Delhi to string when no one in Delhi could do so.[3]

---

[1] Tod's *Rajasthan*, Vol. II, pp. 55,56
[2] Tod's *Rajasthan*, Vol. I, p. 355
[3] Tod's *Rajasthan*, Vol. II, p. 254

"Homer's heroes," says Col. Tod, "were pigmies to the Kurus, whose bracelet we may doubt if Ajax could have lifted."[1]

Colonel Tod says, "Let us take the Rajput character from the royal historians themselves, from Akbar, Jehangir, Aurangzeb. The most brilliant conquests of these monarchs were by their Rajput allies; though the little regard, the latter had for opinion alienated the sympathies of a race, who, when rightly managed, encountered at command the Afghan amidst the snows of Caucasus, or made the furthest Chersonese tributary to the empire. Assam, where the British arms were recently engaged and for the issue of which such anxiety was manifested in the metropolis of Britain, was conquered by Rajput prince, whose descendant is now an ally of the British Government."[2]

"The Moghals were' indebted for half their conquests to the *Lakh Talwar Rohtaran*" (hundred thousand swords of the Rathores). "But the Imperial princes knew not how to appreciate or to manage such men who, when united under one who could control them, were irresistible."[3]

Religious bigotry and Imperial vanity eventually disgusted the Rajputs, who were the bulwark of the Mughal throne, with the result that the empire came to an end sooner than was expected. "The spirit of devotion in this brave race, by whose aid the Mughal power was made and maintained, was irretrievably alienated," [4] when Delhi was invaded by Nadir Shah. Even in the times of the great Mughal Emperor, Aurangzeb, the Hindu princes of Rajputana though disunited and jealous of each other, were some of them individually too strong to be openly defied by the Emperor. Jaswant Singh of Jodhpur was poisoned at

---

[1] Tod's *Rajasthan*, Vol. II, p.81
[2] Tod's *Rajasthan*, Vol. I, p.195
[3] Tod's *Rajasthan*, Vol. II, p. 507
[4] Tod's *Rajasthan*, Vol. I, p. 417

Kabul,[1] and his heir Prithi Singh, at Delhi, which freed the heart of Aurang from a terrible nightmare. It was only after these murders that the tyrant thought of imposing the hated Jazia. The great Jai Singh of Jaipur was also poisoned at his instigation by the Raja's son, Kirat Singh. Having recourse to poison, when unable to openly meet a strong opponent, was a favourite practice of the Mughal Emperors of India. Even the much-belauded Akbar, the 'arch-enemy of the Hindus', was not above it. Colonel Tad says, "A desire to be rid of the great Raja Mann of Amber, to whom he was so much indebted, made the emperor to act the part of the assassin. He prepared a *majum*, or confection, a part of which contained poison; but caught in his own snare, he presented the innoxious portion to the Rajput and ate that drugged with death himself."[2] The cause appears to have been a design on the part of Raja Mann to alter the succession, and that Khusro, his nephew, should succeed instead of Salim.

The murder of Maharaja Ajit Singh of Marwar by his own, son, Bakht Singh, at the instigation of the Sayyads-the king makers of India—was another instance of the policy of "covert guile," which became a stronger weapon than the sword in the Hands of some of the Mohamedan rulers of India, who seem to have accepted the recommendation bestowed on this policy by Belial in the assembly of the Fallen Angels.

The inherent strength of the Rajput character, his power of dogged resistance, his invincible attachment to his country, and, above all, the spiritual nature of the ideals that nurture his soul, are fully recognised by the historian of Rajputana, when he says, "What nation on earth would have maintained the semblance of civilization, the spirit or the customs of their forefathers, during so many centuries of overwhelming depression, but one of such singular character

---

[1] Tod's *Rajasthan*, Vol. I, p. 379, and Vol. II, p. 52

[2] Tod's *Rajasthan*, Vol. I, pp. 351, 52

as the Rajput? Though ardent and reckless he can, when required, subside into forbearance and apparent apathy, and reserve himself for the opportunity of revenge. Rajasthan exhibits the sole example in the history of humankind, of a people withstanding every outrage barbarity can inflict, or human nature sustains, from a foe whose religion commands annihilation, and bent to the earth, yet rising buoyant from the pressure, and making calamity a whetstone to courage. How did the Britons at once sink under the Romans, and in vain strive to save their groves, their druids, or the altars of Bal from destruction! To the Saxons they alike succumbed; they, again, to the Danes; and this heterogeneous breed to the Normans. Empire was lost and gained by a single battle, and the laws and religion of the 'conquered merged in those of the conquerors. Contrast with these the Rajputs: not an iota of their religion or customs have they lost, though many a foot of land. Some of their States have been expunged from the map of dominion; and, as a punishment of national infidelity, the pride of the Rathore, and the glory of the Chalook, the over-grown Kanauj and gorgeous Anhilwarra, are forgotten names! Mewar alone, the sacred bulwark of religion, never compromised her honour for her safety, and still, survives her ancient limits; and since the brave Samarsi gave up his life, the blood of her princes has flowed in copious streams for the maintenance of this honour, religion and independence."[1]

As the ancient Hindus were the bravest nation in the world, 'So did they give to the world its greatest hero. Hercules has been universally acknowledged to be the greatest warrior, the bravest and the most powerful man the world has ever produced. And Hercules was, in reality, a Hindu and not a Greek. Hercules was but Balram. This may sound paradoxical to those who have not studied comparative mythology, but to those who have done so there is nothing strange in this statement. The word Hercules is derived from title Sanskrit word Heri-cul-es (हरी-कुल-ईस).

---

[1] Tod's *Rajasthan*, Vol. I, p. 259

Balram emigrated to Greece after the *Mahābhārata*, and in consequence of the display of his wonderful feats of strength and valour there, the people of Greece began to worship him as a god.

Professor Heeren says, "We can hardly doubt that Bacchus and Hercules were both of them Hindu deities, since they are not only represented as objects of general worship, but the particular countries and places are also specified where both the one and the other had temples erected to their services (see *Arrian*, p. 174, and *Strabo*, Vol. 15th p. 489).

Diodorus says that Hercules was born amongst the Indians. "The combats to which Diodorus alludes are those in the legendary haunts of the Hercules during their twelve years exile from the seat of their forefathers."[1]

Colonel Tod says, "Both Krishna and Baldeo (Balram) or Apollo and Hercules are es (lords) of the race (cul) of Heri (Heri-cul-es), of which the Greeks might have made the compound Hercules. Might not a colony after the Great War have migrated Westward? The period of the return of Heraclidae, the descendants of Atreus (Atri the progenitor of the Hericula (हरिकुल) would answer: It was about half a century after the Great War."

After describing the population of Behar, Mr. Pococke says, "Here then the historian is presented with a primitive population in Hellas, not only from the Himalayas, but from Pelasa, Magadha, or Bihar, with corresponding clans to enter Greece, and the cherished memory of their Chiefs, as the foundation of one of the godships of Hellas. Though Baladeva, the elder brother of Krishna, who was supposed to have perished in crossing the Himalaya mountains, succeeded ultimately in reaching Greece, where his renown

[1] Tod's *Rajasthan*, Vol. I, p. 30, Arrian's story of Hercules is the same as that given in the *Purāṇas*.

became great. Krishna was. doomed to perish in a land far distant from that country."[1]

Colonel Tod cannot resist the inference that the Herculas of India and the Heraclidae of Greece were connected. Arrian notices the similarity of the Hindu and Theban Hercules, and cites as his authority the ambassador of Seleucus. Megasthenes, who says, "He used the. same habit with the Theban, and is. practically worshipped by the Sureseni, who have two great cities belonging to them. namely, Mathura and Clisoboros."

The points of resemblance between the Hindu and the Theban Hercules are most striking, and irresistibly lead one to the conclusion that here at least similarity is synonymous with identity.

(1) The Heraclidae claimed their origin from Atreus, the-Hericulas from Atri.

(2) Euristhenes was the first great king of the Heraclidae; Yudhiṣṭhira has sufficient affinity in his name to the first Spartan king not to startle the etymologist -the d and r being always permutable in Sanskrit.

(3) The Greeks or Ionians, are descended from Yavan or' Javan, the seventh from Japhet. The Hericules are also Yavans claiming from Javan or Yavona, the thirteenth in descent from Yayat, the third son of the primaeval patriarch.

(4) The ancient Heraclidae of the Greeks asserted that they were as the sun, older than the moon. May not this boast conceal the fact that the Hericulidae (or Suryavansa) of Greece had settled there anterior to the colony of the Indu (Lunar) race of Hericulas? Col. Tod says, "Amidst the snows of Caucasus, Hindu legends abandon the Hericulas under their leaders, Yudhiṣṭhira and Baldeo : yet, if Alexander established his altars in Panchalica amongst the sons of Puru and the Hericulas, what

---

[1] *India in Greece*, p. 299

physical impossibility exists that a colony of them under Yudhiṣṭhira and Baldeo, eight centuries anterior, should have penetrated to Greece? Comparatively far advanced in science and arms, the conquest would have been easy."

(5) When Alexander attacked the "free cities"of Panchalika, the Purus and the Hericulas who opposed him evinced the recollections of their ancestor, in carrying the figure of Hercules as their standard.[1]

Comparison proves a common origin to Hindu and Greek mythology, and Plato says "the Greeks derived theirs from Egypt and the East. May not this colony of the Heraclidae who penetrated into Peloponnesus (according to Volney) 1078 years before Christ, be sufficiently near our calculated period of the Great War ?"[2]

"How refreshing,"Colonel Tod concludes, "to the mind yet to discover amidst the ruins of the Yamuna, Hercules (Baldeo) retaining his club and lion's' hide.

---

[1] 'The martial Rajputs are not strangers to armorial bearings, now so indiscriminately used in Europe. The great banner of Mewar exhibits a golden sun on a crimson field, those of the chiefs bear a dagger. Amber displays the *Pañcraṅga*, or five-coloured flag. The lion rampant on an argent field, is extinct with the State of Chanderi. In Europe, these customs were not introduced till the period of the Crusades, and were copied from the Saracens, while the use of them among the Rajput tribes can be traced to a period anterior to the war of Troy.' *India in Greece*,' p. 92.

[2] Tod's *Rajasthan*, Vol. I, p. 51

1.8. POSITION OF WOMEN

Oh, fairest of creation! last and best
Of all God's works! Creature in whom excell'd
Whatever can to sight or thought be formed
Holy, divine, good, amiable, or sweet.

—MILTION: *Paradise Lost*

Mr. Herbert Spender, the great apostle of individual freedom, says that the position of women supplies a good test of the civilisation of a people.

Colonel Tod also says, "It is universally admitted that there is no better criterion of the refinement of a nation than the condition of the fair sex therein."[1]

The high position Hindu women have always occupied in India would, if this is true, argue a very advanced state of civilisation in that country. Even of the modern Hindu society, Colonel Tod says, "If devotion to the fair sex be admitted as a criterion of civilisation, the Rajput must rank very high. His Susceptibility is extreme and fires at the slightest offence to female delicacy, which he never forgives. A satirical impromptu, offending against female delicacy, dissolved the coalition of the Rathores and Kutchwahas, and laid each prostrate before the Marathas, whom when united they had crushed; and a jest, apparently trivial, compromised the right of primogeniture to the throne of Chitor, and proved more disastrous in its consequences than the arms either of Moghuls or Marathas."[2]

Professor H. H. Wilson says, "And it may be confidently asserted that in no nation of antiquity were women held in so much esteem as amongst the Hindus."[3]

---

[1] Tod's *Rajasthan*, Vol. I, p. 609
[2] Tod's *Rajasthan*, Vol. I, p. 276
[3] Mill's *History of India*, Vol. II, p. 51

In Ancient India, however, they not only possessed equality of opportunities with men but enjoyed certain rights and privileges not claimed by the male sex. The chivalrous treatment of women by Hindus is well known to all who know anything of Hindu Society.

"Strike not even with a blossom a wife guilty of a hundred faults," says a Hindu sage, "a sentiment so delicate," says Colonel Tod "that Reginald-de-Born, the prince of Troubadours, never uttered any more refined."[1]

Manu (Chapter V. 130) says, "The month of a woman is constantly pure" and he ranks it with the running waters and the sunbeam."[2] He also says, (Chapter II. 33), "Where the females are honoured, there the deities are pleased; but where dishonoured, there all religious rites became useless."

The Hindus seem to have laid special stress on honouring the wife and treating her with ever increasing delicacy. The nearest approach to these ideas are the views of Mr. Herbert Spencer, who in a letter dated the 18th March 1845, to his friend Lott, says, "And on this ground I conceive that instead of there being, as is commonly the case, a greater familiarity and carelessness with regard to appearances between husband and wife, there ought to be a greater delicacy than between any other parties."[3]

A rather forcible illustration of this view is the reply of the Hariji, queen of the famous Raja Jai Singh of Jaipur. One day when the Rājā was alone with the queen, he began playfully to contrast the sweeping *jupe* of Kotah with the more scanty robe of the belles of his capital; and taking up a pair of scissors, said he would reduce it to" an equality with the latter. Offended at his levity, she seized his sword, and

---

[1] Tod's *Rajasthan*, Vol. I, p. 611

[2] The women are recommended to preserve a cheerful temper and to remain always well-dressed. 'If the wife be not elegantly attired she will not exhilarate her husband. A wife gaily adorned, the whole house is embellished.'

[3] Herbert Spencer's *Autobiography*, Vol. I, p.268

assuming a threatening attitude, said, "that in the house to which she had the honour to belong, they were not habituated to jests of this nature; that mutual respect was the guardian not only of happiness but of virtue;" and she assured him that if he ever again so insulted her, he would find that the daughter of Kotah could use a sword more effectively than the prince of Amber the scissors.[1]

Manu commands that "whoever accosts a woman shall do so by the title of sister, and that way must be made for her even as for the aged, for a priest, a prince, or a bridegroom;" and, in the law of hospitality, he ordains that pregnant women, brides, and damsels shall have food before all the other guests." (Education, art. 129).

The legal status of a wife in ancient India and her equal treatment with her husband is thus defined by Manu, the great lawgiver of the Humankind:

I. If a wife dies, her husband may marry another wife. (Manu, Chapter V, verse 168).

If a husband dies, a wife may marry another husband (Manu, quoted by Madhava and Vaidyanātha Dikṣita; Parāśara, Nārada; Yājñavalkya; quoted by Krishnacharya Smriti; *Agni Purāṇa*; *Smṛti*, quoted by Chetti Koneri Ācārya and Janārdana Bhaṭṭa).

I. If a wife becomes 'fallen by drunkenness or immorality, her husband may marry another. (Manu, Chapter IX, verse 80; Yājñavalkya, page 416, verse 73).

If a husband becomes fallen, a wife may remarry another husband. (Manu, quoted by Madhava and several other authorities above mentioned).

If a wife is barren, her husband may marry another wife. (Manu. Chapter IX, verse 81).

---

[1] Tod's *Rajasthan*, Vol. I, p. 626

If a husband is impotent she may marry another husband. (Manu, and several other authorities quoted above).

IV. In particular circumstances, a wife may cease to cohabit with her husband. (Manu, Chapter IX, verse 79).

V. If a husband deserts his wife, she' may marry another. (Manu, Chapter IX, verse 76, and several others).

VI. If a wife treats her husband with aversion, he may cease to cohabit with her. (Manu, Chapter IX, verse 77).

VII. A husband must be revered (Manu, Chapter V, verse 154).

VIII. A wife must be honoured by the husband (Manu, Chapter III, verse 55).

IX. A good wife irradiates the house and is a goddess of wealth (Manu, Chapter IX, verse 26).

A good husband makes his wife entitled to honour (Manu, Chapter IX, verse 23).

The high ethical teachings of the Indian *Śāstras* prepared the men to assign to women a peculiarly privileged position, keeping them safe from the rough and degrading work that now often falls to their lot in the West, in consequence of the severe struggle for existence raging there. While providing the freest possible scope for the exercise of their peculiar gifts, which enabled them to achieve in the superlative degree, the high and noble work which it is the privilege of women to perform for the well-being and advancement of a people, the ancient Hindu constitution not only accorded to them the position which the mothers, the sisters, the wives, and the daughters of the highest and the lowest in the nation are justly entitled to, but which enabled their true feminine nature and character to receive full development, so as to fulfil their high destiny of giving to the world a race of men yet unequalled in intellect, character and energy.

In Europe, as well as in India, the woman is styled "the half of the man"-in Europe, as "the better half," in India, simply as *Ardhāṅginī* (lit. half self). In Europe, however, it is a meaningless phrase, rather pointing to the desirability of assigning woman a position which is hers by nature than signifying the position actually occupied by her–showing the desirable but yet unattained ideality rather than, as amongst the Hindus, an actual reality. No doubt there are women in Europe, who as, wives, are treated by their husbands with the same respect and generous consideration as Hindu ladies command in all truly Hindu families. True, in every grade of European society women are to be met with, whose position, domestic as well as social, is not only perfectly happy and satisfactory but, to all outward appearance, looks higher than that enjoyed by their Hindu sisters: True also, that European women enjoy in some respects and in certain directions, privileges neither enjoyed by any Asiatic women nor desired by them. They enjoy a freedom of action in certain matters which is not only one of the distinguishing features of the European civilization but emphasises the negation of all that is meant by *Ardhāṅginī* or the half. In Europe, a woman has a distinct individuality of her own, which flourishes independently of man, though by his side and connected with him. Both men and women there lead separate, distinct, independent lives, albeit Nature and necessity compel them to live together. Not so in India. A woman has no distinctive, independent individuality in Hindu social polity. From her birth to her death she is a part of man, and cannot be separated from him. With marriage, she merges her individuality into her husband's, and both together form a single entity in society. The one without the other is only a part and not a whole.

It must not, however, be supposed that the woman loses herself in the man, and is, therefore, inferior to him. The man too, after his union with a woman, is, like her, only a part of the social entity. All important religious, social, and domestic concerns of life recognise the entity only when it is complete, i.e., formed of a man and a woman.

In Europe, the power and position enjoyed by a woman are not recognised by the authority which sanctions all social laws and on which the entire fabric of society is ultimately based. What position and privilege she enjoys she evidently cannot claim as of right–a right inherent in and inseparable from womanhood. In some of the most important concerns of life, she is utterly ignored. Not so amongst the Hindus. In India, she is in possession of her rights, which no power on earth can take away from her. The Hindu woman is not indebted, like her European sister, for her position to a man's love or affectionate regard or to the exigencies of social life. It is her birthright, inalienable. and recognised by all; it lives with her and dies with her.' The man is as much subject to it as the woman is to a man's. Take, for instance, the most important concern of life, the marriage. In Europe, the father gives away the daughter; in his absence, the brother, or the uncle or some near male relation, as the case may be. He by himself performs this sacred and most important function in life. Where comes in the better half of the father, the brother, the uncle or the other relation? She has no place in the rite, no locus standi, no indispensable, inalienable position in the function. She is not a necessary party. She may be happy in the event and join the festivities, but she is an utter outsider so far as the rite itself–the right of giving away–is concerned. But what do we find in India? Amongst the Hindus, in order that the ceremony of giving away (called *Kanyādāna*) may be complete, the *Ardhāṅginī*, or the wife of the father, the brother, the uncle or the other male relative must take part in it. The "giving away" is not complete till the husband and the wife both do it. Nay, there is something more to mark the unalterable position of the wife as the "other half" of the husband. If owing to any cause-death, illness or unavoidable absence the better half of the father, brother or the other relative cannot be present at the Sacrament, a piece of cloth or something else is placed by his side as a substitute for her, to show that he, by himself, is only an incomplete individual, and cannot perform the most important functions of life unless and until joined by his wife. And it is not so with marriage only. From the marriage down to a dip in the sacred Ganges; the worship of the sacred *bar* tree (the Ficus Indica) in the *Bar Tirat* ceremony;[1] the worship of the household gods, and other simple, ordinary duties, ordained by religion or sanctioned by social usage, no ceremony is complete unless the wife joins the husband in its performance. What a difference here between the respective positions of the European and the Hindu woman! How inferior is the position of a European woman to that of her Hindu sister! With all the love and devotion she receives and the freedom of action she enjoys, she in Europe is even now as far away from the position of the other half of a man as she was two thousand years ago. But society in Europe is still in its making. Important and far-reaching changes will yet have to be made before it arrives at a stage of evolution when it will come into line 'with its sister organisation, the Hindu society, as it is found in the *Śāstras*.

In the West, women's sphere is yet limited; women's position yet precarious, owing to the selfish and hypocritical conduct of man, the product of a material civilisation divorced from spiritual ideals. Their principal interest in public affairs, however, is directed to secure for themselves rights which they regard as essential to assure their position in the cold, pitiless struggle for existence, which respects neither age nor sex. In ancient India, people never thought of usurping from women their rights and privileges. They were safe from the turmoil of life; they were secure against the attacks which all have to meet who are governed by the complicated machinery of a civilisation based on the worship of Mammon, with its horizon bounded by the desires, aspirations and capabilities of the physical man.

Sri Madhavacharya says that Draupadi's part in the administration of the empire was to instruct the subjects as to the duties and rights of women, superintend the

---

[1] When the wife keeps a fast for three days.

management of the Palace and its treasuries, to assist in the management of the finances of the empire, and to supervise the religious institutions of the nation.

The character and ideals of Hindu women may be inferred from the conduct of Maitreyee, wife of Yajñavalkya, who declined to accept the estate offered to her by her husband, on his entering the third Aśram (*Vānaprastha*). She told him that she also would like to have that which he was going in search of, and that, if the estate had been worth having, he would not have given it away.

Avvayar, Damyanti and Sāvitrī were women whose lives would have purified the national life of any people. The learning of Gārgī, the intellect and character of Tārā, the fidelity of Anasūyā and the devotion and love of Sītā would do honour to any nation.

The courage and valour displayed by Kaikeyī in the battle field by the side of Daśratha are no less remarkable than the heroism displayed by Satyabhāmā, of whom Mādhavācārya says that, when she saw her husband tired and his enemy exulting in strength, she fought with him and deprived him of his arms. These facts show in ancient times the women of India were not unused to warfare, and that they accompanied their husbands everywhere. They did not lead secluded lives; they were not kept in the *zenana*. The pardah system, which marks the advent into India of foreigners of a much lower civilisation, was unknown in ancient India.

It has sometimes been urged by men unacquainted with the "Social life of the Hindus that the fact that daughters do not share in the paternal property in the same way as the sons, and that the widow does not share equally with her sons the property left by the husband, argue a low state of civilization amongst them. In the first place, the law of inheritance in this respect is no proof of the high or the low refinement of a people; or the Arabs would be held to be more refined than the Hindus. In the second place, it is not a fact that women do not inherit or are incompetent to hold property.

Professor Wilson says, "Their right to property is fully recognised and fully secured."[1] He also says, "In the absence of direct male heirs, widows succeed to a life interest in real, and absolute interest in personal property. Next, daughters inherit absolutely. Where there are sons, mothers and daughters are entitled to shares and wives. hold peculiar property from a variety of sources, besides those specified by the text, over which a husband has no power during their lives, and which descends to their own heirs, with a preference in some cases to females. It is far from correct, therefore, to say that women amongst the Hindus are excluded from the rights of property."

Commenting on Mr. James Mill's opinion that according to Manu (Chapter IV, 43) women among the Hindus are excluded from sharing in the paternal property, Professor Wilson says, "The reference is incorrect, so is the law; as the passage in the first volume adverted to might have shown had the writer remembered it. For, after stating in the text, in the same unqualified manner, that daughter are altogether debarred from a share, it is mentioned in a note that those who are unmarried are to receive portions out of their brothers' allotments. It is mere quibbling, therefore, to say they have no shares. But the more important question, as affecting the position of women in society, is not merely the shares of daughters, although this is artfully put forward as if it was decisive of the rights of the whole sex, but what rights women have in regard to property; and as we have already shown, the laws do not very materially differ in this respect from those which are observed in the civilized countries of modern Europe."[2]

Foreigners imbibe unfavourable notions regarding the position of Hindu women from their ignorance of the

---

[1] Mill's *History of India*, p. 446, footnote.

[2] Mill's *History of India*, Vol. I, p. 451

working of Hindu society and of the principles on which it is based. The Hindu law of inheritance in this respect is somewhat different from that obtaining in Europe, but in no way behind the latter in safeguarding the position of women.

When men in all grades of society recognise the rights and privileges of women, and the social system of the nation is so framed as to provide means to enforce those rights, the aid of legislation becomes unnecessary. Those who are acquainted with the working of the social system of the Hindus know that the rights of women are recognised in a far more substantial manner than by giving them a certain portion of the inheritance in final settlement of all their claims on the family.

Respect for feminine nature, considerations of honour and chivalry towards the sex, and the ingrained feeling of regard, and esteem for womanhood urged the Hindus to take measures to safeguard the position of a woman against all possible but avoidable contingencies. A woman accordingly has claims on her father and brothers and sons for a suitable maintenance under all circumstances. A father may leave nothing to his sons, yet they are bound to suitably maintain their mother so long as she is alive.

Sisters claim maintenance, their marriage expenses, and presents on all ceremonial occasions, no matter whether their brothers have inherited any paternal estate or not. And, not daughters and sisters alone enjoy such rights in Hindu society. Their children, too, have certain well-defined claims, and Hindu society possesses means to see that those claims are satisfied. The ceremonial institutions of the Hindus controlled by the caste organisation, recognise and fulfil these obligations. Those who are acquainted with the inner working of Hindu society know that the sisters and the daughters not only enjoy certain rights in connection with every festival and every event of importance in their father's and brother's families–at some of which functions they play the leading part, but that even after their marriages their connection with the families in which they were born is one of a perennial flow towards them of presents and gifts, to which they are entitled by social law, irrespective of the relations existing between them being cordial or strained.

Thus, while their rights are secured against contingencies, women altogether get from their fathers and brothers far more than is generally received by them anywhere else in Europe or Asia. Moreover, the joint Hindu family system is highly conducive to the preservation of their influence in some respects predominant–in the families in which they were born.

Even at the present day, though the women are not so prominent, their influence is supreme. They talk slander and tell mischievous falsehoods who say that the Hindu women are prisoners in the *zenana*, that their condition is a pitiable one, that they claim the philanthropic efforts of men and women to alleviate their hard lot, and that they deserve all the sympathy that suffering humanity may receive. Colonel Tod says, "The superficial observer, who applies his own standard to the customs of all nations, laments, with an affected philanthropy, the degraded condition of the Hindu female, in which sentiment he would find her little disposed to join. He particularly laments her want of liberty and calls her seclusion, imprisonment. From the knowledge I possess of the freedom, the respect, the happiness which Rajput women enjoy, I am by no means inclined to deplore their state as one of captivity." And, who does not know that amongst no people in India is pardah observed more strictly than by the Rajputs?

Every Sanskrit scholar knows in what respect and veneration ladies like Gārgī, Draupadī, Śakuntalā, Mandodarī, Arundhatī and Rukmaṇi[1] were held. Who can listen, without admiration and strong emotion, to the

[1] Within the last 100 years, the name of Mahārāṇī Ahalyābai Holkar was prominently before the world. She is known from the Himalayas to Cape Comorin, and her memory is actually worshipped in some places.

celebrated forest speech of Draupadī, after the banishment of the Pāṇḍavas.

"Hindu female devotion" is a hackneyed phrase. Colonel Tod says, "Nor will the annals of any nation afford more numerous or more sublime instances of female devotion than those of the Rajputs."[1] Even in mediaeval ages, India produced women that would make the darkest page of history resplendent. "The annals of no nation on earth," says Colonel Tod, "record" a more ennobling or more magnanimous instance of female loyalty than exemplified by Dewalde, mother of the Binafur brothers."[2]

As the incident alluded to above throws a flood of light on the high character of the Rajput women, and fully illustrates the commanding influence they exercise in society, a short account of this inspiring episode that occurred when Hindu independence was about to be overthrown, may well be inserted.

While the last Hindu emperor of India, the chivalrous Prithviraj, was returning to Delhi from Sameta, some of the wounded, who covered his retreat, were assailed and put to death by Parmal, the Chandail prince of Mahoba. In order to avenge this insult, the emperor invaded the territory of the Chandail, whose troops were cut to pieces at Sirsa. The Chandail by the advice of his queen, Malundevi, demanded a truce of his adversary, on the plea of the absence of his chieftains, Allah and Udala. The envoy found the Chohan ready to cross the Pahouj. The chivalrous Prithviraj, unused to refusing such requests, granted the truce.

The two brothers, Allah and Udala, the Sardars of Mohaba, had been made to abandon their home because Alhah had refused to part with one of his mares which Parmal desired to possess. They went away to Kanauj, where they were received with open arms by Jai Chand.

---

[1] Tod's *Rajasthan*, Vol. I, p. 613

[2] Tod's *Rajasthan*, Vol.I, p. 614

The bard, Yagnik, now repaired to Kanauj to beg the two heroes on behalf of Parmal to return to Mahoba, as their father land demanded their services. He said, "the Chohan is encamped on the plains of Mahoba, Nursing and Birsing have fallen, Sirsa is given to the flames, and the Kingdom of Parmal aid waste by the Chohan. For one month a truce has been obtained, while to you I am sent for aid in his griefs. Listen, Oh sons of Binafur, bad have been the days of Malundevi since you left Mahoba! Oft she looks towards Kanauj; and, while she recalls you to mind, tears gush from her eyes and she exclaims, "the fame of the Chandail is departing, but when gone, Oh, sons of Jasraj, great will be your self-accusing sorrow! yet, think of Mahoba.'"

"Destruction to Mahoba? Annihilation to the Chandail, who, without fault, expelled us from our home; in whose service fell our father, by whom his kingdom was extended. Send the slanderous Purihara—let him lead your armies against, the heroes of Delhi. Our heads were the pillars of Mahoba; by us were the Goands expelled, and their strongholds, Deogarh and Chandbari, added to his sway. We maintained the field against the Jadoon, sacked Hindown, and planted his standard on the plains of Kuttair. It Was (continued Allah) who stopped the sword of the conquering Kushwaha. The Amirs of the Sultan fled before us. At Gaya we were victorious and added Rewah to his kingdom. 'Anterved' I gave to the flames and levelled to the ground the towns of Mewat. From ten princes did Jasraj bring spoil to Mahoba. This has we done, and the reward is an exile from our home! Seven times have I received wounds in his service, and since my father's death gained forty battles, and from seven has Udala conveyed the record of victory to Parmal. Thrice my death seemed inevitable. The honour of his house I have upheld yet exile is my reward."

The bard replies, "The father of Parmal left him when a child to the care of Jasraj. Your father was in lieu of his own; the son should not abandon him when misfortune makes him call on you. The Rajput who abandons his sovereign in distress will be plunged into hell. Then place on your head the loyalty of your father. Can you desire to remain at Kanauj while he is in trouble who expended thousands in rejoicings for your birth? Malundevi (the queen), who loves you as her own, presses your return. She bids me demand of Dewalde, fulfilment of the oft-repeated vow that your life and Mahoba, when endangered were inseparable. The breakers of vows, despised on earth, will be plunged into hell, there to remain while sun and moon endure."

Dewalde heard the message of the queen. "Let us fly to Mahoba," she exclaimed. Allah was silent, while Udala said aloud.

"May evil spirits seize upon Mahoba. Can you forget the day when, in distress, he drove us forth? Return to Mahoba—Iet it stand or fall, it is the same to me; Kanauj is henceforth my home."

"Would that the gods had made me barren," said' Dewalde, "that I had never borne sons who thus abandon the paths of the Rajput, and refuse to succour their prince in danger." Her heart bursting with grief, and her eyes raised to heaven, she continued, "Was it for this, O universal lord, thou mad'st me feel a mother's pangs these destroyers of Binafur's fame? Unworthy offspring! the heart of the true Rajput dances with joy at the mere name of strife–but ye, degenerate, cannot be the sons of Jasraj some carl must have stolen to my embrace; and from such ye must be sprung." This was irresistible. The young Chiefs arose, their false withered in sadness. "When we perish in defence of Mahoba, and, covered with wounds; perform deeds that will leave a deathless name, when our heads roll in the fields, when we embrace the valiant in fight, and, treading in the footsteps of the brave, make resplendent the blood of both lines, even in the presence of the heroes of the Chohan, then' will our mother rejoice."

The chieftains took leave of the King of Kanauj and returned to Mahoba. On their return, a grand Council assembled at a final deliberation, at which the mother of the' Binafurs and the queen Malundevi were present. The latter thus opens the debate, "Oh. mother of Alha, how may we succeed against the lord of the world? If defeated, lost is Mahoba; if we pay tribute, we are loaded with shame." Dewalde recommends hearing seriatim the opinions of the chieftains, when Alha, thus speaks, "Listen, Oh mother, to your son! he alone is of pure lineage, who, placing loyalty on his head, abandons all thoughts of self, and lays down his life for his prince; my thoughts are only for Parmal. If she[1] lives, she will show herself a woman or emanation of Parvati. The warriors of Sambhur shall be cut in pieces. I will so illustrate the blood of my fathers that my fame shall last for ever. My son, Eendal, Oh prince!, I bequeath to you, and the fame of Dewalde is in your keeping." the queen thus replies: "The warriors of the Chohan are fierce as they are numerous; pay tribute, and save Mahoba." The soul of Udala was inflamed, and turning to the queen said "Why thought you not thus when you slew the defenceless? But then I was unheard. Whence now your wisdom? Thrice I beseeched you to pardon. Nevertheless, Mahoba is safe while life remains in me, and in your cause, Oh Parmal! we shall espouse celestial brides."

"Well have you spoken, my son," said Dewalde, "nothing now remains but to make thy parent's milk resplendent by thy deeds. The calls of the peasant driven from his home meets the ear, and while we deliberate, our villages are given to the flames." But Parmal replied, "Saturn rules the day, to-morrow we shall meet the foe". With indignation, Alha turned to the king, "He who can look tamely on while the smoke ascends from his ruined towns, his fields laid waste, can be no Rajput: he who succumbs to fear when his country is invaded, his body will be plunged into the hell of hells, his soul a wanderer in the

[1] Hindus do not call their wives now-a-day by their names.

world of spirits for sixty thousand years; but the warrior who performs his duty will be received into the mansion of the sun, and his deeds will last forever."

The heroes embraced their wives for the last time, and with the dawn, performed their pious rites. Then Alha, ca1ling his son Eendal and Udala, his brother, he once more poured forth his vows to the universal mother, "that he would illustrate the name of Jasraj, and evince the pure blood derived from Dewalde, whenever he met the foe." "Nobly have you resolved," said UdaIa, "and shall not my kirban[1] also dazzle the eyes of Sambhur's lord? Shall he not retire from before me?" "Farewell, my children," said Dewalde, "be true to your salt, and should you lose your heads for your prince, doubt not you will obtain the celestial crown." Having ceased, the wives of both exclaim "what virtuous wife - survives her lord? For, thus says Goriji, "the woman who survives her husband who falls in the field of battle will never obtain bliss but wander a discontented ghost in the region of unhallowed spirits."

The fidelity of a nurse is well exemplified by the conduct of Panna the *Dhai* (nurse) of Udai Singh, son of Rana Sanga, who was a. Kheechee Rajputani, when Bunbir, after killing the Rana, Bikramjit, entered the Rao Lal[2] to kill the heir-apparent, Udai Singh, also. Aware that one murder was the precursor of another, the faithful nurse put her charge into a fruit basket, and covering it with leaves, she delivered it to the bari, enjoining him to escape with it from the fort. Scarcely had she time to substitute her own infant in the room of the prince, when Bunbir entering, enquired for him. Her lips refused their office, she pointed to the cradle and beheld the murderous steel buried in the heart of her babe[3].

---

[1] A Scimitar

[2] Queen's quarters in the palace

[3] Tod's *Rajasthan*, Vol. I, p. 315

The exploits of the heroic Tara Bai of Bednore and those of her gallant husband, Prithviraj, the brother of the celebrated Rana Sanga, who opposed Babar at Biana, would gave a clear idea of the dominating influence which the Rajput fair exercise not only in the formation of Rajput character but on Rajput conduct throughout life.

Colonel Tod says, "Tara Bai was the daughter of Rao Surtan, the chieftain of Bednore. He was of the Solanki tribe, the lineal descendant of the famed Balhara kings of Anhilwara. Thence expelled by the arms of Alha in the thirteenth century they migrated to Central India, and obtained possession of Tonk Thoda and its lands on the Banas, which from remote times had been occupied (perhaps founded) by the Taks, and hence bore the name of Taksilla nagar, familiarly Takitpur and Thoda. Surtan had been deprived of Thoda by Lilla the Afghan, and now occupied Bednore at the foot of the Aravalli, within the bounds of Mewar. Stimulated by the reverses of her family, and by the incentives of its ancient glory, Tara Bai, scorning the habiliments and occupations of her sex, learned to guide the war-horse, and to throw with unerring aim the arrow from his back, even while at speed. Armed with the bow and quiver, and mounted on a fiery Kathiawar, she joined the cavalcade in their unsuccessful attempts to wrest Thoda from the Afghan. Jaimul, the third son of Rana Rai Mul, in person, made proposals for her hand. 'Redeem Thoda', said the star of Bednore, 'and my hand is thine'. He assented to the terms; but evincing a rude determination to be possessed of the prize ere he had earned it, he was slain by the indignant father. Pirthiraj, the brother of the deceased, was then in exile in Marwar, he had just signalised his valour and ensured his father's forgiveness, by the redemption of Godwar, and the catastrophe at Bednore determined him to accept the gage thrown down to Jaimul. Fame and the bard had carried the renown of Pirthiraj far beyond the bounds of Mewar, the name alone was attractive to the fair, and when thereto he who bore it added all the chivalrous ardour of his prototype, the Chohan, Tara Bai, with the sanction of her father, consented to be his, on the simple asseveration that 'he would restore to them Thoda or he was no true Rajput.' The anniversary of the martyrdom of the sons of Alli was the season chosen for the exploit. Pirthiraj formed a select band of five hundred cavaliers and accompanied by his bride, the fair Tara, who insisted on partaking of his glory and his danger, he reached Thoda at the moment the (*Tazzia* or bier containing the martyr-brothers, was placed in the centre of the chowk or 'square'. The prince, Tara Bai .and the faithful Senger Chief, the inseparable companion of Pirthiraj, left their cavalcade and joined the procession as it passed under the balcony of the palace, in which the Afghan was putting on his dress preparatory to descending. Just as he had asked who were the strange horsemen that had joined the throng, the lance of Pirthiraj and an arrow from the bow of his Amazonian bride stretched him on the floor. Before the crowd recovered from the panic, the three had reached the gate of the town, where their exit was obstructed by an elephant. Tara Bai with her scimitar divided his trunk, and the animal flying, they joined their cavalcade, which was close at hand.

"The Afghans were encountered, and could not stand the attack. Those who did not fly were cut to pieces, and the gallant Pirthiraj inducted the father of his bride into his inheritance. A brother of the Afghans, in his attempt to recover it, lost his life. The Nawab, Mulloo Khan, then holding Ajmer, determined to oppose the Sesodia prince in person, who, resolved upon being the assailant, advanced to Ajmer, encountered his foe in the camp at day-break, and after great slaughter entered Gurh Beetli, the citadel, with the fugitives. 'By these act' says the Chronicle, "his fame increased in Rajwarra: one thousand Rajputs, animated by the same love of glory and devotion, gathered round the *inakarras* of Pirthiraj. Their swords shone in the heavens, and were dreaded on the earth, but they aided the defenceless.'[1]

The strong affection of a Hindu wife for her husband is typified in the conduct of Chandandas's wife, so beautifully described in the political drama of *Mudrā Rākṣas*[2].

The Rajput mother claims full share in the glory of her son, who imbibes at the maternal fount his first rudiments of chivalry; the importance of this parental instruction cannot be better 'illustrated than in the ever-recurring simile, "make thy mother's milk resplendent," the full force of which we have in, the powerful though overstrained expression of the Bundi Queen's joy on the announcement of the heroic death of her son.

Nor has the Rajput mother failed to defend her son's rights with exemplary valour, and to teach her son how life should be sacrificed at the altar of the country and in defence of the country's independence. Look at the animated picture given by Ferishta of Durgavati, Queen of Gurrah, defending the rights of her infant son against Akbar's ambition. "Like another Boadecea, she headed her army and fought a desperate battle with Asaf Khan, in which she was defeated and wounded. Scorning flight, or to survive the loss of independence; she, like the antique Roman in such a predicament, slew herself on the field of battle."[3]

Durgavati was only following in the footsteps of the earlier queens, the exploits of some of whom are well known in Rajputana. For instance, after the death of Rana Samarsi, on the field of Thaneshwar, his heir, Kuma, being a minor, Kuma's mother, Korum Devi, a princess of Patun, headed her Rajputs and gave battle in person to Kutbuddin

---

[1] Tod's *Rajasthan*, Vol. I, pp. 673, 74

[2] See Infra, '*Hindu Drama.*'

[3] Tod's *Rajasthan*, Vol. I, p. 642

Aibak, near Amber, when the Viceroy (Kutbuddin) was defeated and wounded."[1]

"In the second Saka of Chitor, when Bahadur, Sultan of Gujrat, invaded that far-famed fortress, the queen mother, Jawahir Bai, in order to set an example of courageous devotion to their country, appeared clad in armour and headed a sally,. in which she was slain."[2]

During the famous assault on Chitor by Akbar, when the command of the fortress fell on Fattah, who was only sixteen years of age at the death of the Chandawat leader, his mother displayed heroism unparalleled in history. Colonel Tod says, 'When the Saloomra fell at the gate of the Sun, the command devolved on Putta (Fatta) of Kailwa. He was only sixteen: his father had fallen in the last shock, and his mother had survived but to rear this the sole heir of their house. Like the Spartan mother of old, she commanded him to put on the 'saffron robe' and to die for Chitor: but surpassing the Grecian dame, she illustrated her precept by example; and lest any soft 'compunctious visitings' for one dearer than herself might dim the lustre of Kailwa, she armed the young bride with a lance, with her descended the rock, and the defenders of Chitor saw her fall, fighting by the side of her Amazonian mother. When their wives and daughters performed such deeds, the Rajputs became reckless of life."[3]

"Nor do I deem him worthy who prefers
A friend, how dear so ever to his country"

SOPHOCLES: *Antigone*

An incident taken from the annals of Mewar will illustrate the strength, the courage and the general character of Rajput women. Ursi, the elder brother of the Rana Ajeysi, "being out on a hunting excursion in the forest of

---

[1] Tod's *Rajasthan*, Vol. I, p. 259
[2] Tod's *Rajasthan*, Vol. I, p. 311
[3] Tod's *Rajasthan*, Vol. I, p. 326

Ondwa, with some young chiefs of the court, in pursuit of the boar entered a field of maize, when a female offered to drive out the game. Pulling one of the stalks of maize, which grows to the height of ten or twelve feet she pointed it, and mounting the platform made to watch the corn, impaled the hog, dragged him before the hunters, and departed. Though accustomed to feats of strength and heroism from the nervous arms of their country-women, the act surprised them. They descended to the stream at hand and prepared the repast, as is usual, on the spot. The feast was held, and comments were passing on the fair arm which had transfixed the boar, when a ball of clay from a sling fractured a limb of the prince's steed. Looking in the direction whence it came, they observed the same damsel, from her elevated stand, preserving her fields from aerial depredators; but seeing the mischief she had occasioned she descended to express regret, and then returned to her pursuit. As they were proceeding homewards after the sports of the day, they again encountered the damsel with a vessel of milk on her head and leading in either hand a young buffalo. It was proposed, in frolic, to overturn her milk, and one of the companions of the prince dashed rudely by her; but without being disconcerted, she entangled one of her charges with the horse's limbs, and brought the rider to the ground. On inquiry, the prince discovered that she was the daughter of a poor Rajput of the Chundano tribe. He returned the next day to the same quarter and sent for her father, who came and took his seat with perfect independence close to the prince, to the merriment of 'his companions, which was checked by Ursi, asking his daughter to wife. They were yet more surprised by the demand being refused. The Rajput, on going home, told the more prudent mother, who scolded him heartily, made him recall the refusal and seek the prince. They were married, and Hamir was the son of the Chundano Rajputni,"[1]

---

[1] Tod's *Rajasthan*, Vol. I, pp. 267, 68, It was this Rana Hamir who attacked, defeated and made prisoner the Khilji king,

"The romantic history of the Chohan Emperor of Delhi abounds in sketches of a female character; and in the story of his carrying off Sanjogta, the princess of Kanauj, we have a faithful picture of the sex. We see her, from the moment when, rejecting the assembled princes, she threw the 'garland of marriage' round the neck of her hero, the Chohan, abandon herself to all the influences of passion, mix in a combat of five days' continuance against her father's array, witness his ;overthrow and the carnage of both armies, and subsequently, by her seductive charms, lulling her lover into a neglect of every princely duty. Yet when the foes of his glory and power invade India, we see the -enchantress at once start from her trance of pleasure, and exchanging the softer for the sterner passions, in accents not less strong because mingled with deep affection, she conjures him, while arming him for the battle, to die for his fame, declaring that she will join him in the 'mansions of the sun.'"

What Hindu can read without emotion the reply of the brave and beautiful Sanjogta, then in the heydey of her honeymoon? On Prithvi's relating to her the dream, he saw the previous night, she said, "Victory and fame to my lord! Oh Sun of the Chohans, in glory or in pleasure, who has tasted so deeply as you? To die is the destiny not only of man but of the gods, all desire to throw off the old garment; but to die well is to live forever. Think not of self, but of immortality; let your sword divide your foe, and I will be your *ardhāṅga* (the other half) hereafter."

The army having assembled and all being prepared to march against the Islamite, the fair Sanjogta armed her lord for the encounter. "In vain she sought the rings of his corslet; her -eyes were fixed on the face of the Chohan, as

---

Mahmud, the successor of Allahuddin Khilji. The king suffered a confinement of three months in Chitor. Nor was he liberated till he had surrendered Ajmer, Ranthambhor, Nagaur and Soe Sopur, besides paying fifty lakhs of rupees and one hundred elephants. See Vol. I, p. 272

those of the famished wretch who finds a piece of gold. The sound of the drum reached the ear of the Chohan; it was as a death-knell on that of Sanjogta: and as he left her to head Delhi's heroes, she vowed that henceforth water only should sustain her. I shall see him again in the region of Surya, but never more in Yoginipur."

A more recent instance of the high spirit, undaunted courage and a high sense of duty and honour displayed by a queen of Marwar, has been recorded by a Frenchman of note. In the Civil War for empire amongst the sons of Shah Jahan, when Aurangzeb opened his career by the deposal of his father and the murder of his brothers, the Rajputs, faithful to the Emperor determined to oppose him. Under the intrepid Rathore, Jaswant Singh, thirty thousand Rajputs chiefly of that clan, advanced to the Narbada, and with a magnanimity amounting to imprudence, they permitted the junction of Murad with Aurangzeb.

Next morning the action commenced, which continued throughout the day. The Rajputs behaved with their usual bravery but were surrounded on all sides, and by sunset left ten thousand dead on the field. The Maharaja retreated to his own country, but his wife, a daughter of the Rana of Udaipur, ... disdained (says Ferishta) to receive her lord, and shut the gates of the castle."

The French traveller, Bernier, who was present in India at the time says, "I cannot forbear to relate the fierce reception which the daughter of the Rana gave to her husband, Jaswant Singh, after his defeat and flight. When she heard he was nigh and had understood what had passed in the battle-that he had fought with all possible courage; that he had but four or five hundred men left; and at last, no longer able to resist the enemy, had been forced to retreat; instead of sending someone to condole him in his misfortunes, she commanded in a dry mood to shut the gates of the castle, and not to let this infamous man enter; that he was not her husband; that the son-in law of the great Rana could not have so mean a soul; that he was to remember, that being grafted into so illustrious a house, he was to imitate its virtue ; in a word, he was to vanquish, or to die. A moment after, she was of another humour. She commands a pile of wood to be laid, that she might burn herself; that they abused her; that her husband must need be dead; that it could not be otherwise, And a little while after she was seen to 'change' countenance, to fall into a passion, and break into a thousand reproaches against him. In short, she remained thus transported eight or nine days, without being able to resolve to see her husband, till at last her mother coming, brought herein time to herself, composed by assuring her that as soon as the Raja had but refreshed himself, he would raise another army to fight Aurangzeb, and repair his honour. By which story one may see a pattern of the courage of the women in that country."[1]

[1] Tod's *Rajasthan*, Vol. I, p. 622

1.9. FOREIGN RELATIONS

"In the theatre of the world
The people are actors all.
One doth the sovereign monarch play;
And him the rest obey."

CALDERON

When such brilliant national character combines with such happy social organisation of the people as to excite the admiration of all who study it, one can easily conceive what noble achievements of peace and war the ancient Indians must have accomplished. It is true, "peace hath her victories no less renowned than war" still a peculiar halo of glory attaches to military achievements. The achievements of the Hindus in philosophy, poetry, sciences and art prove their peaceful victories. But their military achievements were equally great, as will appear from their mastery of the science of war.

Their civilising missions covered the globe, and Hindu civilization still flows like an under-current in the countless social institutions of the world.[1]

In the Aitareya Brāhmaṇa, Emperor Sudāsa is stated to have completely conquered the whole world with its different countries.

That the Indians were quite capable of accomplishing this feat, is clear from the remarkable article that appeared in the *Contemporary Review* from the pen of Mr. Townsend. He says, "If the Prussian conscription were applied in India, we should, without counting reserves or land wehr or any force not summoned in time of peace, have two-and-a-half millions of soldiers actually in barracks, with

---

[1] See Hand's A. B., Vol. II, p. 524

800,000 recruits coming up every year – a force with which not only Asia but the world might be subdued."[1]

General Sir Ian Hamilton, in his Scrapbook on the first part of the Russo-Japanese War, says, "Why there is material in the North of India and in Nepal sufficient and fit, under good. leadership, to shake the artificial society of Europe to its foundation."

The territorial strength of India in ancient and even in mediaeval times was greater than it has ever been during the last thousand years. Pururavā is said to have possessed 13 islands of the ocean. See *Mahābhārata Ādiparva*, 3143, "*Trisdaśa Samudra ye dvipāḥ āsnan Pururvā*, etc."

That the Hindus were a great naval power in ancient times is clear from the fact that one of the ancestors of Rama was "Sagara, emphatically called the Sea-king, whose sixty thousand sons (soldiers) were so many mariners."[2]

Pliny, indeed, states that "some consider the four Satrapies of Gedeosia, Arachosia, Ana and Paropamisus to belong to 'India." "This would include" says Mr. Elphinstone, "about two-thirds of Persia."[3]

Strabo mentions a large part of Persia to have been abandoned to the Hindus by the Macedonians.[4]

Colonel Tod says, "The annals of the Yadus of Jaisalmer state that long anterior to Vikram; they held dominion from Ghazni to Samarkand, that they established themselves in those regions after the *Mahābhārata*, and were again impelled on the rise of Islamism within the Indus." He adds, "A multiplicity of scattered facts and geographical distinctions fully warrants our assent to the general truth of these records, which prove that the Yadu race had dominion

[1] Contemporary Review for June 1888. 'Will England retain India'.

[2] Tod's *Rajasthan*, Vol. I, p.602

[3] *History of India*, p. 232

[4] See *Strabo*, Lib. XV, p. 474

in Central Asia."[1] He also says, "One thing is now proved that princes of the Hindu faith ruled over all these regions in the first ages of Islamism, and made frequent attempts for centuries after to reconquer them. Of these, Baber gives us a most striking instance in his description of Ghazni, or, as he writes, Ghazni, when he relates how when the Rai of Hind besieged Subakhtagin in Ghazni, Subakhtagin ordered flesh of kine to be thrown into the fountain, which made the Hindus retire."[2] The celebrated Balabhi was reduced by the same stratagem.

"Bappa, the ancestor of the Ranas of Mewar, abandoned Central India after establishing his line in Chitor, and retired to Khorasan. All this proves that Hinduism prevailed in those distant regions and that the intercourse was unrestricted between Central Asia and India."[3]

"The Bhatti Chronicle calls the Langas[4] in one page Pathan and in another Rajput, which are perfectly reconcilable, and by no means indicative that the Pathan or Afghan of that early period or even in the time of Rai Sehra was Mohamedan. The title of Rai is a sufficient proof that they were even then Hindus." Colonel Tod adds, "Khan is by no means indicative of the Mohamedan faith."[5]

Eminent Greek writers – eye-witnesses of the splendour of India – bear testimony to the prosperity of the country; which, even in her decline, was sufficiently great to dazzle their imagination. The Indian Court was the happy seat to which Greek politicians repaired as ambassadors, and they all speak of it in glowing terms.

Mr. Weber says, "Thus Megasthenes was sent by Seleucus to Chandragupta,[6] Deimachus again by Antiochus

---

[1] Tod's *Rajasthan*, Vol. II. P. 230
[2] Tod's *Rajasthan*, Vol. II, p. 222
[3] Tod's *Rajasthan*, Vol. II, p. 231.
[4] They were Solanki Rajputs.
[5] Tod's *Rajasthan*, Vol. II, p. 258
[6] Weber's *Indian Literature*, p. 251, footnote.

and Dionysius,[1] and most probably Basilis by Ptolemy II to Amritaghata, son of Chandergupta."

Antiochus the Great concluded an alliance[2] with Sobhagsen about 210 B.C., but was eventually defeated and slain by him. Colonel Tod says, "The obscure legends of the encounters of the Yadus with the allied Syrian and Bactrian kings would have seemed altogether illusory sink evidence exist that Antiochus the Great was slain in these very regions by the Hindu king Sobhagsen."[3]

The Greek king, Seleucus, even gave Chandergupta his daughter to wife.[4] Professor Weber says, "In the retinue of this Greek princess there, of course, came to Patliputra Greek damsels as her waiting-maids, and these must have found particular favour in the eyes of the Indians, especially of their princess. For not only are. . . . . mentioned as articles of traffic for India, but in Indian inscriptions also, we find Yavan girls specified as tribute; while in Indian literature, and especially in Kalidasa, we are informed that Indian princes were waited upon by. Yavanis (Greek damsels); Lassen, I.A.K.ii,551,957, and my Preface to *Mālavikā*, p. XLVII."[5]

The Persian Emperor, Nausherawan the Just, gave his daughter in marriage to the then Maharana of Chitor.

Even the *Rāmāyaṇa* says that in Ayodhyā, ambassadors from different countries resided.[6] According to Justin, the monarch of Ujjain (Malwa) held a correspondence with Augustus[7]. Augustus received a Samos an embassy from India. The ambassadors brought elephants, pearls and

---

[1] Max Dunker's *History of Antiqity*, Vol. IV, p. 453
[2] Wilson's *Viṣṇu Purāṇa*, Vol. II, p. 181
[3] Tod's *Rajasthan*, Vol. II, p. 230
[4] Lassen, I.A.K., ii, 208: T. Wheeler's *History of India* (1874) p. 177.
[5] Weber's *Indian Literature*, pp. 251, 52, footnote
[6] Mrs. Manning's *Ancient and Mediaeval India*, Vol. II, p. 27
[7] See Tod's *Rajasthan*, Vol. II, p.312

precious stones. There was a second embassy from India sent to Emperor Claudius, of which Pliny gives an account. He received from the ambassadors who were four in number, the information about Ceylon which he has embodied in his Natural History. Two other embassies from Hindu princes to Rome were sent before the third century BC., one to Trajan (107 BC.) and another to Antonius Pius. These relations continued as late as the time of Justinian (530 BC.)

Strabo[1] mentions an ambassador from King Pandion to Augustus, who met him in Syria. It appears from Periplus and Ptolemy that Pandion was the hereditary title of the descendants of Pandya, who founded the kingdom in the fifth century B.C.,[2] A Brāhmaṇa followed this ambassador to Athens, where he burnt himself alive.

"In one of Ashoka's inscriptions, five Greek princes appear.(1) Antiochus of Syria,(2)Ptolemy, Philadelphos of Egypt, (3) Antigonos Gonatos of Macedon, (4) Magas of Kerene, (5) Alexander II of Epirus. "Great intercourse," says a writer, formerly subsisted between the Hindus and the nations of the West."[3]

Thus, when even in those days, India was so great as to exact the homage of all who saw her, though her grand political and social institutions had lost their pristine purity and vigour, and those mighty forces which worked for her welfare and greatness were disappearing, when even in her fall she was the idol of foreign nations, how mighty must she have been when she was at the height of her power, at the height of her glory! Her constitution still stands like some tall ancient oak in a forest shorn of foliage, but still defying the discordant elements that rage around it, still looking down, with a majesty and dignity all its own, upon

---

[1] Lib, XV, p. 663

[2] Elphinstone's *History of India*, p.218

[3] See *Asiatic Researches*, Vol. III, pp. 297-298

the new-sprung, prosperous young trees growing round it in happy ignorance of the storms and gusts in store.

It is curious to learn that even in her decline, India was sufficiently strong to defy the great conquerors of the old world. It was threatened by the prosperous empire of Assyria, then at the meridian of her power under the celebrated queen Semiramis. She used the entire resources of the empire in preparations to invade India and collected a considerable army. "After three years spent in these extraordinary preparations, she sent forward her armies, which some writers describe as amounting to several millions of combatants, but the narrative of Ctesias estimates them at three hundred thousand foot, five hundred thousand horse, while two thousand boats and a great number of mock elephants were conveyed on the backs of camels." But what was the result? "The army was utterly routed and Semiramis brought back scarcely a third of her host; some authors even maintain that she herself perished in the expedition."[1]

Horrid suggestion! thinkest thou then the gods
Take care of men who came to burn their altars,
Profane their rites, and trample on their laws?
Will they reward the bad? It cannot be.

SOPHOCLES: Antigone

In later times, the Yadu king, Gaj Singh, who founded Gajni (Ghazni) single-handed 'defeated the combined armies of the Shah Sikandar Roomi and Shah Mamraiz.[2]

---

[1] Murray's *History of India*, p. 30
[2] Tod's Rajasthan, Vol.II, p.222.

1.10. CAUSE OF INDIA'S FALL

"The race of mortal man is far too weak
To grow not dizzy on unwonted heights.

GOETHE: *Iphigenia.*

After Mahābhārata war we find, India again shining forth for a moment in all its glory under Vikramaditya. But this was the last faint glimmering of the consuming fire covered with ashes, the last symptoms of vitality that break upon a dying, man. "There is good reason to believe," says Sir W. Jones, in his Preface to *Śākuntala*, "that the court at Avanti was equal in brilliancy in the reign of Vikramaditya to that of any monarch in any age or country."

The emperors Bhoj, the later ruler of India, made attempts to give some brilliancy to his court by following the example of the great Vikram[1] in adorning them with the famous "*Nau Ratna.*"

India possessed a most capable and heroic leader when it was first threatened with a permanent conquest by the Moslems. The world has never seen a more chivalrous leader of men than the mighty Prithvi Raj of Ajmer. He defeated the Sultan of Gor more than once. Colonel Tod says, "Even the Moslem writers acknowledge that Shahabuddin was often ignominiously defeated before he finally succeeded in making a conquest of Northern India." The Ayeen-I-Akbari says, "In the reign of Raja Pithowra, Sultan Moozeddin Sam made several incursions from Ghazni into Hindustan but never gained any victory. It is said that the Raja gained from the Sultan seven pitched battles."

---

[1] Some European critics, in the fulness of their wisdom, deny that Vikramāditya ever existed. This irresistibly reminds one of Archbishop Whately's famous pamphlet, '*Historic doubts relative to Napoleon Bonaparte.*'

Were it not for the fatal disunion between Prithvi Raj and Jai Chand, and the traitorous conduct of the latter and of the king of Anhilwara Patun and the Haoli Rao Hamir, India might never have fallen under the domination of the invader from Afghanistan and Turkistan.

The *Svayamvara* of Sanjogta, daughter of the King of Kanauj, is an event of world-wide importance – of much greater importance to the world than the rape of Helen by Paris. The lovely 'Sanjogta, in defiance of her father's vain-glorious wishes; and, in contempt of the pretensions of the assembled nobility of Northern India, determined to give her hand only to the "flower of the far-famed Rajput chivalry," Prithvi Raj of Ajmer, threw the *varamālā* (marriage garland) around the golden effigy of that hero, placed by Jai Chand at the portals of the palace. unconsciously as an emblem of the protective might of "the Pride of Rajasthan," and as a tribute to his glory as the defender of his race against foreign aggression. The chivalrous Chohan appeared at the right moment, at the imminent risk of losing his life, as well as of defeating the object of the daring enterprise, to answer the call of a noble female of a royal house, and to carry away, from amidst the united heroism of Hindustan, the prize which had attracted all the important princes of India to Kanauj thus fully vindicating his character as the most intrepid and heroic of the Hindu princes. This magnificent feat cost Prithvi Raj his throne and the Hindu nation their independence. The Trikala Chand truly said that "he preserved his prize: he gained immortal renown, but he lost the sinews of Delhi." In the desperate running fight of five days, Prithvi Raj lost his hundred *sanwants* (heroes) the leaders of his army, the mainstay of his throne. Himself unable to overcome Prithvi Raj, and burning with revenge for his humiliation, Jai Chand now' began to intrigue with the enemy of the Hindus, the Sultan of Ghor.

"The brave deserve the fair." The brave Chohan not only secured the fair of Kanauj, but discovered at Nagore a treasure amounting to seven million in gold. This alarmed his enemies still more. Colonel Tod says, "The princes of Kanauj and Patun, dreading the influence of such sinews of war, invited Shahabuddin to aid their design of humiliating the Chohan."[1]. Abul Fazal says, "Shahabuddin formed an alliance with Raja. Jai Chand, and having raised a large army, came to attack the dominions of Pithowra. The Raja (Prithvi Raj), vain with the remembrance of his former victories, collected together only a small number of troops, and with these, he marched out to attack the Sultan. But the heroes of Hindustan had all perished in the manner above described: besides, Jai Chand, who had been his ally, was now in league with his enemy."

Hamir also joined the traitors. Colonel Tod says, "There were no less than four distinguished leaders of this name (Hamir) among the vassals of the last Rajput Emperor of Delhi, and one of them who turned traitor to his sovereign and joined Shahbuddin was actually a Scythian and of the Ghikar race. The Haoli Rao Hamir, was lord of Kangra and the Ghikars of Pamer."[2]

The result of the encounter is well known. The treacherous plan of operations devised by Jai Chand and adopted by the Sultan against Prithvi Raj 'resulted in the overthrow of the Hindu supremacy in India. Prithvi Raj fell into the hands of' the enemy and was taken to Ghazni. But there he succeeded, with the assistance of the ever faithful Chanderbardai, in administering death to the conqueror of his country. The following couplet of Chanderbardai confirms the popular tradition on the subject—

चर बांस चौबीस गज अंगुल अष्टप्रमाण।
ता ऊपर सुलतान है मत चूको चौहाण।।

Abul Fazal, in his *Ayeen-I-Akbari*, also says, "The faithful Chund followed his prince to Ghazni and contrived to gain the favour of the Sultan. Having obtained an

[1] Tod's *Rajasthan*, Vol. I, p. 256
[2] Tod's *Rajasthan*, Vol. I, p. 560

interview with the Rājā, and administered comfort to his mind, he told him that he would take an opportunity of praising his skill with the bow, which would raise the Sultan's curiosity to see him perform his feats when he might make a proper use of his arrow. In consequence of Chund's representation, the Sultan wished! to see the Rājā exercise his bow, when he seized the opportunity and shot the king dead upon the spot."[1]

The same fate met the next great leader of the Hindus when Babar invaded India. Had not the Taur traitor who led the van of Sanga's army gone over to Baber, Rana Sanga[2] would have settled forever the question of Hindu supremacy in India. Says Colonel Tod, "With all Baber's qualities as a soldier, supported by the hardy clans of the 'cloud mountains' of Karatagin, the chances were many that he and they terminated their career on the 'yellow rivulet' of Biana. Neither skill nor bravery saved him (Baber) from this fate, which he appears to have expected...... To ancient jealousies he was indebted for not losing his life instead of gaining a crown, and for being extricated from a condition so desperate that even the frenzy of religion, which made death martyrdom in this holy war, scarcely availed to expel the despair which so infected his followers that in the bitterness of heart he says, "not a single person who uttered a manly word, nor an individual who delivered a courageous opinion." Colonel Tod describes the sad plight of Baber and the negotiations pending Baber's blockade at Khanua, and gives the name of the traitor, "Who sold the cause of his country."

"Oh, for a tongue to curse the slave
Whose treason like a deadly blight
Comes over the counsels of the brave

---

1 See also Tod *Rajasthan*, Vol. I, p. 194

2 'Sanga organized his forces, with which he always kept the field and ere called to contend with the descendants of Timur, he had gained eighteen pitched battles against the kings of Delhi and Malwa-Tod's. *Rajasthan*, Vol.1, p. 300

And blasts them in their hour of might.'

MOORE: *Fire Worshippers*

After describing the battle, Tod says, "While the battle was still doubtful, the Tuar traitor who led the van (herole) went over to Baber, and Sanga was obliged to retreat from the field, which in the onset promised a glorious victory."[1]

India has fallen a victim to her own internal dissensions and disunion. She has been betrayed by her own sons and not conquered by the foreign invader. Prithvi Raj and Sanga were defeated by their own countrymen, not by their enemies. Thus ended the work of ruin that had begun with the *Mahābhārata*!

---

[1] The traitor was 'the chief of Rayseen, by name Sillaide, of the Tuar tribe.' 'Treason,' says Tod, 'effected the salvation of Babar.' *Rajasthan*, Vol. I, p. 306.

2

HINDU COLONIZATION OF THE WORLD

All places, that the eye of heaven visits
Are to a wise man ports and happy havens;
Teach thy necessity to reason thus;
There is no virtue like necessity.

SHAKESPEARE: *Richard II*

The turning point in the history of India, nay, in the history of the world, was the *Mahābhārata* – the death-stroke to Indian prosperity and glory. Before this catastrophe, Hindu civilisation was in full vigour. It declined gradually after the *Mahābhārata* till it was attacked first by the Arab semi-barbarism, and then by the European civilisation. Simplicity with refinement, honesty with happiness, and glory with power and peace, were the splendid results of the Hindu civilisation: complexity with outward polish, selfishness and cunning with progress and prosperity, success with immoderate vanity, wealth with misery are the offsprings of the latter. The *Mahābhārata* was a war not only between man and man, but between the two - aspects of the heart, the two phases of the mind.

There are two remarkable features of that period, differing in nature but coinciding in their effect on India. These were destruction and emigration. The good and the great men of India either emigrated or were killed: the effect upon India was the same inimical to her prosperity. Whole tribes were killed: whole races emigrated. It is true that, in addition to many civilising expeditions, there had been tribal migrations before that momentous period. But these later emigrations sucked out the life-blood of India. These emigrations, as also the settlements and colonies of ancient Greece, differed in an important respect from the modern settlements of the Europeans. The Grecian settlements attracted the best men of Greece; and the Indian emigrations helped powerfully to set in motion those disintegrating forces that have undermined our national superiority, destroyed our independence and ruined our society and religion.

But there is no evil that is an unmixed evil: to every cloud, there is a silver lining. In the present case, **India's loss was the world's gain. Though India's greatness began to decline, the entire Western' world from Persia to Britain received in the colonists the seeds of their future greatness. The *Mahābhārata* was thus fraught with worldwide consequences.**

Says Mr. Pococke, "But, perhaps, in no similar instance have events occurred fraught with consequences of such magnitude, as those flowing from the great religious war which, for a long series of years, raged throughout the length and breadth of India. That contest ended by the expulsion of 'last bodies of men, many of them skilled in the arts of early, civilisation, and the still greater number of warriors by profession. Driven beyond the Himalayan mountains in the north, and to Ceylon, their last stronghold in the south, swept across the valley of the Indus on the west, this persecuted people carried with them the germs of the European arts and sciences. The mighty human tide that passed the barrier of the Punjab, rolled onward towards its destined channel in Europe and in Asia, to fulfil its beneficent office in the moral fertilisation of the world."[1]

It is, of course, true that emigration from India had been going on from time immemorial. Notwithstanding the marvellous fertility of the soil and the wonderful industries that flourished in the country, India had to plant colonies to provide for her superabundant population. Professor Heeren says, "How could such a thickly-peopled, and in some parts of peopled country as India have disposed of her

---

[1] *India in Greece*, p. 26

superabundant population except by planting colonies; even though intestine broils (witness the expulsion of the Buddhists) had not obliged her to have recourse to such an expedient ?"[1]

The earliest emigration appears to date sometime after Manu. One of the oldest colonies founded by the Hindus was in Egypt; America, with some other countries, was also colonised before the last great Migration. The principal migration to Greece took place soon after the Great War. The word *kapi*[2] for ape appears in the hieroglyphic writings of Greece of the 17th century B.C., which shows that the colonisation of Greece must be dated long anterior to the era of Moses.

It would perhaps be interesting to know the exact time when the *Mahābhārata* took place.

In determining dates our efforts are clogged at every step by the dearth of historical records. But it is not in historical literature alone that we have to mourn this loss. Every branch of literature, every science and art have suffered from the ravages of ignorant fanaticism. Some have disappeared completely; others have come down to us in a more or less mutilated form. The present scarcity of historical works, however, should not be regarded as a proof of the absence of the Art of History any more than the present poverty of the country be accepted as a proof of its indigence in ancient times.

For one thing, the enmity of Aurangzeb towards all historical writings is well known. But it is the Arab, Afghan and Tartar semi-barbarism that is responsible for the destruction of literature, whether in Egypt or in India, in Persia or in Greece. The destruction of the Alexandrian Library was one of those notorious feats by which the progress of humanity was put back by a thousand years. But the loss to humanity by the whole destruction of the libraries

---

[1] *Historical Researches*, Vol. II, p. 310

[2] Weber's *Indian Literature*, p. 3

of India is beyond calculation. That eminent antiquarian and explorer, Rai Bahadur Sarat Chander Dass, says, "In the lofty nine storied temple at Buddha Gaya, which was formerly called the Mahagandhola (Gandhalaya), the images of the past Buddhas were enshrined. The nine-storied temple called Ratandadhi of Dharamganja (university) of Nalanda was the repository of the sacred books of the Mahayana and Hinayana Buddhist Schools. The temple of Odantapuri Vihara, which is said to have been loftier than either of the two (Buddha Gaya and Nalanda) contained a vast collection of Buddhist and Vedic works, which, after the; manner of the great Alexandrian Library, was burnt under the orders of Mohamed Ben Sam, general of Bakhtyar Khilji, in 1212. A.D."[1]

Sultan Alla-ud-din Khilji burnt the famous library at Anhilwara Patan. The *Tarikh Firoz Shahi* says that Firoz Shah Tughlak burnt a large library of Sanskrit books at Kohana. Sayed Ghulam Husein, in his well-known book, *Sair Mutakhreen* (Vol. I, p. 140), compiled in the reign of Aurangzeb, who called himself Secunder Sani, says, "Sultan Sikander (Aurangzeb) was the most bigoted of the Sultans, and burnt the books of the Hindus whenever and wherever he got them."

Instances of such savagery could be multiplied easily. These are all manifestations of that mental aberration to which humanity is evidently subject at intervals, the disease being the same, the occasion may be the outrages committed by the Goths and Vandals of earlier times or the Arabs and the Tartars of the latter day.

Mr. Dow, in the Preface to his *History of Hindustan,* observes,' "We must not, with Ferishta, consider the Hindus as destitute of genuine domestic annals, or that those voluminous records they possess are mere legends framed by Brāhmaṇas." Mr. Wilson, with his usual fairness, remarks

---

[1] *The Hindustan Review* for March, 1906, p. 187 (Universities in Ancient India)

that "it is incorrect to say that the Hindus never compiled a history. The literature of the south abounds with local histories of Hindu authors. Mr. Stirling found various chronicles in Orissa, and Colonel Tod has met with equally abundant material in Rajputana."[1]

Professor 'Heeren says, "Wilson's translation of *Rājataraṅgiṇī*, a history of Kashmir, has clearly demonstrated that regular historical composition was an art not unknown in Hindustan and affords satisfactory grounds for concluding that these productions were once less rare, and that further exertions may bring more relics to light."[2]

Professor Wilson's assertion that "genealogies[3] and chronicles are found in various parts of India recorded with some perseverance," will be supported by all who know Hindu society.

The critics who resolutely deny the existence of the art in Ancient India on the plea that none of the productions of the art are to be found, will do well to consider the fact that even the Vedas would have been lost had the Mohamedan rule continued a century or so longer without giving birth to a Dayanand. When such has been the lot of their most adored possession, what better handling could the poor Art of History have aspired to obtain?

The illustrious Colonel Tod says, "If we consider the political changes and convulsions which have happened in Hindustan since Mahmud's invasion, and the intolerant bigotry of many of his successors, we shall be able to

---

[1] Mill's *India*, Volume II, page 67, footnote.

[2] Heeren's *Historical Researches*, Vol. II, p. 143

[3] The genealogies are still kept and are to be found in almost every part of Hindustan proper. In Rajputana, where they are regularly kept, you may select any man of the *Vaiṣya Varṇa*, and after a little search, you can generally find out the names and abodes of every member of his ancestral family for about twenty generations back. There is a clan named 'Jagas' who have made this their hereditary profession.

account for the paucity of its national works on history, without being driven to the improbable conclusion, that the Hindus were ignorant of an art which was cultivated in other countries from almost the earliest ages. Is it to be imagined that a nation so highly civilized as the Hindus, amongst whom the exact sciences flourished in perfection, by whom the fine arts, architecture, sculpture, poetry and music were not only cultivated, but taught and defined by the nicest and most elaborate rules, were totally unacquainted with the simple art of recording the events of their history, the characters of their princes, and the acts of their reigns?"[1]

He then asks, whence did Abul Fazal obtain the materials of his ancient History of India, if there were no historical records at the time of *Rājataraṅgiṇī*? This, he declares, sufficiently proves the existence of the art. Then, again, he says that in Chund's heroic history of Prithvi Raj, we find notices which authorise the inference that works similar to his own were then extant.[2]

It must not be supposed that the authors of these works were ignorant bards. We find that Chund's history contains chapters on laws for governing empires; lessons on diplomacy, home and foreign. See also the admirable remarks of the French Orientalist, Monsieur Abel Remsat, in his Melanges Asiatiques.

But to return to the point, Swami Dayanand Saraswati, in his Bhūmikā, says that 5,107 years have passed since the beginning of the *Kaliyuga* era. The *Siddhānta Śiromaṇi*, one of the most popular of the Hindu works on Astronomy, says that the *Kaliyuga* era, at the time of the establishment of the *Śālivāhana* era, was 3,179:

---

[1] Introduction to Tod's *Rajasthan*

[2] In Rajputana many historical works are to be found, such as, (1) *Vijaya Vilāsa*, (2) *Sūrya Prakāśa*, (3) *Kheṭa*, (4) *Jagat Vilāsa*, (5) *Rāja Prakāśa*, (6) *Jai Vilāsa*, (7) *Khoman Rāsa*, (8) *Mauna Caritra*. The last two are comparatively of recent date. See Ramsamala or Hindu Annals of the Province of Gujarat, by the Honourable A.V. Forbes; Gujarati Edition, 1890, (Bombay).

याता षण्मनवो युगानि भमितान्यन्यद्युगांघ्रि त्रयम्।

नन्दाद्रीगुणास्तथा शकनृपस्यान्ते कलेर्वत्सराः।।

The *Śālivāhana* era at present (2006 A.D.) is 1928: so that the *Kaliyuga* era should now be 3179+1928 =5107.

The author of the book, *Jyotirvidābharaṇa* – a history of the reign of Vikramaditya, composed in the *Saṁvat* era 24 (*Vikram* era) –says that year corresponded with the year 3068 of the *Kaliyuga* era. This also makes the Kaliyuga era now 3068 - 24+2063=5107.

The *Vṛhat Saṅhitā* of Varāhamihira (contemporary of Vikramaditya) says that the constellation Saptarṣi was in *Maghā Nakṣatra* in the reign of Yudhiṣṭhira. According to *Kaliyuga Rājavṛttānta* of *Rājataraṅgiṇī* (*śloka,* 14), *Saptarṣī* entered *Maghā* constellation 75 years before the commencement of *Kaliyuga*, i.e 3177 BC. and the Śaka era (started by Persian Śaka king Cyrus in 550 BC.)[1] started

---

[1] Note : ƒaka era as mentioned by VarÈhÈmihira was different from the ƒÈlivÈhana ƒaka era started by the great grand son of VikramÈditya ƒÈlivÈhana. After the demise of VikramÈditya in 18 AD. (3120 Kali era), the empire was split into 18 states and there were nvasions from Sakas, Tartaras, and other Dasyu kings. After sixty years, the ƒÈlivÈhana, the great grandson of Vikramaditya conquered and recovered the plundered booty from the invaders. This great and mighty emperor established Salivahan era in 78 AD. This era is known as ƒaka ƒÈlivahana era. But before the days of Vikramaditya, Saka era started by Saka king of Persia named Cyprus was prevalent in North wesern India. The empire of Cyrus was streched up to Panjab in India. He founded the Saka (Cyrus era) in 550 BC.(2556 Kali ear). In his campaigns between 550 and 530 B.C., Cyrus united the Persians and the Mades, then moved his show on the road to Mesopotamia. The Persian style was tolerance and benevolence to all. They respected local customs and traditions, thereby gaining many supporters. For example, the Jews were allowed to go home. Cyrus even gave the money to rebuild their smashed temple.

after the lapse of 2526 years of the Yudhiṭhira's rule. According to this, Yudhishtira reigned 2526+2556=5082 years ago or say in 3076 BC. This period works out to be 26 years after the commencement of Kali era. This period is called the *Svargārohaṇa* period or Yudhiṣṭhira kāla era or Loka era or Laukika era or Saptarṣī era.

Bṛhad Garga Muni also holds that the *Saptarṣī* were in the *Maghā Nakṣatra* at the junction of the *Dvāpara* .and the *Kaliyuga*. He says:

कलिद्वापर–संधौतु स्थितास्ते पितृदैतम् (मघाः)।

मुनयो धर्मनिरताः प्रजानां पालने रताः।।

According to him, therefore, Yudhiṣṭhira flourished at the beginning of the Kaliyuga.

An inscription in a Jain temple on a hill near Aihole, Kaladaggi district, Deccan, says that the temple, built by King Pulkeshi II, of the Chalukya family, was erected 3735 years .after the *Mahābhārata*, and when 556 years of the Saka era had passed, thus proving that the Great War took place 3735–556=3179 years before the Saka era; in other words, 3179+ 1928 (Saka era)=5107 years ago. The inscription runs as follows:

Many cities just opened their gates to Cyrus and asked to be part of his empire. The Persians gave the region uniform coinage, shared technology and roads, and asked only for the allegiance and taxes in return. They ruled in peace over 200 years, until they were conquered by Alexander in 312 B.C. It is clear that Cyrus followed the ancient custom and tradition of Bharat and the Persians were the Indians as the Zoroastrian history tells. Hence there is no wonder why Indians employed Cyrus era of 550 B.C. in their writings. Astronomer *VarÈhamihira*, in his *B,hat SaŠ hitÈ* made use of the Era of Cyrus and explained how to compute it. This era was known as *faka KÈla* and *faka N,pa KÈla*, meaning the time of Saka king. **Editor**

त्रिशत्सं त्रिसहस्रेषु भारतादाहवादितः।
सप्ताब्द शतयुक्तेषु श (ग) तेष्वब्देषु पंचसु (3735)
पंचाशत्सु कलौ काले षट्सु पंचाशतासु च (556)।
समासु समतीतासु शकानामपि भूभुजाम।।

Following evidently the view held by Brahadgarga Muni, the author of the Ayeen-i-Akbari, says that Vikramaditya ascended the throne in the 3,044th year of the Yudhishtira era. This also makes the Yudhishtira era begin 3044+ 2063 (Vikrama era) =5107 years ago.

Thus, the authorities are all agreed that the *Kaliyuga* commenced 5,107 years ago: opinion, however, is divided as to when the Great War took place. Tradition seems to say that the *Mahābhārata* took place at the commencement of the *Kaliyuga*, while the astronomers think that it took place about the middle of the 7th century of the *Kaliyuga* era. Whichever view is correct-the former or the later we know, on a comparison of these times with the dates of Scriptural history, that the *Kaliyuga* era commenced before the birth of Noah, and that the Great War took place either before his time or soon after it.

The migrations from India, as stated before, took place Eastwards as well as Westwards and Northwards. The Eastern migrations were to the Transgangetic peninsula, to China, to the islands of the Indian Archipelago, and to America. The Northern and the North-western to Turkistan, Siberia, Scandinavia, Germany and Britain as well as to Persia, Greece, Rome and Etruria. The Western, to the eastern parts of Africa and thence to Egypt. We find that Egypt, Persia, Assyria, and Greece all derived their learning and civilisation from India and that the Egyptian, the Assyrian, the Grecian, the German, the Scandinavian and the Druidic Mythologies were all derived from the Hindu Mythology.

"Sir Walter Raleigh strongly supports the Hindu hypothesis regarding the locality of the nursery for rearing mankind, and that India was the first peopled country.[1]

The Central Asian theory of emigration is unable to meet the difficulty presented by the fact that "the Astronomy of the Hindus and of the Chinese appear to be the remains rather than the elements of a Science." The advocates of the theory are obliged to assume that in ancient times a nation existed more advanced than either, the remains of whose achievements in Science still survive in the literature of the Hindus and the Chinese.

"That the Hindus, the Persians, the Egyptians and the Chinese, from the earliest periods of their history divided the time alike, namely, the year into 12 months and 3651/4: days, and the day into 24 hours; that they divided the Zodiac alike into 12 signs; that they divided the week alike into seven days, which being an arbitrary division, could not be the result of accident, but proves that they obtained it from the common 'source of an ancient people who already possessed a high -degree of civilization." But what nation flourished anterior to the Hindus, the Chinese and the Persians, no one has yet theorised; much less has it been proved that that primitive nation attained to a high degree of civilisation. On the contrary, all 'competent authorities are unanimous in holding that "Hinduism (Hindu Literature, Science and Arts) developed itself on the 'shores of the Ganges and the Yamuna," and that "the Hindu civilisation originated and attained to its highest pitch only in India."

There is thus an abrupt break in the Central Asian theory of emigration. The theory sketched out in the following pages alone can satisfactorily explain all such difficulties. Count Bjornstjerna[2] says, "It is there (*Āryāvartta*) we must

---

[1] *History of the World*, p. 99. He would at once have found the origin of Ararat had he known that the Hindus call their country, '*Āryāvartta.*'

[2] *Theogony of the Hindus*, p. 168

seek not only for the cradle of the Brāhmaṇa religion, but for the cradle of the high civilization of the Hindus, which gradually extended itself in the West to Ethiopia, to Egypt, to Phoenicia, in the East, to Siam, to China, and to Japan; in the South, to Ceylon, to Java and to Sumatra; in the North, to Persia, to Chaldea and to Colchis, whence it came to Greece and to Rome, and at length to the remote abode of the Hyperboreans."

Colonel Olcott says, "The modern school of comparative Philology traces the migration of Aryan civilisation into Europe by a study of modern languages in comparison with the Sanskrit. And we have an equally, if not a still more striking means of showing the outflow of Aryan thought towards the West in the philosophies and religions of Babylonia, Egypt, Greece, Rome and Northern Europe. One has only to put side by side the teachings of Pythagoras, Socrates, Plato, Aristotle, Homer, Zeno, Hesiod, Cicero, Scaevola, Varro and Virgil with those of Veda-Vyasa, Kapila, Gautama, Patañjali Kaṇāda, Jaiminī; Nārada, Pāṇini, Maricī, and many others we might mention, to be astonished at their identity of conceptions – an identity that upon any other theory than that of a derivation of the younger philosophical schools of the West from the older ones of the East would be simply miraculous. The human mind is certainly capable of evolving like ideas in different ages, just as humanity produces for itself in each generation the teachers, rulers, warriors and artisans it needs. But that the views of the Aryan sages should be so identical with those of the later Greek and Roman philosophers as to seem as if the latter were to the former like the reflection of an object in a mirror to the object itself, without an actual, physical transmission of teachers or books from the East to the West, is something opposed to common sense. And this again corroborates our convictions that the old Egyptians were emigrants from India; nearly all the famous ancient philosophers had been to Egypt to learn her wisdom, from the Jewish Moses to the Greek Plato."[1]

Sir William Jones says, "Of the cursory observations on the Hindus, which it would require volumes to expand and illustrate, this is the result, that they had an immemorial affinity with the old Persians, Ethiopians and Egyptians, the Phoenicians, Greeks, and Tuscans, the Scythians, or Goths, and Celts, the Chinese, Japanese, and Peruvians."[2]

The author of "India in Greece" says, 'Although the province of Pelasa or Bihar sent forth a body of emigrants so powerful as to give a general name to the great Oriental movement which helped to people the mainland and islands of Greece, yet the numbers from this province alone give no adequate idea of the population that exchanged the sunny land of India for the more temperate latitudes of Persia, Asia Minor and Hellas. The mountains of Ghoorka; Delhi, Oude, Agra, Lahore Multan, Kashmir, the Indus, and the provinces of Rajputana, sent forth their additional thousands to feed the living tide that flowed towards the lands of Europe and of Asia. With these warlike pilgrims on their journey to the far West – bands as enterprising as the race of Anglo-Saxons, the descendants, in fact, of some of those very Sakas of Northern India like them, too, filling the solitudes, or facing the perils of the West there marched a force of native warriors, sufficiently powerful to take possession of the richest of the soil that lay before them.

"Though unsuccessful in the great struggle that terminated in the expulsion of themselves and their religious teachers, their practised hardihood left them nothing to fear from the desultory attacks of any tribes who might be bold enough to obstruct their march."[3]

He again says, "The actual extent of the Pelasgic race (which in fact became a synonym for the general population

---

[1] See the *Theosophist* for March 1881, p.124

[2] *Asiatic Researches*, Vol. I, p. 426

[3] *India in Greece*, pp. 29 and 30.

of India. when transplanted to Europe and Asia), far exceeded the idea of Niebuhr. So vast were their settlements, and so firmly footed were the very names of kingdoms, the nomenclature of tribes, that I do not scruple to assert that the successive maps of Spain, Italy, Greece, Asia Minor, Persia, and India, may be read like the chart of an emigrant."[1]

[1] India in Greece, p.32

2.1. EGYPT AND ETHIOPIA

In the afternoon they came unto a land,
In which it seemed always afternoon.

TENNYSON: *Lotus Eaters*

Egypt was originally a colony of the Hindus. It appears that about seven or eight thousand years ago a body of colonists from India settled in Egypt, where they established one of the mightiest empires of the old world. Colonel Olcott says, "We have a right to more than suspect that India, eight thousand years ago, sent a colony of emigrants who carried their arts and high civilisation into what is now known to us as Egypt. This is what Brugsch Bey, the most modern as well as the most trusted Egyptologer and antiquarian, says on the origin of the old Egyptians. Regarding these as a branch of the Caucasian family having a close affinity with the Indo Germanic races, he insists that they migrated from India long before historic memory, and crossed that bridge of nations, the Isthmus of Suez, to find a new father-land on the banks of the Nile.' The Egyptians came, according to their own records, from a mysterious land (now shown to lie on the shore of the Indian ocean), the sacred Punt; the original name of their gods who followed thence after their people who had abandoned them to the valley of the Nile, led by Amon, Hor and Hathor. This region was the Egyptian 'Land of the Gods,' Pa-Nuter, in old Egyptian, or Holyland, and now proved beyond any doubt to have been, quite a different place from the Holyland of Sinai. By the pictorial hieroglyphic inscription found (and interpreted) on the walls of the temple of the Queen Haslitop at Der-el-babri, we see that this Punt can be no other than India. For, many ages the Egyptians traded with their old homes, and the reference here made. by them to the names of the Princes of Punt and its fauna and flora, especially the nomenclature of various precious woods to be found but in India, leave us scarcely room for the smallest doubt that the old civilisation of Egypt is the direct outcome of that of the older India."[1]

Mr. Pococke says, "At the mouths of the Indus dwell a seafaring people, active, ingenious, and enterprising as when, ages subsequent to this great movement; they themselves, with the warlike denizens of the Punjab, were driven from their, native land. to seek the far distant climes of Greece. The commercial people dwelling along the coast that stretches from the mouth of the Indus to the Coree, are embarking on that emigration whose magnificent results to civilisation, and whose gigantic monuments of art, fill the mind with mingled emotions of admiration and awe. These people coast along the shores of Mekran, traverse the mouth of the Persian Gulf, and again adhering to the sea-board of Oman, Hadramant, and Yemen (Eastern Arabia), they sail up the Red Sea; and again ascending the mighty stream that fertilises a land of wonders, found the kingdoms of Egypt, Nubia, and Abyssinia. These are the same stock that, centuries subsequently to this colonisation, spread the blessings of civilisation over Hellas and her islands,"[2]

Mr. Pococke thus summarises his researches: "I would now briefly recapitulate the leading evidence of the colonisation of Africa from North-western India and the Himalaya provinces. First, from the provinces or rivers deriving their names from the great rivers of India; secondly, from the towns and provinces of India or its northern frontiers; thirdly, from the Ruling chiefs styled Ramas (Rameses), &c; fourthly, similarity in the objects of sepulture; fifthly, architectural skill and its grand and gigantic character; and sixthly the power of translating words, imagined to be Egyptian, through the medium of a modified Sanskrit.''[3]

---

[1] See the *Theosophist* for March 1881, p. 123

[2] *India in Greece*, p. 42

[3] *India in Greece*, p. 201

Mr. Pococke then proceeds to subjoin "the opinions of men of sound judgment in connection with the Indian colonization of Egypt."

The name "Nile" was given to the great river of Egypt by the Indian settlers there. "For about 10 miles below the Attock," says a critic, "the Indus has a clean, deep and rapid current, but for above a hundred miles further down to Kalabagh it becomes an enormous torrent. The water here has a dark lead colour and hence the name Nilab or Blue river given as well to the Indus as to a town on its banks, about 12 miles below Attock," As Aboasin (a classical name for the Indus) gave its name to Abusinia (Abyssinia) in Africa, so here "we now observe the Nilab (the blue water) bestowing an appellation on the far-famed "Nile" of Egypt. This is one of those facts which prove the colonisation of Egypt to have taken place from the coast of Scinde."

Apart from the historical evidence, there are ethnological grounds to support the fact that the ancient Egyptians were originally an Indian people. Professor Heeren is astonished at the "physical similarity in colour and in the conformation of the head" of the ancient Egyptians and the Hindus. As. regards the latter point, he adds: "As to the form of the head, I have now before me the skulls of a mummy and a native of Bengal from the collections of M. Blumenbach; and it is impossible to conceive anything more striking than the resemblance between the two, both as respects the general form and the structure of the firm portions. Indeed the learned possessor himself considers them to be the most alike of any in his numerous collections."[1]

After showing the still more striking similarity between the manners and customs, in fact, between the whole social" religious and political institutions of the two peoples, Professor, Heeren says, "It is perfectly agreeable to Hindu manners. that colonies from India, i.e., Banian families

[1] Heeren's *Asiastic Nations*, Vol. II, p. 303

should have passed over into Africa and carried with them their industry, and perhaps also their religious worship."[1] He adds, "It is hardly possible to maintain the opposite side of the question, viz, that the Hindus were derived from the Egyptians, for it has been already ascertained that the country bordering on the Ganges was the cradle of Hindu civilisation. Now, the Egyptians could not have established themselves in that neighbourhood, their probable settlement would rather have taken place on the Coast of Malabar."

The learned professor concludes, "Whatever weight may be attached to Indian tradition and the express testimony of Eusebius confirming the report of migrations from the banks of the Indus into Egypt, there is certainly nothing improbable in the event itself, as a desire of gain would have formed a sufficient inducement." Decisive evidence of the fact, however, may be found in Philostratus and Nonnus. For further information on the subject, *vide* Religion.

After tracing the descent of Philippos of Macedon and his son, Alexander, from Bhili-Pos or Bhil-Prince and Hammon in Afghanistan, Mr. Pococke continues," And these same Bhils, i.e., the Bhil, Brāhmaṇas planted this same Oracle of Hammon in the deserts of Africa whither I have already shown that they had sailed; where they founded Philai, i.e., Bhilai, the city of the Bhils, in lat. 24^0 North, long. 33^0 East.[2]

Mr. Pococke, who made the subject his life-long study, says, "The early civilization, then, the early arts, the indubitably early literature of India are equally the civilization, the arts and literature of Egypt and of Greece – for geographical evidences, conjoined to historical fact and religious practices, now prove beyond all dispute that the two latter countries are the colonies of the former."[3]

---

[1] Heeren's *Historical Researches*, Vol. II, p. 309

[2] *India in Greece*, p. 65

[3] *India in Greece*, p. 74

Ethiopia,[1] as is universally admitted, was colonised by the Hindus. Sir W. Jones says, "Ethiopia and Hindustan were possessed or colonised by the same extraordinary race."[2]

Philostratus introduces the Brāhmaṇa Marcus by stating to his auditor that the Ethiopians were originally an Indian race compelled to leave India for the impurity contracted by slayinging a certain monarch to whom they owed allegiance."[3]

Eusebius states that the Ethiopians emigrating from the River Indus settled in the vicinity of Egypt.[4]

In Philostratus, an Egyptian is made to remark that he had heard from his father that the Indians were the wisest of men and that we Ethiopians, a colony of the Indians, preserved the wisdom and usage of their forefathers and acknowledged their ancient origin. We find the same assertion made at a later period, in the third century, by Julius Africanus, from whom it has been preserved by Eusebius and Syncellus.[5]

Cuvier, quoting Syncellus, even assigns the reign of Amenophis as the epoch of the colonisation of Ethiopia from India.[6]

The ancient Abyssinians (Abusinians), as already remarked, were originally migrators to Africa from the banks of Abuisin, a classical name for the Indus.[7]

---

[1] 'The ancient geographers called by the name of Ethiopia all that part of Africa which now constitutes Nubia, Abyssinia, Sanaor, Darfur, and Dongola,' *Theogony of the Hindus*, p.44

[2] *Asiatic Researches*, Vol. I, p. 426

[3] V.A. III, 6. See '*India in Greece*,' p. 200.

[4] Lemp. Barkers' edition; 'Meroe.'

[5] See '*India in Greece*,' p. 205

[6] p. 18 of his '*Discourse*,' & c.

[7] *Heeren's Historical researches*, Vil. II, p.310.

As will appear from the accounts of the commercial position of India in the ancient world, commerce on an extensive scale existed between ancient India and Abyssinia, and we find Hindus in large numbers settled in the latter country, "whence also," says Colonel Tod, "the Hindu names of towns at the estuaries of the Gambia and Senegal rivers, the Tamba cunda and another Cundas." He continues, "A writer in the *Asiatic Journal* (Vol. IV, p. 325) gives a curious list of the names of places in the interior of Africa, mentioned in Park's Second Journey, which are shown to be all Sanskrit and most of them actually current in India at the present day."[1]

[1] See Tod's *Rajasthan*, Vol. II, p. 309, footnote.

2.2. PERSIA

Not vainly did the early Persian make
His altar the high places and the peak
Of earth-o'ergazing mountains, and thus lake
A fit and unwalled temple, there to seek
The spirit, in whose honour shrines are weak,
Upreared of human hands.

BYRON: *Childe Harold*

Mr. POCOCKE says, "I have glanced at the Indian settlements in Egypt, which will again be noticed, and I will now resume my observations from the lofty frontier, which is the true boundary of the European and Indian races. The Parasus, the people of Parasu Ram, those warriors of the Axe, have penetrated into and given a name to Persia; they are the people of Bharata; and to the principal stream that pours its waters into the Persian Gulf they have given the name of Eu-Bharat-es (Euphrat-es), the Bharat Chief."[1]

Professor Max Müller's testimony is decisive on the point. Discussing the word Arya,' he says, "But it was more faithfully preserved by the Zoroastrians, who migrated from India to the North-west and whose religion has been preserved to us in the Zend Avesta, though in fragments only."[2] He again says, "The Zoroastrians were a colony from Northern India."[3]

Professor Heeren says, "In point of fact the Zend is derived from the Sanskrit, and a passage in Manu (10, 43-45) makes the Persians have descended from the Hindus of the second or Warrior caste."[4]

शनकैस्तु क्रिया लोपादिमाः क्षत्रियजातयः ।
वृषलत्वं गतालोके ब्राह्मणदर्शनेन च ।।

---

[1] *India in Greece*, p. 45

[2] *Science of Language*, p. 242

[3] *Science of Language*, p.253

[4] *Historical Researches*, Vol. II, p. 220

पौण्ड्रकाश्चौल द्रविडाः कम्बोजाः यवनाः शकाः।
परदाः पह्लवाश्चीनाः किराताः दरदाः खशाः।

The old name of the country, Iran, was given by the first settlers there, who were Airan, the descendants of Aira, the son of Pururavas the son of Budha of the Lunar race. (Airan is plural of Aira).[1] These settlers bad been expelled from India after long wars, spoken of by ancient chronicles of Persia as wars between Iran and Turan. Turan being a corrupt form of Suran, Sura the Sun, the sun tribes. The tribe of "Cossoei"seen near the banks of the Tigris are the people of Kasi, the classical name of Benares.

Sir W. Jones says, "I was not a little surprised to find that out of ten words in Du Perron's Zend Dictionary, six or seven were pure Sanskrit."[2]

Mr. Haug, in an interesting essay on the origin of Zoroastrian religion, compares it with Brahminism and points out the originally-close connection between the Brahminical and the Zoroastrian religions, customs and observances. After comparing the names of divine beings, names and legends of heroes, sacrificial rites, religious observances, domestic rites, and cosmographical opinions that occur both in the Vedic and Avesta writings, he says, "In the Vedas as well as in the older portions of the *Zend-Avesta* (see the *Gāthas*), there are sufficient traces to be discovered that the Zoroastrian religion arose out of a vital struggle against a form which the Brahminical religion had assumed at a certain early period" After contrasting the name of the Hindu Gods and the Zoroastrian deities, Professor Haug says, "These facts throw some light upon the age in which that great religious struggle took place, the consequence of which was the entire separation of the Ancient Iranians from the Brāhmaṇas and the foundation of

---

[1] *India in Greece*, p. 161
[2] Sir W. Jones' works, Vol. I, pp. 82 and 83

the Zoroastrian religion, It must have occurred at the time when Indra was the chief god of the Brāhmaṇas."[1]

It is not an easy matter to ascertain the exact period at which the Hindu colonisation of Persia took place. It is certain, however, that it took place long before the *Mahābhārata*. Colonel Tod says, "Ajameda, by his wife Nila, had five sons, who spread their branches on both sides of the Indus. Regarding three the *Purāṇas* are silent, which implies their migration to distant regions. Is it possible they might be the origin of the Medes? These Medes are descendants of Yayat, third son of the patriarch, Menu: and Madai, the founder of the Medes, was of Japhet's line. Aja Mede, the patronymic of the branch of Bajaswa, is from Aja 'a goat.' The Assyrian Mede in Scripture is typified by the goat."[2]

Apart from the passage in Manu,[3] describing the origin of the ancient Persians, there is another argument to support it. Zoroaster, the Prophet of the Ancient Persians, was born after the emigrants from India had settled in Persia, long enough to have become a separate nation. Vyasa held a grand religious discussion with Zoroaster at Balkh in Turkistan, and was therefore his contemporary. Zanthus of Lydia (B.C. 470), the earliest Greek writer, who mentions Zoroaster, says that he lived about six hundred years before the Trojan War (which took place about 1800 B.C.). Aristotle and Endoxus place his era as much as six thousand years before Plato, others five thousand years before the Trojan War (see Pliny: Historia Naturalis, XXX, 1-3). Berosus, the Babylonian historian makes him a king of the

---

[1] Haug's *Essays on the Parsees*, p. 288.
Of great importance for showing the originally-close relationship between the Brahminical and Parsi religions, is the fact that several of the Indian gods are actually mentioned by name in the Zend Avesta, some as demons, others as angles. -Haug's Essay, p. 272.

[2] Tod's *Rajasthan*, Vol. I, p. 41

[3] *Manusmṛti* is admittedly much older than *Mahābhārata*.

Babylonians and the founder of a dynasty which reigned over Babylon between B.C. 2200 and B.C. 2000. It is, however, clear that the Hindu colonisation of Persia took place anterior to the Great War.

In the first chapter (Fargard) of the part which bears the name Vendidad of their sacred book (which is also their most ancient book), Hurmuzd or God tells Zapetman (Zoroaster): "I have given to man an excellent and fertile country. Nobody is able to give such a one. This land lies to the east (of Persia), where the stars rise every evening." "When Jamshed (the leader of the emigrating nation), came from the highland in the east to the plain, there were neither domestic animals nor wild, nor men." "The country alluded to above from which the Persians are said to have come can be no other than the North-west part of ancient India-Afghanistan and Kashmir – being to the east of Persia, as well as highland compared to the Persian plains."[1]

Mr. Pococke says, "The ancient map of Persia, Colchis, and Armeni is absolutely full of the most distinct and startling evidences of Indian colonization, and, what is; more astonishing, practically evinces, in the most powerful manner, the truth of several main points in the two great Indian poems, the *Rāmāyaṇa* and the *Mahābhārata*. The whole map is positively nothing less than a journal of immigration on the most gigantic scale:"[2]

---

[1] *Theogony of the Hindus*
[2] *India in Greece*, p. 47

2.3. ASIA MINOR

The Colchian virgin, whose bold hand
Undaunted grasps the warlike spear.

AESCHYLUS: *Prometheus*

The Chaldeans were originally migrators from India. Chaldea is a corruption of cul (*kula*) (family or tribe) and deva (a god or brāhmaṇa). The country, colonised by the tribe of Devas or 'Brāhmaṇas, was called Chaldea, whence, the word Chaldeans. Count Bjornstjerna says, "The Chaldeans, the Babylonians, and the inhabitants of Colchis derived their civilization from India."[1]

Mr. Pococke says, "The tribe 'Abanti' who fought most valiantly in the Trojan War were no other than the Rajputs of 'Avanti' in Malwa."[2]

The Assyrians, too, were of Hindu origin. Their first king was Bali, Boal or Bel. This Boal or Bali was a great king of India in ancient times. He ruled from Cambodia to Greece Professor Maurice says, "Bali.... was the puissant sovereign of a mighty empire extending over the vast continent of India."

Mr. Pococke says, "Thus, then, at length, are distinctly seen – firstly, the identical localities in the Indian and Tartarian provinces whence Palestine was colonized; secondly, the identity of idolatry is proved between India, the old country, and Palestine the new; thirdly, the identity of the Rajput of India and of Palestine; fourthly, the positive notification of the distinct tribe which the Israelites encountered and overthrew."[3]

---

[1] *Theogony of the Hindus*, p. 168

[2] *India in Greece*, p. 33

[3] *India in Greece*, p. 229

2.4. GREECE

The mountain looks on Marathon
And Marathon looks on the sea;
And musing there an hour alone,
I dream'd that Greece might still be free.

BYRON: *Don Juan*

The Hindu emigrations to Greece have already been mentioned. The subject is of such fascinating interest that eminent scholars and archaeologists have devoted their time and learning to unravel the mystery connected with the origin of the race, whose splendid achievements in peace and war yet stand unrivalled in Europe. Colonel Tod and Colonel Wilford laid the foundations of a system of enquiry in this branch of historical research, on which Mr. Pococke has raised the marvellous structure of "*India in Greece*", now available in the name of 'Indian Origin of Greece and Ancient World' edited by the present editor, which stands firm and solid, defying the violence and fury of the windy criticism of ignorant critics and the hail and sleet of certain writers on Indian Archaeology, blinded by inveterate prejudices. Mr. Pococke quotes chapter and verse in proof of his assertions and proves beyond all shadow of a doubt the Indian origin of the ancient Greeks.

After describing the Grecian society during the Homeric times, Mr. Pococke says, "The whole of this state of society, civil and military, must strike everyone as being eminently Asiatic, much of it specifically Indian. Such it undoubtedly is. And I shall demonstrate that these evidence were but the attendant tokens of an Indian colonisation with its corresponding religion and language. I shall exhibit dynasties disappearing from Western India to appear again in Greece: clans, whose martial fame is still recorded in the faithful chronicles of Northwestern India, as the gallant bands who fought upon the plains of Troy,"[1]

"But, if the evidences of Saxon colonization in this island (Great Britain) I speak independently of Anglo-Saxon history – are strong both from language and political institutions, the evidences are still more decisive in the parallel case of an Indian colonization of Greece – not only her language, but her philosophy, her religion, her rivers, her mountains and her tribes; her subtle turn of intellect, her political institutes, and above all the mysteries of that noble land, irresistibly prove her colonization from India."[2] "The primitive history of Greece," adds the author, "is the primitive history of India."

There are critics who concede the derivation of Greek from the Sanskrit, but stop short of the necessary inference that the people who spoke the former language were the descendants of those who spoke the latter. Of such, Mr. Pococke asks, "Is it not astonishing that reason should so halt half–way in its deduction as to allow the derivation of the Greek from an Indian language, and yet deny the personality of those who spoke it; or, in other words, deny the settlement of an Indian race in Greece ?"[3]

The word Greek itself signifies the Indian origin of the ancient Greeks. The royal city of the Magedhanians or Kings of Magadha was called "Raja Griha" "The people or clans of Griha were, according to the regular patronymic form of their language, styled Graihka, whence the ordinary derivative Graihakos (Graikos) Graecus or Greek."[4] This shows that the Greeks were migrators from Magadha; which fact is still further strengthened when we consider that their predecessors in their adopted country were also inhabitants of Magadha. These people were Pelasgi. They were so-

---

[1] *India in Greece*, p. 12
[2] *India in Greece*, p. 19
[3] *India in Greece*, p. 145
[4] *India in Greece*, p. 295

called because they emigrated from Pelasa, the ancient name for the province of Bihar, in Āryāvartta. Pelasgo is a derivative form of Pelasa, whence the Greek Pelasgo. The theory is further strengthened when we; find that Asius, one of the early poets of Greece, makes King Pilasgus siring from "Gaia." This "Gaia" is no other than the "Gaya," the capital city of Pelaska or Bihar.

Aeubaea was colonised by "Eu-babooyas:' the Bahoojas or warriors par excellence. The Makedonians (Macedon= Magadha} were the inhabitants of Magadha, the same province. The people of Bihar or Maghada, it appears migrated in several tribal groups to Greece; and their migrations are marked by the different names they gave to the part or parts of their adopted country. Says Mr. Pococke, "The Bud, has have brought with them into Thessaly the far-famed mythological but equally historical name of 'Cilas,' the fabulous residence of Cuvera, the (Hindu) god of wealth, and the favourite haunt of Śiva, placed by the Hindus among the Himalayan mountains, and applied to one of the loftiest peaks lying on the north of the Manasa lake."[1]

Many other tribes of the *Kṣatriyas* migrated to Greece and the isles of the Archipelago. The Boeotians were the "Baihootian." Rajput dwellers on the banks of Behoot (Jehlum): the Cossopaei, were the Kashmirians so-called from Casayapa (or Kaśyapa), the founder of Kashmir. The Hellopes were the Chiefs of the Hela tribe and their country "Hellados, Hella-desa." The names, Mount Kerketius (Kertetcha range in Afghanistan), Locman (Lughman of Afghanistan), and Mount Titarus (the Tatara Pass of Afghanistan), Mount Othrys (Sanskrit name of Himalaya), Matan Astae (Matan- Vasti "the dwelling place of the Matans, a tribe of Kashmir), Kestrine (Kṣatriya, warrior caste, and *ina*, chief), all point to the fact that many of the

---

[1] *India in Greece*, p. 99

migrators were originally inhabitants of the North-western parts of India.

Speaking of the Hindus having reared a Mythological superstructure on physical facts in making Mount Kailas. the abode of the gods, Mr. Pococke says, "Thus it was with the native of Indus and of the rocky heights of Hela, when he became a settler in the Hellas; and thus it was with his polished descendant in Athens, who though called a Greek was yet as thoroughly Indian in his tastes, religion, and literature as any of his forefathers."[1]

"The land of Hellas, a name so dear to civilisation and the arts," says Pococke, "was so-called from the magnificent range of heights situated in Balochistan, styled the 'Hela' mountains... The chiefs of this country were called Helaines or the chiefs of the Hella.[2] The formation of the term Helaines in Sanskrit would be identical with the Greek. Hel-en (the Sun-king) is said to have left his kingdom to Aeolus, his eldest son, while he sent for Dorus and Zethus to make conquests in foreign lands. Haya is the title of a renowned tribe of Rajput warriors. They were called Asii or Aśva, and their chiefs, 'Aswa-pas,' and to use the words of Conon, as quoted by Bishop Thirlwall, "the patrimony of Aiolus (the Haiyulas) is described as bounded by the river Asopus (Aswa-pas) and the Enipeus." Such, then was the Asopus, the settlement of the Haya tribes, the Aswa chiefs, the sun worshippers, the children of the Sun-king or Helen, whose land was called in Greek Hellados, in Sanskrit, Hela-des (Hela> Hela, des> land). Of Achilles, sprung from a splendid Rajput stock, I shall briefly speak when developing the parent geography of Dolopes."[3]

---

[1] *India in Greece*, p. 69

[2] *India in Greece*, p. 48-50

[3] *India in Greece*, p. 48-50

2.5. ROME

"Oh Tiber! Father Tiber!
To whom the Romans pray,
A Roman's life, a Roman's arms, '
Take thou in charge this day!

MACAULAY: *Horatius*

Mr. Pococke says, "The great heroes of India are the gods of Greece. They are in fact, as they have been often rationally affirmed, and as plausibly but not as rationally denied! –deified chiefs and heroes; and this same process of deification, both among Greeks and Romans – the descendants of colonists from India, continued, especially amongst the latter people down to and throughout the most historical periods."[1]

The Romans were the descendants of the Trojans, the inhabitants of that part of Asia Minor in which Hindu settlements had long been established. Niebuhr says, "Rame is not a Latin name." Mr. Pococke says it is "Rama." The Sanskrit long "a" is replaced by "o" or "w" of the Greeks, as Poseidon and Poseidin.[2]

Their neighbours, the Etruscans, had a system of religion in many respects similar to that of the Indians. It is remarkable that their religion was as perfect in ceremonial details as the –religion of the Indians, or of the Egyptians (which was a direct outcome of Vedic dharma). But the early Etruscans, too, were a body of colonists from India who penetrated into Italy some time before or about the Hindu colonization of Greece. Of the Asiatic tribe called" Asor,' Count Bjornstjerna says, "1t seems to be the same tribe which came by sea to Etruria."[3]

---

1 *India in Greece*, p. 142
2 *India in Greece*, p. 166
3 *Theogony of the Hindus*, p. 105

2.6. TURKISTAN AND NORTHERN ASIA

"At length then to the wide earth's extreme bounds,
To Scythia are we come, those pathless wilds
Where human footstep never marked the ground."

AESCHYLUS: *Prometheus*

The Turanians extending over the whole of Turkistan and Central Asia were originally an Indian people. Cotonel Tod says, "Abdul Gazi makes Tamak, the son of Turc, the Turuṣka of the *Purāṇas.* His descendants gave their name to Tocharistan or Turkistan."[1] Professor Max Müller says, "Turvas and his descendants who represent Turanians[2] are described in the later epic poems of India as cursed and deprived of their inheritance," and hence their migration.

Colonel Tod says, "The Jaisalmer annals assert that the Yadu and the Balica branches of the Indu race ruled Korassan after the Great War, the Indo-Scythic races of Grecian authors." Besides the Balicas and the numerous branches of the Indo-Medes, many of the sons of Cooru (Kuru) dispersed over these regions: amongst whom we may place Ootooru Cooru (Uttara Kuru) (Northern Kurus) of the *Purāṇas*, the Ottorocurae of the Greek authors. Both the Indu and the Sūrya races were eternally sending their superfluous population to those distant regions."[3]

A Mohamedan historian[4] says that the country of Khatha was first inhabited by a body of emigrants from India.

A band of Hindu settlers left India for Siberia, where they founded a kingdom, with Bajrapur as its capital. It is related that on the death of the king of that country in a

---

[1] Tod's *Rajasthan*, Vol. I, p. 103
[2] *Science of Language*, p. 242
[3] Tod's *Rajasthan*, Vo. I, p. 43
[4] *History of China*, Vol. II, p. 10

battle, Pradyumna, Gāda and Sāmbha, three sons of Śri Krishna Chandra, with a large number of Brāhmaṇas and Kṣ atriyas, went there, and the eldest brother succeeded to the throne of the deceased Raja. On the death of Sri Krishna Chandra they paid a condolence visit to Dwarka.[1]

Colonel Tod says, "The annals of the Yadus of Jaisalmer state that long anterior to Vikrama, they held dominion from Ghazni to Samarkand; that they established themselves in those regions after the *Mahābhārata* or the Great War, and were again impelled on the rise of Islamism within the Indus."[2] He further says, "The Yadus of Jaisalmer ruled Zabulistan and founded Ghazni."[3] They claim Chaghtaes as of their own Indu stock, "a claim which," says Colonel Tod, "I now deem worthy of credit."

The Afghans are the descendants of the Aphgana, the serpent tribe of the Apivansa of ancient India. "According to Abu Haukal, the city of Herat is also called Heri. This adjoins Maru or Murve."[4] The country called Seestan, which the Middle Eastern Question may yet bring more prominently before the public, was a settlement of the Hindus. Colonel Tod says, "Seestan (the region of cold, see-sthan) and both sides of the valley were occupied in the earliest periods by another branch of the Yadus."[5] Colonel Tod again says, "To the Indu race of Aswa (the descendants of Deomida and Bajaswa), spread over the countries on both sides of the Indus, do we owe the distinctive appellation of Asia."[6]

---

[1] *Hari Vaṁśa, Viṣṇu Parva, Adhyāya,* 97

[2] Tod's *Rajasthan*, p. 529

[3] Tod's *Rajasthan*, Vol. I, p. 61, 'The sons of Krishna eventually left Indus behind and passed into Zabulistan, and peopled these countries, even to Samarkand.'- p.85

[4] Tod's *Rajasthan*, Vol. II, p. 231

[5] Tod's *Rajasthan*, Vol. II, p. 230

[6] Tod's *Rajasthan*, Vol. I, p. 63, 'Europa derived from *Surūpa*, of the beautiful face,' the initial syllable su and eu having the same

That the Bactrians were an Indian people has already been shown. And that the Indian migrations extended to Siberia and the northern-most part of Asia is evident from the fact that the descendants of the Aryan migrators are still found there. "The Samoyedes and Tchoudes of Siberia and Finland are really Samayadus and Joudes of India. The languages of the two "former races are said to have a strong affinity and are classed as Hindu-Germanic by Klaproth, the author of Asia Polyglotta.'"[1] Mr. Remusat traces these tribes to Central Asia, .where the Yadus long held sway. Sama, Syam is a title of Krishna. They were Sama Yadus.

---

signification in both languages, viz., good *Rūpa* is countenance.' p. 515

[1] Tod's *Rajasthan*, Vol I, p. 529. The race of Joude is described by Babar as occupying the mountainous range, the very spot mentioned in the annals of the Yadus as their place of halt on quitting India twelve centuries before Christ, and thence called Yadu-ki-dang, or hill of Yadu.

2.7. GERMANY

The press's magic letters
That blessing ye brought forth,
Behold! it lies in fetters
On the soil that gave it birth.

CAMPBELL : *Ode to the Germans*

That the Ancient Germans were migrators from India is proved by the following passage from Muir: "It has been remarked by various authors (as Kuhn and Zeitschrift, IV. 94 ff) that in analogy with Manu or Manus as the father of mankind or of the Aryas, German mythology recognises Manus as the ancestor of Teutons."The English 'man' and the German 'mann' appear also to be akin to the word 'manu', and the' German 'mensch' presents a close resemblance to 'manush' of Sanskrit."[1]

The first habit of the Germans, says Tacitus, on rising was ablution, which Colonel Tod thinks must have been of Eastern origin and not of the cold climate of Germany[2] as also "the loose flowing robe, the long and braided hair tied in a knot at the top of the head so emblematic of the Brāhmaṇas."

The Germans are the Brāhmaṇas or Sharmas of India. Sharma became Jarma and Jarma became Jerman. For in Sanskrit *ś* and *j* and a are convertible into one another, as Arya, Arjya and Arshya (see Max Müller's *Ṛgveda*). Csoma-De-Coras in the Preface to his Tibetan Dictionary, says, "The Hungarians will find a fund of information from the study of Sanskrit respecting their origin, manners, customs and language."

The Saxons are no other than the sons of the Sakas (Śakas) who lived on the North-western frontier of Āryāvartta, when they migrated to Germany. The name

---

[1] Manning's *Ancient and Mediaeval India.* Vol. I, p. 118

[2] Tod's *Rajasthan*, Vol. I, pp. 63 and 80

Saxon is a compound of "Saca" (Sakas) and "*sunu*" (descendants).. They were so-called because they were descendants of the Sakas. Their name for Heaven is the same as that of the Indians. A critic says, "It is from the Himaiaya Mountains of the Sacas that the 'Sac-soons' those sons of the Sacas (Saxons or Sacsons, or the words are at once Sanskrit, Saxon and English) derived their Himmel or Heaven."

Colonel Tod says, "I have often been struck with a characteristic analogy in the sculptures of the most ancient Saxon cathedrals in England, and on the continent to Kanaya and the Gopis. Both may be intended to represent divine harmony. Did the Asi and Jits of Scandinavia, the ancestors of the Saxons, bring them from Asia ?"[1]

---

[1] Tod's *Rajasthan*, Volume I, (People's Edition), p. 570

2.8. SCANDINAVIA

The Swedish sage admires in yonder bowers,
His winged insects and his rosy flowers.

CAMPBELL: *Pleasures of Hope*

The Scandinavians are the descendants of the Hindu Kṣatriyas. The term Scandinavian and the Hindu "Kṣatriya" or the warrior class are identical, "the former being a Sanskrit equivalent for the latter:" "Skanda Nabhi" (Scanda Navi) signifies Scanda Chiefs (Warrior Chiefs).

Colonel Tod says, "The Aswas were chiefly of the Indu race, yet a branch of the Suryas also bore this designation." In the Edda we are informed that the Getes or Jits who entered Scandinavia were termed Asi, and their first settlement was Asigard (Asi garh, fortress of the Asi)."

Pinkerton says, "Odin came into Scandinavia in the time of Darius Hystaspes, 500 years before Christ, and that his successor was Gotama. This is the period of the last Budha, or Mahavira, whose era is 477 before Vikrama, or 533 before Christ. Gotama was the successor of Mahavira."[1]

"In the martial mythology and warlike poetry of the Scandinavians a wide field exists for assimilation."[2]

"We can scarcely question," says Count Bjornstjerna, "the derivation of the Edda (the religious books of ancient Scandinavia) from the Vedas."[3]

The principle on which the seven days of the week are named in India is the saml: on which it has been done in Scandinavia with little bit change of the meaning of Indian Planets into deities.

---

[1] Tod's *Rajasthan*, Vol. I, p. 64
[2] Tod's *Rajasthan*, Vol. I, p. 68
[3] *Theogony of the Hindus*, p. 108

(1) Sunday is called by the Hindus *Ravivāram*, after *Ravi*, the sun, after which also the Scandinavians call the day Sondag.

(2) Monday is called by the Hindus *Somavāram*, from Soma, the moon. Among the Scandinavians it is called Mondag.

(3) Tuesday is called Maṅgalvāram in India after the planet Maṅgala (Mars). It bears the name Tisdag amongst the Scandinavians, after their hero, This.

(4) Wednesday is termed *Budhavāram* by the Hindus, after the planet Budha; by the Scandinavians, it is denominated after Oden (Wodan, Bodham, Budha), Onsdag.

(5) Thursday is called Bṛhaspativāram by the Hindus, after Bṛhspati, or planet Jupiter. It bears the name Thorsdag amongst the Scandinavians, after their principal god, Thor.

(6) Friday is called by the Hindus Sukravāram, after Sukra, the planet Venus; it is named by the Scandinavians after Freja, the goddess of beauty, Frejdag.

(7) Saturday is called *Śanivāram* by the Hindus after Sanaiścara, the planet Saturn; it is named Lordag by the Scandinavians from loger, means bathing.

"We have here," says Count Bjornstjerna, himself a Scandinavian gentleman, "another proof that the Myths of the Scandinavians are derived from those of the Hindus."[1]

---

[1] *Theogony of the Hindus*, p. 169

2.9. THE HYPERBOREANS

"Hail, Mountain of delight!
Palace of glory, blessed by Glory's king!
With prospering shade empower me, while I sing
Thy wonders, yet unreach'd by mortal flight!
Sky-piercing mountain! in thy bowers of love
No tears are seen, save where medicinal stalks
Weep drops balsamic o'er the silvered walks."

HYMN TO INDRA: Sir W. Jones' translation

The Hyperboreans (who formerly occupied the Northernmost parts of Europe and Asia) were the Khyber purians or the inhabitants of Khyberpur and its district. Another Khyber settlement will be seen in 1hessaly on the Eastern branch of Phoenix river. Its name is tolerably well-preserved as Khyphara and Khyphera.[1]

Mr. Pococke says, "While the sacred tribe of Dodo, or the Dadan, fixed their oracle towards the northerly line of the Hellopes, in Thessaly, the immediate neighbours of the Hyperboreans took up their abode towards the south of the holy mountain of To-Maros, or Su-Meru. These were the Pashwaran, or the emigrants from Peshawar, who appear in the Greek guise of Passaron. We now readily see the connection between the settlements of the Dodan (Dodonian Oracle), Passaron (Peshawar people), and the offerings of the Hyperboreans, or the men of Khyberpur, who retained this appellation wherever they subsequently settled."[2]

---

[1] *India in Greece*, p. 129
[2] *India in Greece*, p. 127

2.10. THE GREAT BRITAIN

"Whether this portion of the world were rent
By the rude Ocean, from the Continent
Or thus created; it was sure design'd
To be the sacred refuge of mankind."

WALLER: *To the Protector*

The Druids in ancient Britain were Buddhistic Brāhmaṇas; they adopted the metempsychosis, the pre-existence of the soul, and its return to the realms of universal space.' They had a divine triad, consisting of a Creator, Preserver, and Destroyer, as with the Buddhists. The Druids constituted a Sacerdotal Order which reserved to itself alone the interpretation of the mysteries of religion.

"The ban of the Druids was equally terrible with that of the Brāhmaṇas; even the king against whom it was fulminated 'fell,' to use the expression of the Druids, 'like grass before the scythe.'"[1]

Mr. Pocoeke says, "It was the Macedonian hero who invaded and vanquished the land of his forefathers unwittingly. It was a Napier who, leading the small but mighty army of Britain, drove into headlong flight the hosts of those warlike clans from whose parent stock himself and not a few of his troops were the direct descendants."[2]

Mr. Pococke also says, "The Scotch clans, their original localities and their chiefs in Afghanistan and Scotland, are subjects of the deepest interest. How little did the Scotch officers who perished in the Afghan campaign think that they were opposed by the same tribes from whom they themselves sprang! A work on this subject is in progress.[3]"

---

[1] *Theogony of the Hindus*, p. 104
[2] *India in Greece*, p. 86
[3] *India in Greece*, p. 77

Mr. Pococke says, "It is in no spirit of etymological trifling that I assure the reader, that the far-famed 'hurrah' of his native country (England) is the war cry of his forefather, the Rajput of Britain, for he was long the denizen of this island. His shout was 'haro! haro!' (hurrah! hurrah!) Hark to the spirit-stirring strains of Wordsworth, so descriptive of this Oriental warrior. It is the Druid who speaks:

Then seize the spear, and mount the scythed wheel,
Lash the proud steed, and whirl the flaming steel,
Sweep through the thickest host and scorn to fly,
Arise! arise! for this, it is to die,
Thus, neath his vaulted cave the Druid sire
Lit the rapt soul, and fed the martial fire."

"The settlement of the people of the Draus in this island, the northern part of which was essentially that of the HI-BUDHDES (E-BUDH-DES,) or the land of the Hiya Bud'has at once accounts satisfactorily for the amazing mechanical skill displayed in the structure of Stone Henge, and harmonises with the industrious and enterprising character of the Buddhists throughout the old world; for these are the same people who drained the valley of Kashmir, and in all probability the plains of Thessaly.

The history of the Druids is thus explained, "The Druids were Drui-des. They were, in fact, the same as the Druopes. These venerated sages, chiefs of the tribes of the Draus, were of the *Indu Vañśa* or lunar race. Hence the Symbol of the crescent worn by these Druids. Their last refuge in Britain from the oppression of the Romans was 'the Isle of Saints' or 'Mona' (more properly 'Muni', a Sanskrit term for a holy sage). The Druids were the bards of the ancient Rajputs."

Hark! 't was the voice of harps that poured along
The hollow vale the floating tide of song;
I see the glittering train, in long array,
Gleam through the shades, and snowy splendours play;

I see them now with measured steps and slow,
'Mid arching groves the white-robed sages go.
The caken wreath with braided fillet drest—
The crescent beaming on the holy breast—
The silver hair which waves above the lyre,
And shrouds the strings, proclaim the Druid's quire.
They halt and all is hushed.

That the Hindus lived in Britain in ancient times is clear from the fact that a chief of the twice-born was once brought from Śaka-dvipa (Britain) to India by Viṣṇu's eagle.[1]

For further information regarding the Hindu colonisation of Great Britain see Godfrey Higgins' "Celtic Druids," wherein it has been proved that the Druids were the priests of the Hindu colonists who emigrated from India and settled in Britain.

---

[1] Colebrooke's Miscellaneous Essays, Vol. II, p. 17, Translation of *Jatimala*. The learned Pictet says, 'I here terminate this parallel of the Celtic Idioms with the Sanskrit. I do not believe that after this marked series of analogies, a series which embraces the entire organization of their tongues, that their radical affinity can be contested.
'The Celtic race established in Europe from the most ancient times must have been the first to arrive there. The decisive analogies which these languages still present to the Sanskrit carry us back to the most ancient period to which we can attain by Comparative Philology..' Lettre Humboldt, *Journal Asiatique* (1836), p. 455

2.11. EASTERN ASIA

But, Oh ! what pencil of a living star
Could paint that gorgeous car,
In which as in an ark supremely bright,
The Lord of boundless light
Ascending calm o'er the Empyreum sails,
And with ten thousand beams his beauty veils.

HYMN TO SŪRYA: Translated by S. W. Jones

The eastward wave of Hindu emigration covered the whole of Eastern Asia, comprising the Transgangetic Peninsula, China, Japan; the isles of the Indian Archipelago, Australia, and broke upon the shores of America.

The manners and institutions of the inhabitants of the Transgangetic Peninsula bear so strong an affinity to those of the Hindus that one cannot resist the idea of their having been a Hindu race at some distant period. The fundamental principles which underlie their polity, manners, morality and religion are the same as those of the Hindus. In fact, it may be taken for granted that the Transgangetic Peninsula was but a part and parcel of India so far as society, religion and polity were concerned. There was no general change in India but was also wrought there. The propagation of Buddhism was not confined to India; the people of the Transgangetic Peninsula took their share in it.

Till recently the Peninsula was swayed wholly by Indian thought, but by and by a second power was felt to assert itself. China accepted the religion of the Great Buddha. Thence forward it became a rival power with India in the eyes of the inhabitants of the Peninsula. The Aryas soon reverted to their ancient faith, or rather to a modified form of the ancient faith, but on the people of the Peninsula the grasp of the reformed faith was too firm to be so easily shaken off, and hence the silver cord of friendship that tied the two together was snapped. The inhabitants of the Transgangetic Peninsula thence forward began to look up to the Celestials rather than to the Hindus for enlightenment and instruction. But as their political and social institutions had a Hindu cast, a total overthrow of Hinduism in consequence of this cleavage was impossible. Their civilization, therefore, retained its Hindu basis.

It is a well-known fact that the Purdah system was unknown in ancient India and that it came in the train of the Mohamedan invaders. The present position of the Burmese women in the social and domestic life of Burmah, supports the theory that the Celestial influence over the countries between the Brahmaputra and the Pacific was too strong and deep to allow the people there to follow the Hindus in their revolutionary social changes that were unhappily forced upon them by the wave of a less civilized but a more determined foreign aggression.

"The Burmese, we are told by Symes, call their Code generally, Dharmasath or Sastra; it is one among the many commentaries on Manu. Mr. Syme speaks in glowing terms of the Code."[1]

Mr. Wilson says, "The civilisation of the Burmese and the Tibetans is derived from India."

The name Burma itself is of Hindu derivation and proves the Hindu origin of the Burmans. The name Camboja is frequently mentioned in Sanskrit works, and who that has read accounts of it will deny its identity with Cambodia?[2] In 1882 a Hindu temple was excavated in that country by a Frenchman[3] whose writings prove that In ancient times, if not a part" of the Indian empire, it was most closely connected with it.

---

[1] See Syme's *Embassy to Ava*, p. 326

[2] Compare Cambistholi of Arrian, Camba-Sthala (Sthala=place or district). The word denotes the dwellers in the Kamba or Kambis country. So Kamboja may be explained as those born in Kamba or Kambos. Wilson's *Viṣṇu Purāṇa*, Vol. II, p. 182

[3] The Indian Mirror of the 2nd September 1882.

China, too, was a colony of the ancient Hindus. according to the Hindu theory of emigration, China was first inhabited by the Kṣatriyas from India. Colonel Tod says, "The genealogists of China and Tartary declare themselves to be the descendants of "Awar," son of the Hindu King, "Pururavā."[1]

"Sir W. Jones says the Chinese assert their Hindu origin."[2]

According to the traditions noted in the *Schuking*, the ancestors of the Chinese conducted by Fohi came to the plains of China 2900 years before Christ, from the high mountain land which lies to the west of that country. This shows that the settlers into China were originally inhabitants of Kashmir, Ladakh, Little Tibet, and Punjab, which were parts of ancient India.[3]

The religion and culture of China are undoubtedly of Indian origin. Count Bjornstjerna says; "What may be said with certainty is that the religion of China came from India."

That ancient India had constant intercourse with China no one can deny. China[4] and Chinese products are constantly mentioned in the sacred as well as the profane literature of the time. Chinese authors, too, according to Elphinstone, note Indian ambassadors to the court of China. Professor Heeren says that "the name China is of Hindu origin and

---

[1] Annals of *Rajasthan*, Vol. I, p. 35

[2] Annals of *Rajasthan*, Vol. I, p. 57

[3] It may be reiterated that in the days of the *Mahābhārata* and for long after, Afghanistan was a part of Āryāvartta. The Rājā of Kandahar was a Hindu, and his daughter Khandhari or Gardhari was the mother of Duryodhana. Even at the time of Alexander the Great it was a part of India.

[4] *Rāmāyaṇa* mentions Chinese silks and other manufactures.

came to us from India." See also Vincent, Vol. II, pp. 574,75[1] The word Sinim occurs in the Bible, Isaiah xlix. 12.

The wave of Indian migration before breaking on the shores. of America submerged the islands of the Indian Archipelago.

Colonel Tod says, "The isles of the Archipelago were colonised by the Sūryas (Sūrya-Vañśa, Kṣatriyas) whose mythological and heroic history is sculptured in their edifices and maintained in their writings."[2]

Mr. Elphinstone says, "The histories of Java give a distinct account of a numerous body of Hindus from Kalinga who landed on their island, civilised the inhabitants and established an era still subsisting, the first year of which fell in the seventy-fifth year before Christ:"[3]

"The colonisation of the eastern coast of Java" by Brāhmaṇas is "a fact well established by Sir Stamford Raffles."[4]

Later immigrants from India were evidently Buddhists. Mr. Sewell says, "Native tradition in Java relates that about the beginning of the seventh century (603 A.D. according to Fergusson) a prince of Gujrat arrived on the island with 5,000 followers and settled at Mataram. A little later 2,000 more immigrants arrived to support him. He and his

---

[1] M. De guigues says that Magadha was known to the Chinese by the name Mo-Kiato, and its capital was recognized by both its Hindu names, Kusumpura, for which the Chinese wrote Kia-so-mo-pon-lo and Pataliputa, out of which they made Patoli-tse by translating putra, which means son in Sanksrit, into their own corresponding word, *tse*. *Journal of the Royal Asiatic Society*, Vol. V. (Such translation of names has thrown a veil of obscurity over many a name of Hindu origin. Hindu geography has thus suffered a great loss.)

[2] Tod's *Rajasthan*, Vol. II, p. 218, footnote.

[3] Elphinstone's *History of India*, p. 168

[4] Heeren's *Historical Researches*, Vol. II, p. 303, footnote.

followers were Buddhists, and from his time Buddhism was firmly established as the religion of Java."[1]

"The Chinese pilgrims who visited the island in the fourth century found it entirely peopled by the Hindus."[2] Respecting the inhabitants of Java;"Mr. Buckle says, "Of all the Asiatic islanders this race is the most attractive to the imagination. They still adhere to the Hindu faith and worship."[3]

Dr. Cust says, "In the third group we come once more on traces of the great Aryan Civilization of India; for many centuries ago some adventurous Brāhmaṇas from the Telegu coast (or from Cambodia) conveyed to Java their religion, their sacred books and their civilization, and Java became the seat of a great and powerful Hindu dynasty?[4] As regards Borneo, the largest island of the Archipelago, another traveller[5] observes that "in the very inmost recesses of the mountains as well as over the face of the country, the remains of temples and pagodas are to be seen similar to those found on the continent of India bearing all the traits of Hindu mythology; and that in that country of Wahoo, at least 400 miles from the coast, there are several of very superior workmanship with all the emblematic figures so common in Hindu places of worship."

Sir Stanford Raffles while describing the small island of Bali, situated towards the east of Java says, "Here, together with the Brahminical religion, is still preserved the ancient form of Hindu municipal polity."[6]

The Bugis of the island of Celebes trace back their history to the Savira Geding, whom they represent to have

---

[1] *Antiquartian Notes in Java, Journal, R.A.S.*, p.402 (1906)
[2] See *R.A.S. Journal*, Vol. IX, pp. 136, 38 on the History of Java.
[3] *Beauties, Sublimities and Harmonies of Nature*, Vol. I.
[4] *Linguistic and Oriental Essays.*
[5] See Dalten's account of the Diaks of Borneo in the *Journal of the Asiatic Society*, Vol. VII, p. 153
[6] *Description of Java*, Vol. II, p. 236

proceeded in immediate descent from their heavenly mediator *Baitara Guru* (which is distinctly a Hindu name), and to have been the first chief of any celebrity in Celebes.

As regards Sumatra, M. Coleman says, "Mr. Anderson in his account of his mission to the coast of that island (Sumatra) has, however, stated that he discovered at Jambi the remains of an ancient Hindu temple of considerable dimensions, and near the spot various mutilated figures, which would appear to clearly indicate the former existence of the worship of the Vedantic philosophy."[1]

Australia was probably deserted soon after its settlement. But that the wave of Hindu civilisation and emigration did at one time break on the shores of Australia is evident from the fact that many extraordinary things are found there. Among other things, the native races have got a kind of arrow, which clearly betrays its Hindu origin. This arrow called boomerang by the natives is exactly the same that used by Arjuna and Karan in the *Mahābhārata*. Its great merit is that it returns to the archer if it misses the aim.[2]

---

[1] Coleman's *Hindu Mythology*, p. 361

[2] For further information on the point see '*Military Science*.'

2.12. AMERICA

America! half brother of the world!
With something good and bad of every land;
Greater than thee have lost their seat,
Greater scarce none can stand.

BAILEY: *Festus*

The fact that a highly civilized race inhabited America long before the modern civilisation of Europe made its appearance there, is quite clear from the striking remains of ancient and his refinement existing in the country. Extensive remains of cities which must have been once in a most flourishing condition, of strong and well-built fortresses, as well as the ruins of very ancient and magnificent buildings, tanks, roads and canals that meet the eye over a very wide area of the southern continent of America, irresistibly force us to the conclusion that the country must have been inhabited at one time by a very highly civilized nation. But whence did this highly civilised nation. But whence did this high civilisation spring?

The researches of European antiquarians trace it to India. Mr. Coleman says, "Baron Humboldt, the great German traveller and scientist describes the existence of Hindu remains still found in America."[1]

Speaking of the social usages of the inhabitants of Peru, Mr. Pococke says, "The Peruvians and their ancestors, the Indians, are in this point of view at once seen to be the same people."[2] The architecture of ancient America resembles the Hindu style of architecture. Mr. Hardy says, "The ancient edifices of Chichen in Central America bear a striking resemblance to the tops of India."[3] Mr. Squire also says, "The Buddhist temples of Southern India, and of the islands

---

[1] *Hindu Mythology*, p. 350
[2] *India in Greece*, p. 174
[3] *Eastern Monachism*.

of the Indian Archipelago, as described to us by the learned members of the Asiatic Society and the numerous writers on the religion and antiquities of the Hindus, correspond with great exactness in all their essential and in many of their minor features with those of Central America."[1] Dr. Zerfii remarks, "We find the remarkable temples, fortresses, viaducts, aqueducts of the Aryan group."[2]

A still more significant fact proves the Hindu origin of the civilisation of ancient America. The mythology of ancient America furnishes sufficient grounds for the inference that it was a child of Hindu mythology. The following facts will elucidate the matter:

(1) Americans worshipped Mother Earth as a mythological deity, as the Hindus still do *dhartimātā* and *pṛthvī mātā* are well-known and familiar phrases in Hindustan.

(2) Footprints of heroes and deities on rocks and hills were worshipped by the Americans as devoutly as they are done in India even at the present day. Mexicans are said to have worshiped the footprints of Quetzal Coatle, as the Indians worship the footprints of Buddha in Ceylon, and of Krishna in Gokula near Mathura.[3]

(3) The Solar and Lunar eclipses were looked upon in ancient America in the same light as in modern India. The Hindus beat drums and make noises by beating tin pots and other things. The Americans, too, raise a frightful howl and sound musical instruments. The Carecles (Americans) think that the demon Maleoyo, the hater of light, swallows the moon and the sun in the same way as the Hindus think that the demons Rāhu and Ketu devour the sun and the moon.

---

[1] *Serpent Symbol.*

[2] *A Manual of Historical Development of Art.*

[3] The Marwarees of Ajmer worship the footprints of Ajaipal, the founder of Ajmer, on a rock near the city.

(4) The priests were represented in America with serpents round their heads, as Siva, Kali and others are represented by the Hindus.

(5) The Mexicans worshipped the figure made of the trunk of a man with the head of an elephant. The Hindus, as is too well-known, still worship this deity under the name or Ganesh. Baron Humboldt thus remarks on the Mexican deity, "It presents some remarkable and apparently not accidental resemblance 'with the Hindu Ganesh."

(6) The legend of the Deluge[1] as believed in by the Hindus was also prevalent in America.

(7) The Americans believed that the sun stood still at the word of one of their saints. In India, it is said that the cries of Arjuna at the death of Krishna caused the sun to stand still.

(8) The tortoise myth is common to India and America. Mr. Tylor says, "The striking analogy between the tortoise myth of North America and India is by no means a matter of new observation; it was indeed noticed by Father Latvian nearly a century and a half ago. Three great features of the Asiatic stories are found among the North American Indians in their fullest and clearest development. The earth is supported on the back of a huge floating tortoise, the tortoise sinks under and causes a deluge, and the tortoise is conceived as being itself the earth floating upon the face of the deep."[2]

(9) The serpent-worship was common to both countries. In India. even to the present day, the serpent is the emblem of 'wisdom. power, duration, life, eternity and a symbolic representation of the sun. The fact that serpent-

---

[1] Brahma caused the deluge when only one pious man named Satyavrata, and his family and some animals were saved. *Asintic Researches*, Vol. I

[2] *Early History of Mankind*

worship is common to the Hindu, the Egyptian, the Syrian, the Grecian, the Chinese, the Scandinavian and the American mythologies has been held to be another proof of the Hindu mythology being the parent of these systems of mythology. Their philosophy was also .derived from India. Their belief in the doctrine of the transmigration of souls stamps their philosophy also as being of Hindu origin.

Apart from mythology, the manners, customs and habits of the ancient Americans bore a very close resemblance to those of the Hindus. Their dress, costume, and sandals prove them to be of Indian origin. The dress of American women was the same as the national dress of Hindu women.

All that can be safely asserted as to the date of the Hindu colonisation of America is, that it took place after the time of Sri Ram Chandra. That America was frequently visited by the Hindus till long after the *Mahābhārata* is amply proved by historical records of the Hindus.

Sri Ram Chandra and Sita are still worshipped in America, and, remarkably enough, under their original names. In America, an annual fair takes place, which closely corresponds with the Dashera (Ram Chandrajee-ka-Mela) of the Hindus.[1] Sir W. Jones says, "Rama is represented as a descendant from the sun, as the husband of Sita, and the son of a princess named Kausalya. It is very remarkable that Peruvians, whose Incas boasted of the same descent, styled their greatest festival Rama, Sitva; whence we may suppose that South America was peopled by the same race who imported into the farthest parts of Asia the rites and the fabulous history of Rama. [2]

Mythology, architecture, philosophy, traditions, manners, and legends of ancient America all argue the Hindu origin of the Americans. This is supported by what we find in the *Purāṇas*, the *Mahābhārata* and other historical

---

[1] For full particulars see the Theosophist for 1886

[2] *Asiatic Researches*, Vol. I, p. 426

writings. It is expressly stated in the *Mahābhārata* that Arjuna conquered *Pātāla Deśa*, and married Ulupī, daughter of the king of that country, named Kuru, and that the fruit of this union was Aravan[1], who afterwards distinguished himself as a great warrior.

A word regarding the route to America used by the Hindus. They seem generally to have taken the sea route from Ceylon or from some place in the Bay of Bengal to Java, Bali, or Borneo and thence to America – to Mexico, Central America or Peru. But more adventurous spirits appear sometimes to have chosen the land passage to America through China, Mongolia, Siberia, Behring Straits (which, as geology has proved, was not in existence until recent times), and North America.

It has been urged that the Hindus, being prohibited from crossing the sea or even the river Attock, could not have gone to foreign climes in considerable numbers, either as traders or as settlers. Such criticism, however, only betrays ignorance of Hindu literature and Hindu history. Colonel Tod says, "It is ridiculous with all the knowledge now in our possession, to suppose that the Hindus always confined themselves within their gigantic barriers, the limits of modern India."[2]

The most ancient as well as the most authoritative work in Indian literature, the Veda, enjoins mankind to go to foreign countries in steamers and Airplanes or Rockets. The *Yajurveda* (*Adhyāya*, 6, *Mantra,* 21), says:

समुद्रं गच्छ स्वाहा अन्तरिक्षं गच्छ स्वाहा देवं सवितारं गच्छ स्वाहा।

"Oh men, who are fit to do administrative work righteously, go to the seas in big, fast-going steamers, and to the high heavens in Airplanes or Rockets built on scientific principles." Also :

ओं तच्चक्षुर्देवहितं पुरस्ताच्छुक्रमुच्चरत्। पश्येम शरदः शतं जीवेम

---

[1] *Mahābhārata, Bhīṣma Parva, Adhyāya,* 91

[2] Tod's *Rajasthan*, Vol. II, p. 218

शरदः शतं शृणुयाम शरदः शतं प्रब्रवाम शरदः शतमदीनाः स्याम
शरदः शतं भूयश्च शरदः शतात् ।। यजुर्वेद, 36.24

Manu says:

एतद्देशप्रसूतस्य सकाशादग्रजनमनः ।
स्वं स्वं चरित्रं शिक्षेरन् पृथिव्यां सर्वमानवाः ।। मनुस्मृति, 2.20

"Let mankind from the different countries of the world acquire knowledge from learned men first born in this country (India)."

With regard to the adjudication of disputes regarding the amount of fares, Manu says:

समुद्रयान कुशलादेशकालार्थदर्शिनः ।
स्थापयन्ति तु यां वृद्धिं सा तत्राधिगमं प्रति ।।

"The final decision as to what is the suitable fare will rest with traders, who are fully acquainted with sea routes as well as land-routes."

Manu again says:

दीर्घध्वनि यथादेशं यथाकालान्तरीभवेत् ।
नदीतीरेषु तद्विद्यात् समुद्रे नास्ति लक्षणम् ।। मनुस्मृति, 8..406

There are numerous instances on record of political and religious leaders of India having gone to Europe and America on political and religious missions. Maharṣi Vyāsa with Śukhdeoji went to America and lived there for some time. Sukhadeoji eventually returned to India via Europe (Hari Deśa), Persia and Turkistan. The journey took him three years and is succinctly described in the *Mahābhārata*, *Śānti Parva*, (*Śukhotpatti*, *Adh.* 326).

Just before the Great War the Pāṇḍavas started on a conquering expedition to foreign countries. The journey was twice undertaken. On the first occasion they went to Burma, Siam, China, Tibet, Mongolia, Tartary, Persia and returned to India via Herat, Kabul, Kandahar and Baluchistan. At Kandahar (Gandhar) they were the guests of the father-in-law of Dhṛtarāṣṭra. The second Mission was toward the

West. Starting from Ceylon (Siṅhala-Dvīpa) they went to Arabia, thence to Egypt, to Zanzibar and other parts of Africa. See *Mahābhārata*, *Sabhā Parva*, *Adhyāyas*, 26-28.

The Great Arjuna, in the course of a voyage, visited the following islands: (I) Agastya Tīrtha, (2) Plum Tīratha, (3) Subhadra Tīrtha, (4) Karandham Tīrtha, (5) Bharadvāja Tīrtha. See *Mahābhārata*, *Ādi Parva.*

The Emperor Sagarji's extensive foreign conquests are also well known. His conquest of the islands of the Indian Archipelago is mentioned in the ancient traditions of those islands, Where he is still worshipped as the "God of the Sea." See also *Rāmāyaṇa*, *Bālakāṇḍa*, V.2.

The succession of the sons of Sri Krishna to the throne of Bajrapura[1] in Southern Siberia (to the north of the Altai Mountains) has already been mentioned.

It is also well known that the emperors and kings of India often married foreign princesses. In addition to Dhṛtarāṣṭra's marriage with the daughter of the king of Afghanistan, and Arjuna's with that of the American King Kuru, we find that Unardhaji, the grandson of Sri Krishna, married the princess Ukha daughter of Ban, King of Shoont which belonged to Egypt[2] Maharaja Chandragupta married the daughter of Seleucus, King of Babylon; and the then Maharana of Udaipur (Rajputana} married the daughter of Nausherwan the Just, King of Persia.

The obnoxious prohibition to cross the Attock is of recent origin. The Hindu possession of the Afghan and Persian, territories was a relic of their ancient conquest. So late even as the first few centuries of the Christian era, the Hindus lived in thousands in Turkistan, Persia and Russia. For an account of the Hindu commercial colony at Astrakhan, see the account given by Professor Pallas, Mr. Elphinstone says, "Even at the present day, individuals of a

---

[1] See *Hari Vañśa Purāṇa*, *Viṣṇu Parva*, *Adhyāya*, 97

[2] See Hari Vañśa, *Viṣṇu Parva*, *Adh.* 116-127

Hindu tribe from Shikarpur settle as merchants and bankers – in the towns of Persia, Turkistan and Russia.[1] The same may be said of a large number of the natives of Jaisalmer.

A few passages from ancient Sanskrit works of historical importance may be quoted to show that the original founders and forefathers of many of the different nations of the world before they migrated to their respective countries, were inhabitants of India. As quoted above, Manu (Chapter X, page 43) says:

शनकैस्तु क्रियालोपादिमाः क्षत्रिय–जातयः।
पौण्ड्रकाश्चौल द्रविडाः कम्बोजाः यवनाः शकाः।।
परदाः पह्लवाश्चीनाः किराताः दरदाः खशाः।

मुखबाहूरुपज्जोनां यालोके जायतो बहिः।
म्लेच्छवाचश्चार्यवाचः सर्वैते दस्यवः स्मृताः।।

"The following tribes of Kṣatriyas have gradually sunk into the state of Vṛṣalas (outcastes) because of the extinction of Vedic rites, and because they did not try to reach the learned Vedic scholars to revive the lost Vedic traditions among themselves. These outcasts are known now as Pauṇḍrakas, Cholas, Draviḍas, Kambojas, Yavanas, Śakas, Pāradas, Pahlavas, Chinas, Kirātas, Daradas and Khasas, etc."

Sir W. Jones, in his treatise on the Chinese[2], understands "by Chinas, the Chinese, who, as the Brāhmaṇas report, are descended from the Hindus." The other names, which are apparently those of other nations, may be thus explained. The ancient Sacae. The Pahlavis were Medes speaking Pahlavi or the ancient Persian. The Cambojas were the inhabitants of Kamboja; or Cambodia[3];

---

[1] *Elphinstone's History of India*, p. 135

[2] Sir W. Jones' Works, Vol. I, p. 99

[3] That Kambojas meant the inhabitants of Cambodia is supported by two verses from the *Mahābhārata*, where they are said to be living towards the north-east :

the Yavans, as is well known, were the Greeks. The Dravids may be the Druids of Great Britain. The Kirats were the inhabitants of Baluchistan, Daradas of Dardastan in the Chinese territory. The Khasis[1] were probably some people of Eastern Europe.

The *Mahābhārata* (*Anuśāsana Parva*, Verses 2103 and 2104) while giving us a further view of the origin of the various nations of the world, says:

द्राविडाश्च कलिंगाश्च पुलिन्दाश्चाप्युशीनराः।
शकाः यवनाः काम्बोजा कोलिसर्पा।। 2103
महिषकास्तास्ताः क्षत्रियजातयः।
वृषलत्वं परिगता ब्राह्मणानामदर्शनात्।। 2104

These tribes of Kṣatriyas, viz. Śakas, Yavanas, Kambojas, Dravidas, Kaliṅgas, Pulindas[2], Uśinaras, Kolisarpas, and Mahiṣakas, have become outcasts (and exiled) since they were discarded from the Vedic religion.

This is repeated in verses 2158,59, where the following additional tribes are named Mekalas, Latas, Konvasiras, Soṇḍikas, Darvas, Chauras, Savaras, Barbaras, Kiratas and Yavanas.[3]

दरदान्सह काम्बोजैरजयतत्पाकशासनिः।
प्रागुत्तरां दिशं ये च वसन्त्याश्रित्यदस्यवः।। महाभारत, सभापर्व, 1031–32

'The son of Indra conquered the Daradas with the Kambojas and the Dasyus who dwelt in the north east region. *Mahābhārata*, Book II, 1031, 32.

[1] This people is mentioned in the Ramayana also.

[2] The Andhras, Puṇḍras, Śabaras, Pulindas, Mutibas, are also mentioned 1. the *Aitareya Brāhmaṇa.*

[3] Viṣṇu *Purāṇa* names over two hundred different peoples known to the Hindus, including Chinas, Pahlvas, Yavanas, Barbaras, Bahlikas, (people of Balkh) and Huns. See Wilson's *Viṣṇu Purāṇa*, Vol. II, p. 136.

मेकला द्रविडा लाटा पौण्ड्राः कोला उशिनरास्तथा।
शौण्डिका दरदा दर्वाश्चौरा बर्बरा शर्वराः।।
किराता यवनाश्चैव तास्ताः क्षत्रियजातयः।
वृषलत्वमनुप्राप्ता ब्राह्मणानाममर्षणात्।।

महाभारत, अनुशासन पर्व, अध्याय 34

The Kambojas, Śakas, Śabaras, Kiratas, and Varvaras are again mentioned in the *Mahābhārata*, *Droṇa Parva* to have become outcasts because they were not pardoned by the Vedic Scholars for their anti-Vedic activities. Verse 4747:

काम्बोजानां सहस्रैश्च शकानां न विशांपते।
शबराणां किरातानां बर्बराणां तथैव च।।
अगम्बरूपां पृथिवीं मांस–शोणित कद्‌र्दमाम्।
कृतवांस्तत्र शैनेयः क्षपयैस्तावक्रं वलम्।।
दस्यूनां सशिरस्त्राणैः शिरोभिर्लूनमूर्डजैः।
दीर्घकूचैर्महीं कीर्णाावियहैरण्जैरिव।।

महाभारत, द्रौणपर्व, अध्याय 116

"Sameya destroying the host, converted the beautiful earth into a mass of mud with the flesh and blood of thousands of Kambojas, Śakas, Śabaras, Kiratas and Barbaras. The ground was covered with the shorn and hairless but long-bearded heads[1] of the Dasyus, and their helmets as if with birds bereft of their plumes."

As many as 16 different foreign tribes are said in *Sānti Parva* (Section 65 line, 2429 ft.) to have descended from the Hindus. King Mandhatri asks Indra:

यवनाः किराता गांधाराश्चीनाः शबर–बर्बराः।
शकास्तुशारा कंकाश्च पह्लवाश्चान्ध्रमद्रकाः।।

पौण्ड्राः पुलिन्दा रमठाः काम्बोजाश्चैव सर्वशः।
ब्रह्मक्षत्र प्ररूताश्च वैश्याः शूद्राश्च मानवाः।।

कंतधर्माचरिष्यन्ति सर्वे विषयवासिनः।

---

[1] Compare the hairless but long bearded heads of the Arabs.

मद्विधैश्च कथं स्यात्या सर्वे वै दस्युजीवनः।।

एतदिच्छाम्यहं श्रोतुं भगवंस्तद्ब्रूहि मे।
त्वं बन्धुभूतं ह्यस्माकं क्षत्रियाणां सुरेश्वरः।।

महाभारत, शान्तिपर्व, अध्याय 1

"The Yavanas, Kiratas, Gandharas, Chinas, Sabaras, Barbaras, Śakas, Tuśāras, Kaṅkās, Pahlavas, Andhras, Madras. Pauṇḍras, Pulindas, Ramaṭhas, Kambojas men sprang from Brāhmaṇa and from Kṣatriyas, Vaiśyas and Śūdras. How shall all these people of different countries practice duty, and what rules shall kings like me prescribe for those who are living as Dasyus? Instruct me on these points, for they are the friend of our Kṣatriya race."

Manu's account of the origin of the Yavanas, Śakas, etc., is supported by the *Viṣṇu Purāṇa.* When Sagara learnt from his mother all that had befallen his father, Bahu, being vexed at the loss of his paternal kingdom, he vowed to exterminate the Haihayas and other enemies who had conquered it.

"Accordingly he destroyed nearly all the Haihayas. When the Śakas, Yavanas, Kambojas, Pāradas and Pahlavas were about to undergo a similar fate, they had recourse to Vasiṣṭha, the king's family priest, who interposed on their behalf in these words addressed to Sagara, representing them as virtually dead: 'You have done enough, my son, in the way of pursuing these men, who are as good as dead. In order that your vow might be fulfilled, I have compelled them to abandon the duties of their caste, and all association with the twice born.' Agreeing to his spiritual guide's proposal, Sagara compelled these tribes to alter their costume. He made the Yavanas shave their heads, the Śakas shave half their heads, the Paradas wear long hair and the Pahlavas beards. These and other Kṣatriyas he deprived of the study of the Vedas and the *Vaṣaṭkāra.* In consequence of their abandonment of their proper duties and of their desertion by the Brāhmaṇas, they became Mlechhas."

The *Harivanśa Purāṇa* also says :

Śakaḥ Yvanaḥ Kambojaḥ Pāradāḥ, Pahlavāḥ, tathā Kolisarpāḥ, Samahiṣāḥ,

Darvāḥ, Cholāḥ, Keralāḥ sarve te Kṣatriyas tathā teṣāṁ dharmo nirākṛtāḥ.

Vasiṣṭha-vacanād rājan Sāgareṇa Mahātmanāḥ

The Śakas, Yavanas, Kambojas, Pāradās, Pahlavas, Kolisarpas, Mahiṣas, Darvas, Cholas and Keralas had been all Kṣatriyas but deprived of their social and religious position by the great Sagara (Hindu king) in accordance with the advice of Vashishtha. Some other tribes are also mentioned in the next verse to have received similar treatment.[1]

Priyavrata, Svayambhuva's son, divided the earth into seven *dvipas*:

(1) *Jambu Dvipa* (Asia)

(2) *Plakṣa* (South America)

(3) *Puṣkara* (North America)

(4) *Krauñca* (Africa)

(5) *Śaka* (Europe)

(6) *Śālmali* (Antarctica, Australia)

(7) *Kuśa* (Oceania)

Col. Wilford, however, thus interprets them, which is obviously wrong:

---

[1] Mr. Colebrooke (*Transactions of the Royal Asiatic Society*, Vol. I. p. 453) quotes an ancient Hindu writer, who states that the Barbaric tongues are called the Parsica, the Yavana, the Romaka and the Barbara; 'the first three of which,' says he, 'would be the Persian, the Greek and the Latin. But which is the fourth and how Latin became known in India, it is difficult to say.' And yet it is a well authenticated fact that in the time of Vikramāditya there was constant intercourse between India and Rome.

Plakṣa includes Lesser Asia and America.
Kuśa answers to the countries between the Persian Gulf, the Caspian Sea, and the Western boundary of India.
Krauñca includes Germany.
Śaka means the British isles.
Puṣkara is Ireland.
Sālmali is countries by the Adriatic and Baltic.
Jambu Dvipa is India.

Owing to the destruction of the greater part of Sanskrit literature, it is impossible now to interpret correctly these geographical facts, not only because these are only the fragmentary remains of the Science of Geography inextricably mixed up with Puranic mythology, and theology but to a great extent because many of these ancient *dvipas* and countries have been so materially altered in consequence of the Cataclysm called the Deluge, as to have become impossible of identification now. The father of the modern geological science, Cuvier, express the following opinion regarding this Deluge in his *Discours Sur Jes Revolutions de la Surface du Globe*, p. 283 (5th Edition): "I consider with Messrs. Deluc and Dolomieu that if there is anything established in geology, it is the fact that the surface of the earth has been the subject of a great and sudden revolution, the date of which cannot go much further back than five or six thousand years; that this revolution has sunk (enforce) or caused to disappear (*fait-disparaitre*) some of those lands which were formerly inhabited by men, together with those species of animals which are now the most common."

We thus find that the Hindu civilisation overran the entire universe and that its landmarks are still to be seen all over the globe. Nay, it still lives and breathes around us. Says Monsieur Delbos: "The influence of that civilisation worked out thousands of years ago in India is around and about us every day of our lives. It pervades every corner of the civilised world. Go to America and you find there, as in Europe, the influence of that civilisation which came originally from the banks of the Ganges."

3

LITERATURE

Was it not wisdom's sovereign power,
That beamed her brightest, purest flame,
T'illume her sages' soul the thought to frame,
And clothe with words his heaven-taught lore?

AESCHYLUS: *Prometheus Chained*

There is no surer test of the real greatness of a nation than its literature. Literature embodies not only the intellect of .a nation but also its spirit. It is a record of the learning, the wisdom, the refinement, the achievements, the civilisation of a nation – a record of all that a nation thinks, says and does. Literature thus holds a mirror to the state of a nation and serves as an index to mark its position in the scale of civilization and greatness.

Mr. W. C. Taylor thus speaks of Sanskrit literature, "It was an astounding discovery that Hindustan possessed, in spite of the changes of realms and chances of time, a language of unrivalled richness and variety; a language, the parent of all those dialects that Europe has fondly called classical-the source alike of Greek flexibility and Roman strength. A philosophy, compared with which, in point of age, the lessons of Pythagoras are but of yesterday, and in point of daring speculation Plato's boldest efforts were tame and commonplace. A poetry more purely intellectual than any of those of which we had before any conception; and systems of science whose antiquity baffled all power of astronomical calculation. This literature, with all its colossal proportions, which can scarcely be described without the semblance of bombast and exaggeration claimed, of course, a place for itself – it stood alone, and it was able to stand alone.

"To acquire the mastery of this language is almost the labour of a life: its literature seems exhaustless. The utmost stretch of imagination can scarcely comprehend its boundless. mythology. Its philosophy has touched upon every metaphysical difficulty; its legislation is as varied as the castes for which it was designed."[1]

Count Bjornstjerna says, "The literature of India makes us. acquainted with a great nation of past ages, which grasped every branch of knowledge, and which will always occupy a distinguished place in the history of the civilisation of mankind."[2]

"The Hindu", says Mr. W. D. Brown, "is the parent of the. literature and the theology of the world."[3] Professor Max Müller says, "Although there is hardly any department of learning which has not received new light and new life from the ancient literature of India, yet nowhere is the light that comes to us from India so important, novel, and so rich as in the study of religion and mythology."[4]

General Cunningham says, "Mathematical science was so perfect and astronomical observations so complete that the paths of the sun and the moon were accurately measured. The philosophy of the learned few was perhaps for the first time, firmly allied with the theology of the believing many, and Brāhmaṇism laid down as articles of faith the unity of God, the creation of the world, the immortality of the soul, and the responsibility of man. The remote dwellers upon the Ganges distinctly made known that future life about which Moses is silent or obscure, and that unity and Omnipotence of the Creator which were unknown to the polytheism of the Greek and Roman multitude, and to the dualism of Mithraic legislators, while Vyāsa perhaps surpassed Plato in keeping

---

[1] *Journal of the Royal Asiatic Society*, Vol. II (1834) W.C. Taylor's paper no Sanskrit Literture.

[2] *Theogony of the Hindus*, p. 85

[3] *The Daily Tribune* (Salt Lake City) for February 20, 1884.

[4] Max Müller's *India : What can it teach us*? P. 140

the people tremblingly alive to the punishment which awaited evil deeds."[1]

Professor Heeren says, "The literature of the Sanskrit language incontestably belongs to a highly cultivated people, whom we may with great reason consider to have been the most informed of all the East. It is, at the same time, a scientific and a poetic literature."[2] He also says, "Hindu literature is one of the richest in prose and poetry."

Sir. W. Jones says that "human life would not be sufficient to make oneself acquainted with any considerable part of Hindu literature."

Professor Max Müller says, "The number of Sanskrit works which Mss. are still in existence amounts to ten thousand. This is more, I believe, than the whole classical literature of Greece and Italy put together."[3] (But the number is 100 times more).

The Indian Sanskritist, Pandit Shyamji Krishnavarma, in his paper on the use of writing in Ancient India, speaks of Sanskrit 1iterature as a Iiterature more extensive than the ancient literatures of Greece and Rome combined.[4]

Rev. Mr. Ward says, "No reasonable person will deny to the Hindus of former times the praise of very extensive learning. The variety of subjects upon which they wrote proves that almost every science was cultivated among them. The manner also in which they treated these subjects proves that the Hindu learned men yielded the palm of learning to scarcely any other of the ancients. The more their philosophical works and law books are studied, the more will the enquirer be convinced of the depth of wisdom

---

[1] Cunningham's *History of the Sikhs.*

[2] Heeren's *Historical Researches*, Vol. II, p. 201

[3] Max Müller's India : *What can it teach us*? P. 84

[4] *Asiatic Researches*, Vol. I,p.354

possessed by the authors."[1] Mrs. Manning says, "The Hindu had the widest range of mind of which man is capable."[2]

The high intellectual and emotional powers of the ancient Hindus were in any case destined to produce a literature remarkable for its sublimity and extent; but when these great gifts had the most perfect, melodious, and the richest language in the world to work with, the result could not but be a literature not only the most fertile and fascinating in the world but wonderful in range and astonishing in depth.

SANSKRIT LANGUAGE

Sir. W. Jones the most intellectual of the European critics of Sanskrit literature, pronounced the Sanskrit language to be "of a wonderful structure, more perfect than the Greek, more copious than the Latin, and more exquisitely refined than either."[3]

Professor Bopp[4] also says that "Sanskrit is more perfect and copious than the Greek and the Latin and more exquisite and eloquent than either."

Professor Max Müller calls Sanskrit "language of languages," and remarks that "it has been truly said that Sanskrit is to the Science of language what Mathematics is to Astronomy."[5]

Professor Wilson says, "The Hindus had a copious and a cultivated language." "The Sanskrit" says Professor Heeren, "we can safely assert to be one of the richest and most refined of any. It has, moreover, reached a high degree of cultivation, and the richness of its philosophy is no way

---

[1] Ward's *Antiquity of Hinduism*, Vol. IV, conclusion.

[2] *Ancient and Mediaeval India*, Vol. II, p. 148

[3] *Asiatic Researches*, Vol. I, p. 422, 'Sanskrit has the most prodigious compounds, some of them extending to 152 syllables' *Asiatic Researches*, Vol. I, p. 360

[4] *Edinborough Review*, Vol. XXXIII, p. 43

[5] *Science of Language*, p. 203.

inferior to its poetic beauties, as it presents us with an abundance of technical terms to express the most abstract ideas."[1]

The distinguished German critic, Schlegel, says, "Justly it is called Sanskrit, i.e., perfect, finished. In its structure and grammar, it closely resembles the Greek, but is infinitely more regular and therefore more simple, though not less rich. It combines the artistic fullness indicative of Greek development, the brevity and nice accuracy of Latin; whilst having a near affinity to the Persian and German roots, it is distinguished by expression as enthusiastic and forcible as theirs."[2] He again says, "The Sanskrit combines these various qualities, possessed separately by other tongues: Grecian copiousness, deep-toned Roman force, the divine afflatus characterising the Hebrew tongue."[3] He also says, "Judged by an organic standard of the principal elements of language, the Sanskrit excels in grammatical structure, and is, indeed, the most perfectly developed of all idioms, not excepting Greek and Latin."[4]

The importance of this "language of languages" is clarity recognised when we consider, with Sir W.W.

---

[1] *Historical Researches*, Vol. II, pp. 109, 110.
As an example of Mr. James Mill's perverted taste and inveterate prejudice against everything Hindu, the following may be cited Le Pere Paolino says that 'Sanskrit is more copious than Latin. It has several words to express the samething. The sun has more than 30 names, the moon more than 20; a house has 20, a stone 6 or 7, a least 5, an ape 10, and a crow 9.' Mr. James Mill, thereupon says that 'the highest metit of language would consist in having one name for everything which required a name and no more than one.' On this Prof. Wilson exclaims, 'what would become of poetry, of eloquence, of literature of intellect, if language was thus shorn of all that gives it beauty, variety, grace and vigour' *Mill's India,* Vol. II, p. 91

[2] Schlegel's *History of Literature*, p. 117

[3] *Ibid*, p. 105

[4] *Ibid*, p. 106

Hunter, the fact that "the modern philology dates from the study of Sanskrit by the Europeans."[1]

Sir W. Jones' assertion that "*Devanāgarī* is the original source whence the alphabets of Western Asia were derived"[2] not only proves the great antiquity of the Sanskrit literature but points out the channel through which Sanskrit philosophy and learning flowed towards the west, and, working in the new and fresh materials available there, produced Homer, Hesiod, Pythagoras Socrates, Plato, Aristotle, Zeno, Cicero, Scaevola, Varro, Virgil and others to divide the laurels of literary reputation with Vyasa, Kapila, Gautama, Patañjali, Kaṇāda, Jaiminī, Nārada, Pāṇini, Maricī and Vālmīki. The study of comparative philology, in so far as it has advanced, tends to show that Sanskrit is the mother of all Indo-European languages. From the Sanskrit were derived the original roots and those essentially necessary words which form the basis of all these languages. In other words, the part that is common to all or most of the languages of this group is supplied to each language by the Sanskrit.

Mr. Pococke says, "The Greek language is a derivation from the Sanskrit."[3] The learned Dr. Pritchard says, "The affinity between the Greek language and the old Parsi and Sanskrit is certain and essential. The use of cognate idioms proves the nations who used them to have descended from one stock. That the religion of the Greeks emanated from an Eastern source no one will deny. We must, therefore, suppose the religion as well as the language of Greece to have been derived in great part immediately from the East."[4]

---

[1] *Imperial Gazetteer*, '*India*' p. 264. The foundation of the science of comparative philology was laid by the publication of Bopp's *Comparative Grammar* in 1848 A.D.

[2] Asiatic Researches, Vol.1, p.423. Professor Heeren (Hist. Researches, Vol. II, 201 & 202) says that Sanskrit Literature is not only very rich but also extremely ancient.

[3] *India in Greece*, p. 18

[4] Dr. Pritchard's *Physical History of Man*, Vol. I, p. 502

Sir W. Jones says, "I was not a little surprised to find that out of ten words in Du Perron's Zend Dictionary six or seven were pure Sanskrit."[1]

Professor Heeren says, "In point of fact, the Zend is derived from the Sanskrit."[2]

As the Devanāgarī is the source from which the alphabets of Western Asia are derived, so are the Sanskrit names of the figures 1 to 10 the source from which most languages have derived their names of the said figures.

The scale of calculation is common to all nations and owes its origin to the Hindus. Dr. Ballantyne is inclined to support the theory that Sanskrit is the mother of all Aryan (Indo-European) languages. (See Chart)

NUMERALS

Sanskrit	Zend	Greek (Doric)	Latin	Gothic
Prathama	Frat'hema	Prota	Prima	Fruma
Dvitīya	Bitya	Deutera	Altera	Ant'hara
Tritīya	Thritya	Trita	Tertia	Thridyo
Caturtha	Turiya	Tetarta	Quarta	Fidvordo
Pañcama	Pugdha	Pempta	Quinta	Fimfto
Ṣaṣṭa	Cstva	Hekta	Sexta	Saishto
Saptma	Haptat'ha	Hebdoma	Septima	Sibundo
Aṭṣama	Aṣṭema	Ogdoa	Octava	Ahtudo
Navama	Nauma	Ennota	Nova	Niundo
Daśama	Dasema	Dekata	Decima	Taihundo

---

[1] Sir W. Jones Works Vol. I, pp. 82, 83

[2] Heeren's *Historical Researches*, Vol. II, p. 220

Sanskrit	Latin	Greek	Lithunian	Welsh
Eka	Un	Hen	Wein	Un
Dva	Du	Du	Du	Dau
Tri	Tri	Tri	Tri	Tri
Catur	Quatur	Tessar	Kettuar	Pedwar
Pañca	Quinque	Pente	Penki	
Ṣaṭ	Sex	Hex	Szestzi	
Sapta	Septem	Hepta	Septyni	Saith
Aṣṭa	Octo	Okto	Asztuni	
Nava	Movem	Ennea	Dewyni	Naw
Daśa	Decem	Deka	Deszimt	Deg

To these numerals we subjoin a brief conspectus of the

ANALOGY OF VERBS

Singular

Sanskrit	Zend	Greek	Latin
Dad-a-mi	Dadha-mi	Dido-mi	Do
Dada-s	Dadha-si	Dido-s	Da-s
Dada-te	Dadha-te	Dido-ti	D-a-t

Plural

Dad-mas	Dade-mahi	Dido-mes	Da-mus
Dat-tha	Dasta ?	Dido-te	Da-tis
Dad-te	Dade-nti	Dido-nti	Da-nt

GENERAL VIEW OF THE PERSONS OF THE VERB

First Person

Sanskrit	Zend	Greek	Latin
Tiṭhāmi	...Histami	...Histemi	...Sto
Dadāmi	...Dadhami	...Didomi	...Do
Asmi	...Ahmi...	...Emmi	...Sum
Bahrāmi	...Barami	...Phero	...Fero
Vahāmi	...Vazami	...Eko...	...Veho
Second Person			
Asi	...Ahi...	...Essi...	...Es
Tiṣṭhasi	..Histht'hahi	...Histes...	...Stas
Dadasi	...Dadhahi	...Dios...	...Das
Bharasi	...Barahi	Phereis	...Fers
Dadhyas	...Daidhyao	...Didoies	...Des
Bhares	...Bharois	...Pherois	...Feras

Second Person Plural

Tiṣṭhatha	..Hist'hat'ha	...Histate	...Statis
Bharatha	...Bara'ha	...Pherete	...Fertis
Tiṣṭhaha	...Histaeta	...Histaite	...Stetis
Dadyata	...Daidhyata	...Didoiete	...Detis
Bhareta	...Baraeta	...Pheroite	...Feratis

Third Person

Ast...	...Ashti	...Esti	...Est
Tiṭhati	...Histhtoti	...Histate	...Stat

Dadati	...Dadha	...Didote..	...Dat
Barati	...Baraite	...Phere(t)i	...Fert
Bharet	...Baroit...	...Pheroi	...Ferat
Dadyat	...Daidhyat	...Dedoie	...Det
Third Person Plural			
Santi...	...Hente...	...(S) enti	...Sunt
Tiṣṭhanti	...Histenti	...Histanti	...Stant
Dadati	...Dadenti	...Didonti	...Dant
Bharanti	...Barenti	...Pheronti	...Ferunt
Vahanti	...Vazenti	...Ekhonti	...Vehunt

VIEW OF "DIDOMI" IN THE FUTURE TENSE

Singular

Zend		Greek.
Da-symi	...	...Do-so.
Da-saysi	...	...Do-seis
Da-syati	...	...Do-sei
Dual		
Da-syat'has	...	...Do-seton
Da-syatas	...	...Do-seton
Plural		
Da-syamas	...	...Do-somen
Da-syatha	...	...Do-sete
Da-syanti	...	...Do-sonti

SUPINES AND INFINITIVE		
Sanskrit		Latin
Sthā-tum, to stand	...	...Statum
Dā-tum, to give	...	...Datum
Jñā-tum, to know	...	...No-tum
Pātum, to drink	...	...Potum
E-tum, to go	...	...Itum
Stra-tum, to stew	...	...Stratum
Aṅk-tum, to anoint	...	...Unctum
Svani-tum, to sound	...	...Son-i-tum
Sarp-tum, to go	...	...Serptum
Vami-tum, to vomit	...	...Vomitum
Pesh-tum, to bruise	...	...Pistum
Jani-tum, to beget	...	...Gen-i-tum

Mr. Boop[1] says that at one time Sanskrit was the one language spoken all over the world.

Louis Jacoliot[2] says that Sanskrit is the original source of all the European languages of the present day.

Miss Carpenter[3] says that though the original home of Sanskrit is Āryāvartta, yet it has now been proved to have been the language of most of the countries of modern Europe in ancient times.

A German critic says that "Sanskrit is the mother of Greek, Latin and German languages and that it has no other relation to them: this is the reason why Max Müller calls it the ancient language of the Aryas."

1 *Edinborough Review*, Vol. XXXIII, p. 43

2 *Bible in India*

3 *Journal of the Indian Association.*

The great antiquity of Indian civilisation is unquestionably beyond comparison, and the antiquarians are unanimous as to the incomparable antiquity of the Sanskrit literature also. The oldest writings of the oldest nations except the Hindus are, according to some Orientalists, the records of various developments of Buddhism which took its rise in India after the decline of the Vedic religion. Count Bjornstjerna[1] says, "The so-called Hermes Scriptures (the names of all the sacred writings of the Egyptians) contain metaphysical treatises in the form of dialogue between Hermes (Spiritual wisdom) and Todh, Bodh, Buddh (earthly wisdom), which throughout exhibit the doctrines of Buddhism." Again, "the early Egyptian writing which in the translation is called *Pimander's Hermes Trismegistus*, and forms a dialogue between Pimander (the highest intelligence) and Thodt, (Bodha, Buddha) which develops the metaphysics of the Buddhists touching the trinity."

Mr. Weber says, "While the claims of the written records of Indian literature to a high antiquity are thus indisputably proved by external geographical testimony, the internal evidence in the same direction, which may be gathered from their contents is no less conclusive."[2]

---

[1] *Theogony of the Hindus*, p. 110
[2] Weber's *Indian Literature*, p. 5

3.1. ART OF WRITING

This introduces us to the important literary question as regards the art of writing in Ancient India. Apart from Mr. Weber's acceptance of "the claims of the written records of Indian literature to a high antiquity," Professor Wilson says, "The Hindus have been in possession of that (writing) as long as of a literature."[1]

Professor Heeren says, "Everything concurs to establish the fact that alphabetical writing was known in India from the earliest times, and that its use was not confined to inscriptions but extended. also to every purpose of common life."[2] Bjornstjerna says that the Hindus possessed "written books of religion" before 2800 B.C., or 800 years before Abraham.[3] Professors Goldstucker, Bohtlingk, Witney and Roth hold that the authors of the *Prātiśākhyas* must have had written texts before them.[4]

Considering the backwardness of other nations in the invention of the art of writing, and finding it impossible to give the second place to the nation to whom they owe all their learning and wisdom, the advocates of the theory of "Greek Culture" hesitate to assign high antiquity to the Hindu art of writing.

Professor Max Müller, for one, allows no written work before 350 B.C. This strange and absurd supposition is wholly inexplicable. Apart from the internal and direct evidence, one fact alone is sufficient to refute the supposition. When geometry and astronomy flourished so highly' and extensively in India more than 3,000 years before Christ, according to the calculation of the celebrated astronomer, Bailly, is it at all conceivable that writing should have been unknown before 350 B.C.? Professor Max

---

[1] Mill's *India*, Vol. II, p. 49, footnote.

[2] Hereen's *Historical Researches*, vol. II, p. 202

[3] *Theogony of the Hindus*, p. 26

[4] Weber's *Indian Literature*, p. 22, footnote.

Dunker says that according to Max Müller's theory the Brāhmaṇas must have been retained in memory till 350 B.C., but "it seems to me," he says, "quite impossible considering their form." He adds, "If the Brāhmaṇas which cite the Vedas accurately in their present arrangement, and speak not only of syllables but of letters arose between 800 and 600'B.C., it appears to me an inevitable conclusion that the Vedas must have been existing in writing about 800 B.C."[1]

Mr. Shyamji Krishna Varma, Oriental Lecturer of Balliol College, Oxford, in the paper he read before the International Congress of Orientalists at Leiden in 1883, which he attended as the delegate of the Government of India, has dealt with the subject in a masterly way, and shown that the art of writing has been in use in India since the Vedic times. He says, "I feel no hesitation in saying that, there are words and phrases – occurring in the *Saṁhitas* of the Vedas,[2] in the *Brāhmaṇas* and in the *Sūtra*

---

[1] For further particulars see his *History of Antiquity*, Vol. IV, pp. 156-157.

[2] To the objection that the word *Śruti*, as a synonym of Veda. conveyed the idea of what was learnt and taught by hearing, thus proving the absence of written books, he neatly replies that the word *Smṛti*, derived from *Smṛ*, to remember (as *Śruti* comes from *Śru* to hear), would equally convey the same idea and prove the same thing, though it is admitted by all that the art of writing was known to the authors of the *Smṛtis.* After quoting a part of a hymn in the 10th *Maṇḍala* of the *Ṛgveda*, some on seeing the speech does not see it, while another hearing does not hear it,'' and showing that one could not see the speech unless it assumed some tangible shape like that of a book or manuscript; also, that one could not possibly count a million without an acquaintance with writing, not to speak of having technical names for a million, a hundred million, nay, for a hundred thousand million, as we find them given in the seventh Chapter of the white *Yajurveda* –for we find that in Greece before writing became known. the highest number of what could be technically expressed was only 10,000 and in Rome only a

works, which leave no doubt as to the use of the written characters in ancient India. It may be confidently asserted that the systematic treatises in prose which abounded at and long before the time of Pāṇini could never have been composed without the help of writing. We know for certain that with the exception of the hymns of the *Ṛgveda*, most of the Vedic works are in prose, and it is difficult to understand how they could possibly have been composed without having recourse to some artificial means."

Kātyāyana says: यत्रपवत्वमपत्रो लेखकः सहसादिभिः "When the writer and the witnesses are dead." Yājñavalkya mentions written documents, and Nārada and others also bear testimony to their existence. Even Max Müller himself is compelled to admit that "writing was known to the authors of the *Sūtras.*"

The supposition that writing was unknown in India before 350 B.C. is only one of the many instances calculated to show the strange waywardness of human intellect. If anyone of lesser authority than Max Müller had advanced such a supposition he might have been pronounced a maniac. It was left to the learned Professor to conceive the possibility of a language of the structure of Sanskrit being cultivated to the extent of producing compositions like the

---

thousand – he goes on to show that the words 'Kāṇḍa and Patala' which occur in Vedic literature prove the existence of written books in ancient times. After pointing out that the *Adhikāra*, or heading rule, in Pāṇini's grammar was denoted by Svarita, which proved conclusively that he employed writing and that the sixth chapter of *Aṣṭādhyāyī* says that people in Pāṇini's time used to mark the figures eight and five on the ears of their cattle, he concludes: 'The fact that Pāṇini makes allusion to coins, for instance निष्क and रूप्य, with which latter perhaps the word 'rupee' is connected, and that he actually mentions the two words लिपि and लिबि, both meaning writing, affords palpable proof of his acquaintance with the art of writing, without which. as I have said, he could never have produced his great grammar.

Vedas, the *Brāhmaṇas* and the *Upaniṣads*, and of a people achieving wonderful progress in mathematics and astronomy without being able to write A, B, C, or one, two and three!!![1]

The extraordinary vocal powers of the Hindus, combined with their wonderful inventive genius, produced a language which, when fully developed, was commensurate with their marvellous intellectual faculties, and which contributed materially to the creation of a literature unparalleled for richness, sublimity and range. The peculiar beauties inherent in the offspring of such high intellectual powers were greatly enhanced by its scientific upbringing and by constant and assiduous exercise it has developed into what is now such a model of perfection as to well-deserved the name of *Devavāṇī*, or "the language of the gods." The very excellence of the language and the scientific character of its structure have led some good people to doubt if this polished and learned language could ever have been the vernacular of any people. Fully realising the significance of the fact that, with all their boast of the highest civilisation and culture, they possess a language highly defective and irregular when compared to the Sanskrit; these critics find it difficult to believe that the Hindus ever spoke that perfect language.

Mr. Shyamji Krishna Varma, in the learned paper on the subject he read before the International Congress of Orientalists at Berlin, on 14th September 1881, demolishes all the arguments advanced against the Sanskrit language had ever been a spoken vernacular of India. and proves that not

---

[1] *Ancient Sanskrit Literature*, p. 523, The Greeks praise the beauty of the writing of Indians. See *Strabo*, Lib. XV, p. 493. Megasthenes says that 'the Hindus used letters for inscriptions on mile-stones, indicating the resting places and distances.' Curtius also says that 'the Indians wrote on soft rind of trees.' Nearchus mentions that 'the Indians wrote letters on cotton that had been well beaten together.' Father Pautino says that 'cotton paper was used in India before the Christian era. *Historical Researches*, Vol. II, p.107

only was "Sanskrit, as we find settled in the *Aṣṭādhyāyī* of Pāṇini, the spoken vernacular at the time when that grammarian flourished," but that "it is at present extensively used as a medium of conversation and correspondence among learned men in all parts of India, from Kashmir to Cape Comorin."

Professor Max Müller says, "Yet such is the marvellous continuity between the past and the present in India, that in spite of repeated social convulsions, religious reforms and foreign invasions, Sanskrit may be said to be still the only language that is spoken over the whole extent of the vast country." He adds, "Even at the present moment, after a century of English rule and English teaching, I believe that Sanskrit is more widely understood in India than Latin was in Europe at the time of Dante."[1]

Who after this can say that Sanskrit was or is a dead language?

---

[1] *India : What can it teach us*? pp. 78, 79

3.2. THE VEDIC LITERATURE

Veil after veil will-lift- but there must be
Veil upon veil behind

Buddha's Sermon[1]

Professor Max Müller says, "The Vedic literature opens to us a chapter in what has been called the education of the human race, to which we can find no parallel anywhere else."[2]

The Vedic literature consists of (I) The Vedas, (2) The *Brāhmaṇas*, (3) The *Sūtras.* The Vedas are four in number and are called the *Ṛgveda*, the *Yajurveda*, the *Atharvaveda*, and the *Sāmaveda.* The *Ṛgveda* and the *Yajurveda* are the most important of the Vedas, as they respectively deal with the knowledge of things physical, mental and spiritual and the application of that knowledge.

The Vedas are universally admitted to be not only by far the most important work in the Sanskrit language but the greatest work in all literature.

It is nothing short of a miracle that while important works in almost all departments of human learning that were cultivated in ancient India have perished, the most important of them all, the Vedas, the fountainhead of all knowledge and the parent of all literature and science, have come down to us secure and intact. While most of the important Sanskrit works from *Manusmṛti*, the most ancient code of law in the world, to the Rama yana and the Mahābhārata have been tampered with. The Vedas, by the very inimitable grandeur of their language, and the unequalled sublimity of their contents have defied all attempts at interpolation. As, however, the study of the Vedas has long been neglected and a thorough knowledge of the *Sūtras* and *Vedāṅgas* by which

---

1 *Light of Asia*, p. 21

2 *India : What can it teach us*? P. 89

alone the Vedic *mantras* may be interpreted is very rare. The Vedas are rarely well understood even by the learned amongst the Hindus.

When the *Yajurveda* was presented to Voltaire, he expressed his belief that it was the most precious gift for which the West had been ever indebted to the East.[1]

Guigault says, "The *Ṛgveda* is the most sublime conception of the great highways of humanity."

Mons. Leon Delbos speaks enthusiastically of the grandeur and sublimity of the Vedas. "There is no monument of Greece or Rome," he asserts "more precious than the *Ṛgveda*."[2]

Professor Max Müller says, "In the history of the world, the Veda fills a gap which no literary work in any other language could fill."[3] He also says, "I maintain that to everybody who cares for himself, for his ancestors, for his history, for his intellectual development, a study of Vedic literature is indispensable."[4] The Hindus hold the Vedas to be the Revelation, and its study accordingly is indispensable to every man.

The Vedas are admittedly the oldest books in the world. "The age of this venerable hymnal (*Ṛgveda*)," says Sir W.W. Hunter, "is unknown." "They (the Vedas) are the oldest of books in the library of mankind," says Professor Max Müller. "They are without doubt," says Professor Heeren, "The eldest works composed in the Sanskrit."[5] Even the most ancient Sanskrit writings allow the Vedas as already existing." No country except India and no language

---

[1] Wilson's Essays, Vol. III. P. 304

[2] Mons. Leon Delbos's paper on the Vedas read before the International Literary Association at Paris, on 14th July 1884, the venerable Victor Hugo being in this chair.

[3] Wilson's Essays, Vol. III, p. 339

[4] Max Müller's *India: What can it teach us*?. P.121

[5] *Historical Researches*, Vol. II, p. 146

except the Sanskrit can boast of a possession so ancient or venerable. No nation except the Hindus can pretend to stand before the world with such a sacred heirloom in its possession, unapproachable in grandeur and infinitely above all in glory. The Vedas stand alone in their solitary splendour, serving as a beacon of divine light for the onward march of humanity.

The Hindus hold that the Vedas contain the germs of all knowledge and that their teachings are in complete consonance with the doctrines of true science.[1] The late lamented P. Guru Datta of Lahore attempted to interpret a few mantras of the *Ṛgveda* on the strength of Swami Dayanand Sarasvati's commentary on the Vedas. The result was astonishing. Interpreting the *mantra* of the second *Sūkta* of *Ṛgveda* (1.2.17) —

मित्रं हुवे पूतदक्षं वरुणं च रिशादसम्। धियं घृताचीं साधन्ता।।

P. Guru Datta says, "This *mantra* describes the (*dhiyam*) process, or steps whereby the well-known of liquids, water, can be formed by the combination of two other substances (*ghṛtācīm sādhantā*). The word *sādhantā* is in the dual

---

[1] See P. Guru Datta's Vedic Texts, No.2, printed at the Virjanand Press, Labore. Those who read their own historical theories in the Vedas will do well to consider the words of Professor Barth. After pointing out some of the metaphysical theories contained in the Vedas he proceeds : 'These alone are sufficient to prove, if necessary, how profoundly sacredotal this poetry is, and they ought to have suggested" reflections to those who have affected to see in it only the work of primitive shepherds celebrating the praises of their gods as they lead their flocks to the pasture' Barth's. *Religions of India*, p. 38.
Professor Thielve of Leyden, too, expresses the same opinion, only more strongly in *Theologische Tijdochrift* for July 1880. As Professor Max Müller admits, the Europeans are still on the mere surface of Vedic literature,' and must not reject it as useless if they do not find in it corroboration of their preconceived theories of anthropology and sociology. See *India: What can it teach us* ? p. 113.

number indicating that it is two elementary bodies which combine to form water. What those two elementary substances according to this *mantra* are, is not a matter of least importance to determine. The words used to indicate those two substances are *Mitra* and *Varuṇa.*

"The first literal meaning of *Mitra*[1] is measurer. The name is given to a substance that stands, as it were, as a measurer or as a standard substance. It is the measurer of density, or of value, otherwise known as quantivalence. The other meaning of *Mitra* is 'associate.' Now in this *mantra, Mitra* is described as an associate of *Varuṇa*[2]. It will be shown how *Varuṇa* indicates oxygen gas[3]. Now it is well-known that hydrogen is not only the lightest element known, nor is it only monovalent, but that it has a strong affinity for oxygen; hence it is that it is described as an associate of *Varuṇa.* Many other analogies in the properties of *Mitra* and hydrogen go on to suggest that what is in Vedic terms styled as mitra is, in fact, identical with hydrogen. *Mitra,* for instance, occurs as synonymous with *udāna* in many parts of the Vedas, and *udāna* is well characterized by its lightness or by its power to lift up.

"The second element with which we are concerned is *Varuṇa. Varuṇa* is the substance that is acceptable to all. It is the element that every living being needs to live. Its well-known property is *riṣādaḥ*, i.e., it eats away or rusts all the base metals, it burns all the bones, etc, and physiologically purifies the blood by oxidising it and thereby keeping the

---

[1] The word *Mitra* is formed by adding the *uṇādi* suffix *kra* to the root, *mi*, according to the *sūtra* अमिचिमिशसिभ्यः क्रा।। उणा0 4. 164. The meaning is मिनोतोमान्यं करोतिमित्रं or one that measures or stands as a standard of reference.

[2] *Varuṇa* is formed by adding *uṇādi* suffix *unan* to root *vṛ* to accept कृवृदारिभ्य उनन्।। 53।। Hence it means that which is acceptable to all or seeks all.

[3] Again, we have in *Nighaṇṭu*, the Vedic Dictionary, Chapter V. Section 4, मित्र इति पदनामसु पठितम्।। Hence *Mitra* means that which approaches or seeks association with other.

frame alive. It is by these properties that *Varuṇa* is in general distinguished; but it is especially characterised here as *riṣādaḥ*. No one can fail to perceive that the substance thus distinctly characterised is oxygen gas.

"Another word used in the *mantra* is *puta dakṣam*. *Puta* is pure, free from impurities. *Dakṣa* means energy. *Dakṣam* is a substance pure possessed of kinetic energy. Who that is acquainted with the kinetic theory of gases cannot see in *puta dakṣa* the properties of a gas highly heated?

"The meaning of the *mantra* taken as a whole is this. Let one who is desirous to form water by the combination of two substances take pure hydrogen gas highly heated and oxygen gas possessed of the properties *riṣādaḥ*, and let him combine them to form water."

The *Brāhmaṇas*, too, are sometimes held by the ignorant to be part of the Vedas: but as Professor Weber says, "Strictly speaking, only the *Saṅhitas* are Vedas." The Brāhmaṇas are either commentaries on the Vedas or philosophical disquisitions based on them.

Of the period when these *Brāhmaṇas* were composed, Professor Weber says, "We have here a copy of the period when *Brāhmaṇas* with lively emulation carry on their enquiries into the highest questions the human mind can propound; women with enthusiastic ardour plunge into mysteries of speculation, impressing and astonishing men by the depth and loftiness of their opinion, and who solve the questions proposed to them on sacred subjects."[1]

The *Brāhmaṇas*, composed by some of the wisest sages of the ancient world, though not enjoying the authority of the Vedas are of the highest value to the student of the Vedic literature.

The *Sūtras* are divided into

(1) *Sikṣā* (phonetic directory)

---

[1] Weber's *Indian Literature*, p. 22

(2) *Chanda* (metre)
(3) *Vyākaraṇa* (grammar)
(4) *Nirukta* (explanation of words)
(5) *Jyotiṣa* (astronomy)
(6) *Kalpa* (ceremonial)

This division will show that the study of language was cultivated by the Hindus from the earliest times on scientific principles.

Speaking of the *Prātiśākhya* (a sub-division of *Sikṣā*) of the white *Yājuṣ*. Professor H.H. Wilson says, "Such laborious minutiae and elaborate subtleties relating to the enunciation of human speech are not to be met with in the literature of any other nation."[1]

Professor Wilson again says, "It is well known how long it took before the Greeks arrived at a complete nomenclature for the parts of speech. Plato only knew of noun and verb as the two component parts of speech, and, for philosophical purposes, Aristotle, too, did not go beyond that number. It is only in discussing the rules of rhetoric that he is led to the admission of two more parts of speech – conjunctions and articles. The pronoun does not come in before Zenodotus, and the preposition occurs first in Aristarchos. In the *Prātiśākhya*, on the contrary, we meet at once with the following exhaustive classification of the parts of speech."[2]

Mr. Alexander Thomson, the late talented and able Principal of the Agra College, and one of the best philologists in India used to say that the consonantal division of the alphabet of the Sanskrit language was a more wonderful feat of human genius than any the world has yet seen. Even now the Europeans are far behind the Hindus in this respect. Professor Macdonell says, "We Europeans, 2,500 years later, and in a scientific age, still employ an alphabet which is not only inadequate to represent all the

---

[1] Wilson's *Essay on Sanskrit Literature*, Vol. III, p. 317

[2] Wilson's *Essay on Sanskrit Literature*, Vol. III, p. 321, (3rd edition)

sounds of our language, but even preserves the random order in which vowels and consonants are jumbled up as they were in the Greek adaptation of the primitive Semitic arrangement of 3,000 years ago."[1]

Rev. Mr. Ward says, "In philology, the Hindus have, perhaps, excelled both the ancients (Greeks and Romans) and the moderns."[2]

Professor Max Müller says, "The idea of reducing a whole language to a small number of roots, which in Europe was not attempted before the sixteenth century by Henry Estienne, was perfectly familiar to the *Brāhmaṇas* at least 500 years before Christ."[3]

"The science of language, indeed," says Sir W.W. Hunter, "had been reduced in India to fundamental principles at a time when the grammarians of the West still treated it as accidental resemblances."[4]

Another branch of the science of language, the grammatical treatment of it, was cultivated to a degree which not only defies comparison but is unique in the annals of literature. The most eminent Indian grammarian, *Pāṇini* Muni, sits on the hallowed throne of unrivalled literary reputation, having achieved the most perfect work of its kind of which the human mind is capable. Professor Weber speaks in rapturous terms of *Pāṇini's* achievement. He says, "We pass at once into the magnificent edifice which bears the name of *Pāṇini* as its architect, and which justly commands the wonder and admiration of everyone who enters, and which, by the very fact of its sufficing for all the phenomena which language presents, bespeaks at once the

---

[1] *History of Hindu Chemistry*, Vol. I, p. 25

[2] *Mythology of the Hindus.*

[3] Max Müller's *Lectures on the Science of Language*, p.80. For H. Estienne, see Sir John Stoddart, Glossology.

[4] *Imperial Gazetteer*, 'India,' p. 214

marvellous ingenuity of its inventor and his profound penetration of the entire material of the language."[1]

Sir W. Hunter says, "The grammar of *Pāṇini* stands supreme among the grammars of the world, alike for its precision of statement and for its thorough analysis of the roots of the language and of the formative principles of words. By applying an algebraical terminology, it attains a sharp succinctness unrivalled in brevity, but at times enigmatical. It arranges in logical harmony the whole phenomena which the Sanskrit language presents and stands forth as one of the most splendid achievements of human invention and industry. So elaborate is the structure that doubts have arisen whether its innumerable rules of formation and phonetic change, its polysyllabic derivatives, its ten conjugations with its multiform aorists and long array of tenses could ever have been the spoken language of a people."[2]

Manning says, "The celebrated Pāṇini bequeathed to posterity one of the oldest and most renowned books ever written in any language."[3] "The scientific completeness of Sanskrit .grammar appeared to Sir W. Jones so unaccountable that he wrote about it with amazement and admiration."[4]

In Europe, generally speaking, grammatical science does not yet treat of those high principles which underlie the life and growth of language. It is not fair to Panini to compare with his *Vyākaraṇa*, the grammars of modern Europe, where

---

[1] Weber's *Indian Literature*, p. 216. Those rules (of grammar) are formed with the utmost conciseness, the consequence of very ingenious methods.' -Colebrooke on Sanskrit and Prakrit languages, Asiatic Researches, Vol. VII.

[2] *Imperial Gazetteer* of India, Art, 'India,' p. 214

[3] *Ancient and Mediaeval India*, Vol. I, p. 384

[4] *Ancient and Mediaeval India*, Vol. I, p. 379. 'The grammatical works of the Hindus are so remarkable that in their own department they are said to exceed in merit nearly all, if not all, grammatical productions of other nations.' P. 583

the grammatical science has not yet grasped those principles of the formation and development of a language, which it is the unique honour of Sanskrit grammars to classify and explain.

Mrs. Manning says, "Sanskrit grammar is evidently far 'superior to the kind of grammar which for the most part has contented grammarians in Europe."[1]

"*Vyākaraṇa*," says the same authoress, "was not merely grammar in the lower acceptation of being an explanation of declension, conjugation and other grammatical forms, but was from its commencement a scientific grammar or grammatical science in the highest sense which can be attributed to this term."[2]

Mr. Elphinstone says, "His works (Pāṇini's) and those of his successors have established a system of grammar, the most complete that ever was employed in arranging elements of human speech."[3]

Professor Max Müller says, "Their (Indians) achievements in grammatical analysis are still unsurpassed in the grammatical literature of any nation."

"Pāṇini, Kātyāyana, and Patañjali, are the canonical triad of grammarians of India," and, to quote Mrs. Manning once more, "such (grammatical) works are originated as are unrivalled in the literary history of other nations."[4]

Mr. Ward says, "Their grammars are very numerous, and reflect the highest credit on the ingenuity of their authors."[5]

---

[1] *Ancient and Mediaveval India*, Vol. I, p. 381

[2] See Glodstucker's *Pāṇini*, p. 196. *Vyākaraṇa*=undoing or analysis.

[3] Elphinstone's *History of India*, p. 146

[4] *Ancient and Mediaeval History of India*, Vol. I, p. 381. 'Hindu grammarians have been engaged in the solution of interesting problems from times immemorial.' p. 381

[5] Ward's *Mythology of the Hindus*

Professor Sir Monier Williams remarks, "The grammar of Pāṇini is one of the most remarkable literary works that the world has ever seen, and no other country can produce any grammatical system at all comparable to it, either for originality of plan or analytical subtlety." The Professor again says, "His *Sāstras* are a perfect miracle of condensation."[1]

A commentary on Pāṇini's grammar was written by Katyayana, author of *Vārttikas.* He was reviewed by Patañjali, who wrote the *Mahābhāṣya*, which is, according to Professor Sir Monier Williams, "one of the most wonderful grammatical works that the genius of any country has ever produced.

The following grammarians are said to have preceded Pāṇini, Āpiśali, Kaśypa, Gārgya, Gālava, Sakravarmana, Bharadvāja, Sākaṭāyana, Sākalya, Senaka, and Sphoṭāyana.

As regards lexicons, the Reverend Mr. Ward says, "Their dictionaries also do the highest credit to the Hindu learned men, and prove how highly the Sanskrit was cultivated in former periods."

---

[1] *Indian Wisdom.* p. 172

3.3. POETRY

Blessings be with them and eternal praise,
The poets who on earth have made us heirs
Of Truth and pure delight by heavenly lays.

Wordsworth

Count Bjornstjerna says, "Poetry rules over all in India; it has lent its forms, its colouring, and its charms ever to the most abstract sciences, yea, even to religion."[1]

Professor Max Dunker says, "The treasures of poetry in India are inexhaustible."[2] Among such a "poetical people" as the Hindus – as Professor Heeren[3] aptly terms them–poetry flourished in wonderful luxuriance, and its various branches were cultivated with marvellous success. Professor Heeren says, "The various branches of poetry, such as the narrative and the dramatic, the lyric as well as the didactic and the apologue, have all flourished in Sanskrit literature, and produced the most exceJlent results."[4]

Mr. Elphinstone says, "All who have read the heroic poems in the original are enthusiastic in their praise, and their beauties have been most felt by those whose own productions entitle their judgment to most respect. Nor is this admiration confined to critics who have peculiarly devoted themselves to Oriental literature. Milman and Schlegel vie with Wilson and Tones in their applause; and from one or other of these writers we learn the simplicity and originality of the composition; the sublimity, grace and

---

[1] *Theogony of the Hindus*, p. 80

[2] *History of Antiquity*, Vol. IV, p. 27

[3] *Hist. Researches*, Vol. II, p.186

[4] *Hist. Researches*, Vol. II. P. 147

pathos of particular passages; the natural dignity of actors; the holy purity of manners, and the inexhaustible fertility of imagination in the authors."[1]

[1] Elphinstone's *History of India*, p. 155

3.4. EPIC POETRY

And here the singer for his art: Not all in vain may plead,
The song that nerves a nation's heart, Is in itself a deed.

—Tennyson

Professor Heeren says, "The literature of the Hindus is rich in epic poetry."[1] The *Rāmāyaṇa* and the *Mahābhārata*, however, are the principal epics, the epics par excellence of India. Professor Monier Williams thus speaks of them, "Although the Hindus, like the Greeks, have only two great epic poems, namely, the *Rāmāyaṇa* and the *Mahābhārata*, yet to compare these with the Iliad or the Odyssey is to compare the Indus and the Ganges rising in the snows of the world's most colossal ranges, swollen by numerous tributaries spreading into vast shallows or branching into deep divergent channels, with the streams of Attica or the mountainous torrents of Thessaly. There is, in fact, an immensity of bulk about this, as about every other department of Sanskrit literature, which to a European, accustomed to a more limited horizon, is absolutely bewildering."[2]

Of these remarkable poems, the *Rāmāyaṇa* is the older, while the *Mahābhārata* is the larger of the two. Apart from their high poetical merits, in which they defy rivalry and discard comparison, their enormous bulk is a standing puzzle to the European critics. A comparison with other great epics of the old world will give an idea of their enormous size.

Mahābhārata has 2,20,000 lines
Rāmāyaṇa has 48,000 lines
Homer's *Iliad* has 15,693
Virgil's *Aeneid* has 9,868

---

[1] *Historical Researches*, Vol. II, p. 147

[2] *Indian Epic Poetry*, p.1

The *Iliad* and *Odyssey* together contain 30,000 lines. Schlegel calls *Rāmāyaṇa* - the noblest of epics.

"*Rāmāyaṇa*," says Professor Monier Williams, "is undoubtedly one of the greatest treasures in Sanskrit literature. Sir W. Jones says, "The *Rāmāyaṇa* is an epic poem on the story of Rama, which, in unity of action, magnificence of imagery and elegance of style far surpasses the learned and elaborate work of Nonnus."[1]

After giving the argument of the *Rāmāyaṇa*, Prof. Heeren, with his usual moderation, says, "Such, in few words, is the chief subject of *Rāmāyaṇa*, while the development and method of handling this simple argument is so remarkably rich and copious as to suffer little from a comparison in this respect with the most admired productions of the epic muse."[2]

Professor Sir M. Monier-Williams says, "There is not in the whole range of the Sanskrit literature a more charming poem than the *Rāmāyaṇa*. The classical purity, clearness and simplicity of its style, the exquisite touches to true poetic feeling with which it abounds, its graphic descriptions of heroic incidents, nature's grandest scenes, the deep acquaintance it displays with the conflicting workings and most refined emotions of the human heart, all entitle it to rank among the most beautiful compositions that have appeared at any period or in any country. It is like a spacious and delightful garden, here and there allowed to run wild, but teeming with fruits and flowers, watered by

---

[1] *Asiastic Researches*, p. 255. A writer in the *West-minister Review* for April 1868 offers *Mahābhārata* such a remote antiquity as to leave behind not only Manu but even the writings of Āśvalāyana, etc. Count Bjornastjerna dates it at 2000. B.C. Dr. Mittra points out that 'the *Mahābhārata*, in the course of its thousands of verses, nowhere alludes to Buddhism and Buddha, and must therefore, and on other grounds not worth naming here, date from before the birth of Sākya.' *The Indo Aryans*, Vol. I, p. 38.

[2] Heeren's *Historical Researches*, Vol. II, p. 194

perennial streams, and even its most tangled jungle intersected with delightful pathways. The character of Rama is nobly portrayed. It is only too consistently unselfish to be human. We must, in fact, bear in mind that he is half a god, yet though occasionally dazzled by flashes from his superior nature, we are not often blinded or bewildered by it. At least in the earlier portion of the poem he is not generally represented as more than a heroic, noble-minded, pious, virtuous man, whose bravery, unselfish generosity, filial obedience, tender, attachment to his wife, love for his brothers and freedom from all resentful feelings, we can appreciate and admire. When he falls a victim to the spite of his father's second wife, he cherishes no sense of wrong. When his father decides on banishing him, not a murmur escapes his lips. In noble language, he expresses his resolution to sacrifice himself rather than allow his parent to break his pledged word. As to Sita, she is a paragon of domestic virtues."[1]

Sita is the noblest ideal of a woman., Her noble and calm devotion to her lord, her unbounded love, her exalted conception of the eternal, nay, divine relation of a wife to her husband are ideals unparalleled for loftiness and sublimity in any language or literature. What can be more noble than her address to Rama when she pleads for permission to accompany him into banishment?

A wife must share her husband's fate. My Duty is to follow thee

Wherever thou goest. Apart from thee, I would not dwell in heaven itself

Deserted by her lord, a wife is like a miserable corpse.

Close as the shadow would I cleave to thee in this life and hereafter.

Thou art my king, my guide, my only refuge, my divinity.

---

[1] *Indian Epic Poetry*, p. 12

It is my fixed resolve to follow thee. If thou must wander forth.

Through thorny trackless forests, I will go before thee treading down.

The prickly brambles to make smooth thy path. Walking before thee.

Shall feel no weariness: the forest thorns will seem like silken robes.

The bed of leaves a couch of down. To me the shelter of thy presence.

Is better far than stately palaces and paradise itself.

Protected by thy arm, gods, demons, men shall have no power to harm me

With thee I'll live contentedly on roots and fruits. Sweet or not sweet.

If given by thy hand, they will to me be like the food of life.

Roaming with thee in desert wastes, a thousand years will be a day;

Dwelling with thee, e'en hell itself should be to me a heaven of bliss.

"Juliet," says Prof. Dowden, "is but a passionate girl before this perfect woman," meaning, Brutus' Portia, but what becomes of Portia herself before this heavenly woman, this ethereal being, this celestial Sita?

As for Rama, his character simply stands unrivalled in all literature, ancient or modern, Asiatic or European.

Principal Griffith says, "Well may the *Rāmāyaṇa* challenge the literature of every age and country to produce a poem that can boast of such perfect characters as a Rama and a Sita." He adds, "Nowhere else are poetry and morality so charmingly united, each elevating the other as in this really holy poem."

Miss Mary Scott says, "The *Rāmāyaṇa* is full of poetry, and Sita one of the sweetest types of womanhood that I have ever read."[1]

As for the *Mahābhārata*, Professor Herren says, "It will scarcely be possible to deny the *Mahābhārata* to be one of the richest compositions in Epic poetry that was ever produced."[2]

Dr. F.A. Hassler of America thus waxes eloquent in praise of the *Mahābhārata*, "In all my experience in life, I have not found a work that has interested me as much as that noble production of the wise, and I do not hesitate to say, inspired men of ancient India. In fact, I have studied it more than any other work for a long time past, and have made at least 1,000 notes which I have arranged in alphabetical order for the purpose of the study. The *Mahābhārata* has opened to me, as it were, a new world, and I have been surprised beyond measure at the wisdom, truth, knowledge, and love of the right which I have found displayed in its pages. Not only so, but I have found many of the truths which my own heart has taught me in regard to the Supreme Being and His creations set forth in beautiful, clear language.[3]

The Hamilton Daily Spectator (May 31st, 1888) thus speaks of the *Mahābhārata,* "This poem is really a series of religious, moral, metaphysical, philosophic and political disquisitions strung upon a thread of the narrative. This not only gives to the modern world a living picture of Indian life, morals, manners, politics, religion and philosophy as they existed more than 2,000 years ago, but they transmit to us some of the most sublime poetry and some of the deepest

---

[1] Letter to P.C. Roy, dated London, the 8th December, 1883

[2] *Historical Researches*, Vol. II, p. 164

[3] Letter to P.C. Roy, dated 21st July, 1888. See Roy's *Mahābhārata*.

and noblest thoughts that have ever been given to the world."

Krishna, the greatest politician of the world, says:

"The wise grieve not for the departed', nor for those who yet survive.

Ne'er was the time when I was not, nor thou, nor yonder Chiefs, and ne'er

Shall be the time when all of us shall be not; as the unbodied soul

In this corporeal frame moves swiftly on through boyhood, youth & age,

So will It pass through other forms hereafter–be not grieved thereat?

The man whom pain and pleasure, heat and cold affect not, he is fit

For immortality: that which is not cannot be – and that which is

Can never cease to be Know this: the being that spread this universe

Is indestructible; who can destroy the Indestructible?

Bodies that enclose the everlasting soul, inscrutable.

Immortal have an end–but he who thinks the soul can be destroyed,

And he who deems it a destroyer, are alike mistaken: it

Kills not, and is not killed; it is not born, nor doth it ever die;

It has no past nor future-unproduced, unchanging, infinite: he

Who knows it fixed. unborn, imperishable, indissoluble,

How can that man destroy another, or extinguish aught below?

As men abandon old and threadbare: clothes to put on others new,

So casts the embodied soul its worn out frame to enter other forms.

No dart can pierce it; flame cannot consume it, water wet it not,

Nor scorching breezes dry it: indestructible, incapable

Of heat or moisture or aridity–eternal, all-pervading,
Steadfast, immovable; perpetual, yet imperceptible,
Incomprehensible, unfading, deathless, unimaginable."

Miss Mary Scott says, "The characters are splendidly portrayed. It is a thoroughly martial poem, and one can enter into the battles between the Pandus and Kurus." Professor Sylvian Levi of Paris says, "The *Mahābhārata* is not only the largest, but also the grandest of all epics, as it contains throughout a lively teaching of morals under a glorious garment of poetry."[1]

The American ethnologist, Jeremiah Curtin, writing to Babu P.C. Roy, the enterprising publisher of an English translation of the *Mahābhārata*, says, "1 have just finished reading carefully from beginning to end, 24 numbers of your translation of the *Mahābhārata*, and can honestly say that I have never obtained more pleasure from reading any book in my life.[2] The *Mahābhārata* will open the eyes of the world to the true character and intellectual rank of the Aryans of India. You are certainly doing a great work, not only for Hindustan, but for the Aryan race in other countries. The *Mahābhārata* is a real mine of wealth not entirely known, I suppose, at present to any man outside your country, but which will be known in time and valued in all civilized lands for the reason that it contains information of the highest import to all men who seek to know in singleness of heart, the history of our race upon the earth, and the relations of man with the Infinite Power above us, around us and in us."

Saint Hilaire Bartholemy thus speaks of the *Mahābhārata* in the *Journal Des Savantes* of September 1886: "When a century ago (1785) Mr. Wilkins published in Calcutta an extract from the grand poem (*Mahābhārata*), and made it known through the episode of the *Bhagvadgītā*, the world was dazzled with its magnificence. Vyasa, the reputed author of the *Mahābhārata*, appeared greater than even

---

[1] Letter to P.C. Roy, dated the 17th March 1888.

[2] See Roy's Translation of *Mahābhārata*, part XXX

Homer, and it required a very little indeed to induce people to place India above Greece. It has not the less been admitted that this prodigious Hindu epic is one of the grandest monuments of its kind of human intelligence and genius."

The Watertown Post (Tuesday, June 22, 1886), calls *Mahābhārata*, "one of the most wonderful poems of which we have any record," and says, "The poem is the *Mahābhārata*, the oldest, the most voluminous, and, according to Wheeler, the historian of India, the most valuable epic in any language. It consists of some 2,20,000 lines, is fourteen times longer than the *Iliad*."

Sir Edwin Arnold, in his "Indian Idylls," claims for parts of it "an origin anterior to writing; anterior to Puranic theology, anterior to Homer, perhaps to Moses." He further says, .'What truer conception of a wife than this, written more than three thousand years ago: "She is a true wife who is skilful in household affairs: she is a true wife whose heart is devoted to her lord; she is a true wife who knoweth none but her lord. The wife is man's half: the wife is the first of friends: the wife is the root of salvation. They that have wives have the means of being cheerful: they that have wives can achieve good fortune. Sweet-speeched wives' are as friends on occasions of joy: they are as mothers in hours of sickness and woe. A wife, therefore, is one's most valuable possession. No man even in anger should ever do anything that is disagreeable to his wife, seeing that happiness, joy and virtue, everything depended on the wife," and concludes by saying, "we may well accept this great poem as one of the priceless possessions of the East."

Mr. Titus Munson Coan, in the *New York Times* (4th March 1888), says, "The Hindu epics have a nearer significance for us than anything in the Norse mythology. The *Mahābhārata*, one of the longest of these poems, has a wider romantic element in it than King Frithiof's Saga; its action is cast upon a grander scale, and its heroes belittle all others in mythology. The Hindu poems, early though they are, contain ethical and human elements that are unknown to the Norseman. It is in this that their enduring and growing interest remains for the mind of Europe and of America."

The Hamilton Daily Spectator of 31st May 1888, after speaking of the *Rāmāyaṇa* and the. *Mahābhārata* as "immoral works," says that the great epic of India, "*Mahābhārata*, is the longest and in some respects, the greatest of all epic poems."

Mon. A. Barth says, "Some portions of the *Mahābhārata* may well compare with the purest and most beautiful productions of human genius.[1] The *Rāmāyaṇa* is three times as large as Homer's Iliad, and the *Mahābhārata* four times as large as the Ramayana. Homer's Iliad and *Odyssey* have thirty thousand lines, the *Mahābhārata* has two hundred and twenty thousand lines, and, in addition, a supplement of sixteen thousand three hundred and seventy-four couplets. But it is not in size alone that the sacred epics of Vālmīki and Vyāsa excel. They enchant by the wondrous story they tell of ancient Aryan life, faith and valour. There is also a lively teaching of morals under a glorious garment of poetry." "Matchless vivacity, unsurpassable tender and touching episodes, and a perfect storehouse of national antiquities. literature and ethics."[2]

Speaking of a certain part of the *Mahābhārata*, a critic says, "We know of no episode, even in Homeric poems, which can surpass its grandeur or raise a more solemn dirge over the desolation of the fallen heart of men."[3]

---

[1] *Revue De L' Historic Des Religions.* Faris 1889, p.38

[2] *The Montreal Herald*, (Thursday, Nov. 12th, 1891). Trubner's American. European and Oriental Literary Record, new Series, Vol. VII, No.3, speaks of the *Mahābhārata* as 'the wonderful epic,' and regrets 'how little has up to the present been done to unrarvel the mysteries it contains, or ever to smooth a path leading to its golden treasures!'

[3] *The Westminister Review* for October 1842. 'Many of its (*Mahābhārata*'s) episodes of themselves would make perfect

The characters of the five Pāṇḍavas, of Kṛṣṇa, Duryodhana, Droṇa, Bhiṣma and Karṇa, are drawn with a true poetic feeling "and with much artistic delicacy of touch." Yudhiṣṭhira, Arjuna, Bhima, are portraits worthy of the highest poets, and can only be drawn by men of extraordinary imagination, and by soaring intellects as Vyasa.

Perfection is a merit known only to the Hindus. "A European poet would have brought the story to an end" after the termination of the war in favour of the Pāṇḍavas, but "the Sanskrit poet has a far deeper insight into man's nature," and would not end there, to the dissatisfaction of the reader, but would wind up the story and end with the translation of the Pāṇḍavas to Heaven.

"There are many graphical passages," says Professor M. Williams, "in the *Rāmāyaṇa* and *Mahābhārata*, which for beauty of description, cannot be surpassed by anything iIi Homer,... that the diction of Indian epics is more polished, regular and cultivated, and the language altogether in a more advanced stage of development than that of Homer." Then, as to the description of scenery,[1] in which Hindu poets are certainly more graphic and picturesque than either Greek or Latin... he adds, "Yet there are not wanting indications in the Indian epics of a higher degree of cultivation than that represented in the Homeric poems. The battlefields of the *Rāmāyaṇa* and the *Mahābhārata* are not made barbarous by wanton cruelties, and the description of Ayodhya and Lanka imply far greater luxury and refinement than those of Sparta and Troy." *Rāmāyaṇa* and *Mahābhārata* rise above the

---

poems of the first grade and would stand comparison with any European poems. There is a touching episode, full of true poetic felling, in *Ādiparva* 6104, called *Bakabadha*, as there are a thousand other.' Monier williams' *Epic Poetry of India*.

[1] 'In Homer, the description of scenery and natural objects are too short and general to be really picturesque. Twining says that the Greek poets did not look upon Nature with a painter's eye.'

Monier Williams, *Indian Epic Poetry*.

Homeric poems also in the fact "that a deep religious meaning appears to underlie all the narrative, and that the wildest allegory may be intended to conceal a sublime moral, symbolizing the conflict between good and evil, teaching the hopelessness of victory in so terrible a contest with purity of soul, self-abnegation and the subjugation of the passions."[1]

Mr. Herbert Spencer, the greatest of the modern European thinkers, condemns the Iliad among other things for the reason "that the subject matter appeals continually to brutal passions and the instincts of the savage."[2]

Sir Monier Williams says, 'And in exhibiting pictures of domestic life and manners, the Sanskrit epics are even more valuable than the Greek and Roman. In the delineation of women, the Hindu poet throws aside all exaggerated colouring and draws from Nature. Kaikeyi, Mandodari, Kausalya, and even Manthra, are all drawn to the very life. Sita, Draupadi, and Damayanti engage our affections far more than Helen or even that Penelope. Indeed, Hindu wives[3] are generally perfect patterns of conjugal fidelity: nor can it be doubted that in these delightful portraits of the *pativratā*, or devoted wife, we have true representations of the purity and simplicity of Hindu domestic manners in early times."

"Nothing," says the author further on, "can be more beautiful and touching than the picture of domestic and social happiness in the *Rāmāyaṇa* and the *Mahābhārata*. It is indeed in depicting scenes of domestic affection, and expressing those universal feelings and emotions which

---

[1] *Indian Epic Poetry*, p. 4

[2] Herbet Spencer's *Autobiography*, Vol. I, p. 262

[3] Count Bjornstjerna says, 'Among other remarkable particulars in this poem is the pure light in which it sets the noble character and high minded devotion of the women of India.' *Theogony of the Hindus*, p.82.

belong to human nature in all time and in all places, that Sanskrit epic poetry is unrivalled."[1]

In addition to these two most celebrated epics, there are a large number of smaller epics which would well stand comparison with similar poems of any country. Mr. Colebrooke Speaks of *Raghuvañśa* in the highest terms, and says, "*Śiśupālavadha* is another celebrated epic poem."[2] "*Kirātārjunīyam* is remarkable," according to Colebrook "for the variety of measures and the alliteration,[5] while M aha Kavyas appears to the European reader very remarkable for verbal ingenuity." "Bhattikāvya, by Bhartarihari, is a poem of considerable reputation"[3] "*Kumārsambhava* is charming and fanciful," and, adds Mr. Griffith, "the author must have tried all the fertility of resource, the artistic skill, and the exquisite ear of the author of Lala Rookh."[4]

Nalodaya, which is attributed to Kālidāsa, "is remarkable for showing the extraordinary powers of the Sanskrit language, and – it is impossible not to wonder at the ingenuity of that workman."[5]

The *Rāghava Pāṇḍava Vijaya*; by Kaviraja, "is rather a curiosity than a poem." Mr. Colebrooke speaks of it as an instance of a complete poem, every canto of which exhibits a variety of metre. "This," says Mrs, Manning also, "is an extraordinary poem."

---

[1] *Indian Epic Poetry*, pp. 57, 58. 'Contrast with the respectful tone of Hindu children towards their parents the harsh manner in which Telemachus generally speaks to his mother. Filial respect and affection is quite as noteworthy a feature in the Hindu character now as in ancient times. I have been assured by Indian officers that it is common for unmarried soldiers to stint themselves almost to starvation point that they may send money to their aged parents. In this, the Hindus might teach us (Englishmen) a lesson.' Sir Monier Williams.

[2] *Ancient and Mediaeval India*, vol. 11, p. 134

[3] Manning's *Ancient and Mediaeval India*, Vol. II, p. 135

[4] Preface to Griffith's translation of the '*Birth of the War God.*'

[5] *Old Indian Poetry*,

Of *Nala Damayanti*, Professor Herren says, Remarkable as this episode appears for inventive merit it is not at all inferior in point of style, and some passages would do credit even to Homer himself"[1]

The imagination of the ancient 'Hindus was unrivalled infertility and range; in fact, like the whole face of nature, like those stupendous mountains, majestic rivers, and boundless. the expanse of the country around them, the ancient Hindu standards of strength and splendour are bewildering to some critics, who are accustomed to a more limited horizon." Their (Hindu) creations are, therefore, not only unrivalled but unapproachable in beauty, richness and grandeur.

To the European, everything is grand, sublime and magnificent in India, whether you look at the outward expression of nature, or at the physical and mental, resources of the country, look at the creation of God or the creation of man, you are absolutely struck with amazement and awe! The snowy peaks of her sublime Himavat seem to raise their heads higher than the highest heaven, while before their Indra and Brahma the European Apollo and Jupiter sink into insignificance.

"If we compare, ''says Professor Heeren, "the mythology of the Hindus with that of the Greeks, it will have nothing to apprehend on the score of intrinsic copiousness. In point of aesthetic value, it is sometimes superior, at others, inferior to the Greek: while in luxuriance and splendour it has the decided advantage. Olympus, with all its family of gods and goddesses, must yield in pomp and majesty to the palaces of Viṣṇu and Indra."[2] "The Hindu mythology," he says, "like the sublime compositions of Milton and Klopstock, extends its poetic flight far into the regions of unlimited space." He adds, "The Hindu Epic has a greater resemblance to the religious

---

[1] Heeren's *Hist. Researches*, Vol. II. P. 167

[2] Heeren's *Historical Researches*, Vol. II. P. 215

poetry of the Germans and the English than Greeks, with this, the difference, that the poet of India has a wider range afforded to his imagination than the latter."

Some critics hold that the *Rāmāyaṇa* is the origin of the *Iliad*[1], that the latter is only an adaptation of the former to the local circumstances of Greece, that Homer's description of the Trojan war is merely a mythological account of the invasion of Laṅkā by *Rāmachandra.* The main plot, of course, is the' same. Troy stands for Laṅkā (Tabrobane), Sparta for Ajodhia (Ayodhya), Menelaus for Rāma, Paris for Révaṇa. Hector for Indrajīt and Vibhīṣaṇa; Helen for Sītā, Agamemnon for Sugriva, Patroclus for Lakṣmaṇa, Nestor for Jāmvant. Achilles is a mixture of Arjuna, Bhima and Lakshmana.

Indeed, it is very improbable, if not impossible, that the Greeks should produce all at once poems which stand amongst the greatest feats of human genius, and occupy a place in literature inferior only to the Indian epics (in some respects). Anterior to Homer, Greek literature has no existence, even no name, and it is difficult to believe that, without any previous cultivation whatever, some of the highest and the noblest work in the whole range of literature should come into existence. The English literature did not begin with Milton, or the Roman with Virgil; nor does the Sanskrit with Valmiki or Vyasa, as the Greek does with Homer.

Apart from external circumstances, the subject-matter lends support to the theory in a remarkable manner. The plot, the characters and the incidents resemble those of the Hindu epic poetry so strongly that it is difficult to explain this phenomenon, except by assuming that the one has drawn extensively, if not wholly, from the other. And if we consider the external circumstances, the state of civilisation

---

[1] 'Even the action of the Hindu Epic is placed in an age far anterior to historical computation.' Heeren's *Historical Researches.*

of the two nations, their literature, wealth and constitution, the learning and character of their creators, little doubt remains as to who were the real creators and who the adapters. M. Hippolyte Fauche, in the Preface to his French translation of the *Rāmāyaṇa*, says that "*Rāmāyaṇa* was composed before the Homeric poems and that Homer took his ideas from it."

Apart from the fact that the main story has been adopted, and that the underlying plot of the one (*Rāmāyaṇa*) and the principal characters of the other (*Mahābhārata*) have been taken and fused together into a national epic by the Greeks, it is clear that episodes and separate incidents from the Indian epics have been taken and versified in the Greek tongue. Colonel Wilford asserts that "the subject of the Dionysus of Nonnus was borrowed from the *Mahābhārata*."[1] About Ravana's invasion of the kingdom of Indra, Count Bjornstjerna says, "This myth is probably the foundation of the ancient Greek tradition of the attempt of the Titans to storm Heaven."[2]

Professor Max Dunker says, "When Dion Chrysostom remarks that the Homeric poems are sung by the Indians in their own language – the sorrows of Priam, the lamentations of Hecuba and Andromache, the bravery of Achilles and Hector–Lassen is undoubtedly right in referring this statement to the *Mahābhārata* and putting *Dhṛtarāṣṭra* in the place of Priam, Gāndhārī and Draupadī in the places of Andromache and Hecuba, Arjuna and Karṇa in the places of Achilles and Hector."[3]

---

[1] *Asiatic Researches*, Vol. IX, p. 93

[2] *Theogony of the Hindus*, p. 81

[3] *History of Antiquity*, Vol. IV, p. 81

3.5. DRAMA

To wake the soul by tender strokes of art,
To raise the genius and to mend the heart,
To make mankind in conscious virtue bold,
Live o'er each scene, and be what they behold.

POPE: *Pro. to Addison's Cato*

The dramatic writings of the Hindus are equally remarkable. External nature, as might be expected in a country which is "the epitome of the world,"[1] is the special forte of the Hindu poets, and, in no country, ancient or modern, has Nature (in contradistinction to man) been treated so poetically or so, extensively introduced in poetry. But, though outward nature must attract, by its magnificence and its beauties, the attention of a people gifted with such marvelous powers of observation and sense for beauty, yet, the Hindus being a people given more than any other nation to analyzing thoughts and feelings and investigating mental phenomena, have made explorations in the realms of mind that exact the homage of mankind and defy emulation. To this reason, therefore, is due that the internal nature of man, the human mind with all its thoughts, feelings, volitions, all its desires and affections, its tendencies and susceptibilities, its virtues and failings and their developments are all drawn with a pencil at once poetic and natural. Creation in perfect harmony with nature is a feature of the Hindu drama. The characters are all creations, perfect in themselves and in their fidelity to nature. Extravagance, contradiction and unsuitability in the development - either of the plot or the characters is never permitted. The dramas hold the mirror to Nature and, in this respect, the Shakespearean dramas alone can be compared to them: while, as regards the language, Sanskrit must of course always stand alone in beauty and sublimity.

With regard to the extent to which the dramatic literature has been cultivated in India, Sir W. Tones says that the

Hindu theatre would fill as many volumes as that of any nation of modem Europe.

The Mohamedan conquest of India resulted in the effectual repression of Hindu dramatic writings. Instead of receiving further development, the Hindu drama rapidly declined, and a considerable part of this fascinating literature was forever lost.

Professor Wilson says, "It may also be observed that the dramatic pieces which have come down to us are those of the highest order, defended by their intrinsic purity from the corrosion of time." *Rūpaka* is the Hindu term for "Play," and "*Daśarūpaka*," or description of the ten kinds of theatrical' compositions, is one of the best treatises on dramatic literature and shows the extent to which dramatic literature was cultivated by the Hindus.

A writer says, "We might .also conveniently transfer to them (Hindu dramas) the definitions of the European stage, and class them under the head of Tragedy, Comedy, Opera, Ballet, Burletta, Melodrama and Farce." Professor Heeren says, "There are specimens of Hindu comedy still extant no way inferior to the ancient Greek."[1]

Hindu drama, however, is in many respects superior to the Greek drama.

(1) Among the Hindus, there are nine rasa or effects to be produced on the spectator. They are love, mirth, tenderness, fury, heroism, terror, disgust, wonder and tranquillity. "The serious part of this list is much more comprehensive than the Greek tragic rasa of terror and pity."

(2) "The love of the Hindus is less sensual than that of the Greek and Latin comedy." Wilson

(3) Valour, whenever displayed in the Hindu drama, is calm, collected and dispassionate. The calm intrepidity

---

[1] *Historical Researches*, Vol. II, p. 191

of the hero of Vir Charitra presents a very favourable contrast to the fury of Tidides or the arrogance of a Rinaido. The Hindu taste is much finer.

(4) Females were represented in general by females. "Boy Cleopetra" was unknown to the Hindu stage.

(5) The precise division of the Hindu plays into acts is a feature unknown to the Greeks. The division into acts proves higher development.[1]

(6) There was, moreover, no want of instruction for stage business, and we have the "asides" and "aparts" regularly indicated as in the modern theatre in Europe.[2]

Following nature more closely, the Hindu drama usually blended "seriousness and sorrow with levity and laughter." In this respect, the Hindu drama may be classed with much of the Spanish and English drama to which, as Schlegel observes, "the terms tragedy and comedy are wholly inapplicable, in the sense in which they are employed by the ancients."

The higher purpose of the dramatic art was never lost sight of by the Hindus. This is a distinguishing feature of the Hindu drama. Professor Wilson says, "We may, however, observe the honour of the Hindu drama, that *Parakīyā*, or she who is the wife of another person, is never to be made the object of a dramatic intrigue: a prohibition that would have sadly cooled the imagination and curbed the wit of Dryden and Congreve."

---

[1] 'In respect of dress and decorations, the resources of the Hindu theatre are sufficiently ample.' -Heeren's *Historical Researches*, Vol. II.

[2] On Mill's instituting a comparison between the Chinese and the Hindu drama, Professor Wilson says, 'The action of the Chinese plays is unskillfully conducted, and they are wanting in the highpoetic tone which distinguish those of the Hindus : at the same time they are ingenious and often interesting, They represent manners and feelings with truth. They are the works of a civilized people.' Mill's *India*. Vol. 11, p. 60

Sir W. Jones says, "The dramatic species of entertainment must have been carried to great perfection when Vikramaditya, who reigned in the first century before Christ gave encouragement to poets, philologers, and mathematicians." "But what a course of preliminary mental improvement," says Professor Heeren, "must the nation have gone through ere they could possess a writer like Kālidāsa! ere they could understand and appreciate his genius!"

Greater masters of drama, however, lived and died in India before Kalidāsa; Daṇḍī was one of them. Unhappily, however, to the eternal misfortune and regret of the civilised world, his works have met the same fate as productions of the highest class in many other departments of Hindu literature and science have done.

Love or *Sṛngāra*, the emotion which after hunger is the most powerful emotion in the world, is a leading principle in the dramatic literature of the world, and Mrs. Manning says, "Nowhere is love expressed with greater force and pathos than in the poetry of India."[1]

The best-known dramatists of the Hindus are Kālidāsa and Bhavabhūti. Kālidāsa, "one of the greatest dramatists the world has ever produced," flourished in the reign of Vikramaditya in the first century B.C.,[2] while Bhavabhūti lived many centuries later.

---

[1] *Ancient and Madiaeval India*, Vol. II, p. 148

[2] Some critics affect to 'think that the author of *Śākuntala* was a contemporary of Rājā Bhoja and not Vikramāditya, because a poet named Kalidasa is also found to have flourished in the court of Bhoja. Professor Wilson says, 'there having been two Kālidāsas in India, and the existence of a Kālidāsa at the court of Bhoja, is no argument against Amar's being contemporary with another bard of the same name, or their both having flourished long anterior to the regin of the prince.' Professor Wilson then proceeds to explain the cause of such wild criticism, which he says is twofold: (1). The disputants run into the opposite vice of

The masterpiece of Kālidāsa. is the play of *Śākuntala.* The plot of this "astonishing literary performance," as a great German critic calls it, is taken from the *Mahābhārata.* Professor Heeren speaks in rapturous terms of this "far-famed drama,"[1] which is incomparable for its beauty; charm, tenderness and fidelity to nature, and which, in fact, stands at the head of the dramatic literature of the world. He says, "And we must, in truth, allow *Kālidāsa* to be one of those poets who has done honour not merely to their nation but to all civilised mankind."[2]

Augustus Schlegel, the foremost German Sanskritist, says of *Śākuntala,* that it presents "through its Oriental brilliancy of colouring, so striking a resemblance to our (English) romantic drama that it might be suspected that the love of Shakespeare has influenced the translator, were it not that other Orientalists bore testimony to his fidelity."[3]

Alexander von Humboldt also notes the masterly mode in which *Kālidāsa* describes "the influence of nature upon the minds of lovers, his tenderness in the expression of feelings, and above all the richness of his creative fancy."[4] "Her (*Śakuntalā*'s) love and sorrow," says Dr. Sir W.

---

incredulity in order to avoid being thought credlous, (2) 'There opposition to the many claims of Hinduism is not founded so much into greater learning or superior talents as in strong prejudices in favour of their own country and high conceit of their own abilities.' See Mill's *History of India,* vol. I, p. 174

[1] Manning's *Ancient and Mediaeval India,* vol. II, p. 171.

[2] *Historical Researches,* Vol. II, p. 194

[3] Monier Williams' *Śākuntala,* Preface.

Schlegal (History of Literature, p. 115) says, 'What we chiefly admire in their poetry is that tender fondness solitude and the animated vegetable kingdom that so attract us in the drama of *Śākuntala,* the traits of female grace and fidelity and the exquisite loveliness of childhood, of such prominent interest in the older epics of India. We are also struck with the touching pathos accompanying deep moral feeling.'

[4] *Ancient and Mediaeval India,* Vol. II, p. 142

Hunter, "have furnished a theme for the great European poet of our age." Goethe sings:

Wouldst thou the young year's blossom and the fruit of its decline,
And all by which the soul is charmed, enraptured, feasted, fed.
Wouldst thou the Earth and Heaven itself in one sole name combine,
I name thee, O *Śakuntalā*! and all at once is said.

As regards the diction of the Hindu drama, Professor Wilson says, "It is impossible to conceive language so beautifully musical or so magnificently grand as that of the verses of Bhavabhūti and Kālidāsa."[1] No dramatic literature dating earlier than the first century before Christ is extant to enable one to judge of its quality. The earliest specimen available shows the language itself and the study of versification to have reached the highest point of refinement, for the era of Vikramāditya says Professor Heeren, "gave birth to the greatest masterpieces of the art."

Another celebrated play of Kalidāsa is Vikrama and Urvaśī. Comparing this play with Śākuntala, Professor Wilson says, "There is the same vivacity of description and tenderness of feeling in both, the like delicate beauty in the thoughts and extreme elegance in the style. It may be difficult to decide to which the palm belongs, but the story of the present play is perhaps more skillfully woven and the incidents arise out of each other more naturally than in Śākuntala, while, on the other hand, there is perhaps no one personage in it so interesting as the heroine of that drama." He adds, "The chief charm of this piece, however, is its poetry. The story, the situation and the characters are all highly imaginative, and nothing, if partiality for his work

---

[1] Wilson's *Theatre of the Hindus*, vol. I, p. 63. As an instance of the great diversity of composition, I may mention the fact that the first 35 stanzas of *Śākuntala* exhibit eleven kinds of metre.

does not mislead the translator, can surpass the beauty and justice of many of the thoughts."

The story is founded on a legend from the *Śatpatha Brāhmaṇa.* Vikrama (a king) loves Urvasi (a nymph of Heaven), and his love is not rejected; but he is warned that if he is ever seen by her naked or unveiled, she shall be banished. This is a myth, and the high dramatic treatment of this scientific myth does the highest credit to the wisdom, observation and learning of Kālidāsa. Explanations of this myth are given by Max Müller in his "Comparative Mythology," as well as by Dr. Kuhn, wherein 'he alludes also to the ideas of Weber. Max Müller makes Urvaśī=dawn. Another explanation is that Pururavas (or Vikrama) personifies the sun, whilst Urvaśī is the morning mist (see Chamber's Encyclopaedia, S.V. Pururavas). Urvasi is an apsara, and we find in Goldstucker's dictionary that the apsaras "are personifications of the vapours which are attached by the sun and formed into mists or clouds." Apsaras is derived from *ap* =water and *saras*=who moves.[1] Professor Goldstucker holds, therefore, that the legend represents the absorption by the sun of the vapour floating in the air. When Pururavas becomes distinctly visible, Urvaśī vanishes, because when the sun shines forth the mist is absorbed. Urvaśī "afterwards becomes a swan in the *Śatapatha*, but Kālidāsa changes the nymph into a climbing plant. "In Greece, Daphne becomes a laurel, because the country abounds in laurels, which are manifest so soon as the sun has absorbed the mist."

Bhavabhūti's popularity perhaps rivalled that of Kālidāsa. Professor Wilson bears testimony to the extraordinary beauty and power of his language and attributes his peculiar talent for describing nature in her magnificence to his early familiarity with the eternal mountains and forests of Gondwana. His best-known plays are the *Uttra Rām Carita* and *Mālatī Mādhava.* As regards the former, Professor Wilson says, "It has more pretensions to genuine pathos than perhaps any other specimen of Hindu theatre. The mutual sorrows of Rāma and Sītā in their state of separation are pleasingly and tenderly expressed, and the meeting of the father and sons may be compared advantageously with similar scenes with which the fictions of Europe, both poetical and dramatic, abound. Besides the felicitous expression of softer feelings, this play has some curious pictures of heroic bearing and of the duties of a warrior and a prince. A higher elevation can scarcely be selected for either. The true spirit of chivalry pervades the encounter of the two young princes. Some brilliant thoughts occur, the justice and beauty of which are not surpassed in any literature."[1]

As regards *Mālatī Mādhava*, Prof. Wilson says, "It offers nothing to offend the most fastidious delicacy and may be compared in this respect advantageously with many of the dramas of modern Europe, which treat of the passion that constitutes its subject. The manner in which love is here depicted is worthy of observation, as correcting a mistaken notion of the influence which the passion exercises over the minds of the natives of at least one portion of Asia. However intense the feeling – and it is represented as sufficiently powerful to endanger existence – it partakes in no respect of the impetuosity which it has pleased the writers of the West to attribute to the people of the East.

The barbarous nations whose inhuman love
Is wild desire, fierce as the sun they feel.

The heroine of this drama is loved as a woman. She is no goddess in the estimation of her lover. The passion of Malati is equally intense with that of Juliet. The fervour of attachment which unites the different personages of the drama so indissolubly in life and death is creditable to the Hindu national character. Unless instances of such disinterested union had existed, the author could scarcely have conceived, much less pictured, it."

---

[1] Wilson's *Theatre of the Hindus*, vol. I, pp. 383, 84

Altogether, *Mālatī Mādhava* is one of the most charming, powerful and refined representations of the emotion of love to be found in the literature of any nation.

The political life and manners of the Hindus are well depicted by Visakhadatta in this celebrated play, *Mudrā Rākṣasa.* It has the stir and action of city life, the endless ingenuity of political and court intrigue and the "staunch fidelity which appears as the uniform characteristic of servants, emissaries and friends, a singular feature in the Hindu character," which, Professor Wilson remarks, "it has not wholly lost." Professor Wilson adds, "It is a political or Historical drama and unfolds the political policy of Chanakya, the Machiavel of India in a most ingenious manner. The plot of the drama singularly conforms to one of the unities and the occurrences are all subservient to one action – the conciliation of Rākṣasa. This is never lost sight of from first to last without being made unduly prominent." It may be difficult in the whole range of dramatic literature to find a more successful illustration of the rule."[1]

The *Mṛcchakaṭikam,* or the Toy Cart, by Mahārāja Śūdraka, possesses considerable dramatic merit. The interest is rarely suspended, and in every case, the apparent interruption is with great ingenuity made subservient to the Common design. The connection of the two plots is much better maintained than in the play we usually refer to as a happy specimen of such a combination, "The Spanish Friar" The deposition of Palaka is interwoven with the main story so intimately, that it could not be detached from it without injury, and yet it never becomes so prominent as to divert attention from that to which it is only an appendage."[2]

The hero of the play, however, is Sansthānaka, the Rājā's brother-in-law. "A character so utterly contemptible has perhaps been scarcely ever delineated. It would be very

---

[1] Wilson's *Theatre of the Hindus,* Vol. II, p. 254, 'The author is the messenger of the Hindus.' Wilson

[2] Wilson's *Theatre of the Hindus,* Vol. I, p. 181

interesting to compare this drama for its merit of unity with The Merchant of Venice or The Two Noble Kinsmen, two of the best English dramas, in both of which the underplot is so loosely connected with the mainplot"

One more play[1] the celebrated drama, *Prabodha Candrodaya* by Krishna Misra, is much admired by Professor Lassen,[2] who calls it peculiarly Indian, and "unlike anything in the literature of other countries. The allegorical personifications are not only well sustained but are wonderful, and the whole plot constructed with so much ability as to excite the admiration of all readers."

"Much of that of the Hindus," says Professor Wilson, "may compete successfully with the great number of dramatic productions of modern Europe, and offers no affinity to the monstrous and crude abortions which preceded the introduction of the legitimate drama in the West."

---

[1] There are many other dramas of considerable merit and high repute. *Mahāvīra Carita* by Bhava Bhūti, *Ratnāvati* by Sri Harish Deo, Mahārāja of Kashmir, and *Veṇī Saṅhāra* are among those which can be advantageously compared with similar dramas in the literature of other nations.

[2] *Indische Alterthunskunde*, Vol. III, p. 790

3.6. LYRIC POETRY

And fill this song of Jai Deva with thee,
And make it wise to teach, strong to redeem.
And sweet to living' souls. Thou, mystery
Thou, Light of Life! Thou, Dawn beyond the dream!

Hymn to Viṣṇu

The Lyric poetry of the Hindus is the finest of its kind in the world, for the reason that the language in which it is written is the most melodious and musical on earth. As Professor Wilson remarks, the poetry of the Hindus can never be properly appreciated by those who are ignorant of Sanskrit. To judge of the merits of Hindu poetry from translations is to judge it at its worst. Moreover, owing to the peculiarities of life and character of the Hindus, Europeans can hardly be expected to fully appreciate and enjoy their poetry; as they can neither fully understand their character, nor fully enter into their feelings and sympathise with them. To the Hindus, Bharata's conduct in following Rama into the jungle and entreating him to return to Ayodhya is as natural as anything in the world, while to Mr. Talboys Wheeler, the historian of India, it appears, contrary to human nature;" As Mr. Wheeler regards the venerable Daśratha as shamming when he gives vent to sorrow after having sentenced Rama to exile to keep a vow, what should he have thought of the Hindu ladies of the present day had he known that they would die or suffer anything rather than open their lips even to those who are dearer to them than life itself, when they think modesty forbids their doing so, even when life itself is in danger? Hindu ideas of duty, obedience and modesty are much more complex than those of other nations. Still, when Hindu Lyric poetry has been properly judged, the praise has been liberal, and approbation emphatically expressed.

Gīta Govinda is the finest extant specimen of Hindu lyric poetry, and it is difficult to find in any language lyrics that can vie with it in melody and grace, Mr. Griffith says "The exquisite melody "of the verse can only be appreciated by those who can enjoy the original."[1]

Schlegel says, ''Tender delicacy of feeling and elegiac love cast a halo over Indian poetry," and "the whole is recast in the mould of harmonious softness and is redolent of elegiac sweetness."[2]

Gīta Govinda has been analysed by Lassen in his Latin translation, beautifully translated into German by Ruckert, and has been dwelt upon with admiration by Sir W. Jones in his essay on the Mystical Poetry of the Hindus.

Professor Heeren says, "The Hindu lyric surpassed that of the Greeks in admitting both the rhyme and blank verse."[3] He further says, "How much of the beauty of a lyric must inevitably be lost in a prose translation it would be superfluous to remark; and yet it is impossible to read the *Gīta Govinda* without being charmed........It is impossible, however, not to notice "the extreme richness of the poet's fancy, the strength and vivacity of his sentiment particularly observable in his delicate taste for the beauties in general, and which not even the ardour of passion was able to extinguish."[4]

"Gīta Govinda exhibits," says Mr. Elphinstone, "in perfection the luxuriant imagery and the voluptuous softness of the Hindu .school."[5]

Another Hindu lyric is the *Ṛtu Saṅghāra*, something like "Thompson's Seasons" in the English language. Mrs. Manning says about it: "*Ṛtu Saṅghāra*, a lyric poem by

---

[1] *Ancient and Mediaeval India*, Vol. II, p. 269

[2] Schlegel's *History of Literature*, p. 117

[3] *Historical Researches*, Vol. II, p. 187

[4] *Ancient and Mediaeval India*, pp. 189, 190. Jaideva, its author was born, as he himself says, at Kenduli, situated either in Kaliṅga or in Burdwan.

[5] *History of India*, p. 156

Kālidāsa, is much admired not only by the natives of India, but by almost all students of Sanskrit literature."[1]

Mr. Griffith, in his translation of "*Ṛtu Saṅghāra,*" says - "Sir W. Jones speaks in rapturous terms of the beautiful and natural sketches with which it 'abounds;" and, after expressing his own admiration, adds, "it is much to be regretted that it is impossible to translate the whole."[2]

Lyric poetry was extensively cultivated in India. Sir W. Hunter says, "The Mediaeval *Brāhmaṇas* displayed a marvellous activity in theological as well as lyric poetry."

Special charm must attach to the lyric poetry of the Hindus for, as Mrs. Manning remarks, "Nowhere is love expressed with greater force or pathos than in the poetry of the Hindus."[3]

Megha Dūta is an excellent example of purely descriptive poetry. Mrs. Manning says, "It is the most important of its kind, and is a favourite with the Europeans too."[4] Professor' H. H. Wilson says, "The language (of *Megha Dūta*) although remarkable for the richness of its compounds, is not disfigured by their extravagance, and the order of the sentences is, in general, the natural one. The metre combines melody and dignity in a very extraordinary manner, and will bear an advantageous comparison with the best specimens of uniform verse in the poetry of any language, living or dead."[5]

---

[1] *Historical Researches*, Vol. II, Professor Von Bohlen translated it into German and Latin in 1840 A.D.

[2] Manning's *Ancient and Mediaeval India*, Vol. II, p. 265

[3] Manning's *Ancient and Mediaeval India*, Vol. II, p. 148

[4] Manning's *Ancient and Mediaeval India*, Vol. II, p. 257

[5] Wilson's Essay, Vol. II, p. 312

3.7. ETHICO-DIDACTIC POETRY

Thy power the breast from every error frees
And weeds out all its vices by degrees.

GIFFORD: *Juvenal*

The Hindu achievements in this branch of literature establish once for all their intellectual superiority. It is this part of their literature that has made its way to the remotest corners of Europe and America. Its sway over the mind of the civilised world is almost despotic and complete.

Professor Wilson says, "Fable constitutes with them (Hindus) practical ethics – the science or *Nīti* or Polity – the system of rules necessary for the good government of society in all matters not of a religious nature – the reciprocal duties of the members of an organised body either in their private or public relations. Hence it is specially intended for the education of princes, and proposes to instruct them in those obligations which are common to them and their subjects, and those which are appropriate to their princely office; not only in regard to those over whom they rule, but in respect to other princes, under the contingencies of peace and war. Each fable is designed to illustrate and exemplify some reflection on worldly vicissitudes or some precept for human conduct, and the illustration is as frequently drawn from the intercourse of human beings as from any imaginary adventure of animal existence, and this mixture is in some degree a peculiarity of the Hindu plan of fabling or story telling."[1]

It is now admitted by the learned everywhere that the fabulous literature of the world, which is such an important and, in some respects, so necessary a part of the education of young men all over the world, apart from it being one of

---

[1] Wilson's *Essays on Sanskrit Literature* Vol. II, p. 85

the most amusing, interesting and instructive diversions from labour and severe study, owes its origin solely to the intelligence and wisdom of the ancient Hindus.

Pañcatantra is far and away the best masterpiece in the whole fabulous literature of the world; nay, it is the source of which the entire literature of fables, Asiatic or European, has directly or indirectly emanated. Mr. Elphinstone says, "In the composition of tales and fables they (Hindus) appear to have been the instructors of the rest of mankind.[1] The most ancient known fables (those of Bidpai) have been found almost unchanged in their Sanskrit dress; and to them, almost all the fabulous relations of other countries have been clearly traced by Mr. Colebrooke, the Baron-de-Sacy and Professor Wilson."

Dr. Sir W.W. Hunter says, "The fables of animals, familiar to the Western world from the time of Aesop downwards, had their original home in India. The relation between the fox and the lion in the Greek versions has no reality in nature, but it was based on the actual relation between the lion and his follower, the jackal, in the Sanskrit stories. *Pañcatantra* was translated into the ancient Persian in the sixth century A.D., and from that rendering, all the subsequent versions in Asia Minor and Europe have been derived. The most ancient animal fables of India are at the present day the nursery stories of England and America. The graceful Hindu imagination delighted also in fairy tales; and the Sanskrit compositions of this class are the original

---

[1] *History of India*, pp. 156, 157. For a guide to further inquiry as to Hindu origin of European fables, see Transactions of the R.A.S., Vol. p. 156. 'the complicated system of story-telling, tale within tale like the Arabian Nights, seems also to have been of their invention, as are the subjects of many well-known tales and romances, oriental and European.' Elphinstone's *History of India*, p.157

source of many of the fairy stories of Persia, Arabia and Christendom."[1]

Professor Max Müller says, "The King of Persia, Khusro Nausherwan (531-579 AD.) sent his physician, Borzoi, to India in order to translate the fables of the *Pañcatantra* from Sanskrit into Pahlavi.[2] *Hitopadeśa* (*hita*= good and *Upadeśa* = advice) as Mrs. Manning says, is the form in which the old Sanskrit fables became introduced into the literature of nearly every known language.

Fabel maintains the Indian origin of the fables common to India and Greece, which proves the antiquity of the Hindu fables.[3]

Professor Weber says, "Allied to the fables are the fairy tales and romances, in which the luxuriant fancy of the Hindus has, in the most wonderful degree, put forth all its peculiar grace and charm."[4]

Professor Wilson says, "The Fables of the Hindus are a sort of machinery to which there is no parallel in the fabling literature of Greece and Rome."[5] He also says that the Hindu literature contained collections of domestic narrative to an extent surpassing those of any other people.

Mrs. Manning thus remarks on the *Pañcatantra*, "Each fable will be found to illustrate and exemplify some reflection on worldly vicissitude or some precept for human conduct; and instead of being aggregated promiscuously or

---

[1] *Imperial Gazetteer*, 'India,' p. 238

[2] *India: What can it teach us*? P.93. 'The *Pañcatantra* was translated into Persian in the sixth century by order of Nausherawan and thence into Arabic and Turkish and lastly into French.' Heeren's *Historical Researches*, Vol. II, p. 200.

[3] Weber's *Indian Literature*, p. 211, 'The fabe reported by Arrian of Hercules having searched the whle Indian Ocean and found the pearl with which he used to adorn his daughter, is oof Hindu origin.' Heeren's *Historical Researches*, Vol. II, p. 271.

[4] Weber's *Indian Literature*, p.213

[5] Wilson's *Essays*, Vol. II, p. 85

without method, the stories are all strung together upon a connected thread and arranged in a framework of continuous narrative, out of which they successively spring."[1]

A careful study of the subject will show that even the books which appear to have a distinctive Persian character and are generally regarded to be of Persian origin are in reality Hindu to the core. Count Bjornstjerna remarks, "The thousand and one Nights, so universally known in Europe, is a Hindu original translated into Persian and thence into other languages. In Sanskrit, the name is *Vṛhat Kathā*."[2] Professor Lassen of Paris asserts that "the Arabian Nights Entertainments are of Hindu origin."[3]

Despite the authority of so many learned Orientalists in favour of the Hindu origin of this literature, and the express historical evidence as to the transmission of the Hindu fables to Arabia and Persia, there is overwhelming internal evidence in the fables themselves to support the assertion that the Hindus have been the teachers of the rest of mankind in this important branch of literature. Take, for instance, the case of a particular fable. In the Panchtantra there is a story of a female bird who wished to make her nest further inland because on the day of the full moon the sea would be sweeping over the place where she then Mls. But the male bird objects, believing that he was as strong as the sea and that it could not encroach upon his nest. (Benfey Vol. II, pp. 87-89). Now this story is, as Professor Wilson remarks, one of the decisive proofs of the Indian origin of the fables. The name of the bird in Arabic is Titawi, a word which cannot be resolved to any satisfactory Arabic root. It is "only a transcript of the Sanskrit *Ṭiṭṭibha*, Bengali *Titib* and Hindi *Ṭiṭiharī*.

Wilson remarks that in the translation of *Pañcatantra*, Kalalawa Damna, the name of the ox in Sanskrit was

---

[1] *Ancient and Mediaeval India*, Vol. II, p. 274

[2] *Theogony of the Hindus*, p. 85

[3] See his *ind. Alt.* IV, p. 902

Sañjīvaka, whence the Arabic Shanzebeh, and those of the jackals, Karataka and Damnaka, whence the Arabic Kalala and Damna." The tale of Ahmad and Pari Banu betrays palpably its Indian origin. Pari Bhanu is decidedly a Hindu name. The eldest of the three princes, Prince Husein, in search of some extraordinary rarity which may entitle him to the hand of the Princess Nuran Nihar, repairs to the Indian city, Bisnagar (decidedly an Indian name) a metropolis of extraordinary wealth and population.

Mr. Deslongchamps says,' "The book of Sindbad is of Indian origin, and adds that the under-mentioned three stories were in a special degree derived from the original. (I) The Arabic story of a King, his Son, his favourites and seven Viziers. (2) The Hebrew romance of the Parables of Sendebar and (3) the Greek' romance of Syntipas. From the Hebrew Romance above described, Deslongchamps derives, "the history of the seven sages of Rome," Historia septem sepiculan Romoe, a very popular work in Europe for three centuries.

Professor Wilson says, "In a manuscript of the Parable of "Sendebar, which existed in the British Museum, it is repeatedly asserted in anonymous Latin notes that the work was translated out of the Indian language into Persian and Arabic, and from one of them into Hebrew. Sendebar is also described as a chief of the Indian Brāhmaṇas, and Beibar, the King, as a King of India." Ellis' Metrical Romances, Vol. III.

A decisive proof of Sindabad being an Indian is the direct evidence on the subject of the eminent Arabic writer, Masudi. In his "Golden Meadows" (Mirajul-Zeheb), in a chapter on the ancient kings of India, he speaks of an Indian philosopher named Sindebad, who was contemporary with *Kurush*, and was the author of the work entitled, "*The Story of Seven Vaziers*, the tutor, the young man and the wife of the king." "This is the work," he adds, "which is called the book of Sendebad."

By his interesting analysis of the Syntipas and the Parables of Sendebad[1], Professor Wilson clearly shows that the stories are one and all of Hindu origin.[2] He' also shows that the "Seven Sages of Rome" is also of Hindu origin. Besides these fables and stories, says Professor Wilson, "various narratives of Indian origin forced their way individually and unconnectedly to Europe." [3]

Sir John Malcolm says, "Those who rank the highest among Eastern nations for genius have employed their talents in works of fiction, and have added to the moral lessons they desired to convey so much of grace and ornament that their volumes have found currency in every nation of the world."[4]

It is thus clear that the Hindus have produced a branch or literature the kind of which, in any considerable degree, has never been produced by any other nation in the world:

---

[1] Wilson's *Sanskrit Essays*, Vol. II, pp. 99, 100

[2] *Ibid.* p.101

[3] Wilson's Sanskrit Essays, Vol. II, p.101.

[4] He fixes the Crusades as the time of the emigration to Europe of some of the well-known works of this kind, such as (1) the Kathā Sarita Sāgara, (2) the *Vetāla Pañcaviñśati*, (3) The *Siṅghāsana Dvātriñśati*, and (4) The *Śukasaptati.* The first of these works was composed for the amusement and instruction of Sri Harish of Kashmir by the order of his grandmother, Suryavati, who became *sati* in 1093 AD. But that the stories of which it is made up were of great antiquity is proved from the fact of one of them occurring in Odyssey. In the fifth book of *Kathā Sarita Ségara*, there is a story of a man who being shipwrecked is caught in a whirlpool, and escapes by jumping up and climbing the branch of a fig tee, apparently the bunyan (Ficus Indica) celebrated for its pendulous roots. Professor Wilson here refers to Odyssey. XII, pp.101-104., where Ulysses escapes from a whirlpool by jumping up and clinging to the branches of a fig tree-probably the Indian fig tree or bunyan, the pendulous branches of which would be more within reach than those of the Sicllian fig; and Homer, he thinks may have borrowed the incident from some old Eastern fiction

Asiatic or European, ancient or modern. This 'wonderful phenomenon is thus explained by Professor Heeren "The poetry of no other nation exhibits in such a striking manner the didactic' character as that of the Hindus; for, no other people were so thoroughly imbued with, the persuasion that to give and receive instruction was the sole and ultimate object of life."[1]

---

[1] *Historical Researches*, Vol. II, p. 197

3.8. THE *PURĀṆAS*

"We are the voices of the wandering wind
Which moan for rest and rest can never find.
Lo! As the wind is, so is mortal life,
A moan, a sigh, a sob, a storm, a strife,"

Devas' Song to Prince Siddhartha

The *Purāṇas* are looked upon as semi-religious books. As a matter of fact, they are, as it were, the storehouses, the vast treasuries of universal information, like the English "*Encyclopaedia Britannica*" with a unity of purpose and a theological bent. They contain dissertations and discussions on Theology, Mythology, History, War, Polity, Philosophy, Sciences, Arts and other things. In course of time, with the decline and fall of the Hindu nation, when the ideals of the nation were lowered, when plain living and high thinking ceased to be the national characteristics of the race, when the pure and sublime teachings of the Vedas and the *Upaniṣ ads* began to be neglected, interpolations inculcating the worship of different gods and goddesses, celebrating the praises of holy places of India were made in these books from time to time, and they began to be looked upon with greater and greater reverence, with the result eventually that the most spiritual and scientific religion in the world was replaced by a mixture of Theology, Mythology and Sociology.

When the Hindus became too weak to defend themselves from the attacks of the invaders from the Northwest, in order to preserve their literature from the destruction they assigned it to .the care of a class of men whom they invested with special sanctity and accorded them a privileged position in society. In time, the exclusive spirit of these men urged them to look upon learning as their peculiar prerogative and induced them, with the object of preserving the sacerdotal character of their class, to gradually put a bar to other classes acquiring a knowledge of the Hindu *Śāstras.*

A glance at the contents of the *Purāṇas*, however, would reveal their real character; and the common sense of the Hindus can be relied on to assign these books their true place in the literature of the nation.

The world is moving fast, and forces over which the nation, which long revelled in isolation and exclusiveness to its serious detriment and undoing, has no control are now working so as to demand the utmost circumspection on the part of its leaders and thinkers in husbanding its resources, and preventing its energies from being frittered away in following false ideals. If the fate of the ancient Egyptians, the Persians, the Babylonians and the Greeks is to be avoided, it behoves all well-wishers of the nation not only to hold the mirror to its wretched condition for the edification of the masses, but by making proper use of the useful and valuable lessons contained in parts even of this heterogeneous – half sacerdotal, half profane – literature, direct its course towards the realization of aims truly and clearly laid down in the sublime and pure teaching of the Vedas and the *Upaniṣads.*

Professor Heeren[1] says that the *Purāṇas* are not the work of a Vālmīki or Vyāsa, but, like the poems of Tzetzes and other grammarians, the fruit of extraordinary diligence combined with extensive reading." He" is, nevertheless, far from considering them all together as an invention of modern times, that is, of the Middle Ages.

The literal meaning of the word *Purāṇa* is "old" and the *Purāṇas* profess to teach what is old. "They are," says Mrs. Manning, "written in verse with a view to public recitation at festivals, as vehicles for conveying such instruction as the people might be presumed to require. Philosophically, they blend *Sāṅkhya* philosophy with *Vedānta*, and practically they were a code of ritual as well as a summary of law."[2]

---

[1] *Historical Researches*, Vol. II, p. 177

[2] *Ancient and Mediaeval India*, Vol. I, p. 244

The *Purāṇas* have been compiled at different periods and by different men. They seem to have adopted different innovations made into them by Śāṅkarācārya, Rāmānuja, Mādhavācārya, and Vallabhācārya. "The invariable form of the *Purāṇas* is that of a dialogue, in which some person relates its contents in reply to the inquiries of another." The immediate narrator is commonly, though not constantly, Lomaharṣaṇa or Somaharṣaṇa, the disciple of Vyāsa, who is supposed to communicate what was imparted to him by his preceptor.

The *Purāṇas* are divided into three classes:

1. *Sāttvika*, or "Pure," including *Viṣṇu, Nārada, Bhāgavat, Garuḍa, Padma* and *Varāha Purāṇas.*
2. *Tāmasa*, or "*Purāṇas* of Darkness," including *Matsya, Kūrma, Linga, Śiva, Skanda* and *Agni Purāṇas.*
3. *Rājasa* or "Passionate," including *Brahmāṇḍa, Vaivarta,* Mārkaṇḍeya, *Bhaviṣya, Vāmana* and *Brahma Purāṇas.*

The first six *Purāṇas* are Vaiṣṇava, the next six are Śaiva, and the last six advocate the Gossain and Vallabhachari religions.

There are eighteen *Purāṇas*, and it is said that there are 18 *Upa-Purāṇas.* "The eighteen *Purāṇas* are said to have 4,00,000 *ślokas* or 16,00,000 lines. They are fabled to be but an abridgment; the whole amounting to a crore or 10 millions of stanzas, even a 1,000 million." And Professor Wilson adds, "If all the fragmentary portions claiming in various parts of India to belong to the *Purāṇas* were admitted, their extent would much exceed the lesser, though it would not reach the larger enumeration."[1]

To give an idea of their contents, a brief survey of two of the most important *Purāṇas* is subjoined. *Śri Bhāgvat Purāṇa*, "that in which ample details of duty are described

[1] There is a little confusion in the names of the 18 *Purāṇas* according to the different *Purāṇas* themselves.

and which opens with the *Gāyatrī*: that in which the death of the Asura Vṛtra is told, and in which the mortals and the immortals of the *Sārasvata Kalpa*, with the events of that period, are related is called the *Bhāgavat Purāṇa*, and consists of eighteen thousand verses." It is perhaps the most important of all the *Purāṇas*.

Its philosophy is Vedantic, and it opens with a cosmogony mixed with mysticism and allegory; then follow an account of the creation and of the *Varāha Avatāra*, creation of Prajāpatis, Svayambhū, and then Kapila Avatāra, the author of *Sāṅkhya* Philosophy; an account of the *Manvantras*, different legends of Dhruva, Vena, Pṛthu and an account of the universe follow. Other legends follow, including that of Prahlāda, of the churning of the ocean, and the fish Avatārs and others, and then a history of two Hindu dynasties. The tenth book which gives the history of Krishna is the most popular part of the *Purāṇa*. The eleventh book describes the destruction of the Yadavas and the death of Krishna his teaching Yoga to Uddhava. The twelfth book contains the lives of the kings of Kaliyuga and gives an account of the deterioration of all things and their final dissolution. As this *Purāṇa* was recited by Sukhadeva to Parīkṣita, who was awaiting the snake-bite, the king was actually bitten by the serpent and expired. It terminates with an account of Vyāsa's arrangement of the Vedas and the *Purāṇas* and with praises of its own sanctity.

Agni Purāṇa. That *Purāṇa* which describes the events of the *Iśāna Kalpa* and was related by Agni to Vaśīṣṭha is the *Agni Purāṇa*. It consists of 16,000 *ślokas*. It commences with an account of the Avatāras of Rāma and Krishna, and devotes some chapters to "mystical forms of Śiva worship." A description of the earth, genealogies, etc., follow. Then comes a system of medicine, and the work winds up with treatises on rhetoric, prosody, grammar, archery and military tactics, etc. It also contains several systems of *nīti* (polity).

The 18 *Upa-Purāṇas* are enumerated as follows:

1. *Sanatkumāra*	7. *Narsiṁha*	13. *Durvāsa*
2. *Nāradīya*	8. *Parāsara*	14. *Maheśvara*
3. *Śiva*	9. *Kapila*	15. *Mānava*
4. *Varuṇa*	10. *Sāmba*	16. *Nandī*
5. *Auśanasa*	11. *Kalika*	17. *Saura*
6. *Āditya*	12. *Bhāgavat*	18. *Vaśīṣṭha*

The foregoing brief survey of the contents of two of the *Purāṇas* is quite inadequate to enable the reader to form an idea of their importance, as light-houses to a great Past. The *Agni Purāṇa*, for instance, contains particulars of the military organisation of the Hindus, which in consequence of the loss of the *Dhanurveda* are of especial importance. The *Deva Purāṇa* mentions the *brahmāstra*, which proves the use of atomic weapons by the Hindus in those days. The *Padma Purāṇa* contains a treatise on the geography of India in particular and the Universe in general, which is of very great importance. *Matsya Purāṇa* explains the source from which the Jewish, the Christian and the Mohame-dan story of the Deluge and their cosmogony are derived. *Garuda Purāṇa* contains a treatise on precious stones, astrology and palmistry; a system of medicine is contained in the *Agni Purāṇa*, while theories of creation are to be found in almost all of them. Some *Purāṇas* throw important light on the industries and arts of ancient India, and may if properly understood and followed, yet help the Indians to improve their position in the industrial world. It must, however, be admitted that sometimes, with a grain of useful information, there will be found a lot of useless chaff. On the whole, the *Purāṇas* have as much claim to be regarded as the religious books of the Hindus as the *Encyclopaedia Britannica* has to be accepted as the religious books of Englishmen. As to the antiquity of their contents, there is no doubt. Professor H. H. Wilson says, "And the testimony that establishes their existence three centuries before Christianity carries it back to a much more remote antiquity – to an antiquity that is probably not surpassed by any of the prevailing fictitious institutions or beliefs of the ancient world."

4

PHILOSOPHY

How charming is divine philosophy,
Not harsh and crabbed, as dull fools suppose
But musical as Apollo's flute,
And a perpetual feast of nectar'd sweets
Where no crude surfeit reigns.

MILTON: *Comus*

Philosophy is the real ruler of the globe: it lays down principles which guide the world. Philosophy shows how a transcendent genius exacts homage consciously or unconsciously from lower intellects. It is a philosophy that blows the trumpet blast, and it is a philosophy that blunts the edge of the sword. Philosophy reigns supreme, undisputed and absolute. It conquers the conqueror and subdues the subduer.

If it is true that a great nation alone can produce great philosophers or a complete system of philosophy, the ancient Indians may, without hesitation, be pronounced to have been the greatest nation, ancient or modern. "Philosophers," says Professor Max Müller, "arise after the security of a State has been established, after wealth has been acquired and accumulated in certain families, after schools and universities have been founded and taste created for those literary pursuits which even in the most advanced state of civilization must necessarily be confined to but a small portion of an ever toiling community."[1]

To what high pinnacle of civilisation, then, must the ancient Indians have reached, for, says Professor Max

[1] *Ancient Sanskrit Literature*, pp. 564, 65

Müller further on that "the Hindus were a nation of philosophers"[1]

The philosophy of the Hindus is another proof of their superiority in civilisation and intellect to the moderns as well as the ancients. Manning says, "The Hindus had the widest range of mind of which man is capable."[2]

Schlegel speaks of the noble, clear and severely grand accents of Indian thought and says, "Even the loftiest philosophy of the Europeans, the idealism of reason, as is set forth by Greek philosophers, appears in comparison with the abundant light and vigour of Oriental idealism like a feeble Promethean spark in the full flood of heavenly glory of the noonday sun – faltering and feeble and ever ready to be extinguished."[3]

Professor Weber, speaking of Hindu philosophy says, "it is in this field and that of grammar that the Indian mind attained the highest pitch of its marvellous fertility."[4] "The Hindus," says Max Müller, "were a people remarkably gifted for philosophical abstraction."[5] Schlegel says, "India is pre-eminently distinguished for the many traits of original grandeur of thought and of the wonderful remains of immediate knowledge."[6]

Like all other things in India, the Hindu philosophy, too, is on a gigantic scale. Every shade of opinion, every mode of thought, every school of philosophy has found its expression in the philosophical writings of the Hindus and received its full development. Sir W. Hunter says, "The problems of thought and being of mind and matter and soul apart from both, of the origin of evil, of the sommum bonum of life, of necessity and free will, and of the relations

---

[1] *Ancient Sanskrit Literature*, p. 31

[2] *Ancient and Mediaeval India*, Vol. I, p. 114

[3] *History of Literature.*

[4] Weber's *Indian Literature*, p. 27

[5] *Ancient Sanskrit Literature*, p. 565

[6] *History of Literature*, p. 126

of the creator to the creature, and the intellectual problems, such as the compatibility of evil with the goodness of God and the unequal distribution of happiness and misery in this life, are endlessly discussed. Brahmin Philosophy exhausted the possible solutions of these difficulties and of most of the other great problems which have since perplexed Greeks, Romans, Mediaeval school men and modern men of science."[1]

Speaking of the comprehensiveness of Hindu philosophy, Dr. Alexander Duff is reported to have said in a speech delivered in Scotland, that "Hindu philosophy was so comprehensive that counterparts of all systems of European philosophy were to be found in it."

Professor Goldstucker[2] finds in the *Upaniṣads* "the germs 'of all the philosophies, Count Bjornstjerna says, "In a metaphysical point of view we find among the Hindus all the fundamental ideas of those vast systems which, regarded merely as the offspring of phantasy,' nevertheless inspire admiration on account of the boldness of flight and of the faculty of human mind to elevate itself to such remote ethereal regions. We find among them all the principles of Pantheism, Spinozism and Hegelianism, of God as being one with the universe; of the eternal spirit descended on earth in the whole spiritual life of mankind; of the return of the emanative sparks after death to their divine origin; of the uninterrupted alternation between life and death, which is nothing else but a transition between different modes of existence. All this we find again among the philosophers of the Hindus exhibited as clearly as by our modern philosophers more than three thousand years since."[3]

---

[1] *Indian Gazetteer*, pp. 213, 214

[2] *Ancient and Mediaeval India*, Vol. I, p.149

[3] *Theogony of the Hindus*, pp. 29, 30. As an instance of Mr. James Mill's stupidity, if stupidity is compatible with learning, one may cite his opinion that the Hindus were extremely barbarous, for they cultivated metaphysics so largely. Prof.

Even with the limited knowledge of Hindu philosophy and science that could be obtained at the time, Sir William Jones could say, "I can venture to affirm without meaning to pluck a leaf from the never fading laurels of our immortal Newton, that the whole of his theology, and part of his philosophy, may be found in the Vedas, and even in the works of the Sufis. The most subtle spirit which he suspected to pervade natural bodies, and lying concealed in them, to cause attraction and repulsion, the emission, reflection and refraction of light, electricity, calcification sensation and muscular motion, is described by the Hindus as the fifth element, endued with those very powers."

Mrs. Besant says, "Indian psychology is far more perfect a 'Science than European psychology."[1]

As Professor Max Müller has observed, "the Hindus talk philosophy in the streets," and to this reason is due to the thoroughly practical character of their philosophy. "In this respect," says Bjornstjerna, "the Hindus were far in advance of the philosophers of Greece and Rome, who considered the immortality of the soul as problematical."[2] "Socrates and Plato with all their longings could only feel assured that the soul had more of immortality than ought else."[3] In India,

Wilson takes exception to it, and says, "With regard to the writer's theory that the cultivation of metaphysics is a proof rather of barbarism than of civilization, it may be asked if Locke, Descartes, Leibnitz, Kant, Schelling were barbarous." - Mill's *History of India*, Vol. I, p. 74, footnote. Mr. James Mill is a conspicuous instance of a man whose mind becomes completely warped by prejudice. Mill's mind could conceive most absurd impossibilities. ŞMr. Mill¿, says Wilson, Şseems inclined to think that It was not impossible that the Pyramids had dropped from the clouds or sprung out of the soil.¿ How this perverted intellect could educate one of the greatest English thinkers is a problem of some psychological interest.

[1] Lecture on National University in India (Calcutta), January, 1906

[2] *Theogony of the Hindus*, p.27

[3] Phoedo, Taylor's translation, IV, p.324

however, the doctrine has not been accepted in theory only, it moulds the conduct of the whole nation. This is true of philosophy. And it is due to its practical character that Hindu philosophy has extended its sway over so wide an area of the globe. Hindu philosophy even now holds undisputed sway over the minds of nearly half the inhabitants of the world, whilst its partial influence is no doubt universal.

In ancient times people came to India from distant lands to acquire learning and gain wisdom, and Hindu philosophy thus worked silently for centuries. That the Egyptians derived their religion, mythology and philosophy from the Hindus has been dearly established by Count Bjornstjerna; and that the Greek philosophy, too, was indebted almost wholly to the Hindu philosophy for its cardinal doctrines has also been shown by eminent Orientalists. The resemblance"between the Hindu and the Greek philosophy is too close to be accidental. The Hindus being far more advanced must be the teachers, and the Greeks, the disciples Dies. Mr. Colebrooke, the eminent antiquarian, decides in favour of Hindu originality and says, "The Hindus were, in this respect, the teachers and not the learners."[1]

A Frenchman observes that "the traces of Hindu philosophy which appear at each step in the doctrines professed by the illustrious men of Greece abundantly prove that it was from the East came their science and that many of them no doubt drank deeply at the principal fountain." The great Greek philosopher, Pythagoras, came to India to learn philosophy, and here imbibed the doctrine of the transmigration of soul propounded by the Hindu sages. Dr. Enfield says, "We find that it (India) was visited for the purpose of acquiring knowledge by Pythagoras, Anaxarchus,

---

[1] Transactions of the R.A.S., Vol. 1, p. 579

Pyrrho, and others who afterwards became eminent philosophers in Greece."[1]

Discussing the question as to what constitutes human nature according to the Hindus, the Swedish Count says, "Pythagoras, and Plato hold the same doctrine, that of Pythagoras being probably derived from India, whither he travelled to complete his philosophical studies."[2] Mr. Pococke says, "Certain it is that Pythagoras visited India, which I trust I shall make self-evident."[3]

Schlegel says, "The doctrine of the transmigration of souls. was indigenous to India and was brought into Greece by Pythagoras."[4]

Mr. Princep says, "The fact, however, that he (Pythagoras) derived his doctrines from an Indian source is very generally admitted. Under the name of Mythraic, the faith of Buddha had also a wide extension"[5] Sir M. Monier Williams says that Pythagoras and Plato both believed in this doctrine and that they were indebted for it to Hindu writers.[6]

Pyrrhon, according to Alexander Polyhistor, went with Alexander the Great to India, and hence the scepticism of Pyrrhon is connected with the Buddhist philosophy of India.[7] Even Ward says, "The author is persuaded he (the reader) will not consider the conjecture improbable that Pythagoras

---

[1] History of Philosophy, by Dr. Enfield, Vol. I, p. 65. 'Some of the doctrines of the Greeks concerning nature are said to have been derived from the Indians.' p.70

[2] *Theogony of the Hindus*, p. 77

[3] Pococke's *India in Greece*, p. 353

[4] History of Literature, p. 109

[5] *India in Greece*, p. 361. 'Pythagoras, according to Mr. Pococke, was a Buddhist Missionary. He was

Sanskrit,	Bud'ha-Gurus,
Greek,	Putha-Goras Bud'has Spiritual Teacher
English	Pytha-Goras

[6] *Indian Wisdom*, p. 68

[7] Max Müllers's *Science of Language*, p. 86

and others did really visit India and that Gautama and Pythagoras were -contemporaries."[1]

Professor H. H. Wilson says, "We know that there was an active communication between India and the Red Sea in the early ages of the Christian era and that doctrines, as well as article of merchandise, were brought to Alexandria from the former. Epiphanius and Eusebius accuse Scythianus of having imported from India in the second century, books on magic and heretical notions leading to Manichaeism; and it was during the same period that Ammonius Saccas instituted the sect of the New Platonists at Alexandria. The basis of the heresy was that true philosophy derived its origin from the Eastern nations."[2]

Mr. Davies says, "Scythianus was a contemporary of the Apostles and was engaged as a merchant in the Indian trade. In the course of his traffic, he often visited India and made himself acquainted with Hindu philosophy. According to Epiphanius and Cyril, he wrote a book in four parts, which they affirm to be the source from which the Manichaean doctrines were derived."[3]

It is thus clear that the Hindu philosophy is the fountainhead of the Greek philosophy with regard to some of its cardinal points. True philosophy, in fact, originated with the Hindus. Man first distinguished the Eternal from the perishable, and next he perceived within himself the germ of the Eternal. "This discovery," says Professor Max Müller, "Was an epoch in the history of the human mind, and the name of the discoverer has not been forgotten. It was

---

[1] Ward's *Mythology of the Hindus*, p. xxiii (Introduction). 'According to Greek tradition, Thales, Empedocles, Anaxagoras, Democritus and others undertook journeys to Oriental countries in order to study philosophy.' *History of Hindu Chemistry*, Vol. I, p.2

[2] Wilson's *Viṣṇu Purāṇa*, Preface, p. xiv

[3] Davies *Bhagavat Gītā*, p. 196

Śāṇḍilya who declared that the self within the heart was Brahmā."[1]

Excluding the extensive atheistic and agnostic systems of philosophy propounded by Charvaka and others, and those by the Jain and Buddhistic philosophers, the principal Hindu schools. of philosophy are known as the *Darśanas.* But much of the philosophical literature of the Hindus is lost., Professor Goldstucker, too, thinks that "probably besides the *Upaniṣads,* there were philosophical works which were more original than those now preserved, and which served as the common source of the works which have come down to us as the six Darśanas."

The *Darśanas* are: *Nyāya* and *Vaiśeṣika*; *Sāṅkhya* and *Yoga*; and *Pūrva* and *Uttara Mimānsas.*

---

[1] *Ancient Sanskrit literature*, p. 20

4.1 *NYĀYA*

The *Nyāya* system was founded by Gautama, who says that the way to salvation is the true knowledge of पदार्थ substance or being, which he classifies as under:

(I) *Pramāṇa* (2) *Prameya*

(3) *Sañśaya* (4) *Prayojana*

(5) *Dṛṣṭānta* (6) *Siddhānta* (principle).

(7) *Avyaya* (portion) (8) *Tarka* (logic).

(9) *Nirṇaya* (10) *Vāda*[1]

(11) *Jalpa*[2] (12) *Vitaṇḍā*[3]

(13) *Haitvābhāsa* (parallelogism)

(14) *Chala* (15) *Jāti*

(16) *Nigrahasthāna* (when one is pushed to an utterly untenable position)

The author then discusses (1) the nature of the argument and the proof, and their different kinds (प्रमेय वा प्रमाण), (2) the nature of the soul as apart from senses, body and the mind. The relation of the soul with the body is through the medium of the mind or man. The soul and the body cannot affect each other directly but only through the medium of the mind. He then proceeds to prove the transmigration of souls, the omnipresence and omniscience of God and declares that He is separate from the souls who are countless in number. The author believes the Vedas to be the Revelation and advises all mankind to follow their teachings. The material cause of the universe, he declares, is *Paramāṇu* (atoms). The *Paramāṇus* are eternal. The author then

---

[1] *Vāda*=a discussion with a sincere desire to get at the truth.

[2] *Jalpa*=a discussion to refute the oppoenent.

[3] *Vitaṇḍā*=when one obstantely clings to his own doctrine and does not listen to the other side.

proceeds to refute Atheism and ends by giving reasons for a belief in God. An English critic says, "The great prominence given to the method by means of which truth might be ascertained has sometimes misled European writers into the belief that it is merely a system of logic. Far from being restricted to mere logic, the *Nyāya* was intended to be a complete system of philosophical investigation, and dealt with some questions – such as the nature of the intellect, articulated sound, genus, variety, and individuality – in a manner so masterly as well to deserve the notice of European philosophers."[1] Mrs. Manning, after giving a brief outline of the Naiyāyika syllogistic proof, says, "Even the bare outline here given shows Gautama's mental powers and practical mode of dealing with the deepest question which affects the human mind."[2]

European logic employs phraseology founded upon classification, while the *Nyāya* system makes use of terms upon which a classification would be founded. The one infers that "kings are mortal because they belong to the class of mortal beings." The other arrives at the same conclusion, because mortality is inherent in humanity, and humanity is inherent in kings. The proposition given above would, as we have seen, be stated by a European logician as, "All men are mortal;" by a Hindu as, "Where there is humanity there is mortality." The reasoning is the same, but the Hindu method appears to be simpler.[3]

---

[1] *Chamber's Encyclopaedia*, '*Nyāya*.'

[2] *Ancient and Mediaeval India*, Vol. I, p. 173. Mrs. Manning says, 'His clearness of aim and his distinct perception of right means towards its attainment continue to be the invaluable guide of successive generations.'

[3] The European is assisted by the abstract ideas of Class; the Hindu makes use of what in Sanskrit is termed *Vyāpti*. 'It is difficult' remarks Dr. Roer, 'to find an adequate word in English for this term' For further information see Translation of *Bhāṣāparicheda*, pp. 31 and 32, note.

The German critic, Schlegel, says, "The *Nyāya* doctrine attributed to Gautama, from all that we can learn, was an idealism constructed with a purity and logical consistency of which there are few other instances and to which the Greeks never attained."[1]

As regards the logical system of the Hindus, Max Dunker says, "The logical researches of the Hindus 'are scarcely behind the similar works of modern times."[2] Mr. Elphinstone says, "An infinity of volumes have been produced by the Brāhmaṇas on the subject (Logic)."[3]

---

[1] Schlegel's *History of Literature*, p. 126

[2] *History of Antiquity*, p. 310

[3] Elphinstone's India, p. 122. Mrs. Manning says : 'To the ability of the author may be attributed the yet continued popularity of the work (*Nyāya*).'

4.2. *VAIŚEṢIKA*

The *Vaiśeṣika* is said to have been written not to oppose but to complete the *Nyāya* system with slight modifications it is only a fuller development of the *Nyāya*. In Sanskrit, these two schools of philosophy are comprised under one head, "*Mānava Śāstra.*" Kaṇāda, the founder of *Vaiśeṣika*, reduces the contents of the universe under six categories only. They are

1. *Dravya* (substance).
2. *Guṇa* (quality).
3. *Karma* (action or motion).
4. *Sāmānya* (generality or class).
5. *Viśeṣa* (atomic individuality or difference).
6. *Samvāya* (intimate relation).
7. *Abhāva* (non-existence) was added afterwards.

Kaṇāda's work is divided into ten books, of which the first book, after reducing the sixteen पदार्थ of the *Nyāya* to six only, as given above, discusses the nature of *Abhāva* or non-existence. The second book discusses the nature of *Dravya*. In the third are discussed *Ātmā* and *Antaḥkaraṇa* and their relation to each other. The *Ātmā* and *Antaḥkaraṇa* correspond with the *Jīva* and *mana* (मन) of the *Nyāya*. The fourth book discusses the nature of the human body and the external nature as affecting it, while the Vedic *Dharma* is upheld in the sixth book. The seventh book discusses Guṇa and *Samvāya*, their natures, kinds and effects. The eighth book shows the way to what the Hindus call *Jñāna*, or true knowledge of the mysteries of existence, non-existence and other metaphysical topics. The intellect and the *Viśeṣa* are discussed in the ninth book. The tenth book contains a detailed discussion on *Ātmā* and its *guṇas*, etc.

The points of difference between the *Nyāya* and the *Vaiśeṣika* are only two. (1) The *Nyāya* distributes the contents of the universe into sixteen categories, while the *Vaiśeṣika* does so into seven only. (2) The *Nyāya* accepts four kinds of *Pramāṇa* or arguments. The *Vaiśeṣika* accepts only two - *Pratyakṣa* and *Anumāna* – and rejects the remaining two, *Upamāna* and *Śabda*.

In the interesting introduction which Dr. Roer appends to the translation of *Bhāṣāparicheda* he compares Kanada's doctrine of atoms to that of Democritus, the Greek philosopher, and pronounces the former to be vastly superior.

'*Vaiśeṣika*," says Mrs. Manning,[1] "leans towards physical science rather than metaphysical." The theory of sound propounded by the Hindus seems to be in accordance with the latest European advancement in science. After distinguishing between the articulate and the inarticulate sounds, Viśvanātha, the author of *Bhāṣāpariccheda*, says, "Some say its (sound) production takes place like a succession of waves; according to others, like the bud of *Kadamba plant*" (verses 165, 166). The *Tarka Saṅgraha*, another work. of this school, says, "It is ether in which there resides the quality of sound. It is one, all-pervading and eternal."[2]

The author of the History of Hindu Chemistry says, "His. theory of the propagation of sound cannot fail to excite our wonder and admiration even at this distant date. No less remarkable is his statement that light and heat are only different forms of the same essential substance. But Kaṇāda is anticipated in many material points by Kapila, the reputed originator of the *Sāṅkhya* philosophy."[3]

According to the *Vaiśeṣika*, as also according to *Nyāya*, there are five members of the syllogism instead of three as in the English syllogism.

---

[1] *Ancient and Mediaeval India*, Vol. I, p.1

[2] *Ancient and Mediaeval India*, Vol. I, p. 189

[3] *History of Hindu Chemistry*, Vol. J. p. 1

They are - (I) Proposition. (2), Reason, (3) Example, (4) Application, (5) Conclusion.

For instance, (l) The mountain is fiery.

(2) Because it smokes.

(3) Whatever smokes is fiery, as a culinary hearth.

(4) This does smoke.

(5) Therefore it is fiery as aforesaid.

A charge of deficiency, "inaccuracy of definition," has been brought against the five-membered syllogism. Dr. Ballantyne thus meets the accusation, "The five-membered expression, so far as the arrangement of its parts is concerned, is a summary of the Naiyāyika's views in regard to rhetoric, 'an offshoot from logic' (see Whateley's Rhetoric, p. 6.), and one to which, after the ''ascertainment of the truth by investigation, belongs the establishment of it to the satisfaction of another."[1] To this Mrs. Manning adds the following: "In fact Gautama appears to have expressed bare logic in two member argument, and to have added two other members, when he sought to convince, rhetorically, After the declaration and the reason, he inserts an 'example' confirmatory and also suggestive, and an 'application' that is, he shows in the fourth member of his syllogism that his example possesses the required character; and then he winds up with the conclusion or Q. E. D., which is common to all syllogisms."

Evidently, the difference between the Hindu and the Greek syllogism (for the Europeans have no syllogism of their own)[2] is due to the difference of aim of the reasoning

[1] Ballantyne on the *Nyāya* system. -The Pandit, Vol. I, p. 39

[2] Three are only two nations in the whole history of the world who have conceived independently, and without any suggestion from others, the two sciences of Logic and Grammar, the Hindus and the Greeks'- Max Müller's *Ancient Sanskrit Literature*, p. 158. Considering that the Greek philosophers derived their philosophy

of the two nations. The Greek wanted to prove his contention, but the Hindu, being more practical and thorough, wanted to convince his adversary.

---

from India, there may be a doubt regarding the Greek originality.

4.3. *SĀṄKHYA*

This remarkable system of philosophy was founded by Kapila and is the oldest in the world. It teaches that there are twenty-four elements and that the twenty-fifth if it can be so called, is the *Puruṣa* or *Ātmā* (soul). The primary cause of the world is *Prakṛti*, one of the twenty-four. Of itself, *Prakṛti* is non-active, is, in fact. neither produced nor productive, but it becomes active by coming in contact with the *Puruṣa*.

The author holds that there are innumerable souls in the world, which fact constitutes one of its chief differences from the *Vedānta*. *Sāṅkhya* says nothing of God and on this account, some regard it as a system of scientific atheism but that the system is theistic is proved by the fact that such a decided theist as Patañjali vindicates its character and indeed supplements it by his own system, *Yoga*. *Sāṅkhya* differs from *Nyāya* chiefly on the following two points: (1) According to *Nyāya*, *Puruṣa* is the agent, and he again is the legitimate party to enjoy the result of action (*Karma*): *Sāṅkhya*, on the other hand, teaches that in its own nature *Puruṣa* has neither happiness nor misery. It has nothing to do with *Karma* and its results, but by coming into contact with *Prakṛti* it takes upon itself the good or the bad results of *Karma*. This is our ignorance. Knowledge would make us shun good or bad results. We will then be happy. The second point is this: *Sāṇkhya* teaches that there cannot be any thing which has not existed before. We cannot make a body round unless roundness already exists in it. It may not be seen, but still, there it is. *Nyāya* holds the opposite theory.

"*Sāṅkhya* doctrine," says Mrs. Manning, "is a very great effort at unravelling the deep mysteries of our existence. On the one side, it exhibits the worthlessness of the perishable universe, including a man with all his powers and qualities. On the other side, it places the imperishable soul. The Perishable portion of this division is fully and firmly dealt with and has excited the admiration and interest of such men as Wilson, Ballantyne and others. But concerning the soul or the imperishable portion of his subject, one feels that the author is reserved, or that he has more thoughts than he chooses to express."[1]

The word *Sāṅkhya* (*sam*=together and-*khya*=reasoning) indicates that the system is based on synthetic reasoning.

Sir W. Hunter says, "The various theories of creation, arrangement and development were each elaborated, and the views of the modern physiologists at the present day are a return with new light to the evolution theory of Kapila, whose *Sāṅkhya* system is the oldest of the *Darśanas.*"[2]

---

[1] Manning's *Ancient and Mediaeval India.* Vol. I, p. 153
[2] Indian Gazetteer, '*India,*' p. 214

4.4. *YOGA*

Without a knowledge of *Yoga*,[1] one cannot reach the real depths of human nature, and can never fathom the hidden mysteries and the realities of the heart, and know the nature of the soul and of God. True metaphysics is impossible without *Yoga*, and so is mental philosophy. Patañjali divides his work into four chapters. The first chapter, after discussing the nature of the soul and of *Yoga*, enumerates eight means or stages in the process by which *Yoga* can be accomplished. They are as under:

1. *Yama* (forbearance)

    (1) Not doing injury to living beings

    (2) Veracity

    (3) Avoidance of theft

    (4) Chastity

    (5) Non-acceptance of gifts

2. *Niyama* (Religious observance)

    (1) External and internal purity

    (2) Cheerfulness or contentment

    (3) Austerity

    (4) Chanting Vedic hymns

    (5) Devoted reliance on the Lord

3. *Āsana*'(Postures)

    There are 100 different postures of the body

4. *Prāṇāyāma* (Regulation of the breath)

    (1) Inhalation

---

[1] 'Al-Baruni translated *Saṅkhya* and *Yoga* into Arabic in the reign of Khalifa Al-Mammum' Max Müller's *Science of Language*, p. 165.

(2) Exhalation

(3) Suspension (*Khumbhaka*)

5. *Pratyāhāra* (Restraint of the senses)
6. *Dhārṇā* (focussing the mind)
7. *Dhyāna* (Meditation).
8. *Samādhi* (Trance)

After giving the above-mentioned sub-divisions the author describes the nature of *Samādhi* and its two divisions. The second chapter describes in details the ways and means to perform *Samādhi*. The third chapter describes the powers developed in a Yogī when he has reached the last stage of *Yoga*. *Samādhi* on different objects imparts different powers to the *Yogī*. *Samādhi* on the Moon gives one particular power, on the Jupiter another, and so on. The fourth, chapter treats of *Mokṣa*. Patañjali declares that when a man becomes adept at Samādhi, he gains a knowledge of the past and the future, a knowledge of the sounds of animals, of the thoughts of others, the time of his own death, etc.

It would be difficult to conceive all this but for the unimpeachable testimony of European scholars and officers. In an instance recorded by Prof. Wilson,[1] a Brahmaṇa appeared to sit in the air wholly unsupported and to remain so sitting on one occasion for twelve minutes and on another for forty minutes.

Colonel Olcott records an account of a Yogī described to him by Dr. Rajendralal Mitra, "It is not known when this Yogī went into *Samādhi*, but his body was found about 45 years ago quite lifeless. All manner of tortures were used to bring him back to consciousness, but all to no purpose. He

---

[1] Essays on the Religion of the Hindus, Vol. I, p. 209. See the description of the Yogis given by Oniscritus, a follower of Alexander. Also the account of Calanus.

was then touched by the hand of a female and he instantly came back to his senses."[1]

Dr. McGregor says in his *History of the Sikhs*, "A novel scene occurred at one of these garden houses in 1837. A fakeer who arrived at Lahore engaged in burying himself for any length of time shut up in a box without either food or drink! Runjeet disbelieved his assertions, and determined to put them to proof; for this purpose, the man was shut up in a wooden box, which was placed in a small apartment below the level of the ground. There was a folding door to the box which was secured by a lock and key. Surrounding this apartment there was the garden house, the door of which was likewise locked: and outside of this a high wall having the door built up with bricks and mud. Outside the hole, there was placed a line of *sentries*, so that no one could approach the building. The strictest watch was kept for the space of forty days and forty nights, at the expiration of which period the Maharaja, attended by his grandson and several of his Sirdars, as well as General Ventum, Captain Wade, and myself, proceeded to disinter the fakeer." After describing the condition of the fakeer after disinterment, in a few words, the author says, "When the fakeer was able to converse, the completion of the feat was announced by the discharge of guns and other demonstrations of joy; while a rich chain of gold was placed around his neck by Runjeet himself.

"Another gentleman of unimpeachable veracity describes the wonderful feat of a Lama who became his guest in September 1887 at Darjeeling. After describing his postures, etc., the eye-witness proceeds: 'Suddenly he, still retaining his sitting posture, rose perpendicularly into air to the height of, I should say, two cubits (one yard), and then floated without a tremor or motion of a single muscle, like a cork in still water.' The above are two out of numberless similar

---

[1] Col. Olcott's lecture on '*Theosophy, the scientific basis of religion*,' p. 18

cases. In India not only these things but feats of a far more extraordinary nature are so common that they fail to evoke surprise at all."[1]

Fryer was quite astonished to see Yogis who fixed their eyes towards the sun without losing their sight.

The *Yoga* philosophy is peculiar to the Hindus, and no trace of it is found in any other nation, ancient or modern. It was the fruit of the highest intellectual and spiritual development. The existence of this system is another proof of the intellectual superiority of the ancient Hindus over all other peoples.

---

[1] See also '*The Court and Camp of Ranjit Singh.*'

4.5. *MIMĀNSĀ*

Mimānsā is the collective name of two of the six divisions of Hindu Philosophy. They are the *Pūrva* and the *Uttara Mimānsā.* The terms *Uttara* and *Pūrva*, meaning 'latter and former', do not apply to the relative ages of the *Mimānsās* but to the sacred books which are indicated by them. *Pūrva Mimānsā* treats of the Hindu ritual and *Karmakāṇḍa* as promulgated in the *Brāhmaṇas*, whilst the *Uttara Mimānsā* treats of the nature of God and of the soul as taught in the *Upaniṣads.* And the two *Mimānsās* are so-called because the *Upaniṣads* were composed later than the *Brāhmaṇas*.

The *Pūrva Mimānsā* gives in full detail the *Karma* we have to perform. The *Yajñas*, Agnihotras, gifts, etc. are all treated elaborately and minutely. The author, the venerable Jaiminī, after discussing the nature of the *dharma* and adharma, says that *dharma* consists in following the teachings of the Vedas. *Dharma* is essentially necessary to gain happiness.

The *Uttara Mimānsā* is the work of the celebrated *Vyāsa*, and is one of the most important of the six *Darśanas.* The school of philosophy of which the *Uttara Mimānsā* is the best exposition is called *Vedānta.* The word *Vedānta* means "the end or the ultimate aim of the Vedas," and the Vedanta system discusses the nature of the Brahma and the soul. The *Uttara Mimānsā* is one of the grandest feats of the grand Hindu genius. The *Brahmsūtra* of Vyāsa begins with a refutation of atheism and a vindication of theism. It then lays down that the only way to salvation or *mukti* is *ātmajñāna*, or a true knowledge of the soul.

Professor Max Müller says, "Much that was most dear, that had seemed for a time their very self, had to be surrendered before they could find the self of selves, the old man, the looker on, a subject independent of 'all personality, and existence independent of all life. When that point had been reached then the highest knowledge began to draw, the self within (the *Pratyagātman*) was drawn towards the highest self, (the *Paramātman*), is found its true self in the highest self, and the oneness of the subjective with the objective self was recognised as underlying all reality, as the dim dream of religion – as the pure light of philosophy."

"This fundamental idea is worked out with systematic completeness in the *Vedānta* philosophy, and no one who can appreciate the lessons contained in Berkeley's Philosophy, will read the *Upaniṣads* and the *Brahma Sūtras* without, feeling a richer and a wiser man."[1]

There is a difference of opinion as regards the Vedantic view of the nature of the soul and of God. Ramanuja Swami held that the relation between God and soul was that of a master and servant – that they were separate entities, and that there were innumerable souls. The great Śaṅkarācārya believed that the *Vedānta* taught that there was only one Brahma and all else was māyā or illusion.

Swami Dayanand Saraswati, however, has again reverted to the view originally held of *Vedānta*, and said that the *Brahmasūtras* or the real *Vedānta Sūtra* never taught the unity of God and soul. Popular belief, however, is swayed by the views of Śankara Swami, and the system is held to be an all-absorbing Pantheism. Anyway, it is the most sublime system of philosophy ever propounded by man.

Of Śaṅkara's commentary upon the *Vedānta,* Sir W. Jones says that "it is not possible to speak with too much applause of so excellent a work; and I am confident in asserting that, until an accurate translation of it shall appear in some European language, the general history of philosophy must remain incomplete.

Sir W. Jones says of *Vedānta,* "The fundamental tenet of the Vedantic school consisted not in denying the existence of matter, that is, of a solidity, impenetrability, and extended figure (to deny which would be lunacy), but in correcting

---

[1] *India : What can it teach us?* p. 253

the popular notion of it, and in contending that it has no essence independent of mental perception, that existence and perceptibility are convertible terms, that external appearances and sensations are illusory and would vanish into nothing if the divine energy, which alone sustains them, were suspended but for a moment: an opinion which Epicharmus and Plato seem to have adopted, and which has been maintained in the present century with great elegance, but with little applause, partly because it has been misunderstood, and partly because it has been misapplied by the false reasoning of some popular writers, who are said to have disbelieved in the moral attributes of God, whose omnipresence, wisdom and goodness are the basis of the Indian philosophy." He adds, "The system is built on the purest devotion."[1] Sir James Mackintosh, an English philosopher, 'calls the theory (propounded by *Vedānta*) refined, abstruse, ingenious and beautiful."

The *Mimānsā* method of *Pūrva Pakṣa* (reason contra), *Uttara Pakṣa* (reason pro), and Siddhant (conclusion) of the *Śāstras* excite Professor Max Müller's admiration, who says, "It is indeed one of the most curious kinds of literary

---

[1] Sir W. Jones' Works, Vol. I, p. 165, "We might be able", says Count Bjornstjerna, "to resign ourselves with patient submission to the comfortless doctrine of Pantheism, if it only concerned ourselves, but together with the hope of our own continued existence, to lose at the same time that of seeing again those whom we have most loved upon earth, to break them for ever is a reflection that bruises the heart. What! shall we first be bereaved of these beloved ones, retain nothing of them but memory's faint shadow, and then when we are called to follow them, shall even this shadow fly away 'from us? No such can never be the intention of the all-bountiful Creator; He has not deposited in our hearts the tender feelings of love and of friendship in order at life's goal to rend asunder for ever the band that has been tied by them! They are of a spiritual nature, they follow the spirit beyond the boundary of life where we shall find again those whom we have loved." *Theogony of the Hindus*, p.79. What a misunderstanding of Pantheism!

composition that the human mind ever conceived. It is wonderful that the Indians should have invented and mastered this difficult form so as to have made it the vehicle of expression for every kind of learning."[1]

The six *Darśanas* are rarely read and understood by Europeans, owing partly to the extreme difficulty of the language and a peculiar and difficult philosophic technique difficult to acquire, and partly to the want on their part of that mental equipment which is the result of the – highest intellectual training and great spiritual development.

As is well known, the *Upaniṣads* are the fountainhead of all Hindu philosophy. They are said to be 52 in number. The Upanishads are disquisitions on philosophical subjects and breathe an air of sublimity and spirituality, which is nowhere else to be found. The profound philosophy they teach, the deep wisdom they contain, the infallible truths they establish, and the true principles they set forth are the standing marvels of Indian intellect and monuments of human genius.

In his Philosophy of the *Upaniṣads*, recently translated by Rev. A.S. Geden, M.A., Prof. Deussen claims for its fundamental thought "an inestimable value for the whole race of mankind." It is in "marvellous agreement with the philosophy founded by Kant and adopted and perfected by his great successor, Schopenhauer," differing from it, where it does differ, only to excel. For, whereas the philosophy of Schopenhauer only "represent Christianity in its present form," we must have recourse to the *Upaniṣads* "if we are willing to put the finishing touch to the Christian consciousness, and to make it on all sides consistent and complete." "Professor Deussen, it is true, is kind enough to

---

1 'In this method," says Prof. Max Müller, ''the concatenation of *pros* and *cons* is often so complicated and the reason on both sides defended by the same author with such seriousness that we sometimes remain doubtful to which side the author leans, till we arrive at the end of the whole chapter.'

Christianity to bracket the *New Testament* and the Upaniṣ ads as "the two noblest products of the religious consciousness of mankind," but leaves his readers in no doubt as to which he considers the nobler of the two."

The great German philosopher, Schopenhauer, says, "Oh! how thoroughly is the mind here washed clean of all early engrafted Jewish superstitions and of all philosophy that cringes before those superstitions? In the whole world, there is no Study, except that of the originals, so beneficial and so elevating as that of the *Upaniṣads.* It has been the solace of my life, it will be the solace of my death."

Mr. Elphinstone, in comparing the ancient Greeks with the Ancient Hindus, says, "Their (Hindus) general learning was more considerable; and in the knowledge of the being and nature of God, they were already in possession of a light which was but faintly perceived even by the loftiest intellects in the best days of Athens."[1]

[1] Elphinstone's *History of India*, p. 49

4.6. *BHAGAVATA GĪTĀ*

Bhagavat Gītā has for centuries moulded the thoughts and the conduct of a large section of the Hindu nation. *Bhagavat Gītā* is essentially a work on the *Vedānta* philosophy and appears to have been composed to correct a misconception of that noble system. Owing to a misunderstanding of the teachings of this sublime philosophy, men began to neglect their duties and responsibilities, since there was only one Brahma and all else was an illusion. This alarmed all good and thoughtful men, and as an antidote, this excellent book, *Bhagavat Gītā*, was written. It is the part of the *Mahābhārata.* Taking the battle-field as the fittest place, Vyāsa introduced discussions on such sublime metaphysical questions as the book contains. The book has not only fascinated the minds of Hindus but has charmed Europeans, who speak in rapturous terms of this celebrated poem.

Mrs. Manning says, "*Bhagavat Gītā* is one of the most remarkable compositions in the Sanskrit language."

Professor Heeren says, "The poem certainly abounds in sublime passages, which remind one of the Orphic hymns to Jupiter quoted by Stoboeus."[1]

Mr Elphinstone[2] says, "*Bhagavat Gītā* deserves high praise for the skill with which it is adapted to the general Epic and the tenderness and elegance of the narrative by means of which it is introduced."

---

[1] *Historical Researches*, Vol. II, p. 198

[2] *History of India*, p. 155

5

SCIENCE

5.1. MEDICINE

A wise physician, skill'd our wounds to heal,
Is more than armies to the public weal.

POPE

The science of medicine, like all other sciences, was carried to a very high degree of perfection by the ancient Hindus. Their great powers of observation, generalisation and analysis, combined with patient labour in a country of boundless resources, whose fertility for herbs and plants is most remarkable, placed them in an exceptionally favourable position to prosecute their Study of this great science. Owing, however, to the destruction of a great part of Sanskrit literature, it is impossible to form an accurate estimate of the high proficiency attained by the Hindus in this important science. Unlike philosophy and grammar, on which subjects ancient works still extant furnish sufficient material to enable one to form a correct judgement of their pre-eminence in those branches of learning, medicine is a practical science which has long been neglected owing to a variety of causes.

Lord Ampthill recently (February 1905) said at Madras, "Now we are beginning to find out that the Hindu *Śāstras* also contain a Sanitary Code no less correct in principal, and that the great law-giver, Manu, was one of the greatest sanitary reformers the world has ever seen."

Professor Wilson says, "The Ancient Hindus attained as thorough a proficiency in medicine and surgery as any people: whose acquisitions are recorded. This might be expected because their patient attention and natural shrewdness would render them excellent observers, whilst the extent and fertility of their native country would furnish them with many valuable drugs and medicaments. Their diagnosis is said, in consequence, to define and distinguish symptoms with great accuracy, and their Materia Medica is most voluminous."[1]

Sir William Hunter has the following on the scope of Indian medicine: 'Indian medicine dealt with the whole area of the science. It described the structure of the body, its organs, ligaments, muscles, vessels and tissues. The Materia Medica or the Hindus embraces a vast collection of drugs belonging to the mineral, vegetable and animal kingdoms, many of which have now been adopted by European physicians. Their pharmacy confined ingenious processes of preparation with elaborate directions for the administration and classification of medicines. Much attention was devoted to hygiene, regimen of the body and diet."[2]

Mr. Weber says, "The number of medical works and authors is extraordinarily large."[3]

The *Ayurveda* is the oldest system of medicine and is said to have been revealed by the great Hindu physician, Dhanvantari[4] to his pupil Suśruta. Charaka states that "originally the contents of his own works were communicated by Ātareya Muni; to Agniveśa, and by him to Charaka, who condensed where it was too prolix and expanded where it was too brief." Suśruta and Charaka are now the two most important and well-known works on Hindu medicine.

---

[1] Wilson's Works, Vol. Vol. III, p. 69, '*Materia Medica*,' says Weber, 'generally appears to have been handled with great predilection.' *Indian Literature*, p. 270

[2] *Imperial Indian Gazetteer*, '*India*,' p. 220

[3] Weber's *Indian Literature*, p. 269

[4] The name of this great man, *Dhanvantari*, has become a byeword for an 'adept'. His name is always pronounced before taking medicine in Rajputānā, in consequence of the popular belief that his prescriptions are infallible.

The chief distinction of the modern European science of medicine is surgery. But even in surgery, as will be clear from the following quotations. the ancient Hindus attained a proficiency yet unsurpassed by the advanced medical science to the present day.

Mr. Weber says, "In surgery, too, the Indians seem to have attained a special proficiency, and in this department, European surgeons might perhaps, even at the present day still learn something from them, as indeed they have already borrowed from them the operation of rhinoplasty."[1]

"Their surgery," says Elphinstone, "is as remarkable as their medicine."[2] Mrs. Manning says, "The surgical instruments of the Hindus were sufficiently sharp, indeed, as to be capable of dividing a hair longitudinally."[3]

Dr. Sir W. W. Hunter says, "The surgery of the Ancient Indian physicians was bold and skilful. They conducted amputations, arresting the bleeding by pressure, a cup-shaped bandage and boiling oil practised lithotomy; performed operations in the abdomen and uterus; cured hernia, fistula, piles; set broken bones and dislocations; and were dexterous in the extraction of foreign substances from the body. A special branch of surgery was devoted to rhinoplasty, or operation for improving deformed ears and noses and forming new ones, a useful operation which European surgeons have now borrowed. The ancient Indian surgeons also mention a cure for neuralgia, analogous to the modern cutting of the fifth nerve above the eyebrow. They devoted great care to the making of surgical instruments, and to the training of students by means of operations performed on wax spread on a board or on the tissues and cells of the vegetable kingdom, and upon dead animals. They were expert in midwifery, not shrinking from the most critical operations, and in the diseases of women and

---

[1] Weber's *Indian Literature*, p. 270

[2] *History of India*, p. 145

[3] *Ancient and Mediaeval India*, Vol. II, p. 346

children. Their practice of physic embraced the classifications, causes, symptoms and treatment of diseases, diagnosis and prognosis. Considerable advances were also made in veterinary science, and monographs exist on the diseases of horses, elephants, etc."[1]

The author of the History of Hindu Chemistry says, According to Suśruta, the dissection of dead bodies is a *sine qua non* to the student of surgery, and this high authority lays particular stress on knowledge gained from experiment and observation."[2]

A word with regard to the Veterinary Science. Mr. H. M. Elliot says, "There is in the Royal library at Lucknow a work on the veterinary art, which was translated from the Sanskrit by order of Ghayas-ud-din Mohamed Shah Khilji."

This rare book, called *Kurrait-id-mulk*, was translated as early as A.H. 783=1381 AD., from an original, styled Salotar, which is the name of an Indian who is said to have been a tutor of Suśruta. The Preface says that the translation was made "from the barbarous Hindi into the refined Persian, in order that there may be no more need of a reference to infidels." The book is divided into eleven chapters and thirty Sections.

Chapter	I. On the breeds and names of horses	4 sections
”	II. On their odour, on riding, and breeding	3 ”
”	III. On stable management, and on wasps building nests in a stable	2 ”
”	IV. On colour and its varieties	2 ”
”	V. On their blemishes	3 ”
”	VI. On their limbs	2 ”

[1] *Indian Gazetteer*, 'India', p. 220, See also Weber's *Indian Literature*, pp. 270

[2] *History of Hindu Chemistry*, Vol. I, p. 105

”	VII. On sickness and its remedies	4 ”
”	VIII. On bleeding	4”
”	IX. On food and diet	2”
”	X. On feeding for the purpose of fattening.	2”
”	XI. On ascertaining the age by the teeth	1”

The precise age of this work is doubtful, because, although it is plainly stated to have been translated in A. H. 783, yet the reigning prince is called Sultan Ghayas-ud-din Mohamed Shah, son of Mahmud Shah, and there is no king so named whose reign corresponds with that date. If Sultan Gyas-ud-din Tughlak be meant, it should date sixty years earlier, and if the king of Malwa, who bore that name, be meant, it should be dated one hundred years later; either way, it very much precedes the reign of Akbar.[1]

The translator makes no mention in it of the work on the same subject, which had been previously translated from the Sanskrit into Arabic at Baghdad, under the name of *Kitab-ul-Baitarat.*[2]

Professor Weber says, “In the Vedic period, animal anatomy was evidently thoroughly understood, as each part had its own distinctive name”. He also says, “The chapter of

---

[1] ‘It is curious, that without any allusion to this work, another on the veterinary art, styled Salotari, and said to comprise in the Sanskrit original 16,000 *ślokas,* was translated in the regin of Shahjahān,“when there were many learned men who knew Sanskrit,’by Sayyid Abdullah Khan Bhadur Firoz Jung, who had found it among some of her Sanskrit books, which during his expedition against Mewar, in the reign of Jehangir, had been plundered from Amar Singh, Rana of Chitor. It is divided into twelve chapters, and is more than double the size of the other.’

[2] Elliot’s *Historians of India*, Part I, pp 263, 64

Amarkośa on the human body and its diseases certainly presupposes an advanced cultivation of medical science."[1]

Professor Wilson says, "There is a very large body of medical literature in Sanskrit, and some of the principal works are named by Arabic writers as having been known and translated at Baghdad in the ninth century. These works comprise all the branches of medical science, surgery included, and contain numerous instances of accurate observation and judicious treatment."

The Hindus have, through this branch of knowledge, as through many others, been the benefactors of humanity; for Hindu medicine is the foundation upon which the building of the European medical science has been constructed. His Excellency Lord Ampthill, the late Governor of Madras, while declaring open the Madras King Institute of Preventive Medicine, said, "The people of India should be grateful to him (Col. King) for having pointed out to them that they can lay claim to having been acquainted with the main principles of curative and preventive medicine at a time when Europe was still immersed in ignorant savagery. I am not sure whether it is generally known that the science of medicine originated in India, but this is the case, and the science was first exported from India to Arabia and thence to Europe. Down to the close of the seventeenth century, European physicians learnt the science from the works of Arabic doctors; while the Arabic doctors many centuries before had obtained their knowledge from the works of great Indian physicians such as Dhanvantri, Charaka and Suśruta. It is a strange circumstance in the world's progress that the centre of enlightenment and knowledge should have travelled from East to West, leaving but little permanent trace of its former existence in the East."

Sir W. Hunter says, "The Hindu medicine is an independent development. Arab medicine was founded on

---

[1] Weber's *Indian Literature*, p. 267

the translations from the Sanskrit[1] treatises made by command of the Khalif of Baghdad (950-960 A D.). European medicine down to the 17th century was based upon the Arabic, and the name of the Indian physician, Charaka, repeatedly occurs in Latin translations of Avicenna (Abu Sina), Rhazes (Abu Rasi), and Serapion (Abu Sirabi)."

Mrs. Manning says, "The medical works of India had already attained world-wide celebrity when the Khalif of Baghdad collected the greatest works and summoned the most learned scientific men of their era to give brilliancy to Baghdad as a seat of learning." She adds, "It is impossible to exhibit India's ancient science to Europeans unacquainted with Sanskrit or not having access to the native medical libraries, in which we understand many medical works are strictly withheld from Europeans."[2]

In support of the fact that Hindu medical works were largely translated by the Arabs, and that these translations formed the nucleus of their science, and that after being translated into European languages they formed the backbone of the European science of medicine, the following facts may be cited:

Barzouhyeh, a contemporary of the celebrated Sassanian king, Noshirevan (AD 531-572), visited India to acquire proficiency in the Indian sciences.[3]

According to Professor Sachau, the learned translator of Alberuni, "some of the books that had been translated under the first Abbaside Caliphs were extant in the library of Alberuni, when he wrote his '*India*,' the *Brahma Siddhānta*

[1] Csoma de Koros was the first to announce that the Tibetan Tanjur contains among others translations of the *Caraka*, the *Suśruta* and the *Vāgabhaṭa*.

[2] *Ancient and Mediaeval India*, Vol. I, pp. 353, 54

[3] *History of Hindus Chemistry*, Introduction, p.76

or *Sind-hind*,... the Charaka in the edition of Ali Ibn Zain and the *Pañcatantra*, or *Kalila Damna*."[1]

Almansur or Almanzar, who removed his seat from Damascus to Baghdad between 753 and, 774 AD, caused translations to be made from the Sanskrit of medical scientific works, among which we find particularised a tract upon poisons by Shank (meaning Charaka) and a treatise on medicine by Shashrud[2] (meaning Suśruta).

Mrs. Manning says, "Later Greeks at Baghdad are found to have been acquainted with the medical works of the Hindus, and to have availed themselves of their medicaments."[3] We learn with interest that Serapion, one of the earliest of the Arab writers, mentions the Indian Charaka, praising him as an authority in medicine, and referring to the myrobalans as forming part of Charaka's descriptions."[4]

Rhazes was a greater physician than Serapion. He lived, at Baghdad with Al-Mansur. He wrote twelve books on. chemistry. On two occasions, Rhazes refers to the "Indian Caraka" as an authority for statements on plants or drugs."[5]

Another celebrated medical man is Avicinna (Abu Ali Sina)" called Sheikh Rais, or the prince of physicians, who succeeded Rhazes. He was the most famous physician of his

---

[1] Alberuni's India by Professor Sachau.

[2] Colebrooke's Algebra of the Hindus, Vol. II, p, 512. That Caraka should be changed by Arabic writers into Sarak, Suśruta into Susrud, Nidāna into Badan, Āṣṭāṅga into Asankar, and so forth, need not at all surprise us. Such transformations can well be explained on phonetic principles. Moreover, one must remember that the Indian work translated into Arabic were sometimes derived from pre-existing Pahalvi version, and in the migrations through successive languages the names often got rightfully disfigured.

[3] *Ancient and Mediaeval India*, Vol. I, p. 359

[4] Royle's *Ancient Hindu Medicine*, p. 36

[5] See Royle, p. 38

time. He translated the works of Aristotle, and died in 1036 AD. In treating of leeches, Avicinna begins by a reference to what "the Indians say," and then gives nearly the very words of Suśruta, describing the six poisonous leeches, amongst which are "those called Krishna or black, the hairy leech, that which is variegated like a rainbow, etc."[1]

Emperor Firoz Shah, after capturing Nagarkot, had the Sanskrit medical works translated into Arabic by Ayazuddin Khalid.[2]

In the reign of Harun-ul-Rashed, the Hindu medicine was not only valued by the Arabs, but Hindu physicians were actually invited to Baghdad, who went and resided in his court. For this information, we are indebted to Abu Osaiba, whose biographies are quoted by Prof. Deitz in his Analecta Medica,[3] Wustenfeld, Rev. W. Cureton,[4]. Flu Müller.

Abu Osaiba states that Manka was a Hindu, eminent in the art of medicine and learned in Sanskrit literature. He made a journey from India to Iraq, cured the Khalif Harun-ul-Rasheed of an illness, and translated a work on poison by Charaka from Sanskrit into Persian. Another Hindu doctor named Saleh has also been eulogised by Abu Osaiba. He was, it is said, one of the most learned amongst the Hindus, and greatly skilled in curing diseases according to the Indian mode. He lived in Iraq during Haruil's reign. He travelled to Egypt and Palestine, and was buried when he died in Egypt.

---

[1] Royle's *Ancient Hindu Medicine*, p. 38

[2] Max Müller's *Science of Language*, p. 167

[3] Leipsic Edition of 1833, p. 124

[4] Journal of the R.A. society, VI, pp. 105-115

Gabriel Bactishna, a Syrian, became one of the translators of works on medicine from Sanskrit into Arabic."[1]

Professor Sanchan says, "What India has contributed reached Baghdad by two different roads. The part has come directly in translations from the Sanskrit, the part has travelled through Iran, having originally been translated from Sanskrit (Pali? Prakrit?) into Persian, and farther from Persian into Arabic. In this way, e.g., the fables of *Kalila and Dimna* have been communicated to the Arabs, and a book on medicine, probably the famous Caraka of Fihrist, p. 303.

''In this communication between India and Baghdad, we must not only distinguish between two different roads, but also between two different periods.

"As Sindh was under the actual rule of the Khalif' Mansur (AD 753-774), there came embassies from that part of India to Baghdad, and among them scholars, who brought along with them two books, the *Brahmasidhānta* of Brahmagupta (Sindhind), and his *Khaṇḍakhādyaka* (Arkand). With the help of these pundits, Alfazari, perhaps also Yakub

---

[1] See Deitz's *Analecta Medica.* Dr. Furnell, Dy. Surgeon-General and Sanitary Commissioner, Madras, in his lecture delivered on the 1st April 1882, most vigorously supported the claims of Hindu medicine as one of the most ancient and the most advanced sciences ever cultivated in the world. Speaking of the importance of drinking unpolluted water, he said that ''as the ancient Hindus were superior to all others in other respects, so also were they superior to the others in recognising the importance and value of water, as well as in insisting upon preserving the water from filth of any kind whatever." He added that in his address to the Convocation in 1879 he had said that the Hindu physicians were unrivalled in all branches of medicine at the time when the Britons were savages and used to go about quite naked. He then described the instructions contained in the Hindu medical works with regard to the use of water, which he said were most remarkable.

Ibn Tarik, translated them. Both works have been largely used, and have exercised a great influence. It was on this occasion that the Arabs first became acquainted with a scientific system of astronomy. They learned from Brahmagupta earlier than from Ptolemy.

"Another influx of Hindu learning took place under Harun, AD 786-808. The ministerial family Barmak, then at the zenith of their power, 'had come with the ruling dynasty from Balkh, where an ancestor of theirs had been an official in the Buddhistic temple, Naubehar, i.e., *navavihāra*, the new temple (or monastery). The name Barmak is said to be of Indian descent, meaning *paramaka*, i.e., the superior (abbot of the *vihāra*?). Of course, the Barmak family had been converted, but their contemporaries never thought much of their profession of Islam, nor regarded it as genuine. Induced probably by family traditions, they sent scholars to India, there to study medicine and pharmacology. Besides, they engaged Hindu scholars to come to Baghdad, made them the chief physicians of their hospitals and ordered them to translate from Sanskrit into Arabic, books on medicine, pharmacology, toxicology, philosophy, astrology and other subjects. Still, in later centuries, Muslim scholars sometimes travelled for the same purposes as the emissaries of the Barmak, e.g., Almuwaffak, not long before Alberuni's time."[1]

Mrs. Manning says, "Greek physicians have done much to preserve and diffuse the medical science of India. We find, for instance, that the Greek physician Actuarius celebrates the Hindu medicine called *triphalā*. He mentions the peculiar products of India, of which it is composed, by their Sanskrit name *Myrobalans*.[2] Aetius, who was a native of Amida in Mesopotamia, and studied at Alexandria in the fifth century, not only speaks of the Myrobalans, but

---

[1] Sachau's Translation of *Alberuni's India*

[2] *Ancient and Mediaeval India*, Vol. I, p. 351

mentions them as the proper cure for the disease called elephantiasis."

Among the ancient Hindu physicians of note may be mentioned (1) Ātareya, Agniveśa, Charaka, Dhanvantrī, Suśruta, Bhāradvāja, Kapiṣṭhala, Bhela, Latukarṇa, Parāśara, Hārita, Kashraparu, Āśavalāyana, Bādarāyaṇa, Kātyāyana, Baijvapi, Krisa, Sāmkṛtyāyana, Babhravya Kṛṣ ṇātreya, Auddālaki, Śvetaketu, Pañcāla, Gonardīya, Gonikaputra, Subandhu, Śaṁkara, Kaṅkāyana.

The Englishman (a Calcutta daily), in a leader in 1880, said, "No one can read the rules contained in great Sanskrit medical works without coming to the conclusion that, in point of knowledge, the ancient Hindus were in this respect very far in advance not only of the Greeks and Romans, but of Mediaeval Europe."

Nearchas relates that the Greek physicians did not know how to cure snakebite. But the Hindu physicians cured it and notified their ability to cure all who were afflicted with it if they came to the court of Alexander the Great.[1]

As regards their knowledge of the Science of Chemistry, Mr. Elphinstone says, "Their (Indian) chemical skill is a fact more striking and more unexpected."

It is to be regretted that of the several works on chemistry[2] quoted by Mādhava, Rasārṇava alone seems to have survived to our day.

---

[1] See Wise's *History of medicine*, p. 9

[2] "A famous representative of this art (alchemy) was Nagarjuna, a native of Daihak, near Somnātha. He excelled in it, and composed a book which contains the substance of the whole literature on this subject, and is very rare.' *History of Hindu Chemistry*, Vol, I. p. 54.

'Nagarjuna Bodhisatva was well practised in the art of compounding medicines; by taking a preparation (pill or cake), he nourished the years of life for many hundreds of years, so that neither the mind nor appearance decayed. Satvaha-Raja han

The author of the History of Hindu Chemistry says, "While *Rasaratnākara* and *Rasārṇava* are *Tantras* pure and simple in which alchemy is incidentally dwelt upon, *Rasaratna samuccaya* (a modern work based on old Hindu medical works), in a systematic and comprehensive treatise on materia medica, pharmacy and medicine. Its methodical and scientit1c arrangement of the subject matter would do credit to any modern work, and altogether it should be pronounced a production unique of its kind in Sanskrit Literature."[1]

Dr. Ray says, "We have only to refer our readers to the chapter on the preparation of caustic alkali, in the Susruta, with the direction that the strong lye is to be 'preserved in an iron vessel,' as a proof of the high degree of perfection in scientific pharmacy achieved by the Hindus at an early age. It is absolutely free from any trace of quackery or charlatanism and is a decided improvement upon the process prescribed by a Greek writer of the eleventh century, as unearthed M. Berthelot. As regards dispensaries and hospitals, everyone knows that Buddhistic India was studded with them."[2]

In the European histories of chemistry, the credit of being the first to press chemical knowledge into the service of medicine and introduce the use of the internal administration of mercurial preparations is given to Paracelsus (1493-1541). But, says the author of the *History of Hindu Chemistry*, "we have, indeed reason to suspect that Paracelsus got his ideas from the East."[3]

Dr. Ray says, "From the evidence we have adduced all along there can now be scarcely any question as regards the priority of the Hindus in making mercurial remedies a

---

partaken of this mysterious medicine." Beal's Buddhist Records of the Western World, Vol. II, p. 212.

[1] *History of Hindu Chemistry*, Vol. I, p. L.

[2] *History of Hindu Chemistry*, Vol. I, Introduction, p. viii.

[3] *History of Hindu Chemistry*, Vol. 1, p. 60

speciality; and they are entitled to claim originality in respect of the internal administration of metals generally, seeing that the Charaka and the Suśruta, not to speak of the later *Tantras*, are eloquent over their virtues."[1]

In Europe, however, the medicinal virtues of mercury do not appear to have been at all ascertained even in the days of Pliny the elder; that writer termed quicksilver the *bane* and poison of all things, and what would with more propriety be called *death-silver.* [2]

Mr. Elphinstone says, "They knew how to prepare sulphuric acid, nitric acid and muriatic acid; the oxide of copper, iron, lead (of which they had both the red oxide and litharge), tin and zinc; the sulphurets of iron, copper, mercury, antimony, and arsenic; the sulphate of copper, zinc and iron; and carbonates of lead and iron. Their modes of preparing these substances were sometimes peculiar."[3]

"Their use of these medicines seems to have been very bold. They were the first nation who employed minerals internally, and they not only gave mercury in that manner but arsenic and arsenious acid, which were remedies in intermittent. They have long used cinnabar for fumigations, by which they produced a speedy and safe salivation. They have long practised inoculation.

"They cut for the stode couched for the cataract and extracted the foetus from the womb, and in their early works enumerate not less than 127 sorts, of surgical instruments."[4]

---

[1] *History of Hindu Chemistry*, Vol. I, Introduction, p. (xii)

[2] *Natural History*, lib, 33

[3] For further information see Dr. Royle (p. 44 and on), who particularly refers to the processes for making calomel and corrosive sublimate.

[4] Elphinstone's *History of India*, p. 145. The author also says, 'Their acquaintance with medicines seems to have been very extensive. We are not surprised at their knowledge of simples, in which they gave early lessons to Europe and more recently

In the course of a lecture to the natives of Bengal on national universities in India, delivered at Calcutta, in January 1906, Mrs. Besant said, "In physics and chemistry you have advanced far more. In medicine, you are still more advanced. In the West, it is by no means a science but largely guess work. Indian medicine both of the Hindus and the Mohamedans is superior to the medicine of the West."

In order to give an idea of the advanced state of the Hindu science of medicine and hygiene, as well as of what we may yet expect from the continued researches of the learned in ancient Indian literature in the way of valuable additions to the modem European medical science, I cannot do better than quote the words of His Excellency Lord Ampthill, Governor of Madras, at the opening of the King Institute of Preventive Medicine, in February 1905, "The Mohamedan conquests brought back to India much of the medical knowledge which had been lost for centuries, and we have proofs that the Mughal rulers were great sanitary reformers in the magnificent water works which still exist and perform their functions at various places in the north of India. Now, the British rulers of India have been bringing back yet more of the knowledge which emanated from this country centuries ago; and when we undertake municipal water supply schemes, with filter beds and hydraulic pressure, when we build hospitals and establish medical schools, when we promulgate regulations to check the spread of plague, or when we impose on local bodies the duty of watching over the health of the people, we are not introducing any modern innovations or European fads, but merely doing that which was done centuries ago, and again centuries before that, but which has long since been forgotten by all except the historian and the archaeologist. The study of these questions brings out the truth of the old saying that there is nothing new in the world. Now, this saying is even true as regards preventive medicine, which

---

taught us the benefit of smoking *dhatura* in asthma and the use of cowitch against worms.'

we are all apt to regard as one of the most recent discoveries of modern science. Colonel King gives clear proof that the ancient caste injunctions of the Hindus were based on a belief in the existence of transmissible – agents of disease, and that both Hindus and Mohamedans used inoculation by small-pox virus as a protection against small-pox; and certain it is that long before Jenner's great discovery, or to be more correct, rediscovery of vaccination, this art of inoculation was used for a While in Europe, where it has been imported from Constantinople; and knowledge or medicine which flourished in the Near East at the commencement of the Christian era emanated, as I have already shown you, from India."

He then added, "It is. also very probable, so Colonel King assures me, that the ancient Hindus used animal vaccination secured by transmission of the small-pox virus through the cow, and he bases this interesting theory on a quotation from a writing by Dhanvantri, the greatest of the ancient Hindu physicians, which is so striking and so appropriate to the present occasion that I must take the liberty of reading it to you. It is as follows: 'Take the fluid of the pock on the udder of the cow or on the arm between the shoulder and elbow of a human subject on the point of a lancet, and lance with it the arms between the shoulder and elbows until the blood appears : then mixing the fluid with the blood the fever of the small-pox will be produced.' This is vaccination pure and simple. It would seem from it that Jenner's great discovery was actually forestalled by the ancient Hindus."

His Excellency further said, "1 cannot refrain from mentioning yet another of Colonel King's interesting discoveries, which is that the modern plague policy of evacuation and disinfection is not a wit different from that enjoined in ancient Hindu *Śāstras.*"

5.2. MATHEMATICS

In Mathematics he was greater
Than Tycho Brahe, or Erra Pater.

BUTLER: Hudibras

In mental abstraction and concentration of thought, the Hindus are proverbially happy. Apart from direct testimony on the point, the literature of the Hindus furnishes unmistakable evidence to prove that the ancient Hindus possessed astonishing powers of memory and concentration of thought. Hence all such sciences and branches of study as demand concentration of thought and a highly-developed power of abstraction of the mind were highly cultivated by the Hindus. The science of mathematics, the most abstract of all sciences, must have had an irresistible fascination for the minds of the Hindus. Nor are there proofs wanting to support this statement. The most extensive cultivation which astronomy received at the hands of the Hindus is in itself a proof of their high proficiency in mathematics. The high antiquity of Hindu astronomy is an argument in support of a still greater antiquity of their mathematics. That the Hindus were selected by nature to excel all other nations in mathematics, is proved by her revealing to them the foundation of all mathematics. It has been admitted by all competent authorities that the Hindus were the inventors of the numerals. The great German critic, Schlegel says that the Hindus invented "the decimal cyphers, the honour of which, next to letters the most important of human discoveries, has, with the common consent of historical authorities, been ascribed to the Hindus."[1]

Prof. Macdonell says, "In science, too, the debt of Europe to India has been considerable. There is in the first place, the great fact that the Indians invented the numerical figures used all over The world. The influence which the decimal system of reckoning dependent on those figures

---

[1] Schlgel's *History of Literature*, p. 123

has had not only on mathematics but on the progress of civilisation in general can hardly be over-estimated. During the eighth and ninth centuries, the Indians became the teachers in arithmetic and algebra of the Arabs, and through them of the nations of the West. Thus, though we call the latter science by an Arabic name, it is a gift we owe to India."[1]

Sir M. Monier Williams says, "From them (Hindus) the Arabs received not only their first conceptions of algebraic analysis, but also those numerical symbols and decimal notations, now current everywhere in Europe, and which have rendered untold service to the progress of arithmetical science."[2] Says Manning, 'To whatever cyclopaedia, journal or essay we refer, we uniformly find our numerals trace to India and the Arabs recognised as the medium through which they were introduced into Europe."[3] Sir W. W. Hunter also says, "To them (the Hindus) we owe the invention of the numerical symbols on the decimal scale. The Indian figures 1 to 9 being abbreviated forms of initial letters at the numerals themselves, and the zero, or 0, representing the first letter of the Sanskrit word for empty (*śunya*). The Arabs borrowed them from the Hindus, and transmitted them to Europe."[4]

Professor Weber says, "It is to them (the Hindus) also that we owe the ingenious invention the numerical symbols, which in like manner passed from them to the Arabs, and from these again European scholars. By these latter, who were the disciples die Arabs, frequent allusion is made to

---

[1] *History of Sanskrit Literature*, p. 424
[2] *Indian wisdom*, p. 124
[3] *Ancient and Mediaeval India*, Vol. I, p. 376
[4] *Imperial Gazetteer*, p. 219, 'India'

the Indians and uniformly in terms of high esteem; and one Sanskrit word even (uccha) has passed into the Latin translations of Arabian astronomers."[1]

Professor Wilson says, "Even Delambre concedes their claim to the invention of numerical cyphers."

[1] Weber's *Indian Literature*, p. 256

5.3. ARITHMETIC

Mrs. Manning says, compared with other nations, the Hindus were peculiarly strong in all the branches of arithmetic."[1] Professor Weber, after declaring that the Arabs were disciples of the Hindus, says, "The same thing (i.e.. the Arabs borrowed from Hindus) took place also in regard to algebra and arithmetic in particular, in both of which it appears the Hindus attained, quite independently, to a high degree of proficiency." Sir W. W. Hunter also says that the Hindus attained a very high proficiency in arithmetic and algebra independently of any foreign influence."[2]

The English mathematician, Prof. Wallace, says,"The *Līlāvati* treats of arithmetic, contains not only the common rules of that science, but the application of these to various questions of interest, barter, mixture, combinations, permutations, sums of progression indeterminate problems, and mensuration of surface and solids. The rules are found nearly as simple as in the present state of the analytical investigation. The numerical results are readily deduced, and if they be compared with the earliest specimens of Greek calculation, the advantages of the decimal notation are placed in a striking, light."[3] It may, however, be mentioned that *Līlāvati*, of which Professor Wallace speaks, is a comparatively modern manual of arithmetic; and to judge of the merits of Hindu arithmetic from this book is to judge of the merits of English arithmetic from Chamber's manual of arithmetic.

---

[1] *Ancient and Mediaeval India*, Vol. I, p. 374

[2] *Imperical Gazetter*, 'India,' p. 219

[3] *Edinburgh Review*, Vol. 29, p. 147

It may be added that the enormous extent to which numerical calculation goes in India, and the possession by the Hindus of by far the largest fable of calculation, are in themselves proofs of the superior cultivation of the science of arithmetic by the Hindus.

5.4. GEOMETRY

The ancient Hindus have always been celebrated for the remarkable progress they made in geometry. Professor Wallace says "However ancient a book may be in which a system of trigonometry occurs, we may be assured it was not written in the infancy of the science Geometry must have been known in India long before the writing of the *Sūrya Siddhānta*,"[1] which is supposed by the Europeans to have been written before 2,000 B.C.[2]

Professor Wallace says, "*Sūrya Siddhānta* contains a rational system of trigonometry, which differs entirely from that first known in Greece or Arabia. In fact, it is founded on a geometrical theorem, which was not known to the geometricians of Europe before the time of Vieta, about two hundred years ago. And it employs the sines of arcs; a thing unknown to the Greeks, who used the chords of double arcs. The invention of sines has been attributed to the Arabs, but it is possible that they may have received this improvement in trigonometry as well as the numerical characters from India."[3]

Mr. Elphinstone says "In the *Sūrya Siddhānta* is contained a system of trigonometry which not only goes far beyond anything known to the Greeks, but involves theorems which were not discovered in Europe till two centuries ago."[4]

Ptolemy and the Greek mathematicians in their division of the radius preserved no reference to the circumference. The use of sines, as if was unknown to the Greeks, forms a difference between theirs and the Indian trigonometry. Their rule for the computation of the lines is a considerable

---

[1] Mill's *India*, Vol. II, p. 150

[2] See Mill's *India*, vol. II, p. 3, footnote

[3] *Edinburgh Encyclopaedia*, 'Geometry.' P. 191

[4] *History of India*, p. 129

refinement in science first practised by the mathematician, Briggs."[1]

Count Bjornstjerna says, "We find in *Ayeen-e-Akbari*, a journal of Emperor Akbar, that the Hindus of former times assumed the diameter of a circle to be its periphery as 1,250 to 3,927. The ratio of 1,250 to 3,927 is a very close approximation to the quadrature of a circle and differs very little from that given by Metius of 113 to 355. In order to obtain the result thus found by the Vedic Scholars, even in the most elementary and simplest way, it is necessary to inscribe in a circle a polygon of 768 sides, an operation, which cannot be performed arithmetically without the knowledge of some peculiar properties of this curved line, and at least an extraction of the square root of the ninth power, each to ten places of decimals. "The Greeks and Arabs have not given anything so approximate."[2]

It is thus clearly seen that the Greeks and the Arabs apart, even the Europeans have but very recently advanced far enough to come into line with the Hindus in their knowledge of this branch of mathematics.

Professor Wallace says,"The researches of the learned have brought to light astronomical tables in India which must have been constructed by the principles of geometry, but the period at which they have been framed has by no means been completely ascertained. Some are of opinion that they have been framed from observation made at a very remote period, not less than 3,000 years before the Christian era (this has been conclusively proved by Mons. Bailly); and if this opinion be well founded, the science of geometry must have been cultivated in India to a considerable extent long before the period assigned to its origin in the west; so that many elementary propositions may have been brought from India to Greece."[3] He adds, "In geometry, there is

---

[1] Mill's *India*, Vol. II, p. 150

[2] *Theogony of the Hindus*, p. 37

[3] *Edinburgh Encyclopaedia*, 'Geometry,' p. 191

much deserving of attention. We have here the celebrated proposition that the square on the hypotenuse of a right-angled triangle is equal to the squares on the sides containing the right angle and other propositions, which form part of the system of modern geometry. There is one remarkable proposition, namely, that which discovers the area of a triangle when its three sides are known. This does not seem to have been known to the ancient Greek geometers."

The *Śulva Sūtras*, however, date from about the eighth century B.C., and Dr. Thibaut has shown that geometrical theorem of the 47th proposition, Book 1, which tradition ascribes to Pythagoras, was solved by the Hindus at least two centuries earlier, thus confirming the conclusion of V. Schroeder that the Greek philosopher owed his inspiration to India."[1]

Mr. Elphinstone says, "Their geometrical skill is shown among other forms by their demonstrations of various properties of triangles, especially one which expresses the area in the terms of the three sides, and was unknown in Europe till published by Clavius, and by their knowledge of the proportions of the radius to the circumference of a circle, which they express in a mode peculiar to themselves by applying one measure and one unit to the circumference. This proportion was not known out of India until modern times."[2]

---

[1] *Journal of the Asiatic Society of Bengal*, 1875, p. 227
[2] Elphistone's *History of India*, p. 130

5.5. ALGEBRA

The Hindus have been especially successful in the cultivation of algebra. Professor Wallace says, "In algebra the Hindus understood well the arithmetic of surd roots, and the general resolution of equation of the second degree, which it is not clear that Diophantus knew, that they attained a general solution of indeterminate problems of the first degree, which it is certain Diophantus had not attained, and a method of deriving a multitude of answers to problems of the second degree, when one solution was discovered by trial, which is as near an approach to a general solution as was made until the time of La Grange." Professor Wallace concludes by adopting the opinion of Playfair on this subject, "that before an author could think of embodying a treatise on algebra in the heart of a system of astronomy, and turning the researches of the one science to the purposes of the other, both must have been in such a state of advancement as the lapse of several ages and many repeated efforts of inventors were required to produce." "This," says Professor Wilson, "is unanswerable evidence in favour of the antiquity, originality, and advance of the Hindus mathematical science."[1]

Mr. Colebrooke says, "They (the Hindus) understood well to arithmetic of surd roots; they were aware of the infinite quotient resulting from the division of finite quantities by cipher; they knew the general resolution of equation of the second degree, and had touched upon those of higher denomination, resolving them in the simplest case, and in those in which serves for quadratics; they had attained a general solution of indeterminate problems of the first degree; they had arrived at a method for deriving a multitude of solutions for answers to problems of the second degree from a single answer found tentatively."[2] "And this," says Colebrooke in conclusion "was as near an approach to

---

[1] Mill's *India*, Vol. II, p. 151, Wilson's note

[2] Colebrooke's *Miscellaneous Essays*, Vol. II, p. 419

a general solution of such problems as was made until the days of La Grange."[1]

"Equally decided is the evidence," says Manni, "excellence in algebraic analysis was attained in India independent of foreign aid."

Mr. Colebrooke says, "No doubt is entertained of the source from which it was received immediately by modern Europeans. The Arabs were mediately or immediately our instructors in this study."

Mrs. Manning says, "The Arabs were not in general inventors but recipients. Subsequent observation has confirmed this view; for not only did algebra in an advanced state exist in India prior to the earliest disclosure of it by the Arabians to modern Europe, but the names by which the numerals have become known to us are of Sanskrit origin."[2]

Professor Monier Williams says, "To the Hindus is due the invention of algebra and geometry and their application to astronomy."[3]

Comparing the Hindus and the Greeks, as regards their knowledge of algebra, Mr. Elphinstone says, "There is no question of the superiority of the Hindus over their rivals in the perfection to which they brought the science. Not only is Āryabhaṭṭa superior to Diophantus (as is shown by his knowledge of tile resolution of equations involving several unknown quantities and in a general method of resolving all indeterminate problems of at least the first degree) but he

---

[1] Colebrooke's *Miscellaneous Essays*, Vol. II, pp. 416-418. For the points in which Hindu algebra is more advanced than the Greek, see Colebrooke, p. 16.

[2] *Ancient and Mediaevel India*, Vol. II, p. 375. 'Mr. Colebrooke has fully shown that algebra had attained the highest perfection it ever reached in India before it was ever known to the Arabians. Whatever the Arbas possessed in common with the Hindus, there are good grounds to believe that they derived from the Hindus.' Elphinstone's *India*, p. 133.

[3] *Indian Wisdom*, p. 185

and his successors press hard upon the discoveries of algebraists who lived almost in our own time." "It is with a feeling of respectful admiration that Mr. Colebrooke alludes to ancient Sanskrit treatises on algebra, arithmetic and mensuration."[1]

In the *Edinburgh Review* (Vol. XXI, p. 372) is a striking history of a problem (to find x, so that ax^2+b shall be a square number). The first step towards a solution is made by Diophantus, it was extended by Fermat, and sent as a defiance to the English algebraists in the seventeenth century but was only carried to its full extent by the celebrated mathematician Euler who arrives at the point before attained by Bhāskarācārya."[2]

Another occurs in the same Review (Volume XXIX, p. 153), where it is stated, from Mr. Colebrooke that a particular solution given by Bhāskaracārya is exactly the same as that hit on by Lord Brounker in 1657; and that the general solution of the same problem was unsuccessfully attempted by Euler and only accomplished by De la Grange in 1767 AD. although it had been completely given by Brahmagupta.

"But," says Mr. Elphinstone, "the superiority of the Hindus over the Greek algebraists is scarcely so conspicuous in their discoveries as in the excellence of their method, which is altogether dissimilar to the of Diaphanous (Strachey's *Bīja Gaṇita* quoted in the "Edinburgh Review," Vol. XXI, pp. 374-375), and in the perfection of the

---

[1] Manning's *Ancient and Mediaeval India*, Vol. I, p. 374

[2] Elphinstone's *India*, p. 131. Bhāskarācārya wrote the celebrated books '*Siddhānta Śiromaṇī*,' containing treatises on algebra and arithmetic. His division of a circle is remarkable for its minute analysis which is as follows :

60 *Vikalā* (Seconds)	=	A *Kalā* (Minutes)
60 *Kalā* -	=	A *Bhāga* (Degree)
30 *Bhāga*-	=	A *Rāśi* (Sing)
12 *Rāśi*	=	A *Bhagaṇa* (Revolution)

algorithm (Colebrook's Hindu Algebra quoted in the E.R. Vol. XXIX. P.162)

One of their most favourite processes (that called cattaca) was not known in Europe till published by Bachet de Mezeriac, about the year 1624, and is virtually the same as that explained by Euler (*Edinburgh Review*, Vol. XXIX, p. 151). Their application of algebra to astronomical investigations and geometrical demonstrations is also an invention of their own; and their manner of conducting it is even now entitled to admiration (Colebrooke, quoted by Professor Wallace; and *Edinburgh Review*, Vol. XXIX, p. 158).

Speaking of the Hindu treatises on algebra, arithmetic, and mensuration, Mr. Clebrooke says, "It is not hoped that in the actually advanced condition of the analytical art they will add to its resources and throw new light on the mathematical science in any other respect than as concerns its history, but had an earlier version of these treatises been completed; had they been translated and given to the public when the notice of mathematicians was first drawn to the attainments of the Hindus in astronomy and in sciences connected with it, some additions would have been then made to the means and resources of algebra, for the general solution of problems, by methods which have been re-invented or have been perfected in the last age."[1]

It is thus evident from what Mr. Colebrooke shows that the Hindu literature even in its degenerate state, and when so few works are extant, contains mathematical works that

---

[1] Colebrooke's *Miscellaneous Essay*. Vol. II, p. 419
It may, however be said that in some quarters the genuiness of the independent solution of the problems mentioned above, and the discovery of methods similar to those of the Hindus by modern Europeans have been doubted, and such doubts may well be excused, considering the extensive intercourse that has existed between India and Europe for a long time past.

show an advance in the science in no way behind the latest European achievements.

As an instance of the remarkable and extensive practice and cultivation of mathematics in India may be cited the case of a problem from *Lalita Vistara.* Mons. Waepcke[1], indeed, is of opinion that the account in the *Lalita Vistara* of the problem solved by Buddha on the occasion of his marriage examination, relative to the number of atoms in the length of a *Yojana,* is the basis of the "Arenarius" of the celebrated scientist Archimedes.

The credit of the discovery of the principle of differential calculus is generally claimed by the Europeans. But it is remarkable that similar method existed in India ages ago. Bhaskarācārya, one of the world's greatest mathematicians, has referred to it. Following, however, in the footsteps of his Hindu predecessors he does not expound the method fully, but only gives an outline of it.

Mr. Spottiswoode says, "It must be admitted that the penetration shown by Bhāskarācārya in his analysis is in the highest degree remarkable that the formula which he establishes, and his method, bear more than a mere resemblance they bear a strong analogy to the corresponding process in modern mathematical astronomy; and that the majority of scientific persons will learn with surprise the existence of such a method in the writings of so distant a period and so remote a region."[2]

Mr. Lethbridge says, "Bhāskarācārya is said to have discovered a mathematical process very nearly resembling the differential calculus of modern European mathematicians."[3]

---

[1] *Meam Surla propagation des chiffres Indiens,* Paris, 1863, pp. 75-91

[2] J.R.A. S., Vol. XVII.

[3] School *History of India,* Appendix A., p.ii

5.6. ASTRONOMY

"Ye multiplying masses of increased
And still increasing lights: what are ye? what
Is this blue wild Jerness of interminable
Air where ye roll along, as I have seen
The leaves along the limpid stream of Eden?
Is your course measured for ye? or do ye
Sweep on in your unbounded revelry
Through an aerial universe of endless
Expansion, at which my soul aches to think,
Intoxicated with eternity.

BYRON: *Cain*

A European critic says, "For a man, the most sublime study is that of astronomy." And, indeed, what can be more sublime than the study of Nature in its broadest aspects, of the movements and the functions of those wonderful and splendid bodies with which the boundless expanse of the wide space is thickly studded, where fancy is puzzled and imagination itself staggered?

Heaven
Is as the book of God before thee set
Wherein to read His wondrous words.

MILTON: *Paradise Lost*

The science of astronomy flourishes only amongst a civilised people. Hence, considerable advancement in it is itself a proof of the high civilisation of a nation Hindu astronomy, or what remains of it, has received the homage of European scholars. Dr. Sir William Hunter says, "The Astronomy of the Hindus has formed the subject of excessive admiration." "Proofs of very extraordinary proficiency'', says Mr. Elphinstone, "In their astronomical writings are found."[1]

---

[1] *History of India*, p.129.

The Hindu astronomy not only establishes the high proficiency of our ancestors in this department of knowledge and exact admiration and applause: it does something more. It proves the great antiquity of the literature and the high literary culture of the Hindus. "Mons. Bailly, the celebrated author of the History of Astronomy, inferred from certain astronomical tables of the Hindus, not only the advanced progress of the science but a date so ancient as to be entirely inconsistent with the chronology of the Hebrew Scriptures. His argument was laboured with the utmost diligence and was received with unbounded applause. All concurred at the time with the wonderful learning, wonderful civilisation and wonderful institutions of the Hindus."[1] It must not, however, be forgotten, as this celebrated astronomy (Mons. Bailly) holds, that Hindu astronomy is "the remains rather than the elements of a science."[2]

Mr. Weber says, "Astronomy was practised India as early as 2780 BC"[3] But some of the greatest modern astronomers have decided in favour of a much greater antiquity. Cassini, Bailly, Gentil and Playfair maintain "that there are Hindu observations extant which must have been made more than three thousand years before Christ, and which evince even then a very high degree of astronomical science."[4]

Count Bjornstjerna proves conclusively that Hindu astronomy was very far advanced even at the beginning of the *Kaliyuga*, (about 5,000 years ago). He says, "According to the astronomical calculations of the Hindus, the present period of the world, *Kaliyuga*, commenced 3,102 years before the birth of Christ, on the 20th of February, at 2

---

[1] Mill's *History of India*, Vol. II, pp. 97, 98

[2] See *Bailly's Historie de l' Astronomie Ancienne (Plutot les debris que les elemens d'une Science*)

[3] Weber's *Indian Literature*, p. 30, Biot regards the 2357 B.C. as the earliest point when the course of the moon was first watched for astronomical use.' Dunker's *History of Antiquity*, p. 284

[4] *Theogony of the Hindus*, p. 32

hours 27 minutes and 30 seconds, the time being thus calculated to minutes and seconds. They say that a conjunction of the planets then took place, and their tables show this conjunction. Bailly states that Jupiter and Mercury were then in the same degree of the ecliptic, Mars at a distance of only eight, and Saturn of seven degrees; whence it follows, that at the point of time given by the Brāhmaṇas as the commencement of *Kaliyuga*, the four planets above mentioned must have been successively concealed by the rays of the sun (first Saturn, then Mars, afterwards Jupiter and lastly Mercury). They thus showed themselves in conjunction; and although Venus could not then be seen, it was natural to say, that a conjunction of the planets then took place. The calculation of the Brāhmaṇas is so exactly confirmed by our own astronomical tables, that nothing but an actual observation could have given so correspondent a result." The learned Count continues, "He (Bailly) further informs us that Laubere, who was sent by Louis XIV as ambassador to the King of Siam, brought home, in the year 1687, astronomical tables of solar eclipses, and that other similar tables were sent to Europe by Patouillet (a missionary in the Karnatic), and by Gentil, which latter were obtained from the Brāhmaṇas in Tirvalore, and that they all perfectly agree in their calculations although received from different persons, at different times, and from" places in India remote from each other. On these tables, Bailly makes the following observation. The motion calculated by the Brāhmaṇas during the long space of 4,383 years (the period elapsed between these calculations and Bailly's), varies not a single minute from the tables of Cassini and Meyer; and as the tables brought to Europe by Laubere in 1687, under Louis XIV are older than those of Cassini and Meyer, the accordance between them must be the result of mutual and exact astronomical observations." Then again, "Indian tables give the same annual variation of the moon as that discovered by Tycho Brahe, a variation unknown to the school of Alexandria, and also to the Arabs, who followed the calculations of this school."

"These facts," says the erudite Count, sufficiently show the great antiquity and distinguished station of astronomical science among the Hindus of past ages." The Count then asks "if it be' true that the Hindus more than 3,000 BC., according to Bailly's calculation, had attained so high a degree of astronomical and geometrical learning, how many centuries earlier must the commencement of their culture have been, since the human mind advances only step by step on the path of science."[1]

There are, however, many other arguments to establish a far higher antiquity of the Hindu astronomy than what is assigned by Bentley. The equation of the sun's centre, according to the Indian tables, is 20^0 $10^{1/2}$; whereas the same quantity according to the modern observations is only 1^0 55 $^{1/2}$. It is one consequence of the mutual disturbances of planets that the eccentricity of the solar orbit on which the equation just mentioned depends, was greater in former ages than it is at the present time. From the quantity which the Hindus assign to this astronomical element, M. Bailly has drawn an argument in favour of the antiquity of the Indian tables, which it must be confessed is of great weight when the difference of the Indian and European determination is considered as arising from the gradual alteration of the planetary orbits.

2. The quantities which the Indian tables assign to other astronomical elements, viz., the mean motions of Jupiter and Saturn, have been found to agree almost exactly not with what is observed at the present time, but with what the theory of gravity shows would have been observed at the beginning of the *Kaliyuga*. Laplace discovered it after the publication of the *Astronomie Indian* and inserted it in the *Journal des Savans*.

3. Mr. Bailly has shown that the place of the aphelion of Jupiter's orbit, determined by the Indian tables for the beginning of the *Kaliyuga* agrees with the modern tables of

---

[1] *Theogony of the Hindus*, p. 37

Lalande when corrected by the theoretical equations of La Grange. The same thing is true of the quantity which the Hindus assign to the equation of Saturn's centre.

4. Another argument to vindicate the great antiquity of Hindu astronomy is derived from the obliquity of the ecliptic which the Indians state at 24^0. Both observation and theory concur in showing that the obliquity of the ecliptic has been diminishing slowly for many ages preceding the present.

5. The length of the Hindu tropical year as deduced from the Hindu tables is 365 days, 5 hours, 50 minutes, 35 seconds, while La Calle's observation gives 365-5-48-49. This makes the year at the time of the Hindu observation longer than at present by 1′ 46″. It is, however, an established fact that the year has been decreasing in duration from time immemorial and shall continue to decrease. In about 49 centuries the time of the year decreases about $40^{1/2}$. This, then, is an unmistakable proof of the very high antiquity of Indian astronomy. The observation by the Hindus must have been made in the *Dvāpara* (more than 5,000 years ago).

It should now be quite Clear that in India astronomy was cultivated and wonderful progress in the science made at a period when the rest of the world, including the whole of Europe. was completely enveloped in ignorance.

Sir. W. Hunter says, "In some points, the *Brāhmaṇas* made advances beyond Greek astronomy. Their fame spread throughout the West and found entrance into the Chronicon Paschalo (commenced about 330 AD and revised under Heraclius 610-641).[1]

Mr. Elphinstone says, "In addition to the points already mentioned in which the Hindus have gone beyond the other nations, Mr. Colebrooke mentions two in astronomy. One is in their notions regarding the precessions of the Equinoxes, in which they were more correct than Ptolemy, and as much

---

[1] *Indian Gazetteer*, Vol. IV, p. 218

so as the Arabs, who, did not attain to that degree of improvement till a later period; the other relates to the diurnal revolution of the earth on its axis which the *Brāhmaṇas* discussed in the fifth century BC"[1]

Sir. W. Hunter says, "The Sanskrit term for the apex of a planet's orbit seems to have "passed Into the Latin translations of the Arabic astronomers. The Sanskrit *ucca* became the aux (gen. *augis*) of the later translators." (Reinaud. P. 325 and Weber, p. 257).

"Professor Weber says, "The fame of Hindu astronomers spread to the West, and the Andubarius (or probably, Ardubarius), whom the Chronicon Paschale places in primeval times as the earliest Indian astronomer, is doubtless none other than Āryabhaṭṭa, the rival of Pauliśa, and who is likewise extolled by the Arabs under the name of Arjabahar."[2]

Professor Wilson says, "The science of astronomy at present exhibits many proofs of accurate observation and deduction, highly creditable to the science of the Hindu astronomers. The division of the ecliptic into lunar mansions, the solar zodiac, the mean motion of the planet, the precession of the equinox, the earth's self-support in space, the diurnal revolution of the earth on its axis the revolution of the moon on her axis, her distance from the earth, the dimensions or the orbits of the planet, the calculations of eclipses are parts of a system which could not have been found amongst an unenlightened people."[3]

But the originality of the Hindus is not less striking than their proficiency. It is remarkable that the Hindu methods are all original and peculiar. Professor Wilson says, "The originality of Hindu astronomy is at once established, but it is also proved by intrinsic evidence, and although there are some remarkable coincidences between the Hindu and other

---

[1] *History of India*, p. 132, footnote.

[2] Weber's *Indian Literature*, p. 255

[3] Mill's *History of India*, Vol. II, p. 106

systems, their methods are their own."[1] Mr. Elphinstone says, "In the more advanced stages, where they are more likely to have borrowed, not only is their mode of proceedings peculiar to themselves but it is often founded on principles, with which no other ancient people were acquainted, and showed a knowledge of discoveries not made even in Europe till within the course of the last two centuries."[2]

In the sixth volume of the *Journal of the American Oriental Society*, Professor Whitney published an English translation of *Sūrya Siddhānt* by the Rev. E. Burgess, with an elaborate commentary by himself. This paper excited comments from M. Biot, the late venerable astronomer of Paris, and from Professor Weber of Berlin. Biot believed that the Hindus derived their system of *Nakṣatras*, or moon stations, from the Chinese, but Professor Whitney contributed two other papers to the said Journal, in which he clearly shows that the Hindu *Nakṣatra* does not mean the same thing as the Chinese Sieu. Sieu means a single star, whereas *Nakṣatra* expresses a group of stars, or rather a certain portion of the starry heavens. Again, professor Weber shows that the Chinese Sleu is not traceable further than two or three centuries before Christ, while *Nakṣatras* are amongst the heavenly objects mentioned in the Vedic hymns."[3] The great antiquity of the science, however, is the best proof of its originality.

The Arabs were the disciples of the Hindus in this branch of knowledge also. Professor Weber says that Hindu astronomers are extolled by the Arabs. He adds, "For, during the eighth and ninth centuries the Arabs were, in astronomy, the disciples of Hindus, from whom, they borrowed the lunar mansions in their new order, and whose Siddhāntas they frequently worked up and translated in part

---

[1] Mill's *History of India*, Vol. II, p. 107

[2] Elphinstone's *History of India*, p. 132

[3] W.D. whitney, '*Views of Weber and Biot respecting the Relations of the Hindu and Chinese Asterism*, p. 25

under the supervision of Indian astronomers themselves, whom the Khalifs of Baghdad, etc., invited to their courts."[1]

Dr. Robertson says, "It is highly probable that the knowledge of the twelve signs of zodiacs was derived from India."[2]

Sir W.W. Hunter says, "The Arabs became their (Hindus) disciplines in the eight century, and translated Sanskrit treatises, Siddhāntas, under the name *Sind hinds.*"[3] Professor Wilson says, "Indian astronomers were greatly encouraged by the early Khalifs, particularly Harun-ul-Rashid, and Almamun; they were invited to Baghdad, and their works were translated into Arabic. The Hindus were, fully as much as the Greeks, the teachers of the Arabians."[4]

There are nine '*Siddhāntas*[5]: (I) *Brahma Siddhānta*, (2) *Sūrya Siddhānta*, (3) *Soma Siddhānta*, (4) *Bṛhaspati Siddhānta,* (5) *Gārgya Siddhānta*, (6) *Nārada Siddhānta*, (7) *Parāśara Siddhānta*, (8) *Pulastya Siddhānta*, and (9) *Vasīṣṭha Siddhānta.* Of these, the work best known to Europeans is the *Sūrya Siddhānta* which is the oldest of the extant *Siddhāntas.*[6] There is internal evidence to show that *Sūrya Siddhānta* is a very old book. The author in two *ślokas* (*Madhyan Adhāya*, *ślokas* 22, 23) gives the date when the book was written. He says:

कल्पादस्मात् मनवः षड्व्यतीताः ससन्धयः ।
वैवस्वतस्य च मनोर्युगानां त्रिघनो गतः ।। 22 ।।

अष्टाविंशाद्युगादस्माद्यतमे तत्कृतं युगम् ।।

---

[1] Weber's *Indian Literature*, p. 255

[2] *Disquisition concerning India*, p. 280

[3] *Indian Gazetteer*, 'India,' p. 218

[4] Mill's *History of India*, Vol. II, p. 107

[5] The *Pañca Siddhāntas*, or the five principal astronomical works in general use are : (1) The *Pauliśa Siddhānta*, (2) the *Romaka Siddhānta*, (2) The *Vaśiṣṭha Siddhānta*, (4) The *Saura Siddhānta*, *Brāhma Siddhānta*, (5) The *Paitāmaha Siddhānta.*

[6] *Indian Wisdom*, pp. 184, 185

अतः कालं प्रसंख्याय य संख्यामेकत्र पिण्डयेत् ।। 23 ।।

"Six *Manvantras* have passed since the beginning of this *Kalpa* (present world): and of the seventh *Manvantra*, 27 *Caturyugis* bave passed. The *Satyuga* of the 28th *Caturyugī* has also passed. From this, the time of the compilation of this book may be inferred." This makes the book nearly 2,165,000 years old.

Mr. Davis calculates that the celebrated Hindu astronomer, Parāśara, judging from the observations made by him, must have lived 1391 years before Christ,[1] and consequently, says Bjornstjerna, "had read in the divine book of the heavenly firmament long before the Chaldees, the Arabs and the Greeks."[2]

Mr. Haughton says, "From a text of Parāśara it appears that the equinox had gone back from the tenth degree of *Bharaṇī* to the first of Aśvini, or 23 degrees and 20 minutes between the days of that Indian philosopher and the year of our Lord 499, when it coincided with the origin of the Hindu ecliptic, so that Parāśara probably flourished near the close of the twelfth century before Christ."

After Parāśara Muni came Āryabhaṭṭa, who was a great astrologer too. He was born in 2765 BC. He was the man who, according to the Europeans, first brought to light "diurnal revolution of the earth on its axis, and to have known the true theory of the causes or the lunar and solar eclipses, and notice the motion, of solstitial and equinoctial points."[3]

His principal works are: (1) *Āryabhaṭiyam* (2) *Daśa Gītikā*, (3) *Āryaśtaka*

The best-known astronomer who flourished after Āryabhaṭṭa's time is Varāhamihira (123 BC.), who became pre-eminent in astrology. Mrs. Manning says,

---

[1] *Asiatic Researches*, Vol. II, p. 288

[2] *Theogony of the Hindus*, pp. 33, 34

[3] See Chamber's Encylopaedia

"Varāhamihira may be cited as a celebrated astronomer to whom astrology was irresistibly attractive;" and again, "He is called an astronomer, but it is for astrology that we find him most celebrated. He attained excellence in each branch of the *Saṁhitā*, and before writing his celebrated treatise called the *Bṛhat-Saṁhitā* he composed a work on pure astronomy."[1] Varāhamihira lived in the first century before Christ and was one of the nine gems at the court of Vikramāditya. The nine gems or *Navaratnas* were:

धन्वन्तरिः क्षपणकोमरसिंहशंकू।
वेतालभट्ट–घटखर्पर–कालिदासाः।।

Varāhamihira's chief works are (1) *Vṛhat Jātaka* (2) *Vṛhat Saṁhitā*, (3) A Summary of the Original *Pañca Siddhāntas*. Mrs. Manning says, "Richness of detail constitutes the chief attraction of the book (*Vṛhat Saṁhitā*), a merit which was appreciated by the Arab astrologer, Alberuni, as it will be by ourselves; for although professedly astrological, its value for geography, architecture, sculpture, etc., is unequalled by any Sanskrit work as yet published."[2]

The last Hindu astronomer of eminence, however, was Bhaskarācārya, who is said by Europeans to have flourished so late as the twelfth century. He expounded the law of gravity with peculiar felicity, while his mathematical works place him in the forefront of the world's great mathematicians.

The roundness of the earth and its diurnal rotation, however, were known to the Hindus from the earliest times. Says a Rishi in the *Aitareya Brāhmaṇa,* "By this great inauguration similar to Indra's, Tura, son of Kavaṣa, consecrated Janamejaya and thereby did he subdue the earth completely round."[3] In *Āryabhaṭṭīyam* we read:

---

[1] *Ancient and Mediaeval India*, Vol. I, pp. 368, 369

[2] *Ancient and Mediaeval India*, Vol. I, p. 370, See also Dr. Kern's Bib. Ind., Introduction, p. 27

[3] Haug's *Atareya Brāhmaṇa*, Vol. II, p. 242

बृत्तभ पंजरमध्ये कक्षयापरिवेष्टितः खमध्यगतः।

मृज्जलशिखिवायुमयो भूगोलः सर्वतोवृत्तः।।

"The earth, situated in the middle of the heavens and composed of five elements, is spherical in its shape." Bhaskarācārya, in *Golādhayāya* says:

सभोयेतः स्यात्परिधेः शतांशः पृथ्वी पृथ्वी च नितरान्तर्नायान्।

नरस्य तत्पृष्ठगतस्य कृष्णा समेवतस्यप्रतिभात्यतः सा।।

"A hundredth part of the circumference of a circle appears to be a straight line. Our earth is a big sphere, and the portion visible to man being exceedingly small, the earth appears to be flat."

Dr. H. Kern, in his paper on "Some fragments of Āryabhaṭṭa," translates a passage as follows: "The terrestrial globe, a compound of earth, fire, water, air, entirely round, and compassed by a girdle, i.e., equator, stands in the air," etc., etc.

As regards the annual motion of the earth, the *Ṛgveda* says:

या गौर्वर्त्तनिं पर्य्येति निष्कृतं पयो दुहाना व्रतनीरवारतः।
सा प्रब्रुवाणा वरुणाय दाश्रुषे देवेभ्यो दाशविशा विवस्वते।।

The diurnal motion is thus described in the *Yajurveda*.

आयं गौः पृश्निरक्रमोद सदन्मातरं पुरः।
पितरं च प्रयन्त्स्वः।।

The *Aitareya Brāhmaṇa* explains that the sun neither sets nor rises, that when the earth, owing to the rotation on its axis is lighted up, it is called day," and so on.[1]

अथ यदेनं प्रातरुदेतीति मन्यन्ते रात्रेरेव तदन्तमित्वा अथात्मानं विपर्यस्यते अहरेवावस्तात् कुरुते रात्रिम् पुरस्तात्। स वै एष न कदाचन निम्लोचति। न ह वै कदाचन निम्लोचति।।

[1] Haug's *Aitareya Brāhmaṇa*, Vol. II, p. 242

As regards the stars being stationary as compared to the motion of the earth, Āryabhaṭṭa[1] says:

भपंजरः स्थिरो भूरेववृत्यावृत्यप्रातिदैवासिकौ।
उदयास्तमयौ संपादयते ग्रहनक्षत्राणाम् ।।

"The starry vault is fixed. It is the earth which, moving round its axis, again and again, causes the rising and setting of planets and stars." He starts the question, "Why do the stars seem to move ?" and himself replies, "As a person in a vessel while moving forwards, sees an immovable object moving backwards, in the same manner, do the stars, however immovable, seem to move daily."[2] The Polar days and nights of six months are also described by him.

विषुवद्वृत्तद्युसदां क्षिते जित्वमितं तथा च दैत्यानाम्।
उत्तरयाम्यौ क्रमाशो मूर्द्धार्द्धेगताधुरवायस्तेषाम।।्
उत्तरगोले क्षितिजादुर्द्धे परितो भ्रमन्तमादित्यम्।
हव्यक्षिदशः सततं पश्यन्त्यसुराः असन्यगं याम्ये।।
लङ्कापुरेऽर्कस्ययदोदयः स्यात्तदादिनार्द्धयमकोटिपुर्य्याम्।
भवेत्तदासिद्धपुरेऽस्तकालः स्याद्रोमकेरात्रिदलंतदैव।।

"When it is sunrise at Lanka (0^0 latitudes), it is midday at Yavakoṭi (90^0 west of 0^0 lat.), sunset in Siddhapura (180^0 lat.) and midnight at Romaka (90^0 east of lat.)"

As regards the size of the earth, it is said:

प्रेक्तोयोजन संख्ययाकुपरिघेः सप्ताङ्गनन्दाबधयस्तद्मतः।
कुभुजस्यमायकभुवः सिड्वांशकिनाधिकाः।।

"The circumference of the earth is 4,967 *yojanas*, and its diameter is $1{,}581^{1/24}$.'' A *yojana* is equal to five English miles, the circumference of the earth would, therefore, be 24,835 miles and its diameter $7{,}905^{5/24}$ miles.

---

[1] Colebrooke's *Miscellaneous Essays*, Vol. II, p. 392

[2] *Journal of the R.A.S.*, Vol. XX, p. 372

The *Yajurveda* says that the earth is kept in space owing to the superior attraction of the sun.

आकृष्णेन रजसा वर्तमानो निवेशयन्नमृतं मर्त्यं च।

हिरण्ययेन सविता रथेना देवो याति भुवनानि पश्यन्।।

The theory of gravity is thus described in the *Sidhānta Śiromaṇī* centuries before Newton was born.

आकृष्टिशक्तिश्च मही तया यत्।

स्वस्थं गुरुस्वामिमुखं स्वशक्त्या।।

आकृष्यते तत् पततीव भाति।

समे समन्तात् क्वपततित्वयं रवेः।

"The earth, owing to its force of gravity, draws in things towards itself, and so they seem to fall towards the earth." etc. etc.

That the moon and the stars are dark bodies is thus described:

भूगृहभानांगोलार्द्धानिव स्वच्छाययाविवर्णानि।

अट्वीनियथासारं सूर्य्याभिमुखानि दीप्यन्ते।।

"The earth, the planets and the comets all receive their light from the sun: that half towards the sun being always bright, the colour varying with the peculiarity of the substance of each."

The *Atharvaveda* says, "दिवि सोमो अधिश्रितः।" "The moon is dependent on the sun for its light."

As regards the atmosphere it is stated:

भुमेर्बहिर्द्वादशयोजनानि भूवायुस्वाम्बुदविद्युदाद्यम्।

"The atmosphere surrounds the earth, and its height is 12 *yojanas* (60 English miles), and the clouds, lightning etc. are, phenomena connected with it."

Mr. Colebrooke says, "Āryabhaṭṭa affirmed the diurnal revolution of the earth on its axis. He possessed the true theory of the causes of solar and lunar eclipses and disregarded the imaginary dark planets of mythologists and astrologers, affirming the moon and primary planets (and even the stars) to be essentiality dark and only illuminated by the sun."[1]

As regards the solar and lunar eclipses, it is stated:

छादमत्यर्कमिन्दुर्विधुं भूमिभाः ।।

"When the earth in its rotation comes between the sun and the moon, and the shadow of the earth falls on the moon, the phenomenon is called lunar eclipse, and when the moon comes between the sun and the earth the sun seems as if it was being cut off – this is solar eclipse."

The following is taken from Varahamihira's observations on the moon. "One half of the moon, whose orbit lies between the sun and the earth, is always bright by the sun's rays; the other half is dark by its own shadows, like the two sides of a pot standing in the sunshine."[2]

About eclipses, he says, "The true explanation of the phenomenon is this: in an eclipse of the moon, he enters into the earth's shadow; in a solar eclipse, the same thing happens to the sun. Hence the commencement of a lunar eclipse does not take place from the west side, nor that of the solar eclipse from the past." [3]

Kālidāsa says in his *Raghuvañśa*:

छायाहि भूमेः शशिनो मलत्वेनारोपिता बुद्धिमतः प्रजाभिः ।

Jai Deva sings in the *Gīta Govinda,* "His heart was agitated by her sight, as the waves of the deep are affected by the lunar orb."[4]

India has from time immemorial been the land of Philosophers, poets, astronomers and mathematicians, and

---

[1] Colberooke's Essays, Appendix G. p. 467

[2] *Bṛhat Saṅhitā*, Chapter V, v. 8

[3] *Bṛhat Saṅhitā*, Chapter V, v. 8

[4] Tod's *Rajasthan*, Vol. I, p. 543

every now and then it produced a great genius. Less than two centuries ago, Rajputānā produced an astronomer, no doubt the greatest of his time. This astronomer was no other than the famous Jai Singh of Jaipur. Sir William Hunter says, "Raja Jai Singh II constructed a set of observatories at his capital, Jaipur. Mathura, Benaras, Delhi and Ujjain, and was able to correct astronomical tables of De La Hire published in 1702 AD. The Raja left as a monument of his skill, a list of stars collated by himself known as the Zij Mohammed Shahi or Tables of Mohammed Shah. His observatory at Benaras survives to this day."

The celebrated European astronomer. Mr. Playfair, says, "The Brahmaṇa obtains his result with wonderful certainty and expedition in astronomy."[1] This speaks volumes in favour of the original, advanced and scientific methods of the Hindus and their marvellous cultivation of the science. Professor Sir M. Williams says, "It is their science of astronomy by which they (Hindus) heap billions upon million, trillions upon billions of years and reckoning up ages upon ages, aeons upon aeons with even more audacity than modern geologists and astronomers. In short, astronomical Hindu ventures on arithmetical conceptions quite beyond the mental dimensions of anyone who feels. Himself incompetent to attempt a task of measuring infinity."

A strange confession of inferiority! Well may Mrs. Manning exclaim, "The Hindus had the widest range of mind of which man is capable."[2]

In astronomy, as in other sciences, what scanty records remain not only show the astonishing proficiency of the Hindus in the science, but contain theories not yet understood by others. Sir M. Mon. Williams says, "A very strange theory of the planetary motion is expounded at the

---

[1] Playfair on the astronomy of the Hindus. Transactions of the R.A.S. of Great Britain and Ireland, Vol. II, pp. 138, 139

[2] *Ancient and Mediaeval India*, Vol. I p. 114

commencement of the *Sūrya Siddhānta*, Chapter II," which is unknown outside India.[1]

[1] Monier Williams' *Indian Wisdom*, p. 189, Mr. C.B. Clarke, F.G.S. , says in his Geographical Reader:- 'Till of late years we did not known with extreme exactness the longitudes of distant place.' The ancient Hindu method of finding the longitude by first finding out the Deshantra Gathika, with the aid of observations made at the time of the lunar eclipse, is not only scientific but infallible.

5.7. MILITARY SCIENCE

My voice is still for war,
Gods! can a Roman Senate long debate
Which of the two to choose, slavery or death?

ADDISON: *Cato*

CAPTAIN Troyer says, "All the traditions of the Hindus are filled with wars, in which religion certainly had its share. I have shown this sufficiently already, without being obliged to go back so far as the contests between the *Suras* and the *Asuras.*"[1]

War as an art as well as a science was equally well understood in ancient India. The nation which overran nearly the whole of the habitable globe and produced Hercules, Arjuna, Sagar, Bali could scarcely be considered inferior to any other people in their proficiency in military science.

Being skilful sailors from time immemorial, the Hindus were adepts at naval warfare. Colonel Tod says, "The Hindus of remote ages possessed great naval power."[2]

Being the greatest commercial nation in the ancient world, and enjoying sea trade with nearly every part of the world (see "Commerce"), they were compelled to look to their navy to guard their trade and to make it sufficiently strong to ensure their position as the "mistress of the sea." Their position in the ancient world being similar to that of England in the modern world so far as maritime affairs are concerned, their navy, too was equally eminent and powerful. Manu mentions navigation to have existed among the Hindus from time immemorial. Strabo mentions a naval department in addition to the others in the Indian army.

---

[1] Troyer on the *Rāmāyaṇa* in the Asiatic Journal for October, 1844, p. 514

[2] Tod's *Rajasthan*, Vol. II, p. 218

Dhanurveda, the standard work on Hindu military science being lost, the dissertations on the science found in the *Mahābhārata*, the *Agni Purāṇa*, and other works are the only sources of information on the subject left to us. Dr. Sir W. Hunter says, "There was no want of a theory of regular movements and arrangements for the march, array, encampments, and supply of troops. They are all repeatedly described in the *Mahābhārata*."[1]

Mr. Ward says, "The Hindu did not permit even the military art to remain unexamined. It is very certain that the Hindu kings led their own armies to the combat, and that they were prepared for this important employment by a military education; nor is it less certain that many of these monarchs were distinguished for the highest valour and military skill."[2]

The ancient Hindu tactics of war were as original as valuable. It is said that the Hindus divided their army in the following manner: (1) *Uras* or centre (breast), (2) *Kakṣas* or the flanks, (3) *Pakṣas* or wings, (4) *Praligraha* or the reserves, (5) *Koṭi* or vanguards, (6) *Madhya* or centre behind the breast, (7) *Pṛṣṭha* or back – a third line between the *madhya* and the reserve.[3]

Array of forces in action is generally termed *vyūha*.

Some *vyūhas* are named from their object. Thus: (1) *Madhyabhedī* =one which breaks the centre, (2) *Antara bhedi* = that which penetrates between its division. More commonly, however, they are named from their resemblance to various objects. For instance (1) *Makaravyūha*, or the army drawn up like the *Makara*, a mire monster (2) *Syenavyūha*, or the army in the form of a hawk or eagle with wings spread out. (3) *Śakaṭavyūha*, or the army in the shape of a waggon. (4) *Ardhacandra*, or half moon. (5)

---

[1] *Indian Gazetteer*, 'India' p. 223

[2] See the *Theosophist* for March 1881, p. 124

[3] The sage *Bṛhaspati* was a great teacher of military science, but unfortunately none of his works is now extant.

Sarvatobhadra, or hollow square (6) *Gomutrikā*, or echelon (1) *Daṇḍa* or staff, (2) *Bhoja* or column; (3) *Maṇḍala* or hollow circle, (4) *Asaṅhata* or detached arrangements of the different parts of the forces, the elephants, cavalry, infantry severally by themselves. Each of these vyuhas has subdivisions; there are seventeen varieties of the *Daṇḍa*, five of the *Bhoja* and several of both the *Maṇḍala* and *Asaṅhata*.[1]

In the *Mahābhārata* (Vol.VI., pp. 699-729), Yudhiṣṭhira suggests to Arjuna the adoption of the form of *Sūcimukha*, or the needle point array (similar to the phalanx of the Macedonians), while Arjuna recommends the *vajra* or thunderbolt array for the same reason. Duryodhana; in consequence, suggests *Abhedya*, or the impenetrable.

In their land army, the Hindus had, besides the infantry and the cavalry, elephants and chariots also. The elephants, "the living battering rams," as Macaulay calls them, were a source of great strength when properly managed and skilfully supported by other arms. Of the elephants given by Chandragupta to Seleucus, Professor Max Dunker says, "These animals a few years later decided the day of Ipsus in Phrygia against Antogonus, a victory which secured to Seleucus the territory of Syria, Asia Minor, etc." According to Ctesias, Cyrus was defeated and killed by the enemy, only because of the strong support the latter received from the Indian elephants.[2]

---

[1] See *Agni Purāṇa.* "The most important part of Hindu battles is now a cannonade. In this they greatly excel, and have occasioned heavy losses to us in all our battles with them. Their mode is to charge the front and the flanks at once, and the manner in which they perform this maneuver has sometimes called forth the admiration of European antagonists. Elphinstone's *History of India*, p. 82.

[2] 'The proficiency of the Indians in this art (management of elephants) early attracted the attention of Alexander's successors; and natives of India were so long exclusively employed in this service, that the term Indian was applied to every elephant-

As regards the soldierly qualities of the Indians even of the present day, Sir Charles Napier, one of the highest authorities on the subject, says, "Better soldiers or braver men I never saw, superior in sobriety, equal in courage, and only inferior in muscular strength to our countrymen. This appears to me, as far as 1 can judge, the true character of the Indian army in the three Presidencies, and 1 have had men of each under my command."[1]

The chivalrous conduct of the Indian sepoys on the occasion of the defence of Arcot by Clive, and when, towards the close of the war with Tipu in 1782, the whole of the force under General Mathews were made prisoners is well known. The sepoys magnanimously and spontaneously contrived with great personal risk to send every pie of their petty savings to their imprisoned officers, saying, "We can live upon anything, but you require mutton and beef." The conduct of the Indian sepoys shown on such occasions sheds lustre on the whole profession. General Wolseley, in a paper on "Courage," contributed to a journal, highly eulogised the bravery of the Indian sepoys. "During the siege of Lucknow," he said, "the sepoys performed wonderful feats of valour."

Mr. Elphinstone says, "The Hindus display bravery not surpassed by the most warlike nations and will throw away their lives for any considerations of religion or honour.

---

driver, to whatever country he might belong." Wilson's *Theatre of the Hindus*, Vol. I, p.15.

'In war, the King of India was preceded by 10,000 elephants and 3,000 of the strongest and the bravest followed him." Max Dunker's *History of Antiquity*.

'Sixty years after the death of the Enlightened, the Indians assisted the Persian King, the successor of Darius in the invasion of Greece, when they trod the soil of Hellas and wintered in Thessaly. They defeated the Greeks and saw the temple of Athens in flames. Max Dunker's *History of Antiquity*, Vol. IV, p. 384

[1] *The Indian Review* (Calcutta) for November, 1885, p. 181

Hindu sepoys, in our pay have in two instances advanced after troops of the king's service have been beaten off; and on one of these occasions, they were opposed to French soldiers. The sequel of this history will show instances of whole bodies of troops rushing forward to certain death."[1]

Clive, Lawrance, Smith, Coote, Haliburton and many others speak of the sepoys in the highest terms.

Now as regards the weapons used by the Hindus. Professor Wilson is assured that the Hindus cultivated archery most assiduously, and were masters in the use of the bow on horseback. Their skill in archery was wonderful. "Part of the archery practice of the Hindus consisted in shooting a number of arrows at once, from four to nine at one time." Arjuna's feats in archery at the tournament before Draupadi's marriage, and again on the deathbed of Bhishma, must excite universal admiration.

The archery of the Hindus had something mysterious about it. The arrows returned to the archer if they missed their aim. This was considered absurd until the discovery of the "bomerang" in the hands of the Australians.[2]

Warlike weapons and splendid daggers were presented at the International Exhibitions of 1851 and 1862, and a critic speaking of them, says, "Beautiful as the jewelled arms of India are, it is still for the intrinsic merit of their steel that they are most highly prized."[3]

That the ancient Hindus were celebrated for their sword fight is evident from the Persian phrase, "to give an Indian answer," meaning "a cut with an Indian sword." The Indian swordsmen were celebrated all over the world. In an Arabic

---

[1] Elphinstone's *History of India*, p. 198

[2] Besides bows, other missiles as the discuss, short iron clubs, and javelins, swords, maces, battle axes, spears, shields, helmets, armour and coats of mail, etc. are also mentioned. See Wilson's *Essays*, Vol. If, pp. 191, 92.

[3] Manning's *Ancient and Mediaeval India*, Vol. II, p. 365

poem of great celebrity, known as *Sabaa Moalaqa*, there occurs the passage, "The oppression of near relations is more severe than the wound caused by a Hindu swordsman."[1]

Ctesias mentions that the Indian swords were the best in the world.[2]

The following fivefold classification of Hindu weapons is exhaustive: (1) Missiles thrown with an instrument or engine called *yantramukta*; (2) Those hurled by hand or *hastamukta* ; (3) Weapons which may or may not be thrown, or *muktāmukta*, as javelins, tridents etc. ; (4) Which are not thrown, as swords, maces, etc.; (5) Natural weapons, as fists, etc. *Bhindipāla*, *Tomara*, *Nārāca*, *Prāśa*, *Ṛṣṭi*, *Paṭṭiśa*, *Kṛpāṇa*, *Kṣepaṇī*, *Pāśa*, etc., are some of the arms of the ancient Hindus now extinct.

The chief distinction of the modern military science is the extensive employment of fire-arms, their invention being attributed to the Europeans, and it being supposed that fire-arms were unknown in ancient India. Nothing, however, is farther from the truth. Though the Hindu masterpieces on the science of war are all lost, yet there is sufficient material available in the great epics and the *Purāṇas* to prove that firearms were not only known and used on all occasions by the Hindus, but that this branch of their armoury had received extraordinary development. In mediaeval India, of course, guns and cannons were commonly used. In the twelfth century, we find pieces of the ordinance being taken to battle-fields in the armies of Prithviraj. In the 25th stanza of *Prithvirāja Raso* it is said, "The cavillers and cannons made a loud report when they were fired off, and the noise which issued from the ball was heard at a distance of ten *kosa*."

नृप पंग नयर छूटे अराब।

---

[1] The Tafsir Azizi says: *Teghi-i-Hindi va Khanjar-i-roomi-Na Kunad aanki intiazar Kunad.*

[2] Max Dunker's *History of Antiquity*, Vol. IV, p. 436

कोटह कंगूर चढ़ि चढ़ि सिताब।।

जंबूर तोप छूटहि झंनकि।
दश कोश जाय गोला मनकि।।

सिरदार भार बाराह रोह।
लंगी अभंग बर हनै कोह।।

An Indian historian, Raja Kundan Lall, who lived in the court of the king of Oudh, says that there was a big gun named lichmā in the possession of His Majesty the King (of Oudh) which had been originally in the artillery of Mahārājā Prithviraj of Ajmer. The author speaks of a regular science of war, of the postal department, and of public or common roads. See *Muntakhab Tafsee-ul-Akhbar*, pp. 149, 50.

"Maffei says that the Indians far excelled the Portuguese in their skill in the use of fire-arms."[1]

Another author quoted by Bohlen speaks of a certain Indian king being in' the habit of placing several pieces of brass ordnance in front of his army.[2]

"Faria-e Souza speaks of a Gujrat vessel in AD. 1500 firing several guns at the Portuguese[3], and of the Indians at Calicut using fire vessels in 1502, and of the Zamorin's fleet carrying in the next year 380 guns."[4]

But let us turn to ancient India. Professor Wilson says, "Amongst ordinary weapons one is named *vajra*, the thunderbolt, and the specification seems to denote the employment of some explosive projectile, which could not have been in use except by the agency of something like gunpowder in its properties."[5]

---

[1] Hist. Indica, p. 25

[2] Das Aite Indien, Vol. II, p. 63

[3] Asia Portuguesa, Tom I, Part I, Chapter 5.

[4] *Ibid*, Chapter 7

[5] Wilson's Essays, Vol. II, p. 302. The Indians are from time immemorial remarkable for their skill in fireworks. The display of fire works has been from olden days a feature of the Dasehra

As regards "gunpowder," the learned Professor says, "The Hindus, as we find from their medical writings, were perfectly well acquainted with the constituents of gunpowder–sulphur, charcoal, saltpetre, and had them all at hand in great abundance. It is very unlikely that they should not have discovered their inflammability, either singly or in combination. To this inference, *a priori* may be added that drawn from positive proofs, that the use of fire as a weapon of combat was a familiar idea, as it is constantly described in the heroic poems."[1]

The testimony of ancient Greek writers, who, being themselves ignorant of fire-arms used by Indians, give peculiar descriptions of the mode of Hindu warfare is significant. ''The mistius mentions the Brāhmaṇa fighting at a distance with lightning and thunder."[2]

Alexander, in a letter to Aristotle, mentions "the terrific flashes or flame which he beheld showered on his army in India." See also Dante's Inferno, XIV, 31-7.

Speaking of the Hindus who opposed Alexander the Great, Mr. Elphinstone says, "Their arms, with the exception of fire arms, were the same as at present."[3]

Philostratus thus speaks of Alexander's invasion of the Punjab "Had Alexander passed the Hyphasis he could never have made himself master of the fortified habitations of these sages. Should an enemy make war upon them, they drive him off by means of tempests and thunders as if sent

---

festival. Mr. Elphinstone says, 'In the Dasehra ceremoney the combat ends in the destruction of Laṅkā amidst a blaze of fireworks which' would excite admiration in any part of the world. And the procession of the native prince on this occasion presents one of the most animating and gorgeous spectacles ever seen.' Elphinstone's *History of India*, p. 178.

[1] Essays, Vol. II, p. 303

[2] Orat, XXVII, p. 337. See Ap. Duten's *Origin of the discoveries attributed to the Moderns*, p. 196.

[3] Elphinstone's *History of India*, p. 241

down from Heaven. The Egyptian Hercules and Bacchus made a joint attack on them, and by means of various military engines attempted to take that place. The sages remained unconcerned spectators until the assault was made when it was repulsed by fiery whirlwinds and thunders which, being hurled from above, dealt destruction of the invaders."[1]

Commenting on the stratagem adopted by King Hal in the battle against the king of Kashmir, in making a clay elephant which exploded, Mr. Elliot says, "Here we have not only the simple act of explosion but something very much like a fuse, to enable the explosion to occur at a particular period."[2]

Viśvāmitra, when giving different kinds of weapons to Rāma, speaks (in the *Rāmāyaṇa*) of one as āgneya, another as *śikhara*.

आग्नेयमस्त्रन्दयितं शिखरन्नाम नामतः।

"Carey and Marshman render *śikhara* as a combustible weapon."[3]

In the *Mahābhārata* we read of "a flying ball emitting the sound of a thunder-cloud which Scholiast is express in referring to artillery."[4]

The *Harivaṁśa* thus speaks of the fiery weapon:

आग्नेयमस्त्रं लब्ध्वा च भार्गवात्सगारे नृपः।

---

[1] Philostrati Vit: Apollon, *Lib* II, C. 33

[2] Elliot's *Historians of India*, Vol.I, p. 365

[3] Various kinds of weapons are mentioned, some of which are extraordinary. As it is not known how they were made, what they were like, and how they were used, people think they are only poetic phantasies. Mr. Elliot says, ''Some of these weapons mentioned above were imaginary, as for instance, the *vāyava* or airy." But who would not have called the gramaphone, the cinematograph and wireless telegraphy imaginary only 50 years ago

[4] Bohlen, *Das Alte Indien*, II, 66

जिगाय पृथिवीं हत्वा तालजंघान्सहैहयान्।।

"King Sagara having received fire-arms from Bhargava. conquered the world, after slaying the Tāljaṅghas and the Haihayas." M. Langlois says that "these fire-arms appear to have belonged to the Bhargavas, the family of Bhṛgu."[1] Again,

ऊर्ध्वस्तु जातकर्म्मादि तस्य कृत्वा महात्मनः।
अध्याप्य वेदानखिलांस्ततोऽस्त्रम्प्रत्यपादयत्।।

आग्नेयस्तु महाबाहुरमरैरपि दुस्सहम्।
स तेनास्त्र बलेनाजी बलो च समन्वितः।।

"Aurva having performed the usual ceremonies on the birth of the great-minded (prince), and having taught him the Vedas instructed him in the use of arms; the great-armed (Aurva presented him the fiery weapon, which even the immortals could not stand."

Brahmāstra is repeatedly mentioned in Sanskrit works. Professor Wilson, in his Sanskrit Dictionary, calls *Brahmāstra* "a fabulous weapon, originally from Brahmā." For its use see Śri Bhāgvat describing the fight between the son of Droṇa and Arjuna with the *Brahmāstra*. The Rev. KCM. Banerjee in his work, "*The Encyclopaedia Bengalensis*," says that the *Brahmāstra* was probably a piece of musketry not unlike the modern matchlocks." Madame Blavatsky, in her *Isis Unveiled*, also shows that "fire arms were used by the Hindus in ancient times."[2] *Brahmāstra*, in fact, was an atomic weapon invented by Brahmā."

In the description of Ayodhyā is mentioned the fact of *yantras*[3] being mounted on the walls of the fort, which shows that cannons or machines of some kind or other were used in those days to fortify and protect citadels.

---

[1] *Harivañśa*, p. 68

[2] *Encyclo. Bengal*, Vol. III, p. 21

[3] *Yantra* means '*that thing with which something is thrown.*'

The *Rāmāyaṇa*, while describing the fortifications, says "As a woman is richly decorated with ornaments, so are the towers with big destructive machines."[1] This shows that cannons or big instruments of war like cannons, which discharged destructive missiles at a great distance, were in use at that time.

In descriptions of fortresses and battles, *Śataghnis* are often mentioned. *Śataghni* literally means "that which kills hundreds at once." In Sanskrit dictionaries, *Śataghni* is defined as a machine which shoots out a piece of iron and other things to kill numbers of men. Its other name in *Bṛścī Kāli* बृश्चीकाली[2]

Śataghnis and similar other machines are mentioned in the following *ślokas* of the *Rāmāyaṇa*:

Canto	3	--- --- ---	*Ślokas* 12, 13, 16 and 17
"	4	--- --- ---	23
"	21	--- --- ---	last *śloka*
"	39	--- --- ---	36
"	60	--- --- ---	54
"	61	--- --- ---	32
"	76	--- --- ---	32
"	76	--- --- ---	68
"	86	--- --- ---	22

Rāmāyaṇa says that the *Śataghnī* was made of iron. In the *Sundara Kāṇḍa,* it is compared in size with big broken trees or their huge offshoots, and in appearance said to 'resemble trunks of trees." "They were not only mounted on forts but were carried to the battle-fields, and they made a noise like thunder." What else could they, therefore, be but cannons?

---

[1] *Rāmāyaṇa*, *Sundara Kāṇḍa*, Third Chapter, 18th verse.

[2] See Raja Sir Rādhā Kant Deva's *Śabdakalpadruma.*

Besides the *Rāmāyaṇa*, the *Purāṇas* make frequent mention of *Śataghni* being placed on forts and used in times of emergency. See *Matsya Purāṇa* (मत्स्यपुराण)." Art of Government''. The name used in this *Purāṇa* is *Sahasraghani* (शात) and सहस्र mean hundreds and thousands or innumerable)[1] guns and cannons are mentioned as existing in Laṅkā, under Rāvaṇa. They were called *Nhulat Yantras.*

Commenting on the passage in the Code of Gentoo (Hindu) Laws that "the magistrate shall not make war with any deceitful machine or with poisoned weapons, or with cannons and guns, or any kind of fire-arms," Halhed says, "The reader will probably from hence renew the suspicion which has long been deemed absurd, that Alexander the Great did absolutely meet with some weapons of that kind in India, as a passage in Quintus Curtius seems to ascertain. Gunpowder has been known in China, as well as Hindustan, far beyond all periods of investigation. The word fire-arms is literally the Sanskrit *Āgneyāstara*, a weapon of fire; they describe the first species of it have been a kind of dart or arrow tip with fire and discharged upon the enemy from a bamboo. Among several extraordinary properties of this weapon, one was, that after it had taken its flight, it divided into several separate streams of flame, each of which took effect, and which, when once kindled, could not be extinguished: but this kind of Āgneyāstra is now lost."[2] He adds "A cannon is called '*Śataghnī*, or the weapon that kills one hundred men at once,' and, that the *Purāṇa Śāstaras* ascribe the invention of these destructive engines to Viśvakarmā, the Vulcan of the Hindus."

---

1 *Śataghnī* differed widely from *Matvāla* in that the *Matvāla* were roiled down from maintains, while *Śataghnī* was an instrument from which stones and iron balls were discharged. *Jamera* was another machine that did fatal injury to the enemy by means of stones. See accounts of battles with Mohamed Kasim.

2 Halhed's *Code of Gentoo Laws, Introduction*, p. 52 See also *Amarakoṣa* and *Śabda Kalpadrum*, Vol. I, p. 16

Mr. H. H. Elliot, Foreign Secretary to the Government of India (1845), after discussing the question of the use of fire-arms. in ancient India, says "On the whole, then, we may conclude that fire-arms of some kind were used in early stages of Indian history, that the missiles were explosive, and that the time and mode of ignition was dependent on pleasure; that projectiles were used which were made to adhere to gates and buildings, and machines setting fire to them from a considerable distance; that it is probable that saltpeter, the principal ingredient of gunpowder, and the cause of its detonation, entered into the composition, because the earth of Gangetic India is richly impregnated with it in a natural state of preparation, and it may be extracted from it by lixiviation and crystallization without the aid of fire; and that sulphur may have been mixed with it, as it abundant in the north-west of India."[1]

"Rockets," says Professor Wilson, "appear to be of Indian invention, and had long been used in native armies when Europeans came first in contact with them."

Col. Tod says, "Jud Bhan (the name of a grandson of Vajra, the grandson of Krishna), 'the rocket of the Yadus,' would imply a knowledge of gun-powder at a very remote period."

Rockets were unknown in Europe till recently (1906AD.). "We are informed by the best authorities that rockets were first used in warfare at the siege of Copenhagen in 1807."[2] Mr. Elliot says, "It is strange that they (rockets) should now be regarded in Europe as the most recent invention of artillery."[3]

There were in ancient India machines which, besides throwing balls of iron and other solid missiles, also threw peculiar kinds of destructive liquids at great distances. The

---

1 *Bibliographical Index to the Historians of M. India*, Vol. J. p. 373.

2 Tod's *Rajasthan*, Vo. II, p. 220

3 *Penny Encyclopaedia*, V, 'Rocket.'

ingredients of these liquids are unknown: their effects, however, are astonishing.

Ctesias[1], Elian[2] and Philostratus[3] all speak of an oil manufactured by Hindus and used by them in warfare in destroying the walls and battlements of towns that no "battering rams or other polioretic machines can resist it," and that "it is inextinguishable and insatiable, burning both arms and fighting men."

Lassen says, "That the Hindus had something like 'Greek fire' is also rendered probable by Ctesias, who describes their employing a particular kind of inflammable oil for the purpose of setting hostile towns and forts on fire."[4]

Eusebe Salverte, in his Occult Sciences, says, "The fire which burns and crackles on the bosom of the waves denotes that the Greek fire was anciently known in Hindustan under the name of *baḍavā*."[5]

But what establishes the superiority of the ancient Hindus over the modern Europeans in the noble game of war is the *Astra Vidyā* of the former. "The *Astra Vidyā*, the most important and scientific part (of the art of war) is not known to the soldiers of our age. It consisted in annihilating the hostile army by involving and suffocating it in different layers and masses of atmospheric air, charged and impregnated with different substances. The army would find itself plunged in a fiery, electric and watery element, in total thick darkness, or surrounded by a poisonous, smoky, pestilential atmosphere, full sometimes of savage and terror-striking animal forms (snakes and tigers, etc.) and frightful noises. Thus they used to destroy their enemies.[6] The party

---

[1] Ctesie, *Indica Exerpta*, XXVII (ed. Baer), p. 356

[2] *De Natura Animal, Lib.* V., cap. 3

[3] *Philostrati Vita Apollonu*, Lib. III, cap. 1

[4] Lassen's *Ind. Alt.* II, p. 641

[5] English Translation, Vol. II, p. 223

[6] *Theosophist*, March 1881, p. 124

thus assailed counteracted those effects by arts and means known to them, and in their turn assaulted the enemy by means of some other secrets of the *Astra Vidyā*. Col. Olcott 'also says, "*Astra Vidyā*, a science of which our, modern professors have not even an inkling, enabled its proficient use to completely destroy an invading army, by enveloping it in an atmosphere of poisonous gases, filled with awe striking shadowy shapes and with awful sounds." This fact is proved by innumerable instances in which it was practised. *Rāmāyaṇa* mentions it. Jalandhar had recourse to it when he was attacked by his father, Mahādeva (Śiva), as related in the *Kārtika Mahātmya*.

Another remarkable and astonishing feature of the Hindu science of war which would prove that the ancient Hindus cultivated every science to perfection, was that the Hindus could fight battles in the air. It is said that the ancient Hindus "could navigate the air, and not only navigate it but fight battles in it, like so many war-eagles combating for the dominion of the clouds. To be so perfect in aeronautics, they must have known all the arts and sciences relating to the science, including the strata and currents of the atmosphere, the relative temperature, humidity and density and the specific gravity of the various gases."[1]

Vimāna Vidyā was a science which has now (by the time of 1906 AD.) completely disappeared. A few years ago, facts concerning this science found in ancient records were rejected as absurd and impossible of belief. But wireless telegraphy and the recent developments in ballooning have prepared the Europeans to entertain the idea of the possibility of human knowledge advancing so far as to make it practicable for men to navigate the air as they navigate the sea. And a day will come as assuredly as that the day will follow the night, when not only will the ancient Hindu greatness in this science be recognised, but the results

---

[1] Colonel Olcott's lecture at Allahabad in 1881. See the Theosophist for March 1881.

achieved by them will again be achieved by men to mark their rise to the level of the ancient Hindus.

5.8. MUSIC

Music exalts each joy, allays each grief.
Expels diseases, softens every pain.
Subdues the rage of poison and the plague.
And hence the wise of ancient days adored.
One power of physic, melody and song.

ARMSTRONG: *A. P. H.*

Music is the natural expression of a man's feelings. It comes naturally to man, woman and child in all conditions, at all times and in all countries. "The very fact of musical utterance," says Sir Hubert Parry, "implies a genuine expansion of the nature of the human being, and is in 'a varying degree a trustworthy revelation of the particular likings, tastes and sensibilities of the being that gives vent to it."

The Chinese emphasise its importance by calling it "the science of sciences."

"An eminently poetical people,'' as the ancient Hindus were, could not but have been eminently musical also. Anne C. Wilson, in what is perhaps the latest attempt on the part of a European to understand Hindu music, says, "The people of India are essentially a musical race..........To such an extent is music an accompaniment of existence in India, that every hour of the day and season of the year has its own melody."[1]

Mr. Coleman says, "Of the Hindu system of music the excellent writer whom I have before mentioned (Sir W. Jones) has expressed his belief that it has" been formed on better principles than our own."[2]

---

[1] *A short Account of the Hindu System of Music*, by Anne C. Wilson (1904), p. 5

[2] Coleman's *Hindu Mythology*, Preface, p.ix.

Colonel Tod says, "An account of the state of musical science amongst the Hindus of early ages and a comparison between it and that of Europe is yet a desideratum in Oriental literature. From what we already know about the science, it appears. to have attained a theoretical precision yet unknown to Europe, and that at a period when even Greece was little removed from barbarism." The antiquity of this most delightful art is the same as the antiquity of the Sanskrit literature itself. Anne C. Wilson says, "It must, therefore, be a secret source of pride to them to know that their system of music, as a written science, is the oldest in the world. Its principal features were given long ago in Vedic writings. . . . . Its principles were accepted by the Mohamedan portion of the population in the days of their preeminence, and are still in use in their original construction at the present day."[1]

Music has been a great favourite[2] with the Hindus from the earliest times. Even the Vedas (e.g., *Sāmaveda*) treat of this divine art. The enormous extent[3] of which the Hindus have cultivated this science is proved by their attainments in it. But, unhappily, the masterpiece on this "Science and Art combined'' the *Gandharva Veda*, is lost, and references to it in Sanskrit works alone remain to point to the high principles on which the Hindu science of music was based.

Even at the present day the *Rāgas* and *Rāgnis* of the Hindus are innumerable, and the majority of them differ so minutely from each other that even the "cultivated ear of the

---

[1] *A Short Account of the Hindu System of Music* by A.C. Wilson, p. 9

[2] Shakespear says :
'The man that hath no music in himself
Nor is not moved with concord of sweet sounds.
Is fit for treason, stratagems and spoils;
Let no such man be trusted.'

[3] 'The Hindu system of music is minutely explained in a great number of Sanskrit books.' Sir W. Jones.

musical Europeans" cannot fully understand and follow them.

Sir W. W. Hunter says, "Not content with the tones and semitones, the Indian musicians employed a more minute sub division, together with a number of sonal modifications which the Western ear neither recognises nor enjoys. Thus, they divide the octave into 22 subtones instead of 12 semitones of the European scale. The Indian musician declines altogether to be judged by the few simple Hindu airs which the English ear can appreciate."[1]

Anne C. Wilson says, "Every village player knows about time, and marks it by beating time on the ground, while the audience claps their hands along with him. He has the most subtle ear for time, and a more delicate perception of shades of difference than the generality of English people can acquire, an acuteness of musical hearing which also makes it possible for him to recognise and reproduce quarter and half tones when singing or playing."[2]

Nor are Europeans able to imitate Hindu music. Mr. Arthur Whitten says, "But I have yet to observe that while our system of notation admits of no sound of less than half a tone, the Hindus have quarter tones, thus rendering it most difficult of imitation by Europeans. The execution of their music, I hold to be impossible to all except those who commence its practice from a very early age."[3]

He also observes, "Few of the ancient Hindu airs are known to Europeans. and it has been found impossible to set them to music according to the modern system of notation, as we have neither staves nor musical characters whereby the sounds may be accurately expressed."[4]

---

[1] *ImperialGazetteer*, 'India,' p. 224
[2] Anne C. Wilson's *Hindu System of Music.*
[3] *The Music of the Ancients*, p. 22.
[4] *The Music of the Ancients*, p. 21

Professor Wilson says, "That music was cultivated on scientific principles is evident from the accounts given by Sir W. Jones and Mr. Colebrooke, from which it appears that the Hindus had a knowledge of the garnet, of the mode of notation, of measurement of time, and of a division of the notes of a more minute description than has been found convenient in Europe."[1] We understand," says Mrs. Manning, "that the Hindu musicians have not only the Chromatic but also the Enharmonic genus."[2]

The Oriental Quarterly Review says, "We may add that the only native singers and players whom Europeans are in the way of hearing in most parts of India are reported by their scientific brethren in much the same light as a ballad singer at the corner of the street by the prime soprans of the Italian opera."[3]

Sir W. W. Hunter says, "And the contempt with which the Europeans in India regard it merely proves their ignorance of the system on which Hindu music is built Up."[4] Professor Wilson says, "Europeans, in general, know nothing of Indian music. They hear only the accompaniments to public processions, in which noise is the

---

[1] Mill's *India*, Vol. II, p. 41

[2] *Ancient and Mediaeval India*, Vol. II, p. 153

[3] *Quarterly Review* for December 1825, p.197

[4] *Imperial Gazetteer*, 'India,' p. 224. Mrs. Anne C. Wilson says: 'Not many Europeans, I fancy, would boast of being even superficially acquainted with the *Dhrupada* style of song, the popular *Tappas*, the *Ṭhumarī* songs of the N. W. P., the *Kharkhas* or war-songs of the Rajputs, the *Huttari* chants, the nursery rhymes, the wedding and cremation songs of Gujrat, the Vernams, Pallam, Kirtans of Madras who amongst us know the lyric poetry of Vidyapati, of Chandidas, Jaideva or the well known family of Ram Bhagan Dutt, sometimes called the 'nest of singing birds ?' p. 41.

chief object to be attained, or the singing of the Mohamedans, which is Persian, not Indian."[1]

There are six male *rāgas*, and associated with them are thirty-six female *rāganīs*, which partake of the peculiar measure or quality of their males but in a softer and more feminine degree. From each of these 36 *rāgnīs* have been born three *rāganīs* reproducing the special peculiarity of their original, and these have in their turn produced offsprings without number, each bearing a distinct individuality to the primary *rāga*, or, to use the poetic Hindu expression, "they are as numerous and alike as the waves of the sea." That the Hindus cultivated music on scientific principles is proved by the fact that, as Mr. Whitten says, these *rāgas* were designed to move some passion or affection of the mind, and to each was assigned' some particular season of the year, time of the day and night or special locality or district, and for a performer to sign a *rāga* out of its appropriate season or district would make him, in the eyes of all Hindus, an ignorant pretender and unworthy the character of a musician."

The six principal *rāgas* are the following:

(1) *Hindaul* : It is played to produce on the mind of the hearers all the sweetness and freshness of spring; sweet as the honey of the bee and fragrant as the perfume of a thousand blossoms.

(2) *Śri Rāga* : The quality of this *rāga* is to affect the mind with the calmness and silence of declining day, to

---

[1] Mill's *India*, Vol. II, p. 41. Professor Wilson adds, "The practice of art among them (Hindus) has declined in consequence probably of its suppression by the Mohamedans.' Sir W. W. Hunter says, "Hindu music after a period of excessive elaboration sank under Mussalmans.' '*Imperial Gazetteer*'', p. 223. "However, it still preserves, in a living state, some of the earlier forms, which puzzle the student of Greek music, side by side with the most complicated development.'' Sir W.W. Hunter, p. 224.

tinge the thoughts with a roseate hue, as clouds are gilded by the setting sun before the approach of darkness and night.

(3) *Megha Malhāra.* This is descriptive of the effects of an approaching thunder-storm and rain, having the power of influencing clouds in times of drought.

(4) *Dīpaka* : This *rāga* is extinct. No one could sing it and live: it has consequently fallen into disuse. Its effect is to light the lamps and to cause the body of the singer to produce flames by which he dies.

(5) *Bhairava* : The effect of this *rāga* is to inspire the mind with a feeling of approaching 'dawn the carolling of birds, the sweetness of the perfume and air,' the sparkling freshness of dew dropping morn.

(6) Malkos. The effect of this *rāga* is to produce on the mind a feeling of gentle stimulation.

There is much that is common to both the Hindu and European systems. Mr. Arthur Whitten says, "Their (Hindus) scale undoubtedly resembles our diatonic mode, and consists of seven sounds, which are extended to three octaves, that being the compass of the human voice.' 'Their voices and music, like ours, are divided into three distinct classes. The bass, called *odarah*, or lowest notes; the tenor, called *madurrah*, or middle notes; the soprano, called the *tarrah*, or upper notes. The similarity of the formation, of the ancient Hindu scale to our modern system is noteworthy. We name the sounds of our scales: *Doh*, *Ray*, *Me*, *Fah*, *Sol*, *La*, *Te*. That common in India is: *Sā*, *Re*, *Gā*, *Mā*, *Pā*, *Dhā*, *Ni.*[1] The reason of this similarity is evident. Sir W. W. Hunter says, "A regular system of notation was worked out before the age of Panini, and seven notes were designated by their initial letters. This notation passed from the *Brāhmaṇas* through the Persians to Arabia, and was thence introduced into European music by Guido d' Arezzo at the beginning of

---

[1] *The Music of the Ancients*, pp. 21, 22

the eleventh century."[1] (Note: The seven sounds of Indian Musical scale sā, re, gā, mā, pā, dhā, ni are based on the seven musical notes of Vedas, viz. *ṣaḍaja, revata, gāndhāra, madhyama, pañcama, dhaivata* and *nicṛta.* Ravi Prakash Arya)

Professor Weber says, "According to Von Bohlen and Benfey, this notation passed from the Hindus to the Persians,[2] and from these again to the Arabs, and was introduced into European music by Guido d' Arezzo at the beginning of the eleventh century."[3]

But the principles of Hindu music were imported into Europe much earlier than this.

Strabo says, "Some of the Greeks attribute to that country (India) the invention of nearly all the science of music. We perceive them sometimes describing the *cittiara* of the Asiatics and sometimes applying to flutes the epithet Phrygian. The names of certain instruments, such as *nabla* and others, likewise are taken from barbarous tongues." Colonel Tod says, "This *nabla* of Strabo is possibly the *tablā*, the small *tabor* of India. If Strabo took his orthography from the Persian or Arabic, a single point would constitute the difference between the N (*nun*) and the *T* (*te*)."[4] He adds, "We have every reason to believe from the very elaborate character of their written music, which is painful and discordant to the ear, and from its minuteness of subdivision that they had also the Chromatic scale, said to

---

[1] *Indian Gazetteer*, p. 223. See Benfey's *Indien Ersch*, p. 299, and Gruber's *Encyclopaedia*, vol. XVIII. 'Some suppose that our modern word gamut comes from the Indian *gama*=a musical scale. Prakrit is *gama*, while its Sanskrit is *grāma*.

[2] Hindu musicians used to go to foreign countries to grace the courts of foreign kings. King Behram of Persia had many Hindu musicians in his court.

[3] Weber's Indian Literature, p. 272

[4] Tod's *Rajasthan*, Vol. I, p. 569 (P. Edition).

have been invented by Timotheus in the time of Alexander, who might have carried it from the banks of the Indus."[1]

Colonel Tod also says, "In the mystic dance, the *Rāsa-Maṇḍala,* yet imitated on the festival sacred to the sun-god, Hari, he is represented with a radiant crown in a dancing attitude, playing on the flute to the nymphs encircling him, each holding a musical instrument. . . . .These nymphs are also called the *nava-rāganī,* from *rāga,* a mode of the song over which each presides, and *nava-rasa,* or nine passions excited by the powers of harmony. May we not in this trace the origin of Apollo and the sacred Nine ?"

Bharata, Iśvara, Parṇa and Nārada were among the great Hindu musicians of ancient India.[2] In more recent times, however, Naik Gopal and Tansen have been the most celebrated ones. About Naik Gopal, Mr. Whitten says, "Of the magical effect produced by the singing of Gopal Naik and of the romantic termination to the career of this sage, it is said that he was commanded by Akbar to sing the *rāga Dīpaka,* and he, obliged to obey, repaired to the river Jumna, in which he plunged up to his neck. As he warbled the wild and magical notes, flames burst from his body and consumed him to ashes."[3] He adds, "It is recorded of

---

[1] Tod's *Rajasthan,* Vol. I, p. 570

[2] Weber's *Indian Literature,* p. 272

[3] *Music of the Ancients,* p. 21. Dr. Tennet says, 'If we are to judge merely from the number of instruments and the frequency with which they apply them, the Hindus might be regarded as considerable proficients in music.'
The instrument *singa,* or horn, is said to have been played by Mahadeo, who alone possessed the knowledge and power to make it speak. Singular stories are related of the wonders performed by this instrument.
The Vīṇā is the principal stringed instrument of music amongst the Hindus at the present day.
'Although not ocean born, the tuneful Beena
Is most assuredly a gem of Heaven
Like a dear friend it cheers the lonely heart
And lends new luster to the social meeting;

Tansen that he was also commanded by the Emperor Akbar to sing the *śri*, or night *rāga* at midday, and the power of the music was such that it instantly became night, and the darkness in a circle round the palace as far as his voice could be heard.' India, it seems, produced Orpheuses even so late as the 17th century AD.

It lulls the pains that absent lovers feel,
And adds fresh impulse to the glow of passion.

5.9. OTHER SCIENCES

What cannot Art and Industry perform?
When Science plans the progress of their toil?
BEATTIE: *Minstrel*

That in addition to the astronomical, the mathematical, the medical and the military sciences, many other equally important sciences flourished in ancient India is evident from the remains of some of the most important achievements of the Hindus. Mr. Elphinstone says, "In science, we find the Hindus as acute and diligent as ever."[1]

Medical science in a flourishing condition presupposes the existence in an advanced state of several other sciences, such as. Botany, Chemistry, Electricity, etc. The *Astra* Vidyā (see Military Science) presupposes the existence of the sciences of chemistry, dynamics, meteorology, geology, physics, and other cognate sciences in a much more advanced state than what we find them in at the present day; while the *Vimāna Vidyā* presupposes an intimate acquaintance with an equally great number of such sciences. The huge buildings of ancient India and "those gigantic temples hewn out of lofty rocks with the most incredible labour at Elephanta, Elora and at many other places," which have not only excited admiration but have been a standing puzzle to some people, could not have come into existence if the ancient Hindus had not been masters of the science of engineering. The engineering skill of the ancients was truly marvellous. With all its advanced civilisation, modern Europe has yet to produce engineers able to build the Pyramids or to turn huge rocks into temples. Mons. de Lesseps was no doubt an admirable representative of triumphant engineering skill and was an honour to France, but the only followed in "the footsteps of his predecessors,' who were equally great, and who, too, had at one time connected the Red Sea with the Mediterranean. Mr. Swayne

---

[1] Elphinstone's *History of India*, p. 133

says, "A French engineer repeats the feat of the old native kings and the Greek Ptolemies in marrying by a canal the Red Sea to the Mediterranean, an achievement which will make the name of Lesseps immortal if the canal can only be kept clear of sand."[1] The sands still maintain a threatening aspect.

As regards the Pyramids, the early fathers of the Church (Christian teachers before 500 AD.), believed them to have fallen from Heaven, while others: in Europe believed them to have sprung out of the earth or to have been built by Satan and his devils.

The *Mahābhārata* shows that the ancient Hindus had achieved wonderful advancement in mechanics. In the description of the *Māyāsabhā* (Exhibition), which was presented by Mayāsura to the Pāṇḍavas, mention is made of microscopes, telescopes, clocks, etc.

An American critic says, "Such, indeed, was the mechanism of the *Māyāsabhā*, which accommodated thousands of men, that it required only ten men to turn and take it in whatever direction they liked." There was, he also says, "the steam or the fire-engine called the *Agni ratha.*"

That there were powerful telescopes in ancient India is, doubtless, quite true. One is mentioned in the *Mahābhārata.* It was given by Vyāsajī to Sanjaya at Indraprastha, in order to witness the battle going on at Kurukshetra.[2]

As regards the science of botany, Professor Wilson says, "They (the Hindus) were very careful observers both of the internal and external properties of plants, and furnish copious lists of the vegetable world, with sensible notices of their uses, and names significant of their peculiarities."[3] If the Akhbar-ul-Sadeeq[4] is to be trusted, a Sanskrit dictionary

---

[1] Swayne's Herodouts (Ancient Classics), p. 41

[2] See *Mahābhārata, Bhīṣma Parva*, Chapter II, *śloka* 10

[3] Mill's *History of India*, Vol. II, p. 97, footnote.

[4] Akbhar-ul-Sadeeq, dated 25th November, 1887, p. 7

of botany in three Volumes was discovered in Kashmir in 1887.

In the play *Mālatī Mādhava*,[1] it is stated that the damsel drew Madhava's heart "like a rod of the ironstone gem," which clearly shows that the Hindus were acquainted with artificial magnets as well as with the properties of the loadstone. Professor Wilson, too, supports this view. He further says, "The Hindus early adopted the doctrine that there is no vacuum in nature, but observing that air was excluded under various circumstances from space, they devised, in order to account for the separation of particles, a subtle element, or ether, by which al1 interstices, the most minute and inaccessible, were pervaded, a notion which modern Philosophy intimates some tendency to adopt, as regards the planetary movements, and it was to this subtle element that they ascribed the property of conveying sound: in which they were so far right that in vacuo there can be no sound. Air again is said to be possessed of the faculty of touch, that it is the medium through which the contact of bodies is effected either keeps them apart air impels them together. Fire, or rather light, has the property of figure – Mr. Colebrooke renders it of colour. In either case, the theory is true; for neither colour nor form is discernible except through the medium of light. Water has the property of taste, an affirmation perfectly true; for nothing is sensible to the palate until it is dissolved by the natural fluids."[2] This shows that the Hindus were in no way behind the scientists of the nineteenth century.

The influence of the moon in causing tides seems to have been known to the Hindus from the earliest times. *Raghuvaṅśa* (V. 61) says:

तं तस्थिवांसं नगरोपकंठे ।
तदागमारूढ़ गुरूत्व हर्षः ।

---

[1] See also Manning's *Ancient and Mediaeval India*, Vol. II, p. 209

[2] Mill's *India*, Vol. II, pp. 95, 96

प्रत्युज्जगाम कथकैशिकेन्द्रः ।

चन्द्रं प्रवृद्धोर्मिरिवोर्मिमाली ।।

"That the Hindus were excellent observers and became great Naturalists becomes clear from Professor Wilson's note on a verse of the drama of *Mṛcchhkatika*, Cārudatta says:

"The elephants' broad front, when thick congealed
The dried-up-dew, they visit me no more."

Wilson says, "At certain periods a thick dew exhales from the elephant's temples. This peculiarity, though known to Strabo, seems to have escaped Naturalists till lately, when it was noticed by Cuvier.[1]

Facts regarding diamonds, pearls, sapphires, etc., are mentioned with care, which show that the ancient Hindus were thoroughly well-versed in the sciences and the arts relating to the fishery and to mining, and- the processes of separating and extracting various substances from the earth.

That the ancient Hindus were masters of the sciences of chemistry, mechanics, meteorology is proved by one of the most wonderful of human achievements. This was the *Vimāna Vidyā.* The balloons of the Western world give us an idea of what *Vimānas* may have been like. Fifty years ago a *Vimāna* was considered an impossibility. But happily those days of Western scepticism are over, and a *Vimāna*; for its practical advantages, is looked upon as an ideal of scientific achievement. A European critic says, "*Vimāna Vidyā* was a complete science amongst the ancient Hindus. They were its masters and used it for all practical purposes."

This indicates their mastery of all the arts and sciences on which the *Vimāna Vidyā* is based, including a knowledge of the different strata and the currents of the atmospheric air, the temperature and density of each, and various other

---

[1] The *Theatre of the Hindus*, Vol. I, p. 22 footnote

minor particulars. *Vimāna Vidyā* thus clearly mentioned in the Vedas. The *Yajurveda* (VI, 21) says:

समुद्रंगच्छ स्वाहा अन्तरिक्षंगच्छ स्वाहा देवं सवितारंगच्छ स्वाहा।।

Manu also says:

संशोध्य त्रिविधं मार्गं षडविधं च बलं स्वकम्।

सांपरायिककल्पेन यायादरिपुं शनैः।।

This science is said by some to have been a part of the more comprehensive science called "the *Vāyu Vidyā*" mentioned in the *Śatapatha Brāhmaṇa*, XI and XIV.

Prof. Weber says, "*Sarpa Vidyā* (serpent science) is mentioned in the *Śatapatha Brāhmaṇa* XIII, as a separate science and *Viṣa Vidyā* (science of poisons) in the *Āśvalāyana Sūtra.*"[1] "Śivadāsa, in his Commentary of Chakrapāṇī, quotes Patañjali as an authority on *Lohasāstra*, or 'the Science of metals or metallurgy',"[2]

The Greeks derived their knowledge of electricity from India. Thales, one of the Greek sages, learned during his tour in India that when amber was rubbed with silk it acquired the property of attracting light bodies.

Not only were the sciences of electricity and magnetism extensively cultivated by the ancient Hindus, but they received their highest development in ancient India. The Vedantist says that lightning comes from rain. This can be easily demonstrated by the well-known experiments of Touilet and others: all these prove that Hindu sages perfectly understood all the electrical magnetic phenomena. The most significant proof of the high development of these sciences is to be found in the fact that they were made to contribute so much to the every-day comfort and convenience[3] of the

---

[1] Weber's *Indian Literature*, p. 265

[2] *History of Hindu Chemistry*, Vol. I, 55

[3] As an instance of such practical adaptations of their scientific discoveries, the following may be useful: Visitors to Simla are familiar with the sight of young native children placed in a

whole community, and that their teachings were embodied in the daily practices of the ancient Hindus, which does the highest credit to their practical wisdom and their scientific temperament.

Sleep is necessary not only to enjoy sound health but to keep the body and soul together. The question now is in what way to sleep to derive the greatest benefit from this necessary operation of nature. Its solution by the ancient Hindus not only proves them to have .been masters of the sciences of magnetism and electricity, but shows the spirit of Hinduism, which cannot be commended too highly for its readiness at all times and in all directions to adopt and assimilate the teachings of science. Every Hindu is instructed by his or her mother and grandmother to lie down to sleep with the head either eastward or southward.

Babu Sitā Nath Roy cites ślokas from the *Śāstras*, which enjoin this practice. The *Ānhika*, *Tattva*, a part of our *Smṛti Śāstras*, says, "1. The most renowned Garga Ṛṣi says that man should lie down with his head placed eastward in his own house, but if he longs for longevity he should lie down with his head placed southward. In foreign places he may lie down with his head placed even westward, but never and nowhere should he lie down with his head placed northward."

---

position in which they are exposed to the constant trickling of a stream of water. This custom is generally considered a cruel one, although it has not been shown that it promotes a high rate of mortality. The object is to put the young ones to sleep, and the means are probably not more injurious than many of the patent foods and medicines which are the civilized substitutes. At the same time it is startling to find that Sir Joseph Fayrer, President of the Medical Society, is, trying to introduce the hill custom in England. He says that the flowing of water on the vertex of the cranium never fails to induce sleep and that parents who are tormented with fretful children have only to pop them under an improvised water-spout.

"2. Mārkaṇḍeya, one of the much revered Hindu sages says that man becomes learned by lying down with his head placed eastward, acquires strength and longevity by lying down with his head placed southward, and brings upon himself disease and death by lying down with his head placed northward."

The learned writer found another *śloka* in the *Viṣṇu Purāṇa*, which says, "Oh king! It is beneficial to lie down with the head placed eastward or southward. The man always lies down with his head placed in contrary directions becomes diseased."

After stating certain facts 'regarding magnetism and electricity necessary to enable a man (unacquainted with the elements of these sciences) to understand his explanation, Babu Sita Nath Roy says, "According to what has been just now said, it is not very difficult to conceive that the body of the earth on which we live is being always magnetized by a current of thermal electricity produced by the sun. The earth being a round body, when its eastern part is heated by 'the sun its western part remains cold. In consequence, a current of thermal electricity generated by the sun travels over the surface of the earth from east to west. By this current of thermal electricity the earth becomes magnetised, and its geographical north pole being on the right-hand side of the direction of the current, is made the magnetic north pole, and its geographical south pole being on the left-hand side of the same current, is made, the magnetic south pole. That the earth is a great magnet requires no proof more evident than that by the attractive and repulsive powers of its poles, the compass needle, in whatever position it is placed, is invariably turned so as to point out the north and the south by its two ends or poles. In the equatorial region of the earth the compass needle stands horizontally, on account of the equality of attraction exerted on its poles by those of the earth; but in the polar region the needle stands obliquely, that is, one end is depressed and the other end is elevated on account of the inequality of attraction exerted on its poles by those of the earth. Such a position of the needle in polar regions is technically termed the dip of the needle.

"It has been found by experiments that the human body is a magnetizable object, though far inferior to iron or steel. That it is a magnetizable object is a fact that cannot be denied, for in addition to other causes there is a large percentage of iron in the blood circulating throughout all the parts of the body.

"Now, as our feet are for the most part of the day kept in close contact with the surface of that huge magnet-the earth the whole human body, therefore, becomes magnetised. Further, as our feet are magnetised by contact with the northern hemisphere of the earth, where exist all the properties of north polarity, the south polarity is induced in our feet, and north polarity, as a necessary consequence, is induced in our head. In infancy, the palms of our hands are used in walking as much as our feet, and even later on the palms generally, tend more towards the earth than towards the sky. Consequently, south polarity is induced in them as it is at our feet. The above arrangement of poles in the human body is natural to it, and therefore conducive to our health and happiness. The body enjoys perfect health if the magnetic polarity natural to it be preserved unaltered, and it becomes subject to disease if that polarity be in the least degree altered or its intensity diminished.

"Although the earth is the chief source whence the magnetism of the human body is derived, yet it is no less due to the action of oxygen. Oxygen gas being naturally a good magnetic substance, and being largely distributed within and without the human body, helps the earth a good deal in magnetising it.

"Though every human, the body is placed under the same conditions with regard to its magnetisation, yet the intensity and permanence of the magnetic, polarity of one are not always equal to those of another. Those two properties of the human body are generally in direct ratio to the compactness of its structure and the amount of iron particles entering into its composition.

"Now it is very easy to conceive that if you lie down with your head placed southward and feet northward, the south pole of the earth and your head, — which is the north pole of your body, and the north pole of the earth and your feet, which are the two branches of the south pole of your body, being in juxtaposition, will attract each other, and thus the polarity of the body natural to it will be preserved; while for the same reason, if you lie with your head placed northward and feet or untoward, the similar poles of your body and 'the earth being in juxtaposition will repel each other, and thereby the natural polarity of your body will be destroyed or its intensity diminished. In the former position the polarity your body acquires during the day by standing, walking and sitting on the ground, is preserved' intact at night during sleep; but in the latter position, the polarity which your body acquires during the day by standing, walking and sitting on the ground is altered at night during sleep.

"Now, as it has been found by experiment that the preservation of natural magnetic polarity is the cause of health, and any alteration of that polarity is the cause of disease, no one will perhaps deny the validity of the *ślokas* which instruct us to lie down with our heads placed southward, and never and nowhere to lie down with our heads placed northward.

"Now, why in those two *ślokas* the eastern direction is preferred to the western for placing the head in lying down, is explained thus, "It has been established by experiments in all works on medical electricity that if a current of electricity pass from one part of the body to another, it subdues all inflammations in that part of the body, where it enters into and produces some inflamnlation in the part of the body whence it goes out. This is the sum and substance of the two great principles of Anelectrotonus and

Catelectrotonus, as they are technically called by the authors of medical electricities.

"Now, in lying down with the head placed eastward, the current of thermal electricity which is constantly passing over the surface of the earth from east to west, passes through our body also from the head to the feet and therefore subdues all inflammation present in the head, where it makes its entrance. Again, in lying down with the head placed westward, the same current of electricity passes through our body from the feet to the head, and therefore produces some kind of inflammation in the head, whence it goes out. Now, because a clear and healthy head can easily acquire knowledge, and an inflamed, or, in other words, congested head is always the laboratory of vague and distressing thoughts, the venerable sage *Mārkaṇḍeya* was justified in saying that man becomes learned by lying down with his head placed eastward and is troubled with distressing thoughts by lying down with his head placed westward."[1]

There are other time honoured practices, which are founded upon a knowledge of the principles of electricity and magnetism. For instance, we find that (I) Iron or copper rods are inserted at the tops of all temples; (2) Mindulies (metallic cells) made of either gold, silver or iron, are worn on the diseased part of the body; (3) Seats made of either silk, wool, *kuśa* grass or hairy skins of the deer and tiger are used at the time of saying prayers. Those who are acquainted with the principles of electricity will be able to account for these practices. They know that the function of the rod of the *Triśula* (trifurcated iron rod) placed at the top of the Hindu temples is analogous to a lightning conductor. The mindulies perform the same functions as electrical belts and other appliances prescribed in the electrical treatment of diseases. The golden temple of Vishveshwar at Benaras is really thunder proof shelter. Professor Max Müller

[1] *Arya Magazine* for December 1883, p. 211

recommends the use of a copper envelope to a gunpowder magazine to exclude the possibility of being struck by lightning. The woollen and the skin *āsanas* (seats) protect our lives during a thunderstorm from the action of a return shock and keeps our body insulated from the earth.

There is another practice among the Hindus which is explained by an Austrian scientist. 'In representation, "around the head of each of the Hindu gods is the aureole." But why they should be so represented was a mystery until now. Baron Von Reichenbach, an Austrian chemist of eminence, thus explains it. He says, "The human system, in common with every animate and inanimate natural object, and with the whole starry heavens, is pervaded with a subtle aura, or, if you please, imponderable fluid, which resembles magnetism and electricity in certain respects, and yet is analogous with neither. This aura, while radiating in a faint mist from all parts of our bodies, is peculiarly bright about the head, and hence the aureole." "In fact," says Col. Olcott, "we see that Reichenbach was anticipated by the Aryans (Hindus) in the knowledge of the odic aura". And yet "we might never have understood what the nimbus about Krishna meant, but for this Vienna chemist, so perfect is the sway of ignorance over this once glorious people."[1]

Another practice of the Hindus which is ridiculed by non-Hindus, and the importance of which is only dimly perceived by some of the European scientists, is that "when they sit down to eat, every man is isolated from his neighbours at the feast; he sits in the centre of a square traced upon the floor, grandsire, father and son, brother and uncle, avoiding touching each other quite as scrupulously as though they were of different castes. If I should handle a Brāhmin's brass platter, his *loṭā* or another vessel for food and drink, neither he nor any of his caste would touch it, much less eat or drink from it until it had been passed

---

[1] Col. Olcott's lecture delivered at the Town Hall, Calcutta, on 5th April, p. 82.

through fire: if the utensil were of clay it must be broken. Why all these? That no affront is meant by avoidance of contact is shown in the careful isolation of members of the same family from each other. The explanation, I submit, is that every member was supposed to be an individual evolution of psychic force, apart from all consideration of family relationship: if one touched the other at this particular time when the vital force was actively centred upon the process of digestion, the psychic force was liable to be drawn off, as a lead jar charged with electricity is discharged by touching it with your hand. The oldest member of old was an initiate, and his evolved psychic power was employed in the *Agnihotra* and other ceremonies. The case of the touching of the eating or drinking vessel, or the mat or clothing of a member by one of another caste of inferior psychic development, or the stepping of such a person upon the ground within a certain prescribed distance from the sacrificial spot, bear upon this question. In this same plate of Baron Reichenbach's, figure F represents the aura streaming from the points of the human hand. Every human being has such an aura, and the aura is peculiar to himself or herself as to quality and volume. Now, the aura of a person of the ancient times was purified and intensified by a peculiar course of religious training – let us say psychic training — and if it should be mixed with the aura of a less pure, less spiritualized person, its strength would of necessity be lessened; its quality adulterated. Reichenbach tells us that the odic emanation is conductible by metals, slower than electricity, but more rapidly than heat, and that pottery and other clay vessels absorb and retain it for a great while. Heat he found to enormously increase quantitatively the flow of odyle through a metal conductor. The person, then in submitting his odylically – tainted metallic vessel to the fire, is but experimentally carrying out the theory of Von Reichenbach.

6

ARTS

6.1. ARCHITECTURE AND SCULPTURE

I asked of Time for whom those temples rose
That prostrate by his hands in silence lie;
His lips disdained the mystery to disclose,
And borne on swifter wings he hurried by!
The broken columns whose? I asked of Fame
(His kindling breath gives life to works sublime);
With downcast looks of mingled grief and shame
She heaved the uncertain sigh and followed Time,
Wrapt in amazement over the smouldering pile
I saw oblivion pass with giant strides,
And while his visage wore Pride's scornful smile,
Haply these vast domes that even in ruin shine
"I reck not whose," he said, "they now are mine."

BYRON

There is another unmistakable proof of the wonderful civilisation of the ancient Hindus–it is their architecture. The magnificent Hindu temples; the splendid palaces, the formidable forts and the wonderful caves are truly monuments of human genius and marvels of human industry and skill. They have excited the admiration of all European critics, and have elicited expressions of wonder and amazement from them. Mrs. Manning says, "The ancient architecture of India is so amazing that the first European observers could not find terms sufficiently intense to express their wonder and admiration, and although the vividness of such emotions subsides on more intimate acquaintance, the most sober critics still allow that it is both wonderful and beautiful."[1]

Strength and durability, beauty and majesty are the characteristics of the Hindu style of architecture. Mahmud Ghaznavi writing to the Khalif from Mathura said that the buildings of India were surely not less strong than the Mohamedan faith. Such expressions of wonder from one of the greatest fanatics that ever lived is significant evidence of the highest development of the art of architecture in India.

Mr. Thornton says, "The ancient Indian erected buildings the solidity of which has not been overcome by the revolution of thousands of years."[2]

After speaking of Hindu sculpture, Professor Weber continues, "A far higher degree of development was attained by architecture of which some most admirable monuments still remain."[3] While describing the structure of a building, Mr. Elphinstone says, "The posts and lintels of the doors, the panels and other spaces are enclosed and almost covered by deep borders of building and a profusion of arabesques of plants, flowers, fruits, men, animals and imaginary beings; in short, of every embellishment that the most fertile fancy could devise. These arabesques, the running patterns of plants and creepers, in particular, are often of an elegance scarcely equalled in any other part of the world."[4]

Mr. Fergusson describes a remarkable temple at Rameshwaram, of which the outer court measures the length of the river face of Parliament House at Westminster by twice their depth. Of the pagoda at Rameshwaram, Lord Valentia says, "The whole building presents a magnificent

---

[1] *Ancient and Mediaeval India*, Vol. I, p. 391

[2] Thornton's Chapters from the *British History of India*

[3] Weber's *Indian Literature*, p. 274

[4] Elphinstone's *History of India* , p.160. The author also says, 'Perhaps the greatest of all the Hindu works are the tanks. The Hindu wells are also very remarkable.'

appearance, which we might in vain seek adequate language to describe."[1]

After giving a description of the pagoda at Chalambron, 27 miles south of Pondicherry, Professor Heeren says, "On the other side of the large tank is the most wonderful structure of all. This is a sanctuary or chapel in the middle of an enormous; hall, 360 ft. long x 260 ft. in breadth, and supported by upwards of one thousand pillars each thirty feet high and. disposed in regular order."[2] Dr. Robertson thus speaks of the Hindu architectural elegance, "Some of the ornamental parts are finished. with an elegance entitled to the ration of the most admiration of the most ingenious artists."[3]

The cave temples are not only peculiar to this country but how the highest artistic genius of the people. Professor Heerena[4] thus speaks of the Elora temples, "All hat is great, splendid and ornamental in architecture is above ground is here seen, also beneath the earth-staircases, bridges, chapels, columns and proticos, obelisks, colossal statues and relief's sculptured on almost all the walls, representing Hindu deities." An English' critic says, "All this wonderful structure, the variety, richness and skill displayed in the ornaments surpass all description."[5] Professor Heeren again

---

[1] Travels. Vol. I, pp. 340, 341. A description of the temple of *Mahākāla* at Ujjain and of the famous temple of Gobind Deoji at Brindaban will give one an idea of the magnificence of Hindu temples.

[2] Heeren's *Historical Researches*, Vol. II, p. 95

[3] Dr. Robertson's Works, Vol. XII, 'Disquisition Concerning India,' p. 16

[4] See *Historical Researches*, Vol. II, pp.60-70. 'Magnitude,' says Professor Wilson, 'is not the only element of beauty in the cavern temples. The columns are carved with great elegance and fitness of design. Notice is taken of the numerous remains of temples in various parts of India in which extreme architectural beauty is to be found. Mill's *History of India*, Vol. II, p. 15

[5] *Asiatic Researches*, Vol. III, p. 405

says, "It is not without an involuntary shudder that we pass the threshold of these spacious grottoes, and compare the weight of these ponderous roofs with the apparent slenderness and inadequacy of its support, an admirable and ingenious effect which must have required no ordinary share of abilities in the architect to calculate and determine!"[1] The learned Professor concludes, "Such are the seven Pagodas or ancient monuments so called, at Mavalipuram on the Coromandel coast, of which extraordinary buildings it will be hardly too much to assert that, they, will occupy a most distinguished place in the scale of human skill and ingenuity."[2]

Baron Dalberg was greatly struck with the architecture of Dwarka" which he calls "the wonderful city," and says, "The natives of that country (India) have carried the art of constructing and ornamenting excavated grottoes to a much higher degree of perfection than any other people;"[3]

Comparing the Hindu with the Greek and the Egyptian architecture, Professor Heeren says, "In the richness of decoration bestowed on their pilasters, and, among other things, in the execution of statues resembling caryatides they (the Hindus) far surpass both those nations (the. Greeks and Egyptians)."

Mrs. Manning says, "The caves are remarkable also for the use of stucco and paint, not merely on the walls but on the roof and pillars. And the frets and scrolls are of such beauty and elegance as to rival those at Pompeii and the Baths of Titus.[4] The Kailas and the other excavations of

---

1 *Historical Researches*, Vol. II, 74, Śākya Pādāmṛta is the name of the sculptor of the Grottoes of Ellora.

2 Heeren's *History of Researches*, Vol. II, p. 78

3 *Geographical Ephemerides*, Vol. XXXII p. 12

4 *Ancient and Mediaeval India*, Vol. I, p. 404, See also Fergusson's *History of Architecture*, Vol. II, pp. 499-501. The Karli cave is the most perfect specimen of the cave temples.

Western India excite our awe and wonder."[1] She adds, "India is most famous for pillared architecture." The pillared colonnades or choultries, connected with the Southern temples are the most extraordinary buildings."[2] Buddhism gave a great stimulus to the development of architecture in ancient India; and with the spread of Buddhism in foreign countries, the Buddhistic style of architecture was largely borrowed by foreign nations. Professor Weber hits the point when he says, "It is, indeed, not improbable that our Western steeples owe their origin to the imitation of the Buddhistic topes."[3]

Col Tod says, "The Saracen arch[4] is of Hindu origin," and yet some would deny the existence of arches in the architectural style of ancient India.[5]

---

[1] *Ancient and Mediaeval India*, Vol. II, p. 420

[2] *Ancient and Mediaeval India*, Vol. I, p. 418

[3] *Indian Literature*, p. 274

[4] Tod's *Rajasthan*, Vol I, p. 781, Colouel Tod, speaking of the Adhai-din-ka-Jhonpra at Ajmer, says, 'I may further, with this temple and screen before us, speculate on the possibility of its having furnished some hints to the architects of Europe. It is well known that the saracenic arch has crept into many of those structures called Gothic, erected in the 12th and 13th centuries, when a more florid style succeeded to the severity of the Saxon or Roman, but I believe it has been doubted whence the Saracene obtained their model: certainly it was neither from Egypt nor from Persia.' He then goes no to surmise that the influence of the early Caliphs of Baghdad (who were as enlightened as powerful), on European society was great, and that the victories of the Caliph's lieutenants produce no trifling results to the arts, that 'this very spot, Ajmer was visited by the first hostile force which Islam sent across the Indus,' and that the arches of the 'temple' at Ajmer may thus be to models of the arches that were subsequently introduced amongst the Saracens.

[5] The finest example of the triumphal arches is at Barnagar, north of Gujrat, which is the richest specimen of Hidu art.' - Elphinston'e *History of India*, p. 163

Sir William Hunter says, "Although Mohamedans brought their new forms of architecture, nevertheless Hindu art powerfully asserted itself the Imperial works of the Mughals, and has left behind memorials which extort the admiration and astonishment of our age. The palace architecture of Gwalior, the mosques and the mausoleums of Agra and Delhi with several of the older temples of Southern India, stand unrivalled for grace of outline and elaborate wealth of ornament."

Mr. Coleman says, "The remains of their architectural art might furnish the architects of Europe with new ideas of beauty and sublimity."[1]

"English decorative art," to quote Sir W. W. Hunter once more, "in our day has borrowed largely from Indian forms and patterns. The exquisite scrolls of the rock temples at Karli and Ajanta, the delicate marble tracery and flat-wood carving of Western India, the harmonious blending of forms and colours in the fabrics of Kashmir, have contributed to the restoration of taste in England;"[2]

Mr. Coleman says, "The ancient Hindu sculpture can boast of an almost unrivalled richness and beautiful minuteness of floral ornaments which claim and excite our warmest admiration." [3]

"The grand temple at Barolli (Rajputana)," says the English translator of Heeren's Historical Researches, "contains unrivalled specimens of sculpture, some parts of which, especially the heads; in the language of an eye witness, would be no disgrace to Canova himself."

---

1 *Hindu Mythology*, Preface, p. ix

2 *Imperial Indian Gazetteer*, Art 'India,' p. 225. 'Indian art work, when faithful to native designs, has obtained the highest honours at the various International Exhibitions of Europe.' Such is Indian art even in these degenerate days.

3 *Hindu Mythology*, Preface, p. vii.

Colonel Tod, after carefully examining and exploring the temple, exclaims, "To describe its stupendous and diversified architecture is impossible; it is the office of the pen alone, but the labour would be endless, Art seems to have exhausted itself, and we are perhaps now for the first time fully impressed with the beauty of Hindu sculpture. The columns, the ceilings. the external roofing where each stone presents a miniatl1re temple, one rising over another until the crown, by the urn-like kalas, distract our attention. The carving on the capital of each column would require pages of explanation, and the whole, in spite of its high antiquity, is in wonderful preservation.

"The doorway, which is destroyed, must have been curious, and the remains that choke up the interior are highly interesting. One of these specimens was entire and unrivalled in taste and beauty."[1]

---

[1] Tod's *Rajasthan*, Vol. II, p. 704. Col Tod says, 'In short, it would require the labour of several artists for six month to do anything like justice to the wonders of Barolli.'

6.2. WEAVING

The whole world without art and dress
Would be one great wildness.

BUTLER

Indians, even of the present day, are remarkable for their delicacy of sense, especially their nicety of touch. Not only is their observation very accurate and minute, which has given a peculiar charm to their poetry and their fine arts, but their delicate and tactile sensibility, with their general delicacy of sense, has enabled them to achieve a peculiar excellence in many of the industrial arts and manufactures. Mr. James Mill says, "The delicate frame of the Hindu is accompanied with an acuteness of external sense, particularly of touch, which is altogether unrivalled, and the flexibility of his fingers is equally remarkable."[1]

Mr. Orme says, "The hand of the Indian cook wench shall be more delicate than that of an European beauty. The skin and features of a porter shall be softer than those of a professed *petit maitres.* The women wind off the raw silk from the pod of the worm. A single pod of the raw silk is divided into 20 different degrees of fineness, and so exquisite is the feeling of these women that whilst the thread is running through their fingers so swiftly "that their eye can be of no assistance, they will break it off exactly as the assortments change at once from the first to the twentieth, from the nineteenth to the second."[2]

It appears that nature herself has bestowed the gift of excellence in arts and manufactures on the patient, skilful Hindu. The other nations appear to be constitutionally unfit to rival the Hindus in the finer operations of the loom, as well as in other arts that depend upon the delicacy of sense.

---

[1] Mill's *India*, Vol. II, p. 17

[2] *People and Government of Hindustan*, pp. 409 and 413

Nature gave India another advantage. Mr. Mill says, "His (Hindu) climate and soil conspired to furnish him with the most exquisite material for his art the finest cotton which the earth produces."[1]

Mr. Elphinstone, speaking of Indian cotton cloth, says, "the beauty and delicacy of which was so long admired, and which, in fineness of texture, has never yet been approached in any country."[2] Mr. Murray says, "Its fabrics, the most beautiful that human art has anywhere, produced, were sought by merchants at the expense of the greatest toils and dangers."[3]

Mr. Thornton says that the Indian muslins are "fabrics of unrivalled delicacy and beauty."[4]

Mr. Both in his work, "*Cotton Manufactures of Dacca*" says that Aurangzeb once reproved his daughter for showing her skin through her clothes. The daughter justified herself

---

[1] Mill's *History of India*, Vol. II. p. 17. This shows that India is capable of producing and in ancient times did produce the finest cotton used in weaving. In those days India had not to look to Egypt and America for cotton of a superior quality to enable her to manufacture finer muslins to clothe her sons and daughters. It would be interesting to many to learn that cotton is thought to have ''reached Europe in the time of the Crusade, through the medium of the Arabs, the Arab word *kuta* becoming our cotton." Mrs. Manning's *Ancient and Mediaeval India*, Vol. II, p. 356

[2] Elphinstone's *History of India*, pp. 163, 164

[3] Murray's *History of India*, p. 27

[4] Thornton's Chapters of the *British History of India*, Buddha forbids the use of fine muslin by religious women, because he ones saw Gang-Dgah-mo (a woman having upon her a-very fine linen which was sent to Gsal-rgzal by the king of Kalighana) naked while she was wearing a full muslim dress. To give an idea of the value of such fine muslins. Dr. Watts says that in 1776 A.D., the finest muslin reached the price of 56 pound (British currency) per piece (*Textile Manufactures*, p. 79).

by asserting that she had on seven suits, or jamas[1]. After comparing the finest fabrics of India and of England, Dr. Wilson decides in favour of the Indian fabrics. He finds the yarn finer than any yet produced in Europe, while the twisting given to it by the Hindus hands makes it more durable than any machine-made fabric.

"Shawls made in Kashmir," says Mrs. Manning, are still unrivalled."[2] Even James Mill says, "Of the exquisite degree of perfection to which 'the Hindus have carried the productions of the loom it would be idle to offer any description; as there are few, objects with which the inhabitants of Europe are better acquainted, Whatever may have been the attainment in this art of other nations of antiquity, (the Egyptians, for example, whose fine linen was so eminently prized), the manufacturer of no modern nation can, in delicacy and fineness vie with the textures of Hindustan."[3]

Mrs. Manning says, "Some centuries before our era they produced muslins of that exquisite texture which even our nineteenth century machinery cannot surpass."[4] The Encyclopaedia Britannica says that the exquisitely fine fabrics of cotton have attained to such perfection that the

---

[1] Mr. Elphihistone says, 'Gold and silver brocades were also favourites, and were, perhaps, original manufactures in India.' See Colebrooke, *Asiatic Researches*, Vol. V, p.61, *Rudrayāmla Tantra*, in an enumeration of Hindu castes, mentions *Puṇḍrakas* or *Pattasūtrakāras*, or feeders of silkworms and silk twisters: this authority, therefore, in conjunction with the frequent allusion to silk in most ancient Sanskrit books, may be considered as decisive of the questions, provided the antiquity of the *Tantra* be allowed, of which Mr. Colebrooke seems to have no doubt. Silk is, moreover, mentioned throughout the Archipelago by its Sanskrit name, Sūtra, which proves its Indian origin.

[2] 'The presentation of Kashmir shawls to Sita supplies an additional proof in favour of the high antiquity of these celebrated fabrics.'

[3] Mill's *History of India*, Vol. II, p. 16

[4] *Ancient and Mediaeval India*, Vol. I, p. 359

modern art of Europe, with all the aid of its wonderful machinery, has never yet rivalled in beauty the product of the Indian loom."

A critic says, "Carpets are made at Masulipatam with unrivalled Hindu taste," to which Mrs. Manning adds, "Carpets have also been made in later days in Government prisons, under British superintendence; the result proves that we must not attempt to teach art to India."[1]

Dr. Forbes Watson, in his work on the Textile Manufactures of India, gives an interesting account of a series of experiments made on both the European and the Indian muslins, to determine their claims to superiority. The result was altogether in favour of the Indian fabrics. He concludes, "However viewed, therefore, our manufacturers have something still to do. With all our machinery and wondrous appliances, we have hitherto been unable to produce a fabric which, for fineness or utility, can equal the woven air of Dacca, the product of arrangements, which appear rude and primitive, but which in reality are admirably adapted for the purpose."

---

[1] *Ancient and Mediaeval India*, Vol. II p. 363. Professor Heeren says, 'The variety of cotton fabrics mentioned even by the author of Periplus as articles of commerce is so great that we can hardly suppose the number to have increased afterwards.'

6.3. OTHER ARTS

Art is long and time is, fleeting.

LONG FELLOW

Professor Weber says, "The skill of the Indians in the production of delicate woven fabrics, in the mixing of colours, the working of metals and precious stones, the preparation of essences and in all manner of technical arts; has from early times enjoyed a world-wide celebrity."[1]

Professor Wilson says, "They had acquired remarkable proficiency in many of the ornamental and useful arts of life."[2]

As regards dyeing, Mr. Elphinstone says, "The brilliancy and permanence of many of the dyes, have not yet been equalled in Europe."[3] He adds, "The brilliancy of their dyes is remarked on as well as their skill in manufactures and imitations of foreign objects."[4]

Dr. Tennet and even Mr. James Mill admit that the Indian colours are the most brilliant on earth. The Hindus were the earliest nation who discovered the art of extracting colours from plants. The names by which several plants are known in foreign countries bear testimony to this fact. *Indigo* is so called after India. Pliny used to write *Indico.*[5]

Bancroft gives much praise to the "native of India for having so many thousand years ago discovered means by which the colourable matter of the plants might be extracted, oxygenated and precipitated from all other matters combined with it. Even Mill is constrained to say, "Among the arts of

---

[1] Weber's *Indian Literature*, p. 275

[2] Mill's *History of India*, Vol. II, p. 233

[3] *History of India*, p. 164

[4] *History of India*, p. 243, See Strabo, lib, xv. P.493

[5] He says, 'Cast the right indico upon the live coals, it yieldeth a flame of most excellent purple' -Manning's *Ancient and Mediaeval India*, Vol. II, p. 355

the Hindus, that of printing and dyeing their cloths has been celebrated; and the beauty and brilliancy, as well as durability of the colours they produce, are worthy of particular praise."[1]

Mr. Elphinstone says, "The taste for minute ornaments fitted them to excel in goldsmith's work."[2]

Professor Heeren says, "The art of working in ivory must have attained a high degree of perfection."

What is most remarkable, however, is the simplicity of their processes and the exceedingly small number of the instruments with which they work. Stavorinus writes, "Their artificers work with so little apparatus and so few instruments, that an European would be astonished at their neatness and expedition."[3]

As regards painting, Mr. Mill says' ''The Hindus copy with great exactness, even from nature .... They draw portraits both of individuals and of groups with a minute likeness."

As regards iron manufactures, Professor Wilson says, "Casting iron is an art that is practised in the manufacturing country (England) only within a few years. The Hindus have

---

[1] Mill's *India*, Vol. II, p. 21, 'In some of the more delicate manufactures, however, says Mill, 'particularly in weaving, spinning, and dyeing, the Hindus rival allnations as in the fabrication of trinkets too.' Professor Heeren says, 'The dress of the Hindus seemed extra ordinarily white to the Greeks.' *Historical Researches*, Vol. II, p. 272

[2] Elphinstone's *History of India*, p. 164. 'The Hindus cut the precious stones, polish them to a high degree of brilliancy and set them neatly in gold and silver.' Mill's *History of India*, Vol. II, p. 30

[3] Stavorinus' Voyage, p. 412. Foster was astonished to see their instruments and their simple processes. -*Asiatic Researches*, vol. II, p. 272

the art of smelting iron, of welding it, and of making steel, and have had these arts from times immemorial."[1]

Dr. Ray says, "Coming to comparatively later times, we find that the Indians were noted for their skill in the tempering of steel. The blades of Damascus were held in high esteem but it was from India that the Persians, and, through them, the Arabs learnt, the secret of the operation. The wrought-iron pillar close to the Kutub, near Delhi, which weighs ten tons and is some 1,500 years old, the huge iron girders at Puri, the ornamental gates of Somnath, and the 24-feet, wrought iron gun at Nurvar, are monuments of a bye gone art, and bear silent but eloquent testimony to the marvellous metallurgical skill attained by the Hindus." Regarding the Kutub pillar, Fergusson says, "It has not, however, been yet correctly ascertained what its age really is. There is an inscription upon it, but without a date. From the form of its alphabet, Prinsep ascribed it to the third or fourth century." Mr. Fergusson continues, "Taking AD 400 as a mean date, and it certainly is not far from the truth – it opens our eye to an unsuspected state of affairs, to find the Hindus at that age capable of forging a bar of iron larger than any that have been forged even in Europe up to a very late date and not frequently even now. As we find them, however, a few centuries afterwards using bars as long as this *lat* in roofing the porch of the temple at Kanaruc, we must now believe that they were much more familiar with the use of this metal than they, afterwards became. It is almost equally startling to find that after an exposure to wind and rain for fourteen centuries it is unrusted, and the capital and inscription are as clear and as sharp now as when putting up fourteen centuries ago. There is 'no mistake about the pillar being of pure iron. General Cunningham had a bit of it analysed in India by Dr. Murray, and another portion was, analysed in the School of Mines here by Dr.

[1] Mill's *History of India* Vol. II, p.47

Percy. Both found it pure malleable iron without any alloy."[1]

Mr. Manning says, "The superior quality of Hindu steel has long been known, and it is worthy of record that the celebrated Damascus blades have been traced to the workshops of Western India." She adds, "Steel manufactured in Kutch enjoys at the present day a reputation not inferior to that of the steel made at Glasgow and Sheffield."[2] Mrs. Manning also says, "It seems probable that ancient India possessed iron more than sufficient for her wants and that the Phoenicians fetched iron with other merchandise from India."[3]

Dr. Royle is of opinion that the system of rotation of crops has been derived from India. The Hindu farmer understands extremely well how to maintain the productive power of his land.[4]

Professor Wilson says, "The use of glass for windows is a proof of civilisation that neither Greek nor Roman refinement presents."[5]

Dr. Forbes Watson says, "The study of Indian art might in numberless ways improve the character of the everyday articles around us (Englishmen)."[6]

Chamber's Encyclopaedia says, "In manufacture, the Hindus attained to a marvellous perfection at a very early

---

[1] *History of Indian and Eastern Architcture*, p. 508, ed. 1899

[2] *Ancient and Mediaeval India*, Vol. II, p. 365

[3] *Ancient and Mediaeval India*, Vol. II, p. 364. See 'Commerce.'

[4] Dr. Roxburgh fully approves of the Hindu system of agriculture. Sir T. Munro calls it a good system.'

[5] Mill's *India*, Vol. II, p. 46

[6] During his Viceroylty, Lord Dufferin once said, 'The West has still much to learn from the East in matters of dress.' Of the much despised *dhoti*, Mrs. Manning says, 'Any dress more perfectly convenient to walk, to sit, to lie in, it would be impossible to invent.' *Ancient and Mediaeval India*, vol. II, p. 368.

period, and the Courts of Imperial Rome glittered with gold and silver brocades of Delhi. The muslins of Dacca were famous ages ago throughout the civilised world. In the International Exhibition of 1852, splendid specimens of gorgeous manufactures and the patient industry of the Hindus were displayed. Textile fabrics of inimitable fineness, tapestry glittering with gems, rich embroideries and brocades, carpets wonderful for the exquisite harmony of colour, enamel of the most brilliant hue, inlaid wares that require high magnifying power to reveal their minuteness, furniture most elaborately carved, swords of curious forms and excellent temper are amongst the objects that prove the perfection of art in India."[1]

---

[1] *Chamber's Encyclopaedia*, p. 543

7

COMMERCE AND WEALTH

7.1. COMMERCE

But chief by numbers of industrious hands
A nation's wealth is counted; numbers, raise
Warm emulation; where that virtue dwells.
There will be traffic's seat; there will she build
Her rich emporium.

DYER: Fleece

Though the Indians have practically no hand now in the commerce of the world, yet there was a time when they were the masters of the seaborne trade of Europe, Asia and Africa. They built ships, navigated the sea, and held in their hands all the threads of international commerce, whether carried on overland or by sea.

As their immense wealth was in part the result of their extensive trade with other countries; so were the matchless fertility of the Indian soil and the numberless products of Hindu arts and industries the cause of the enormous development of the commerce of ancient India. As Cowper says:

"And if a boundless plenty be the robe,
Trade is a golden girdle of the globe."

India, which, according to the writer in Chamber's Encyclopaedia "has been celebrated during many ages for its valuable natural productions, its beautiful manufactures and costly merchandise,[1] 'was', says the *Encyclopaedia Britannica*, "once the seat of commerce."[2]

Mrs. Manning says, "The indirect evidence afforded by the presence of Indian products in other countries coincides with the direct testimony to Sanskrit literature to establish the fact that the ancient Hindus were a commercial people."[3] She concludes, "Enough has now been said to show that the Hindus have ever been a commercial people."[4]

Professor Heeren says, "The Hindus in their most ancient works of poetry are represented as a commercial people."[5]

In Sanskrit books, we constantly read of merchants, traders, and men engrossed in commercial pursuits. *Manusmṛti*, one of the oldest books in the world, lays down laws to govern all commercial disputes having reference to seaborne traffic as well as the inland and overland commerce. Traders and merchants are frequently introduced in the Hindu drama. In *Śakuntalā* we learn of the importance attached to commerce, where it is stated "that a merchant named *Dhanavṛddhi*. who had extensive commerce had been lost at sea and had left a fortune of many millions." In Nala and Damyanti, too, we meet with similar incidents. Sir W. Jones is of opinion that the Hindus "must have been navigators in the age of Manu because bottomry is mentioned in it."[6] In the *Rāmāyaṇa*, the practice of bottomry is distinctly noticed.[7] Mr. Elphinstone says, "The Hindus navigated the ocean as early as the age of Manu's code,

---

[1] *Chamber's Encyclopaedia*, Vol. V. p. 536.

[2] *Encyclopaedia Britannica*, Vol. XI, p. 446

[3] *Ancient and Mediaeval India*, Vol. II, p. 353

[4] *Ancient and Mediaeval India*, Vol. II, p. 354

[5] Heeren's *Historical Researches*, Vol. II, p. 266

[6] *Asiatic Researches*, Vol, II, p. 284. Manu speaks of 'merchants who traffic beyond the sea and bring presents to the king.' *India in Greece.*

[7] See *Rāmāyaṇa*, III, 237

because we read in it of men well acquainted with sea voyages."[1]

According to Professor Max Dunker, ship-building was known in ancient India about 2000 BC. It is thus clear that the Hindus navigated the ocean from the earliest times, and that they carried on trade on an extensive scale with all the important nations of the Old World.

With Phoenicia, the Indians enjoyed trade from the earliest times. In the tenth century BC; Solomon of Israel and Hiram of Tyre sent ships[2] to India, whence they carried away ivory, 'Sandalwood, apes, peacocks, gold, silver, precious stones, etc., which they purchased from the tribe of Ophir.[3] Now Ptolemy says there was a country called Abhiria at the mouth of the River Indus. This shows that some people called Abhir must have been living there in those days. We find a tribe called, 'Abhir" still living in Kathiawar, which must, therefore, be the Ophir tribe mentioned above Professor Lassen thinks "Ophir" was a seaport on the south-west coast of India. Mrs. Manning says it was situated on the western coast of India.

As, however, the authors of Smith's Dictionary of the Bible think that Ophir was situated somewhere in Africa, let us go a little more closely into the question of this tribe. Let us first see if the articles imported by the Navy of Tarshish were procurable in India, and if they were, whetl1er they were procurable in Africa or any other country also.

Among the things sent by the Hindus to Solomon and Hiram were peacocks. Now, these birds were nowhere to be found in those days except India, where they have existed from the earliest times. "We frequently meet in old Sanskrit poetry with sentences like these: ''Peacocks unfolding in

---

[1] Elphinstone's *History of India*, p. 166. 'The word used in the original for sea is not applicable to inland waters.'

[2] Called the '*Navy of Tarshish.*' See also the Book of Chronicies.

[3] Max Dunker's *History of Antiquity*, Vol. IV, and Manning's *Ancient and Mediaeval India*, Vol. II, p. 349

glittering glory all their green and gold; 'peacocks dancing in wild glee at the approach of rain'; 'peacocks around palaces glittering on the garden walls.' Ancient sculpture, too, shows the same delight in peacocks, as may be seen, for instance, in graceful bas-reliefs on the gates of Sanchi or in the panels of an ancient palace in Central India, figured in Tod's Rajasthan (p.405).

At the same time, it is quite certain that the peacock was not generally known in Greece, Rome, or Egypt before the time of Alexander of Macedon, whose followers were astonished to see such a beautiful bird in India. It was after Alexander's time that peacocks came to be imported directly from India or through Persia into Greece. It was the Romans, however, who most delighted in the bird, admired it, and spent immense sums of money on it. It was the height of luxury for the high Roman dames and the old Roman epicures to have tongues of peacocks served to them at their tables.

There is. however, conclusive evidence to prove that Solomon and Hiram got their peacocks from India. This evidence is the name which the bird received in the Holy Land. "The word for peacock in Hebrew is universally admitted to be foreign and Gesenius, Sir Emerson Tennent, and Professor Max Müller appear to agree with Professor Lassen in holding that this word as written in Kings and Chronicles is derived from the Sanskrit language."[1]

Now, with regard to ivory. It was largely used in India, Assyria, Egypt, Greece and Rome. Elephants are indigenous to India and Africa, and the ivory trade must be either of Indian origin or African. But the elephants were scarcely known to the ancient Egyptians,[2] and Professor Lassen decides that elephants were neither used nor tamed in Ancient Egypt.[3]

---

[1] *Ancient and Mediaeval India*, Vol. II, p. 351

[2] *ibid.*

[3] *Alterthumkunde*, Vol. I, p. 354

In Ancient India, however, as is well known, they were largely used and tamed. No description of a king's procession or of a battle is to be met with but elephants are mentioned in it. No chieftain was without his elephants. The elephant is an emblem of royalty and a sign of rank and power. The god Indra, too, has his "Airāvata." Then, the Sanskrit name for a domestic elephant is *ibha*, and in the bazars of India *ibha* was the name by which the elephant's tusks were sold. In ancient Egypt, ivory was known by the name *ebu.* Professor Lassen thinks "that the Sanskrit name ibha might easily have reached Egypt through Tyre, and become the Egyptian *ebu.* It is thus very probable that India first made Egypt acquainted with ivory. Mrs. Manning says, "It is believed that by this name or by words derived from it, ivory have been introduced into Egypt and, Greece. Although, by what process ibha was changed into the Greek elephas, is not satisfactorily explained."

Though ivory was known in Greece before the time of Homer, who speaks of it as largely used, but the elephant itself was unknown to the Greeks until the day of Arabella, where they saw Darius aided by war-elephants with their drivers from India. It was here that the Greeks for the first time saw these animals armed with tusks, which were familiar to them in trade. They gave the name of elephas to the animal itself, whose tusks were known to them by that name. By this name also, Aristotle made the animal famous in Europe. We thus see that from India were first imported ivory and peacocks into Egypt, Greece, Palestine and Persia, and that the "ophiri" is no other than the Ahir tribe of India.

"It would be interesting to many to learn that "it was in India that the Greeks first became acquainted with sugar."[1] Sugar bears a name derived from the Sanskrit. With the

[1] *Ancient and Mediaeval India*, Vol. II, p.353

article, the name travelled into Arabia and Persia, and thence became established in the languages of Europe.[1]

Mr. Maunder says, "In the reign of Seleucidae, too, there was an active trade between India and Syria"[2] Indian iron[3] and coloured cloths and rich apparels[4] were imported into Babylon and Tyre in ships from India. There were also commercial routes to Phoenicia, though Persia, which will be mentioned later on. We have already seen that India exported her merchandise to Egypt. Mr. Elphinstone says, "The extent of the Indian trade under the first Ptolemies, is a well known fact in history."[5]

In the Book of Genesis,[6] we read that Joseph was sold by his brethren to the "Ishmaelites come from Gilead, with their camels bearing spicery, balm and myrrh going to carry it down to Egypt. Here, Dr. Vincent observers, ''We find a caravan of camels loaded with the spices of India and balm and myrrh of Hadramaut." Some suppose that myrrh used to be imported into Egypt by the Abyssinians, in whose country it largely grows. But the most conclusive proof of its importation from India is the name which it took in Egypt. Dr. Royle[7] observes that myrrh is called bal by the Egyptians, while its Sanskrit name is *bola*, bearing a resemblance which leaves no doubt as to its Indian manufacture. Silk, pearls, diamonds, calicoes, and other commodities of India were also imported into Alexandria in Egypt, which remained for ages the chief emporium of the Eastern commerce.

---

[1] See lassen, p. 318

[2] Maunder's *Treasury of History*, p. 775

[3] Phoenicians fetched iron with other merchandise from India.' *Ancient and Mediaeval India*, Vol. II, p. 364

[4] Maunder's *Treasury of History*, p. 775

[5] Elphinstone's *History of India*, Vol. I, p. 141

[6] *Genesis*, Chapter xxvii, p. 25

[7] Royle's *Ancient Hindu Medicine*, 'Myrrh,' p. 119

This trade was carried on from Myos Hormos, the Chief port on the Red Sea, where the Indian fleets arrived. It is said that the articles were carried from here to Coptos, and thence to Alexandria on the Nile[1]. In the middle ages also trade on an extensive scale was carried on between India and Egypt, whence frankincense, an article of perfumery, is said to have been imported from Egypt into India.[2] Periplus clearly says that there was direct intercourse between ancient India and Egypt.[3] Mr. Davies says, "But apart from this occasional intercourse, a constant trade was carried on between Alexandria and Western India. There was also an overland route through Palmyra."[4]

There was also an active trade between India and Greece. The mention of ivory by Homer and of several other Indian articles assign the trade a very ancient date. In addition to ivory, India also supplied indigo[5] (as mentioned in Periplus) to Greece. The writer in Chamber's Encyclopaedia (Vol. V, p. 557) says that indigo was imported into Greece and Rome from India, whence also the inhabitants of the former countries derived their knowledge of its use. In India, it is called *nil*, whence is derived the *anil* of the Portuguese and the neel of the Arabs. Homer knew tin by its Sanskrit name. Prof. Dunker says that Greeks used to wear silken garlands which were imported from India and which excelled 'Sindones', or Tyrian robes.

Rome appears to be the western most city in Europe with which ancient India had a considerable trade. The chief articles exported from India in addition to those already mentioned, are, according to Periplus, cotton, muslin, chintz of various kinds, cinnamon and spices; diamonds, pearls, emeralds and many other inferior stones.

---

[1] *Encyclopaedia Britannica*, Vol. XI, p.459

[2] *Ibid*, p. 446

[3] See Heeren's *Historical Researches*, Vol. II, p. 300

[4] Davie's *Bhagavat Gītā*, p. 195

[5] *Periplus*, p. 28

Ctesias[1] adds steel, drugs, aromatics, calicoes[2] and lac[3]. Spicery appears to have been exported from India from the earliest times. Professor Heeren says, "India is the mother country of spices, and from the most ancient times, she supplied the whole Western world with – that, article.[4]" Pepper was very largely exported from India in the time of Theophrastos,[5] who distinguishes several varieties of it. With pepper, its name also migrated through Persia to the West.[6] Mrs. Manning says, "Nard or spikenard, cassia, calamus, and what appears to be the bdellium of Scripture may be traced to India, where scents were early valued and carefully prepared."[7]

Of the products of the loom; silk was more largely imported from India into ancient Rome than either in Egypt or in Greece. "It so allured the Roman ''ladies,'' says a writer, "that it sold for its weight in gold."[8] It is evident that that "there was a very large consumption of Indian manufactures in Rome. This is confirmed by the elder Pliny, who complained that vast sums of money were annually absorbed by commerce with India."[9] The annual drainage of gold from Rome and its provinces to India was estimated by him at 500 steria, equal to about Rs. 4,000,000.[10] "We are assured on undisputed authority that the Romans remitted annually to India a sum equivalent to 4,000,000 to pay for their investments, and that in the reign of Ptolemies 125 sails of Indian shipping were at one time lying in the ports

[1] *Indica*, Chapter iv.

[2] *Encyclopaedia Britannica*, Vol. XI, p. 459

[3] Ctesias, *Indica*, Chapter xxi.

[4] Heeren's *Historical Researches*, Vol. II, p. 274

[5] Theophrastos : Historical Plant, IX, 22

[6] Sanskrit *Pippali*, whence the Latin *piper* and *pipper*.

[7] *Ancient and Mediaeval India*, Vol. II, p. 353

[8] *Encyclopaedia Britannica*, Vol. XI, p. 459

[9] *Pliny : Historical Nation*, XII, p.18

[10] *Encyclopaedia Britannica*, Vol. XI, p. 460

whence Egypt, Syria, and Rome itself were supplied with the products of India."[1]

Arabia, being the nearest of the countries situated in the west of India, was the first to which the Indian commercial enterprises by sea were directed. The long continued trade with Arabia dates from a remote antiquity. Agarthachides,[2] who lived upwards of 300 years before the time of Periplus, noticed the active commercial intercourse kept up between Yemen and Pattala – a seaport in western India, which Mr. Pottinger identifies with the modern Hyderabad in Sindh. Pattala in Sanskrit means a "commercial town," "which circumstance, if it is true," says Professor Heeren, "would prove the extreme antiquity of the navigation carried on by the Indus."[3] Professor Max Dunker says, "Trade existed between the Indians and Sabaens on the coast of south Arabia before the tenth century BC."[4] the time when, according to the Europeans, Manu lived. In the days of Alexander, when the Macedonian general, Nearchus, was entering the Persian Gulf, Muscat was pointed out to him as the principal mart for Indian products which were transmitted thence to Assyria.

That this trade was chiefly in the hands of the Indians up to the beginning of the last century is proved by what Mr. Cloupet, a not very ancient writer, says, "The commerce of Arabia Felix," he says "is entirely in the hands of the Banians of Gujrat, who from father to son have established themselves in the country, and are protected by the Government in consideration of a certain import levied upon their estimated property.[5]

---

[1] *Life in Western India* (Guthrie) from Tod's *Western India*, p. 221.

[2] Geogr. Min I, p. 66

[3] *Historical Researches*, Vol. II, p.299.

[4] Dunker's *History of Antiquity*, Vol. IV, p. 156.

[5] From the accounts of Mr. Cloupet in Allgem. Geogr. Ephem, for November 1810, p. 235

Egypt was not the only part of Africa with which the Hindus traded in olden days. The eastern coast of Africa called Zanzibar and the provinces situated on the Red Sea carried on an extensive trade with ancient India. Myos Harmos as has been stated before was the chief emporium of Indian commerce on the Red Sea. Of the trade with Zanzibar, Periplus gives us pretty full information. After enumerating the commercial stations on the coast as far as the promontory of Rhapta, now called Delgado, which was the most southerly point of his geographical knowledge, and after describing their mercantile relations with Egypt, he continues, "Moreover" indigenous products such as corn, rice, butter, oil of sesamum, coarse and fine cotton goods, and cane-honey (sugar) are regularly exported from the interior of Ariaka (Konkan), and from Barygaza (Bharuch) to the opposite coast."[1]

This trade is also noticed by Arrian, who adds that "this navigation was regularly managed." Professor Heeren thinks that the trade with the gold countries of Africa will serve to explain the great abundance of this metal in India.

The African trade, too, was in the hands of the Hindus. Periplus[2] calls our attention to the fact that the banians, of India as well as merchants of Greece and Arabia, established themselves at Socotra[3], near the Gulf of Aden, beside the Cape of Guardafui. Professor Heeren[4] says it is a well-known fact the banians or Hindu merchants were in the habit of traversing the ocean and settling in foreign countries. The fact that thousands of Hindus from Gujarat and its neighbouring provinces are even now found settled in the eastern districts of Africa, proves that in ancient times Indians in large numbers had settled in Africa for purposes of commerce.

---

[1] *Periplus*, p. 8

[2] *Periplus*, p. 17

[3] It was formerly called the island of Dioscorids

[4] *Historical Researches*, Vol. II

The Eastern countries with which ancient India traded were chiefly China, Transgangetic Peninsula and Australia. Professor Heeren says that the second direction which the trade of India took was towards the East, that is, to the Ultra-Gangetic Peninsula, comprising Aava[1], Mallaca,[2] etc., etc. The traffic with these countries, would, of course, be carried on by sea only, though the transmission' of goods across the Bay of Bengal could not be attended with much difficulty."[3]

This commerce was actively carried on in the days of Periplus, as it actually mentions a place situated on the Coromandel coast, from which the passage was usually made to Chrysa, which appellation, according to Ptolemy,[4] denoted Malacca, but according to the author of Periplus, the whole of the Transgangetic Peninsula.[5]

Professor Heeren says, "The Hindus themselves were in the habit of constructing the vessels in which they navigated the coast of Coromandel, and also made voyages to the Ganges and the peninsula beyond it. These vessels bore different names according to their size.[6] Nothing, indeed, could furnish better proof that this commerce did not originate from an intercourse with the Greeks, but was the sole product of ancient native industry, a fact which receives additional confirmation from the existence of commercial towns and ports on the confirmation from time immemorial. Masulipatam, with its cloth manufactures, as well as the mercantile towns situated at the mouth of the Ganges, have already been noticed as existing in the time of Periplus; and if we allow these places to have been even then very ancient, of which there is scarcely any doubt, have we not

---

[1] Its Sanskrit name is Auga, which is noticed in the *Rāmāyaṇa*.

[2] Col. Wilford interprets the Sanskrit Yamalo by Mallaca. See *Asiatic Researches*, Vol. VIII, p. 302

[3] *Historical Researches*, Vol. II, p. 296

[4] See Mannert, Vol. V, p.242

[5] *Periplus* p. 34

[6] Some were called Sangara, others Colandiaphonta, and so on.

equal reason for believing their commerce and navigation to be so also?"[1]

[1] *Historical Researches*, Vol. II, p. 296

7.2. CEYLON

A few words regarding the commercial importance of Ceylon will not be out of place. According to Cosmos, Ceylon was at one time the centre of Hindu commerce, for which purpose, indeed, its natural situation and commodious havens afforded singular opportunities.[1]

Ceylon has been known by a variety of names in the East as well as in Europe. It was, called Taprobane, a name first used by "Onesicritus"[2] and ingeniously derived from Tap, an Island and Rahan or Ravan, an ancient king conquered by Mahārāja. Rāma Chandra[3]. Ptolemy remarks that it was formerly called Paloesimundi (which Pliny confirms), but that in his own time it was called Salice, and the natives Saloe (whence Selan and Ceylon). It was called *Siṅhal Dvipa* by the Hindus.

In Ptolemy's accounts of '"Ceylon we find its coasts well furnished with commercial ports[4] Talacori, Modutti, Amurogramum, Moagramum (Māhāgrama, a great city) are among the principal commercial cities described by him. Professor Heeren says, "It (Ceylon) was noted, for commercial navigation before 500 BC"[5]

From Arrian we know that the northern part of Ceylon was in a very highly civilised state, and that it was a seat of extensive commerce with the countries from the farthest China in the East to Italy in the West.[6]

Pliny says, "Taprobane was for a long time considered to be the second world and went by the appellation of

---

[1] Professor Heeren says, 'Commercial History of India is mainly dependent on that of Ceylon.' *Historical Researches*,Vol.II,p. 440

[2] *Historical Researches*, Vol. II, p. 417

[3] *Asiatic Researches*, Vol. V. p. 39

[4] Ptolemy, Chapter XII

[5] *Historical Researches*, Vo. II, p. 437

[6] *Historical Researches*, Vo. II, p. 432

Antichthones" which proves its reputation as a seat of commerce and civilisation.

Some idea of the extent of the ancient commerce of Ceylon can be gathered from the accounts; which Cosmos gives of it though at a comparatively later date. After describing the situation of the island and the name by which the Hindus called it, he says, "From all India, Persia, Ethiopia, between which countries it is situated in the middle, an infinite number of vessels arrive at, as well as go from, Ceylon. From the interior of the continent, as for instance from China and other commercial countries, it receives silk; aloes, cloves, and other productions, which it exports to Malabar, where the pepper, grows and to Calliene (near Bombay), whence is brought steel and cloth, for this ,latter is also a great commercial port. It likewise makes consignments to Sindh on the borders of India, whence come musk and castoreum; and also to Persia, Yemen, and Adule. From all these countries it receives articles of "Produce" which again it transmits into the interior, together with its own productions. Selandiv (Sinhala Dwipa) is consequently a great emporium, and being situated in the middle of the Indian Ocean, it receives merchandise from, as well as sends it to, all parts of the world."[1]

Professor Heeren adds, "From Pliny, who quotes the testimony of ancient historians, namely, those of Alexander's age, who first discovered Taprobane to be an island, we learn that Ceylon enjoyed this commercial, reputation in .the time of the Ptolemies, and even in that of Alexander. If we extend this 'Period but a century and a half further back, which no one surely will consider unreasonable, we come at once to the interesting historical fact that during a space of a thousand years, that is from 500 BC to 500 AD., the island of Ceylon, so conveniently situated for such a purpose, continued to be the great emporium of the Hindu-carrying trade, from Adule on 1he

---

[1] *Historical Researches*, Vol. II, p. 298

coast of Africa, Yemen and Malabar and the Ultra Gangetic Peninsula, even to China." He also says, "Ceylon was the common mart of Australian commerce."[1]

That a considerable portion of ancient India is closely connected with that of Ceylon is clear, not only from the remains of Hindu civilisation still everywhere visible in the island, but also from the express testimony the writers on the subject. The island of Ceylon has been celebrated in the historical and fabulous writings of India as being very prosperous and wealthy.

"Golden Lanka" is a trite, phrase in India. The island was politically, socially, in religion, and, till very recently, even physically – after Ram Chandra's celebrated stone bridge – a part of India. It was inhabited by Hindus, who, so far as nationality, language; religion and civilisation are concerned belonged to the same stock as their brethren of India. It enjoyed, therefore, an equally' considerable refinement and civilisation. When the British first went to Ceylon, "they beheld with astonishment the stupendous remains of ancient civilisation, not merely temples and other edifices, but what is still more extraordinary, tanks of such amazing extent as to deserve the name of lakes." Her ancient prosperity, her material strength, her moral and social achievement have all been testified to by many European writers. Arrian, Cosmos,[2] and a host of other great writers, travellers and annalists of the first centuries of the Christian era unanimously declare that Ceylon occupied the foremost poritions in the commercial transactions of the ancient world.

It has already been remarked that the Alexandrian historians, were the first to discover that Ceylon was an island. Professor Heeren says, "It is. however, quite evident

---

[1] *Historical Researches*, Vol. II, p. 426

[2] A merchant who traveled about 560 A.D. in the reign of Emperor Justinian II as far as 'Abule, at that time a celebrated port belonging to the king of Axume, in Ethiopia, near Arkeeko.

from the testimony of Arrian that much of what is advanced respecting the trade of Ceylon may, with equal justice, be applied to the opposite coast of Malabar."

The sea-coast of India was naturally well furnished with harbours and havens to copy with commerce on a gigantic scale. Professor Heeren says, "Commercial towns and ports existed on the Coromandel coast from time immemorial. The coast of Coromandel, and especially the southern part, is represented by Ptolemy to have been thickly studded with a series of commercial, towns."[1]

Extensive commerce bespeaks advanced civilisation, Mr. Elphinstone says, "The numerous commercial cities and ports for foreign trade which are mentioned in Periplus, attest the progress of the Indians in a department which, more than any other, shows an advanced condition of the nation."[2]

---

[1] *Historical Researches*, Vol. II, p. 297. The chief ports mentioned in Periplus, p. 30, are : (1) Barygaza (Bharouch), (2) Miziris (Mangalore), (3) Nelkynda (Neliceram), (4) Patala (Hyderabad in Sindh), (5) Callience (Gallian, situated over against Bombay), and the islands of Elphanta and Salsette. In addition to these Cosmos names Sindus (Sindh), Orrbota (Surat), Callience, Sibor, Parti, Mangaruth, Salopatana, Nelopatana, Pudapatana.

[2] *History of India*, p. 241.

7.3. LAND TRADE

The land trade of India extended to China, Turkistan, Persia, Babylon, and sometimes also to Egypt, Greece and Rome. Mr. Vincent says, "The country in the north with which India traded was China."[1] The author of Periplus, after describing the geographical position' of China, says: "Silk was imported from that country, but the persons engaged in this trade were the Indians themselves." It may, however, be added, in the words of an English critic[2], "It is not improbable that silk was also indigenous in India even at a remote epoch."[3]

As regards the trade with central and northern Asia, we are told that "the Indians make expeditions for commercial purposes into the golden Ideas, the desert of Gobi, in armed companies of a thousand or two thousand men. But, according to report, they do not return home for three or four years." The Takht-i-Suleman, or the stone tower mentioned by Ptolemy and Ctesias, was the starting point for Hindu merchants who went to China.

Professor Heeren says, "By means of this building it is easy to determine the particular route as well as the length of time employed by the Hindu merchants in their journey to China. If we assume Kabul, or rather Bacteria, as their place of departure, the expedition would take a north-easterly direction as far as the forty-first degree of north latitude. It would then have to ascend the mountains and so arrive at the stone tower through the defile of Hoshan, or Owsh. From thence the route led by Kashgar, beyond the mountains, so the borders of the great desert of Gobi, which it traversed probably through Khotan and Aksu (the Casia and Auxazia

---

[1] Vincent, Vol. II, pp. 574, 575. The author says 'the name China is of Hindu origin and comes to us from India.'

[2] *Asiatic Researches*, Vol. II, p. 286. See also Schlegel, Berlin, Calender, p. 9, (Edition 1829)

[3] See also '*Art of Weaving.*'

of Ptolemy). From these ancient towns the road lay through Koshoters to Se-chow, on the frontiers of China, and thence to Pekin a place of great antiquity, if we are to understand it as the metropolis of Serica, which, indeed, the accounts of Ptolemy would hardly leave any room to doubt. The whole distance amounts to upwards of two thousand five hundred miles."[1]

As regards Western Asia, Professor Heeren says that "the Palmyrians, in addition to their commerce by land, exercised also a sea-trade with India."[2]

"After the decline of Rome," says the Encyclopedia Britannica, "Bassora became the chief commercial mart, and to Ormus merchandise from India was brought."[3]

India traded with Europe by sea as well as by land. The writer quoted above says, "The produce of India was also brought to Europe by other routes, namely (1) by the way of Palmyra, then a flourishing city, and thence to Rome and other Western cities, through the ports of Syria; (2) across the Himalaya mountains to the Oxus, thence to the Caspian Sea, and finally to its ultimate markets of Europe."[4]

Foreign trade of a nation presupposes development of its internal trade. Specially is this true of a large country like India, with its varied products, vast population and high civilisation. Professor Lassen of Paris considers it remarkable that the Hindus themselves discovered the rich, luxurious character of India's product; many of them are produced in other countries, but remained unnoticed until sought after by foreigners, whereas the most ancient Hindus had a keen enjoyment in articles of taste and luxury. Rajas and other rich people delighted in sagacious elephants, swift horses, splendid peacocks, golden decorations, exquisite perfumes, pungent peppers, ivory, pearls, gems, etc., and

---

[1] *Historical Researches*, Vol. II, p. 290

[2] *Historical Researches*, Vol. II, p. 409 (Appendix IX)

[3] *Encyclopedia Britannica*, Vol. XI, p. 460

[4] *Encyclopedia Britannica*, Vol. XI, p. 459

consequently caravans were in continued requisition to carry down these and innumerable other matters between the north and the south, and the west and the east of their vast and varied country. These caravans, it is conjectured, were met at border stations and about ports by western caravans or ships bound to or from Tyre and Egypt, or to or from the Persian Gulf and the Red Sea."[1]

Professor Heeren remarks, "The internal trade of India could not have been inconsiderable, as it was in a certain degree prescribed by nature herself."[2] Royal roads were constructed all over the country from east to west and from north to south, in addition to the numberless rivers, along the banks of which considerable commerce was carried on.

Strabo, Plutarch, and Apollodorus agree in their statements that India had considerable trade roads in all directions, with milestones, and was provided with inns for travellers. (See Strabo, Chap. XV, pp. 474 and 487). And these "roads," says Heeren, "were planted with trees and flowers."[3]

Active internal commerce was carried on in northern India along the course of the Ganges. Here was the royal highway extending from Taxila on the Indus through Lahore to Palibhotra (in Bihar), and which was 10,000 stadia in length.[4]

Rāmāyaṇa, too, mentions another road leading from Ayodhyā (Oudh) by Hastinapur on the Jamna, through Lahore, to the city of Giniberaja, in the Punjab.

Periplus, too, after saying that "the Ganges and its tributary streams were the grand commercial routes of

---

[1] See *Ancient and Mediaeval India*, Vol. II, p.348

[2] *Historical Researches*, Vol. II, p. 267

[3] *Historical Researches*, Vol. II, p. 279

[4] Strabo, p. 1010. Pliny also speaks of it in his Natural History Vol. VI, p. 21

northern India," adds that the "rivers of the Southern Peninsula also were navigated."[1]

According to Arrian, the commercial intercourse between the eastern and western coasts was carried on in the country – built ships.

Periplus again says that "in Dachhanabades (Dakṣiṇa Pradesh of Sanskrit, or the Deccan) there are two very distinguished and celebrated marts, named Tagara and Pluthama[2], whence merchandise was brought down to Barygaza (Bharaunch).

Ozene[3] (Ujjain) was one of the chief marts for internal traffic and supplied the neighbouring country with all kinds of merchandise. It also became the emporium of foreign commerce. It transported Indian products to Barygaza and was a celebrated depot of the produce of more distant and northern countries.

Fairs were an important vehicle of trade and were introduced in every part of the country. A large concourse of people assemble at these fairs in different seasons for the purpose of exchanging merchandise as well as discussing religious and national topics. Even now lakhs of people assemble at Hardwar, Benares, Allahabad, on the banks of Nerbudda and other places.[4]

---

[1] Periplus, p. 39

[2] For the identification of these two places, see Elphinstone's 'India,' p 223, footnot. 'Tagara remained for 2,000 years the great emporium of the Mediterranean commerce.' - Heeren

[3] *Historical Researches*, Vol. II, p. 280.

[4] 'The almost innumerable crowds that yearly flock to Benares, Jagan Nath and elsewhere, amounting to many hundred thousands of souls, would obviously give rise to a species of commerce.' *Historical Researches*, Vol. II, p. 279. (For an account of fairs at Hardwar, see Hardwick's accounts of it in the *Asiatic Researches*, Vol. II, p. 312; where he says that tow-and-a-half lakhs of souls assemble every year, while on the occasion of Kumbh the number is many time larger.)

Regarding these Hindu fairs, Mr. Elphinstone says, "Indian fairs have a strong resemblance to those of England. But no assemblage in England can give a notion of the lively effect produced by the prodigious concourse of people in white dresses and bright coloured scarfs and turban, so unlike the black head-dresses and dusky habits of the North."[1]

Mrs. Manning says that the Hindus traded even in the Vedic period, "and the activity in trade thus early noted has continued to be the characteristic of the country."[2]

The *Encyclopedia Britannica* says, "It (India) exported its most valuable produce, its diamonds, its aromatics, its silks, and its costly manufacture. The country, which abounded In those expensive luxuries, was naturally reputed to be the seat of immense riches, and every romantic tale of its felicity and glory was readily believed. In the Middle Ages, an extensive commerce with India was still maintained through the ports of Egypt and the Red Sea; and its precious produce, imported into Europe by the merchants of Venice, confirmed the popular opinion of its high refinement and its wealth."[3]

---

[1] Elphinstone's *History of India*, p. 179. He also remarks that 'many such places are also amongst the celebrated marts for the transfer of merchandise.'

[2] *Ancient and Mediaeval India*, Vol. II, p. 347

[3] *Encyclopaedia Britannica*, Vol. XI, p. 446. Foreign commerce on such a gigantic scale as described above was one of the principal causes of the immense riches of ancient India.

7.4. WEALTH

Rich in the gems of India's gandy zone.

CAMPBELL: *Pleasures of Hope*

If History proves anything, it proves that in ancient times, India was the richest country in the world. The fact that she has always been the cynosure of all eyes, Asiatic or European, that people of less favoured climes have always cast longing looks on her glittering treasures, and that the ambition of all conquerors has been to possess India, prove that she has been reputed to be the richest country in the world.

Her sunny climate, unrivalled fertility, matchless mineral resources and world-wide exports in ancient times helped to accumulate in her bosom the wealth which made her the happy hunting ground of adventures, and conquerors. Professor Heeren says, "India has been celebrated even in the earliest times for its riches."[1] Dr. Wise says that the wealth, splendour and prosperity of India had made a strong impression on the mind of Alexander the Great, and that when he left Persia for India, he told his army that they were starting for that "Golden India" where there was endless wealth and that what they had seen in Persia was nothing compared to the riches of India. Chamber's Encyclopaedia says, "India has been celebrated during many ages for its wealth."[2] The writer of the article "Hindustan" in the *Encyclopedia Britannica* remarks that India "was naturally reputed to be the seat of immense riches."[3] Milton voiced the popular belief when he sang of the wealth of India:

"High on a throne of royal state which for
Outshone the wealth of Ormuz and of Ind.

---

[1] Heeren's *Historical Researches*, Vol. II, p. 268

[2] *Chamber's Encyclopaedia*, Vol. V, Art. 'India,' p. 536

[3] *Encyclopaedia Britannica*, Vol. XI, p. 446

Or where the gorgeous East with richest hand
Showers on her king barbaric, pearl and gold."

An idea of the immense wealth of India could be gathered from the fact that when Sultan Mahmud Ghaznavi destroyed the far-famed temple of Somnath he found such immense riches and astonishing diamonds cooped up in the single "Idol of Śiva" that it was found quite impossible to calculate the value of that booty.[1] After a stay at Mathura for 26 days, in which he collected large idols of gold and silver in thousands, many set in with priceless jewels, Mahmud went to Kannauj, which so astonished the tyrant and his followers, though long familiar with wealthy cities like Mathura, that they declared that Kanauj was only rivaled in splendour and magnificence by the high heavens.

Gold, the emblem of wealth, was first found in India. India was the home of diamonds and other precious stones in ancient times. Periplus says that "the Greeks used to purchase pieces of gold from the Indians." Nelkynda or Neliceram, a port near Calicut on the Malabar Coast, is said to have been the only market for pearls in the world in ancient times.

Chamber's Encyclopaedia says that the minerals of India are rich and varied. Diamonds, emeralds. plumbago, beryl, topazes, are among its products. Gold has been found in India from time immemorial. The Deccan and the Malabar Coast are believed to be the gold-bearing districts,[2] and at Dharwar, quartz reefs of the richest description have been found.

India has been famous for pearls, topazes, sapphires, rubies, emeralds, lazuli, corals and other jewels. The most

---

[1] See Lethbridge's '*History of India*'.

[2] Periplus (p. 36) speaks of gold mines situated in the lower Gangetic Plain. Pliny speaks of gold and silver mines in the mountains of Capitalia, which are represented by him as the highest of the Ghat Range. Heeren's *Historical Research*, Vol. II.

famous pearls and stones are all of the Indian origin. The pearl presented by Julius Caesar to Servilia, the mother of Brutus, as well as the famous pearl ear-ring of Cleopatra, were obtained from India. The most famous diamonds in the world are natives of India. Though the Pitt (or the Regent as it is now called) weighs 136 $^{7/8}$) carats and is larger in size yet the *Koh-i-noor*, weighing only 106 carats,[1] hallowed by ages of romantic history, is the most famous diamond in the world. Both were taken from India to England. The Pitt however, after being reduced in cutting from 410 to 136$^{7/8}$ carats was, sold in 1717 to the Regent of France the Duke of Orleans. It may still be seen at the Louvre, Paris. It is valued at £ 480,000, the Koh-i-noor at only £140,000. But the mythological and historical value of the *Koh-i-noor* is untold.

It was the wealth of India that impelled the rude Arabs to invade this country and led the half-civilized Tartars to overrun it. It was the wealth of India that attracted that attracted Nadir Shah to India, from whence he returned laden with immense booty, and caused the Abdali chief to renew his attacks on it. May be, as Sophocles sings[2] that,

> "Gold is the worst of ills
> That ever plagued mankind: this wastes our cities,
> Drives forth their natives to a foreign soil,
> Taints the pure heart, and turns the virtuous mind
> To basest deeds."

Yet gold has its virtues. It was gold which not only enabled England to save herself and Europe in the last century but decided the fate of Napoleon Bona parte[3].

---

[1] When the Koh-i-noor first reached England it weighed 186 ¾ carts.

[2] Antigone, Act I.

[3] The representatives of the Allied Powers, assembled at Vinna, declared him an outlaw after his return from Elba, but declined to oppose him for want of funds. On this, England granted them

8

RELIGION

True Religion
Is always mild, propitious and humble,
Plays, not the tyrant; plants no faith in blood,
Nor bears destruction on her chariot wheels,
But stops to polish, succour and redress,
And builds her grandeur on the public good.

J. MILLER

Religion, the balm for afflicted minds, is, as Bacon observes "the chief bond of human society." It is the most powerful factor in the regulation of human affairs. As a man's company gives us a key to the general principles which guide his conduct, so does a nation's religion give us a clue to those general principles and natural forces which are at work in it for good or for evil, and which will lead it either towards civilization and enlightenment or towards degeneration and darkness. As the habitual actions and trifling acts of a man are clearly stamped with the characteristics of his personality, so is the religion of a nation an index to mark its position in the scale of civilisation.

Religion, then, is one of the tests of civilisation. And true religion, which is only another name for *Jñāna* or true knowledge, is a necessary result of pre-eminence in morals, philosophy, literature, science and general culture.

The present religion of the masses in India should not be literally taken to be the religion of their ancestors, and the nature of their religion should not be judged from the religious system of the modern Hindus. The once highly spiritual religion of the Hindus has, so far as the masses are

---

large subsidies, Thus Began the war that ended in the crowing mercy of Waterloo.

concerned, now become thoroughly materialised to mark their degradation, and things earthly are now installed in the place which was once occupied by the eternal principle of all things.

The Vedic religion is the knowledge, the recognition of the eternal principles of being, of God, of spirit and matter, and their relation to one another as revealed to them in the Vedas. Unbounded sympathy with humanity and infinite love for all God's creatures, which are the results of the noblest influences of true religion, found their supreme expression in India. No nobler sacrifice can be imagined than that involved in the resolution of the Indian who said, "Never will I seek nor receive private individual salvation - never enter into final peace alone, but forever and everywhere will live and strive for the universal redemption of every creature throughout he world. Until all are delivered, never will I leave the world of sin, sorrow and struggle, but will remain where I am."[1]

The Hindu religion is the knowledge and the comprehension of those eternal principles which govern nature and man, those immutable laws which in one sphere are called "science," in another "true philosophy." It concerns itself not with things true under certain conditions or at certain times: its precepts are ever true, true in the past, true in the present, true in the future. True knowledge being one; it takes without any distinction, into its fold, Indians, Arabs, Europeans, Americans, Africans and Chinese. Its principles circumscribe the globe and govern all humanity.

The Hindu religion is not like other religions, a confession of weakness, an humble admission of the helplessness of humanity, and an absolute reliance on an external power for the salvation of humankind. The Hindu religion is a confident assertion of supreme manhood – an assertion full of dignity and independence.

---

[1] Buddhist Catena.

Schlegel says, "It cannot be denied that the early Indians possessed a knowledge of the true God. All their writings are replete with sentiments and expressions, noble, clear, severely grand, as deeply conceived as in any human language in which men have spoken of their God."[1]

The Rev. J. Bryce admits that "there is every reason to believe that there existed a period in the Hindu history when the Brahma was the sole object of religious adoration."[2] Rev. Mr. Ward says, "It is true, indeed, that the Hindus believe in the unity of God. 'One Brahma without a second,' is a phrase very commonly used by them when conversing on subjects which relate to the nature of God. They believe also that God is Almighty, All-wise, Omnipotent, Omniscient."

Mr. Charles Coleman says, "The allmighty, Infinite, Eternal, Incomprehensible, Self-existent Being; He who sees everything though never seen. He who is not to be compassed by description, and who is beyond the limits of human conception is Brahma, the one unknown true Being, the Creator, the Preserver and Destroyer of the universe. Under such and innumerable other definitions is the Deity acknowledged in the Vedas or the sacred writings of the Hindus."[3]

Col. Kennedy says, "Every Hindu who is in the least acquainted with the principles of his religion must, in reality, acknowledge and worship God in unity."

Count Bjornstjerna, after giving a quotation from the Vedas says, "These truly sublime ideas cannot fail to convince us that the Vedas recognise only one God, who is Almighty, Infinite, Eternal, Self-existent, the Light and the Lord of the Universe."[4]

---

[1] *Wisdom of the Ancient Indians.*

[2] *Sketch of the State of British India.*

[3] *Mythology of the Hindus.*

[4] *Theogony of the Hindus*, p. 53.

Maurice is assured "that the Brahmin is seeking after one Divine unseen object, nay, that his aim in his whole life and discipline is to purify himself from outward, sensible things, that he may approach nearer to this one source of Illumination."[1] Mr. Colebrooke says that "the ancient Hindu religion, as founded on the Hindu Scriptures, recognised but one God."[2]

"It is very doubtful," says Prof. Monier Williams, idolatry existed in the time of Manu's compilation of the *Smṛti.*"[3]

Of the much-abused institution of *Śrāddhas*, Prof. Max Müller says, "The worship of the ancestors and the offering of *Śrāddhas* have maintained much of their old sacred character. They have sometimes been compared to the communion in the Christian Church, and it is certainly true that many natives speak of their funeral and ancestral ceremonies with a hushed voice and with real reverence. They alone seem still to impart to their life on earth a deeper significance and a higher prospect. I could go even a step further and expressed my belief that the absence of such services for the dead and of ancestral commemoration is a real loss in our own religion. Almost every religion recognizes them as tokens of a loving memory offered to a father, to a mother, or even to a child, and though in many countries they may have proved a source of superstition; there runs through them all a deep well of living human faith that ought never to be allowed to perish."[4]

The distinguishing feature of Hinduism, however, is, that it is a thoroughly scientific religion. Religion and science went hand-in-hand in ancient India. The religious tenets of other nations have been proved, and are admitted

---

[1] *Religions of the World*, p. 44

[2] *Asiatic Researches*, Vol. VIII, p. 385. See also Paterson's *Origin of Hindu religion in the Asiatic Researches.*

[3] *Indian Wisdom*, p. 226

[4] India : Widsom, p.226

by men of culture and thought to be in conflict with the teachings of modern science. In India, however, theology is founded upon philosophy and science. The Vedic religion is, therefore, thoroughly scientific. Major Cunningham says, "In the East, however, philosophy has always been more closely allied to theology than in civilised Greece or modern Europe."[1]

An eminent Frenchman says the Hindu Revelation is "of all Revelations the only one whose ideas are in complete harmony with modern science."

That gifted lady, Mrs. Besant, said at Calcutta, "India is the mother of religion. In her are combined science and religion in perfect harmony and that is the Hindu religion, and it is India that shall be again the spiritual mother of the world."[2]

---

[1] Cunningham's *History of the Sikhs*, p. 25

[2] Mrs. Besant's lecture at the Grand Theatre, Calcutta on 15th January 1906. In the course of the lecture, Mrs. Besant said, 'In the nineteenth century one of the postulates of science was that life thought and consciousness were all results of certain molecular arrangements of matter. Brain, the speaker added, secreted thought as the liver secreted bile. The whole materialistic science tended to show that life was the result of an arrangement of matter. Where the mechanical arrangement of matter failed, there thought failed. Intelligence and consciousness were simply the results of matter. That was the idea repeated in Tyndal's famous treatise – we must see in matter a permanent potency of every form of life.' But Hinduism proclaimed exactly the opposite. It taught that life was primary and matter secondary. Matter was simply tool, instrument, vehicle. This was clearly explained in the *Upaniṣads*, in the problem of *ātmā*. It was shown how the unembodied *ātmā* was in the body. The body was the dwelling-house of the embodied *ātmā*. It is written that the *ātmā* desired to see and the eye was there. The atma desired to hear and the ear was there. The *ālmā* desired to think and the mind was there. Consciousness was primary, *ātmā* was primary, while the senses, organs, the body were secondary. This was the Hindu teaching. The later

The Vedas do not certainly teach such unscientific absurdities as that out of nothing came something, or that the sun was created after the creation of the earth. Miss F. P. Cobbe very justly observes, "For ages back, and markedly since the days of Spinoza, facts have been known to learned men utterly at variance with the received doctrines of the infallibility of Scripture, or even of its historical accuracy."[1]

Mr. Froude says, "The truth of the Gospel history is now more widely doubted in Europe than at any time since the conversion of Constantine."[2]

Bishop Colenso says, "I assert without fear of contradiction that there are multitudes now of the more intelligent clergy who do not believe in the reality of the Noachian deluge as described in the Book of Genesis."[3]

Mr. J. A. Langland says, "This philosophy and the religion of to-day (Christianity) are opposed. The teachings of our divines and the teachings of our thinkers are antagonistic."[4]

The Vedic *dharma*, however, never feared scientific advancement, nor was it ever guilty of the terrors of the

---

discoveries of science also taught that consciousness is the creator and the matter is the form.'The speaker then stated by way of illustration, that ''man had legs as was plain to her audience, and they were able to walk; and such was the case with other senses. But modern science taught exactly the opposite. It declared that creatures with legs desired to walk and legs were gradually formed by slow degrees after repeated efforts. The desire was an aspect of consciousness and not an arrangement of matter. The creatures wanted to move, (so the organs of locomotion were gradually and duly built. The function of sight did not come from the eye; it was the result of perception in consciousness.''

1 *Broken Lights.*

2 *Short Studies on Great Subjects*, Vol. I., p. 278

3 *Pentateuch and Book of Joshua*, Part II Preface

4 *Religious Septicism and infldelity.*

Inquisition. It never shed the blood of a Galilio, a Copernicus or a Bruno.[1]

The Countess of Jersey says in the Nineteenth Century, "But to the higher caste Hindu (provided he knew anything about Hinduism. Christianity offers to his doubts and to his fears. The doctrines of the *Upaniṣads* (the philosophical speculations of the Vedas) satisfy the utmost longings of the mind. The acute logic of the ancient Ṛṣis has raised a bulwark of arguments to support the huge fabric of Hindu thought. The doctrine of Karma offers the simplest and most reasonable answer to the obvious inequalities and striking contrasts in this visible world, of happiness and suffering. The ferment and unrest of the soul in the search, of knowledge, is soothed and laid at rest when the object of contemplation is reduced to a figure-head and finally a point in space. This contemplation of point in space results in a self-absorbing delight which knows no end, and which place the soul high above all carnal wants and aspirations. This is the goal of Hindu philosophy. Christianity has nothing to offer to those who are dissatisfied with Hinduism."[2]

---

[1] 'Although steadfast in his faith, the Hindu is not fanatical; he never seeks to make proselytes. Creator of the world, he says, had given the preference to a certain religion, this alone would have prevailed upon the earth; but as there are many religions, this proves the approbation of them by the Most High..They (the Hindus) regard God as present in the mosques, with those who kneel before the cross, and in the temple where Brahma is worshipped. And is not this faith more in accordance with the true doctrine of Christ than that which lighted the *Auto dafe* for the infallibility of the Popes, for the divinity of Mary, and for the miracles of the saints?' *Theogony of the Hindus*, pp. 67, 68.

[2] Times of India (Weekly edition) for 25th May 1889. Chaplain Della Valle, author of "*A Voyage to East India*," thus concludes the chapter "On the Moralities of the Hindu" : "O! what a sad thing". it is for Christians to come short of Indians even in moralities, come short of those, who themselves believe to come short of heaven' The chaplain thus closes his interesting work on the subject of conversion, which is as remote from

No religion in the world claims to be in complete harmony with the spirit of modern science except the Vedic religion. Buddhism, being only a modified form of Hinduism, does not differ materially from the Vedic religion in its scientific aspects.

It bas been shown that almost every part of the world was, at some remote period, conquered and colonised by the ancient Hindus. Similarly, it will be found that the different nations of the ancient world derived their religion from ancient Āryāvartta.

Even at the present moment more than half of the human race are the express followers of the religions that emanated from India. If the population of the world be taken in round numbers at 1,000,000,000 we shall find from authentic records, that 53,000,000 men profess Hinduism and Buddhism (the religions that originated in India), while only 470,000,000 men follow religions which are of non-Indian origin. Rev. Mr. Ward says, "Their (Hindus) philosophy and religion still prevail over the greater portion of the globe, and that it is Hinduism which regulates the forms of worship and modes of thinking and feeling and acting throughout Japan, China, Tartary, Hindustan, the Burman Empire, Siam, Ceylon, etc."[1]

---

accomplishment at this day as it was at that distant period: 'Well known it is that the Jesuits there, who, like the Pharisees 'that would compass sea and land to make one proselyte" (Matt. 2.25), have sent into Christendom many large reports of their great conversion of infidels in East India. But all these boasting are but reports; the truth is, that they have there spilt the precious water of baptism upon some few faces, working upon the necessity of some poor men, who for want of means, which they give them, are contented to wear crucifixes, but for want of knowledge in the doctrine of Christianity are only in name Christian.' *A Voyage to East India*, pp. 402, 417,418 and 480.

[1] *Mythology of the Hindus*, Preface, p. xviii.

It is equally clear that the religions that did not originate in India have been strongly influenced by Hindu religious thought.

Bjornstjerna says, "Buddhism has also extended its doctrines among most of the other religious system". The Mosaic cosmogony, still believed in by the Jews and others is derived from the Hindu system of cosmogony.

The origin of the Greek Church of Christianity is thus explained by Mr. Princep, "The Buddhists of the West, accepting Christianity on its first announcement, at once introduced the rites and observances which, for centuries had already existed in India. From that country, Christianity derived its monarchical institutions, its forms of ritual and church service, its councils or convocations to settle schisms on points of faith, its worship of relics and working of miracles through them, and much of the discipline and of the dress of the clergy, even to the shaven heads of the monks and friars."[1]

Some of the most important of the Christian ethical teachings may be found a word by word" in – the writings of the Hindu philosophers, who flourished centuries before the birth of the Saviour. The corner stone of Christian ethics, "Do unto others as thou wouldst they should do unto thee," is nothing more than the teaching of Yājñavalkya, who says, "It is not our hermitage, still less the colour of our skin that produces virtue, virtue must be practised. Therefore, let no one do to others what he would not have done to himself."[2]

Mons. Delbos says that "the religious aspirations of that (Hindu) civilisation are found grandly expressed in the *Ṛgveda.* That civilisation pervades in every corner of the

[1] Princep's *Mongolia and Tartary.*
[2] See Max Müller's *India : What can it teach us*? P. 74

civilised world, and is around and about us every day of our lives."[1]

It is an observation, of Hume that one generation does not go off the stage at once and another succeed, as is the case with silkworms and butterflies. There is a varying margin, says Mr. Payne, into which the men of one age and those of the succeeding are blended.

In the same way, one religion never completely dies out to be succeeded by another altogether new and independently developed. As a rule, new religions are evolved out of the old ones, and the old ones are in a way the parents of the new religions. Christianity is evolved out of the Mosaic Scripture, which again is derived from the religion of the ancient Egyptians, which was derived from India. Mohamedanism, some writers hold, is a mixture of the Mosaic Scriptures, Christianity and the Parsee religion (which was derived from Hinduism), strongly tinged with the native spirit and single-mindedness of the Arabs and the democratic principles of their social system.

Buddhism, as is well known, was only a revolt against Brāhmanical tyranny, and was founded by Śākya Singh or Śākya Muni,[2] the son of Śudhodhana, king of Kapilavastu, situated to the north at Bihar. According to Buddhistic writers, however, he was the third Buddha, not the first, there being twenty-two Buddhas in all. There have been several Buddhas who differ among themselves as they differ from the Hindus. But they all agree on the following points: "They acknowledge the Vedic *dharma* as the foundation of their own. (2) They admit, in conjunction with this doctrine, a divine triad, which combines the principle of the Trinity with that of the unity, although frequently under other names than those of the Tinmurtee of the Brāhmaṇas. (3) In acknowledging the doctrine of the transmigration of the

---

[1] Mons. Delbos' paper on the Vedas read before the International Literary Association at Paris on 14th July 1884.

[2] Buddha, as a child, was also called Siddhartha.

soul. (4) Regarding the soul as an emanation of the Divine Being, which, after having accomplished its transmigration, returns to its high origin.[1] Buddhism differs from popular Hinduism in the following particulars. (I) It does not acknowledge the Vedas as a revelation from God, but only regards them as, a highly deserving human composition, containing great but not revealed truths. (2) It does not recognise the division of castes, as Hinduism does. (3) It considers the inferior gods and demigods of the Brahmin religion merely as holy men sent by the Almighty for the benefit of the human race. These Buddhas, therefore, were, like Luther Calvin and Huss, reformers of religion. (4) Their idea of God is different from the Hindu idea.

Sir E. Arnold says, "Buddhism has in it the eternity of a universal hope, the immortality of a boundless love an indestructible element of faith in final good and the proudest assertion ever made of human freedom."[2]

As regards the propagation of Buddhist doctrines, it is probable that at one time they spread over the whole world. In Burma, Siam, in most of the Islands of the Indian Archipelago and Ceylon, in Tibet, Mongolia, Japan. Nepal, Bhutan and the Lesser Tibet it is still the prevailing religion but that at one time it spread to Turkistan, Persia, Egypt, and Rome, and even to Scandinavia and the British Islands, is most probable.[3]

---

[1] This shows the origin of Buddhism to have taken place after the *Mahābhārata*, when the *Vedānta* came to be received as an *Advaita* system. Its rejection of the caste system also points to the same period, as it was after the *Mahābhārata* that the system began to be abused.

[2] *Light of Asia*, Preface, p. xiii.

[3] 'That the true seat of Buddhism, says Bjornstjerna, Ṣin ancient, times was Hindustan is attested by the of temple of Ellora, Elephanta and, Ajanta, of which the greater part were dedicated to Buddha, and also by the most authentic Hindu records. In a conversation with Bogle (the British envoy at Tibet) the Dalai Lama stated that Brahmā, Viṣṇu and Śiva were worshipped by

Count Bjornstjerna says, "it is called Godama's (Gautama's) doctrine in Assam, Pegu, Ava and Ceylon; Samana's doctrine in Siam; Amidha Buddha's in Japan, 'Fo's or Fohi's in China and Cochin-China, Sākya Singh's in Eastern Bengal and Nepal, Dherma Ray's in Bhutan; Adi Buddha's in Great Tibet; Mahamuni's in Lesser Tibet, and Sakia Muni's in Mongolia and Mants-Chouri."[1]

"The Buddhist Monks, Bharana and Matanga, who first carried Buddhism to China, during the reign of the Han Emperor Mingti in A.D,. 65 were natives of Gandhara (Punjab) of which the capital was Takshila. Some authors conjecture the Goeti of the Chinese to be the same as the Greek Scythi, who were no other than the parent stock of the Hindu Śākya race."[2]

The foot-prints of Buddha were worshipped by his followers and were called Prabat. They were engraved on rocks and hills, where people flocked from all parts of the country to worship them. They have now been found to be existing in most countries. These foot-prints are regarded by the Buddhists in the same light as the rainbow in the religions founded on the Mosaic records, namely, as an assurance that the deluge shall not return. Six such Prabats are found in the East, one of them singularly enough in

---

the inhabitants of Thibet, but the lesser gods of India were not otherwise regarded by them than as holy men (Buddhism); that the people of Tibei from 700 to 800 years back possessed many temples in India, but that the Brāhmaṇas had destroyed them, and that India was the real native seat of their gods and doctrines; he therefore begged the English envoy to obtain permission from the Governor General that they might again erect temples on the shores of the Ganges'' *Theogony of the Hindus*, p. 98

[1] *Theogony of the Hindus*, p.86. A.H. Bitchourin, a Russian translator of Chinese religious books, says that Buddhism universally prevails in the highland of Central Asia.

[2] See Sarat Chander Das. '*Universities in India*' in the *Hindustan Review* for March 1906.

Mecca, whither the Buddhists made pilgrimages long before the rise of Islamism."[1] This proves the prevalence of Buddhism in Arabia in ancient times.

Bjornstjerna continues, "But Buddhism has also penetrated to the banks of the Nile, of which we have many proofs. The so-called Hermes Scriptures (the name of the sacred writing; of the Egyptians) contain a metaphysical treatise in the form of a dialogue between Hermes and Thodh, Bodh, Buddh, which throughout exhibits the doctrines of Buddhism; they speak of the pre-existence of the soul, of its transmigrations upon earth (Metempsychosis), of its emanation from the Divine Being, and of its final return to its high original."[2] There is another early Egyptian writing, Pimander's Hermes Trismegistus, in a dialogue form, between Pimander and Thodh, which develops the Buddhist doctrine of Trinity.

Count Bjornstjerna again says, "The Chaldeans, the Babylonians and the inhabitants of Colchis derived their religion and culture from India."[3] "That a system of Hinduism," says Colonel Tod, "pervaded the whole Babylonian and Assyrian empires, Scripture furnishes abundant proofs in the medium of the various type of the Sungod, Bal Nath, whose pillar adorned every mount and every grover."[4]

"The Samaritans in Aram were Buddhists, as also the Essenes in Palestine, at least as to their private doctrine, for outwardly they followed the Mosaic law." The Gnostics were divided into two classes: (1) The Egyptians and (2)

---

[1] *Theogony of the Hindus*, pp.92, 93. After discoursing on Socrates, Epicuras, Zoroaster and Confucius, Schlegel says, 'But they were not so generally revered as benefactors of their country: whilst for numerical influence Gautama Buddha swayed the destinies of more millions of human beings than the four together.' *History of Literature*, p. 124

[2] *Theogony of the Hindus*, p.100

[3] *Theogony of the Hindus*, p.38

[4] Tod's *Rajasthan*, Vol. I, p. 605

The Asiatics; and "the adherents of the latter," says the Swedish Count, "were in fact Buddhists who in a great measure adopted the external forms of Christianity, because they regarded Jesus as a Buddha who had appeared on earth in accordance with their own tenets."[1]

Count Bjornstjrna continues, "Even the Druids in ancient Britain were Buddhists; they adopted the metempsychosis, the pre-existence of the soul and its return to the realms of universal space. They had a divine Triad consisting of a creator, preserver and destroyer as with the Buddhists (and Hindus). The Druids constituted a sacerdotal order which reserved to itself alone the interpretation of the mysteries of religion."[2]

The Druids propagated their doctrines in Gaul during the time of Caesar, whence they penetrated in the West to the Celtic tribes in Spain, and in the East to Germany and the Cimbrian peninsula. The spread of Buddhism to the above-mentioned parts of the world was for the most part anterior to Christianity; simultaneously with the establishment of this creed, Buddhism penetrated so far as the Altai mountains in Asia and the Scandinavian peninsula in Europe. In the lost named peninsula it was introduced by sigg-e-Fri-dulfson, surnamed *Odin* in the ancient Scandinavian dialect Whodin, in it the article which added to Whod, Bhood Budh, makes Whodin—Odin), chief of an Asiatic tribe called Asar."[3]

Buddhism being a particular form of Hinduism, not only is Hinduism the groundwork of Buddhism, but the mythology and the traditions of both are necessarily one and the same Hence, wherever Buddhism has spread through the exertions of the Indians or wherever the Buddhist Hindus migrated, there is found the religion, mythology, and scientific and philosophical writings of India and of those -

---

[1] *Theogony of the Hindus*, p. 101

[2] *Theogony of the Hindus*, p. 10

[3] *Theogony of the Hindus*, p.105. The author says, 'It seems to be the same tribe which came by sea to Etruria.

countries, an affinity too close to be only accidental. In the case of Scandinavia, however, the resemblance is so close that without assuming the migration of the Hindus into the country, it cannot otherwise be explained satisfactorily. All the Indo Scythian invaders of India, says Colonel Tod, held the religion of Buddha, and hence the conformity of manners and mythology between the Scandinavians or German tribes and the Rajputs.[1]

(1) After giving a few questions with their answers from the Edda of the Scandinavians and a few similar ones from the Vedas, the Swedish Count, Bjornstjerna, concludes, 'All these questions are so exceedingly similar to those which the angels make to Brahma and the answers similar to those of Brahma in the Vedas, that we can scarcely question the derivation of the Edda from the Veda.[2]"

(2) "A common symbol of the Creator among the Hindus(from whom it passed into Egypt) was the scarabaeus or beetle. In Scandinavia, likewise, this insignificant insect was secured, and bore the name of the god Thor."

(3) "The resemblance between the serpent of Midgard in the Edda and the serpent or Vishnu in the Veda is also worthy of remark, both being described as having encircled the world."

(4) "But what is, most deserving of observation is the accordance between the gates of Walhall and the Indian ages of the world on *yugas.* According to the Edda, Walhall has 540 gates; if this number be multiplied by 800, the number of Einheriers who can march[3] out abreast from each gate,

---

[1] Tod's *Rajasthan,*Vol. I, p. 65

[2] *Theogony of the Hindus*, pp. 107, 108

[3] Five hundred and forty doors. I believe to be in Walhal. Eight hundred Einheriers can go out abreast when they are to fight against the Ulfven (the wolf). Here is meant the fatal encounter with *Fenris Ulfven* at the end of the world, when Odin, at the head of 432,000 armed Einheriers takes the field against them. (Sec. the Edda)

the product will be 432,000 which forms the very elementary number for the so frequently named ages of the world or *yugas*, adopted both in the doctrine of Brahma and Buddha, of which the one now in course will extend to 432,000 years , the three preceding ones corresponding to this number multiplied by 2, 3, and 4."

Between the nomencalures of the Scandinvian and Hindu mythologies, there is a remarkable resemblance. Love is in Swedish, karlek, Bengali, Karlekeya, Whiel Swerga is the Swedish name of Sweden and is situated near the North Pole, Skand, the God of war, regains there (Scandinavia), and seven steps (zones) lead thither, of which the most northern is named *Thule*, the ancient name of Sweden."[1]

It appears that the Hindu settlers migrated to Scandinavia before the *Mahābhārata*, taking their philosophy and religion with them, but were soon absorbed by the natives owing to their inferiority in numbers.

Count Bjornstjerna says, "We have seen how Buddhism has spread first over the two peninsulas of India and afterwards proceeded to Ethiopia. Egypt, Ghana, Corea, Tibet: it penetrated to Chaldea, Phoenicia, Palestine, Colchis, Greece, Rome, Gaul, and Britain,."[2] It is thus clear that Buddhism, or rather Reformed Hinduism, at one time spread over almost every country of the ancient world. We have already seen (see Colonization) that Egypt and Greece were colonised by the Hindus in ancient times: those settlers must have taken with them their religion from ancient India. Direct and conclusive proofs, however, are available to prove that the religion of the ancient Egyptians and ancient Greeks was derived from India. On comparing, the religious systems of the Egyptians and the Hindus we are struck by their resemblance to each other. "Both proceed from monotheistic principles and degenerate into a polytheistic heathenism though rather of a symbolic than of a positive

---

1 *Theogony of the Hindus*, p. 109.

2 *Theogony of the Hindus*, p. 101

character. The principle of Trinity with that of the Unity, the pre-existence of the soul, its transmigration, the division of castes into priests, warriors, traders and agriculturists are the cardinal points of both systems. Even the symbols are the same on the shores of the Ganges and the Nile. Thus we find the *Liṅgam* of the *Śiva* temple & of India is the Phallus of the Ammon temples of Egypt a symbol also met with on the head dress of the Egyptian gods. We find the lotus flower as the symbol of the sun both in India and in Egypt, and we find symbols of the immortality of the soul in both countries. The power of rendering barren women fruitful, ascribed to the temples of Śiva in India, was also ascribed to the temples of Ammon in Egypt; a belief retained to our days, for the Bedouing women may still be seen wandering around the temple of Ammon, for the purpose of obtaining this blessing."[1]

Several names of Hindu mythology are recognised in Egypt, "Thus, Ammon, the supreme god of the Egyptians corresponds to Aum of the Hindus, and the Brahminical Śiva is found in the temple to which Alexander the Great made his pilgrimage from Egypt and which yet bears this name." These resemblances between the two systems of religion prove that the one is derived from the other. The following arguments advanced by Count Bjornstjerna prove conclusively that the Hindu religion is the source of the Egyptian religion.

(1) "It is testified to by Herodotus, Plato, Solon, Pythagoras and Philostratus that the religion of Egypt proceeded from India.

(2) "It is testified by Niebuhr, Valentia, Champollian, and Waddington, that the temples of Upper Egypt are of greater antiquity than those of Lower Egypt; that the temples in Meroe are more ancient than those of Elephantine and Thebes; these are more ancient than the temples of Tentyra and Abydos; and these again more ancient than those of

[1] *Theogony of the Hindus*, pp. 40, 41

Memphis, Heliopolis and Sais; that consequently the religion of Egypt, according to the testimony of those monuments, proceeded from the South which cannot be from any other land than from Ethiopia and Meroe, to which country it came from India, as testified by the above named Greek authorities.

(3) "The chronicles found in the temples of Abydos and Sais, and which have been transmitted to us by Josephus, Julius Africanus and Eusebius all testify that the religious system of the Egyptians proceeded from India.

(4) "We have Hindu chronologies (besides those of *Purāṇas* concerning the *Yugas*, which are nothing but astronomical allegories) which go still further back in time than the tables of the Egyptian kings, according to Manetho.

(5) "There is a tradition among the Abyssinians which they say they have possessed from time immemorial and which is still equally received among the Jews and the Christians of that country, that the first inhabitants (they say Cush, grandson of Noah, with his family) came over the chain of mountains, which separates the highlands of Abyssinia from the Red Sea and the Straits of Babel-Mandeb from a remote Southern country. The tradition further says that they built the city of Axum early in the days of Abraham, and that from thence they spread themselves following the River Nile downward, until they became (as Josephus says) the Meroetes; namely, the inhabitants of that part of Nubia, which being, situated between the Nile and its conflux the Atbara, forms what is commonly called the island of Meroe, from which they spread farther down the river to Egypt." Count Bjornstjerna thus concludes, "It appears from the above-mentioned grounds that the Hindus have a greater claim to the primogeniture of religion, and consequently to the primogeniture of civilization than the people of Ancient Egypt."[1]

---

[1] *Theogony of the Hindus*, pp. 43, 46

The cosmogony of the whole world has been derived from India. That the Greeks derived theirs from the Hindus may be seen in the accounts which Damascius has given of the doctrine of Orpheus. It is as follows "In the beginning, was Kronos, who out of chaos created other (day) and erebos (night); therein he laid an egg (Hindu) from which came Phanes, furnished with three heads (the Indian *Trimurti*). Phanes created the man and the woman from whom the human race is derived. The cosmogony of the Egyptians also adopts the Hindu egg which, divided into two, formed heaven and earth (vide Diodorus and Plutarch)."[1]

The Mosaic system of cosmogony was derived from India. Count Bjornstjerna says, "If we reflect upon all these testimonies respecting Moses, and consider the place (Heliopolis) where he studied, and if we also recollect that the religion of the Egyptians was derived from India, we thus find clue from whence Moses must partly have obtained his cosmogony, and also his religious system, which, like the Vedas, was constructed upon monotheistic principles."[2]

The present cosmogony prevalent in the Christian and Mohamedan countries is also of Indian origin. The Buddhistic cosmogony is as follows "In the beginning, the earth was uninhabited, at which time the inhabitants of Heaven or of Bhurana (angels) used to visit the earth. These glorious beings consisting of men and women, through the purity of their spirit, had never yet cherished any sensual desires, when Adi Buddha (the supreme God) infused into them the desire to taste the fruit of a tree resembling the almond, which excited the sensual appetite in them, and they afterwards disdained to return to Bhurana, and thus became the parent of the human race."[3] That this is the source from which the Bible and the Quran-derived their common system of cosmogony there can scarcely be any doubt. It is thus

---

[1] *Theogony of the Hindus*, pp. 130, 131

[2] *Theogony of the Hindus*, p. 144

[3] *Theogony of the Hindus*, p. 131

perfectly clear that every system of cosmogony, whether ancient or modern, owes its origin to India.

The mythology of the Greeks, the Egyptians and the Assyrians is wholly founded on the Hindu mythology. Professor Max Müller says, "The poetry of Homer is founded on the mythology of the Vedas,"[1] and without the Veda, he says a little further, "the Science of Mythology would have remained mere guess work and without a safe basis."[2]

The gods and goddesses of Greece are but copies of their Hindu Originals.

Jupiter	-	"	Stands for Indra
Juno	-	"	Durga or Pārvatī Indrāṇī)
Apollo	-	"	Kṛṣṇa
Venus	-	"	Rati
Ceres	-	"	Śri
Cybele	-	"	Pṛthvī
Neptune and Uranus	-	"	Varuṇa
Minerva	-	"	Sarasvati
Mars	-	"	Skand
Pluto	-	"	Yama
Plutus	-	"	Kubera
Vulcan	-	"	Viśvakarmā
Cupid	-	"	Kāma
Mercury	-	"	Nārada
Aurora	-	"	Uṣas

[1] *Chips from a German workshop*, Vol. III, p. 79
[2] *Chips from a German workshop*, Vol. III, p. 96

Aeolus - " Vāyu

Janus - " Gaṇeśa

Dioscuri (CastorAnd Poollux-"Aśvinī Kumars

Styx - " Vaitarṇī

Ida - " Kailāśa

Olympus - " Meru

The *Rāmāyaṇa* and the *Mahābhārata* are the sources of the Homeric poems, and the mythology of the Greeks is, to a great extent, only an adaptation of the Hindu mythology to local life and traditions of Greece.

The Christian mythology, top, is derived from that of the Hindus. Both Mr. Maurice[1] and Sir W. Jones[2] believe Rāma to be Raamah of Scripture, son of Cush (Genesis, Chapter x. verse 7). It is thus clear to a student of comparative mythology that the Hindu deities are, the objects of worship in some form or other throughout the world.

Mr. W.D. Brown says, "By careful examination the unprejudiced mind cannot but admit that Hindu is the parent of the literature and theology of the world. The researches and investigations made in Sanskrit language, which was once spoken in that country, by scholars like Max Müller, Jaccolliot, Sir William Jones and others have found in the ancient records of India the strongest proofs that thence were drawn many or nearly all the favourite dogmas which later theologians have adopted; and the strongest proofs show to the thoughtful student that ancient Hindu were neither the practisers of idolatry nor the unlearned, uncivilized, barbaric race they have usually been thought, but a people enjoying a measure of inspiration that might be envied by more pretentious nations. And I have not the least doubt that these translations of ancient Hindu literature will

---

[1] Maurice's History, Vol. III, p.104

[2] Sir W. Jones in the *Asiatic Researches*, Vol. II, p. 40

confound the so-called modern civilisations, that they will look upon India as a country flower once more coming into full bloom, wafting forth its delicious fragrance, and will beg for a slip from its branches."[1]

[1] *The Daily Tribune*, Salt Lake City, United States, America, Holiday Morning, 20th February 1884.

www.ingramcontent.com/pod-product-compliance
Lightning Source LLC
Chambersburg PA
CBHW071959150426
43194CB00008B/934